Standardized Minds

STANDARDIZED MINDS

The High Price of America's Testing Culture and What We Can Do to Change It

PETER SACKS

PERSEUS PUBLISHING
Cambridge, Massachusetts

A CIP record for this book is available from the Library of Congress
ISBN: 0-7382-0433-1

Perseus Publishing is a member of the Perseus Books Group.

Text design by Jeff Williams
Set in 10-point Minion by the Perseus Books Group

3 4 5 6 7 8 9 10—03 02
First paperback printing, December 2000

Perseus Publishing books are available at special discounts for bulk purchases in the U.S. by corporations, institutions, and other organizations. For more information, please contact the Special Markets Department at HarperCollins Publishers, 10 East 53rd Street, New York, NY 10022, or call 1-212-207-7528.

Find us on the World Wide Web at http://www.perseuspublishing.com

Contents

Acknowledgments

Dozens of kind people lent their precious time, support, and interest to this project. I would like to thank them all for sharing their stories, information, and resources. I am particularly indebted to: John Muffo of Virginia Tech in Blacksburg; Chris Watson of Gainesville, Florida; Chuck Lavaroni of Marin County, California; Al Kauffman of the Mexican American Legal Defense and Educational Fund in San Antonio, Texas; Mary and her daughter Kelly in San Antonio; Karen Price of Smithfield, North Carolina; Kimberly West-Faulkon of NAACP Legal Defense Fund; Gil Medeiros of Walnut Creek, California; Melissa Manly of Porter, Texas; James Parsons of Humble, Texas; Michelle Savage of Sidney Lanier High School in San Antonio; Linda Tims of the South Carolina Department of Education; Monty Neill, Charles Rooney, and Bob Schaeffer of the National Center for Fair and Open Testing (FairTest) in Cambridge, Massachusetts; Carol Weston and her family in New York City; Kami Kim and her family, also of New York; "Jackie" and her family in Boise, Idaho; Bob Zenhausern of St. John's University; Jenifer VanDeusen of the Maine Center for Educational Services in Auburn; Karen Hartke of Boston; George Madaus of Center for the Study of Testing, Evaluation, and Educational Policy at Boston College; Jennifer Ruth of Portland, Oregon; Karl Petruso of the University of Texas at Arlington; Nancy Schulman of the 92nd Street Y Nursery School, Zelda Warner of the Grace Church School, Lucille Porter of the Educational Records Bureau, and Polly Smith Breland of the Hunter College Campus Schools, all of New York City; Clarke Fowler of Salem State College; Debra Andrake of Wenham, Massachusetts; Michael J. Feuer of the National Research Council; Julie Gauthier of Boston; Carmelo Melendez of Texas; Elaine Siegel of Chicago; Don Kleiner of Union, Maine; David J. Morrow of the *New York Times;* William Hiss of Bates College in Lewiston, Maine; Fred Bryant of Loyola University of Chicago; William Crain of the City University of New York; Richard Sander of the UCLA School of Law; Bruce Walker of the University of Texas at Austin; Ann Hayes and John Parker of Roanoak Rapids schools in North Carolina; C. E. "Mack" McCary of the Elizabeth City–Pasquotank schools, also of North Carolina; Amanda Colby, Karina Moltz, and Karen Fletcher, all students at Bates College; Christy Stevens of Foxfire in Mountain City, Georgia; Paulette Acquavito of Freeport, New York; and Chris Gustafson of Seattle.

In addition, I would like to thank Ted Marchese at *Change* magazine, in which a version of the book's opening chapter first appeared as an essay in the March/April 1997 issue.

At Perseus Books, I'm especially indebted to my editor, Marnie Cochran, who provided much support and encouragement for the project. I'm also grateful to Sharon Rice, my publicist, and to Marco Pavia and Myia Williams for their careful efforts in the production of the manuscript.

Finally, I am deeply grateful to my wife, Kathleen Romito, a willing and able reader of countless drafts, whose beliefs in this book and in me remained unwavering.

Peter Sacks

Acronyms

AAMC	Association of American Medical Colleges
AAU	Association of American Universities
ACORN	Association of Community Organizations for Reform
AERA	American Educational Research Association
AGS	American Guidance Service
AP	advanced placement
APSA	Abstract problem-solving ability
ASI	Assessment Systems Inc.
BEP	Basic Education Plan
BGU	Ben-Gurion University of the Negev
BSAT	Basic Skills Ability Test
C-NLSY	Children of the National Longitudinal Study of Youth
CAT	California Achievement Test
CBEST	California Basic Educational Skills Test
CCSSO	Council of Chief State School Officers
CI	Combined index
CLAS	California Learning Assessment System
CTBS	Comprehensive Test of Basic Skills
CUNY	City University of New York
EEOC	Equal Employment Opportunity Commission
EOG	end-of-grade
ERB	Educational Resource Bureau
ETS	Educational Testing Service
FairTest	National Organization for Fair and Open Testing
GATB	General Aptitude Test battery
GDP	Gross domestic product
GED	General equivalency diploma
GPA	grade point average
GRE	Graduate Record Examination
IFHP	Infant Health Development Project
ITBS	Iowa Test of Basic Skills
KELP	Kentucky Elementary Learning Profile
LFT	Learning From Text

LSAT	Law School Admission Test
MALDEF	Mexican American Legal Defense and Educational Fund
MCAT	Medical College Admissions Test
NAACP	National Association for the Advancement of Colored People
NAEP	National Assessment of Educational Progress
NCAA	National Collegiate Athletic Association
NCANC	Next Century Assessment for North Carolina
NCES	National Center for Educational Statistics
NELS	National Educational Longitudinal Study
NRC	National Research Council
NTE	National Teacher's Examination
OTA	Office of Technology Assessment
P-BAT	Performance Based Accountability Program
PGCE	Post Graduate Certificate in Education
PI	Predictive index
PTA	Parent-Teacher Association
R&D	Research and development
SB 2	Senate Bill 2 (North Carolina)
SCE	Select Committee on Education
SEC	Securities and Exchange Commission
STAR	Standardized Testing and Reporting
STAT	Sternberg Triarchic Abilities Test
TAAS	Texas Assessment of Academic Skills
TABS	Texas Assessment of Basic Skills
TEA	Texas Education Agency
TEAMS	Texas Educational Assessment of Minimum Skills
TIERS	Title I Evaluation and Reporting System
TIMSS	Third International Math and Science Study
USES	U.S. Employment Service
VUE	Virtual University Enterprises
WISC-III	Weschler Intelligence Scale for Children, Third Edition
WISC-R	Weschler Intelligence Scale for Children–Revised
WPPSI-R	Weschler Preschool and Primary Scale of Intelligence–Revised

Preface

In my research for this book, I was struck by a profound disconnection between knowledge and practice. I spent some three years scouring the social scientific research on the subject of standardized testing, examining hundreds of articles in dozens of academic journals and government reports. I talked to scores of teachers, administrators, students, workers, and professionals, admissions officials, parents, and testing experts.

The evidence revealed the very troubling and costly effects of our growing dependence on large-scale mental testing to assess the quality of schools, one's merit for college, and a person's aptitude for many different jobs. In light of the evidence, I was dumbfounded that mental testing was continuing to carve out an increasingly entrenched and unquestioned position in our schools, colleges, and workplaces.

There was so much damning evidence having so little effect on the practical world we lived in. Most Americans were not getting the information they needed to think straight about something that had so much influence on their lives. I vowed to write a book that might help change that, and I hope *Standardized Minds* is that book.

In my view, an important reason why the accumulated body of knowledge about testing has had so little effect on practical affairs is that the subject has largely been owned by academicians who have had limited success informing the public about the limitations, effects, and costs of large-scale mental testing in our society.

I am not an academician but rather an independent journalist. I am a former economist who spent several years writing about business and economics as a staff writer at daily newspapers, leaving newspapering to teach and to write about education. I have come to believe education is *the* most important subject for any American concerned about social and economic justice at the turn of the century.

I hope that *Standardized Minds* might complement the work of many others in providing an accessible bridge between the academic sphere of research reports and journal articles and the parents, children, admissions officers, policymakers, and others with a stake in how our schools, colleges, and workplaces measure American minds.

Standardized Minds is a critique of the American testing culture. It is not intended to win popularity contests. As a fuller picture of the evidence about the costs and benefits of our mental testing culture began to emerge, I realized that some very powerful people and institutions would dislike what I had to report, and they would likely defend their power and influence by attacking the messenger.

The Educational Testing Service, which makes the SAT college admissions exam, among dozens of other standardized tests, will probably be offended by this book. The same goes for the College Board, whose members include most major colleges and universities for whom ETS makes the SAT.

Even many politicians, both conservative and liberal, who have touted more testing and higher standards as the panaceas for improving public schools, may well object to this book's message. Regrettably, many state, local, and national public officials have seized on education reform as a means to their own political ends. Elected officials' virtually constant condemnation of American schools and their calls for more and more testing do often serve those ends.

Am I suggesting some pernicious conspiracy afoot here? Hardly. I would merely say to my readers that many organizations, institutions, and testing companies have an enormous stake in preserving America's mental testing enterprise, and there is little question that they will act in their own best interests to preserve their stakes. I expect *Standardized Minds* will be received by either a roaring silence, in hope that its message will soon go away, or cries of protest and indignation over yet another irresponsible book by yet another sensational journalist with an ax to grind. I will let you be the judge.

Introduction

Standardized testing: It's an innocuous sounding term, isn't it? Straightforward, inexpensive, tidy, fair. Americans have grown so accustomed to taking multiple-choice tests to prove themselves that people don't bother to question the tests' legitimacy.

These seemingly innocuous rites of American passage are neither straightforward, inexpensive, tidy, nor fair.

Standardized Minds explores the nation's unhealthy and enduring obsession with standardized mental testing and how this tool of the so-called meritocracy affects us all, from the day we enter kindergarten to when we might apply for a job or seek a new profession.

This book examines why standardized testing continues to dominate the education system. The book will show also how such testing has become a pervasive influence in the workplace as well.

We will explore proven alternatives to such testing and ways to make the American meritocracy more accurate and fair to all people.

The Meritocracy: An American Fascination

Americans in recent years seem fascinated with the mechanisms of the so-called meritocracy.

Recent evidence of this fascination includes the raging controversy over publication a few years ago of *The Bell Curve.*

Socioeconomic class divisions have become more striking than ever in the past ten or fifteen years, fueling concerns and debate over how the meritocracy works—or doesn't work.

In recent years, however, the reach of mental testing in our society, as the linchpin of the meritocracy, has largely escaped public scrutiny.

Sure, newspapers have covered President Clinton's national school testing proposal. You have seen the ups and downs of your schools' test scores splattered every few months across the front page of your local newspaper. You have been told time and again, tests aren't perfect but they're the best we have to make important decisions and judgments.

Is this really true?

What are the flaws of such testing?

Why is one's father's occupation a better predictor of SAT scores than virtually any other factor?

Whose interests does mental testing serve?

Why do the gatekeepers of America's meritocracy emphasize potential over actual accomplishment?

Why have teachers pejoratively called an ambitious, highly motivated child an "overachiever" because her actual performance surpassed what her test scores predicted?

What's the underlying—and little discussed—connection between people who advocate the end of affirmative action and others who argue for more standardized testing?

To be sure, there have been books in the past about America's testing habit. However, many of these came during the peak of a rather short-lived antitesting "rebellion" of sorts by many teachers, parents, and consumers in the late 1970s and early 1980s.

Americans now face an entirely different political environment and an even more entrenched mental measurement establishment.

The use of mental tests has continued to explode. Parents, taxpayers, and students are spending billions of dollars on mental testing each year. To get a job as a wine taster, baseball umpire, teacher, government clerical worker, or even a football player in the NFL nowadays, you need to prove your "competence" via a standardized mental test. No, that's not meant to be funny. As ridiculous as it might sound, we do use standardized tests for such purposes.

In whatever the context, ability is often judged from meaningless tests of "aptitude," regardless of our proven ability to perform the job, do the work, get the grades, or accomplish remarkable things.

We know that the results of such tests tell us precious little about competence. They merely measure one's ability to perform well on tests.

Unfortunately, the public largely accepts the legitimacy of this tool of the meritocracy, believing the exams are accurate predictors of success for individuals and good measures of the quality of our schools. This erroneous view is reinforced constantly in our culture. Educational researchers have found that such tests have proven to be of dubious value in predicting one's ability to perform on practical tasks that really matter.

Yet this emotional and intellectual abuse we call standardized testing continues. Why is this so? Who are the real winners of this game?

I will argue that there are two principal beneficiaries. First, the testing game has largely served the interests of America's elites, further stratifying the society by race and socioeconomic class; second, the companies that produce, administer, score, and coach for standardized tests of all types have gotten rich off the nation's testing habit.

Most previous books on this topic have focused on specific types of tests and institutions, particularly the SAT and the Educational Testing Service, the tax-exempt company that makes the SAT and many other tests. Other books have been academic and highly statistical, aimed at relatively narrow audiences.

Standardized Minds is intended for a general audience, the parents, students, employees, and other consumers of standardized tests. It is also aimed at educators, policymakers, and others who are in a position to help make the meritocracy more accurate, fair, and humane.

Beyond the Testing Trap

What's the answer to the problem of abusive, inaccurate mental testing affecting the lives of virtually all Americans, from kindergarteners to graduate school applicants to city bus drivers?

This book explores the emerging paradigm of "performance assessment," whereby schoolchildren and schools are assessed by what they can actually *do* on activities that really matter, rather than on abstract, multiple-choice tests.

Although these open-ended assessment are not a cure-all for the inequities of standardized tests, evidence suggests alternative "authentic" assessments could lessen the racial and class biases inherent in traditional mental testing, while enhancing the academic standards of schools.

I argue that the nation's swoon over the "accountability" movement is wrongheaded at best, and that true reform of our schools must include a revolution in the way we measure children and in the very meaning of what schooling should be.

Otherwise, we persist in reproducing an education system that leads to rote, superficial, standardized thinking.

In the realm of higher education, I show how many colleges and universities have gone their own way by eliminating the commonly required standardized admissions tests, such as the SAT or ACT, without diminishing academic quality.

Such experiments are completely redefining what it means to have "merit" in American society.

In short, this book examines the pitfalls, biases, and social costs of the device that often determines who wins and loses in the American meritocracy—and what Americans should do about it.

1

Meritocracy's Crooked Yardstick

MOST AMERICANS TAKE STANDARDIZED MENTAL TESTS as a rite of passage from the day they enter kindergarten. Gatekeepers of America's meritocracy—educators, academic institutions, and employers—have used test scores to label people as bright or not bright, as worthy academically or not worthy. Some, with luck, are able to overcome the stigma of poor performance on mental tests. But others do not.

Indeed, not only is it a stigma, but one largely unrecognized in our culture. Meritocracy's gatekeepers brand those who score poorly on standardized tests as somehow deficient, incapable. Educators have used a quasi-clinical term for such people: Remember the teacher or counselor who scornfully labeled an ambitious, competent child an "overachiever" because her academic performance exceeded what the tests predicted? Or recall the hand-wringing over the "underachiever," the student whose brilliant test scores predicted greater things than what he actually accomplished.

These terms are disappearing from public discussion, a result of concerns about standardized testing and its role in the American merit system. Some scholars have forcefully argued against the narrow views of ability measured by traditional mental tests. Many educators have sung the praises of new, authentic alternatives to standardized testing, such as performance assessment. Advocates of performance assessment say schools ought to focus more on what people can do and less on how well kindergarteners, high school students, and prospective teachers take tests.

Although the antitesting bandwagon has gathered new adherents, the wagon itself has crashed head-on into an entrenched system that is obsessed with the testing of American minds. With roots in intelligence testing that go back generations, the mental measurement establishment continues to define merit largely in terms of potential ability rather than actual performance. The case against standardized mental testing is as intellectually and ethically rigorous as any argument about social policy in the past twenty years. And yet such testing continues to dominate the education system, carving further inroads into the employment arena as well, having been bolstered in recent years by a conservative backlash advocating advancement by "merit."

How has the standardized testing paradigm managed to remain entrenched, despite the many criticisms against it? Like a drug addict who knows he should quit, America is hooked. We are a nation of standardized-testing junkies.

The Antitesting Movement

Granted, there has been scattered criticism against standardized testing in American education in the wake of the explosive growth of such testing since the 1960s. Baby boomers were funneled through the school system and tested to death. Sales of standardized tests to public schools, in real dollars, more than doubled between 1960 and 1989 to $100 million a year—even while enrollments were up just 15 percent, according to the U.S. Office of Technology Assessment. That some parents, consumers, and teachers would voice concerns about the effects of standardized testing on schools and schoolchildren was perhaps an inevitable byproduct of its growing cost and presence in American life.

Criticisms of testing became somewhat pronounced during the late 1970s and early 1980s, culminating in a string of successes for test consumers and their advocates. There were books and reports, such as Stephen Jay Gould's *The Mismeasure of Man,* James Crouse and Dale Trusheim's *The Case Against the SAT*, and the 1980 Ralph Nader report, *The Reign of ETS,* about the Educational Testing Service, the company known famously as the maker of the SAT college admission test. New York's 1979 Truth in Testing law gave consumers of standardized mental tests a minimum of protection. Activists and educators launched the National Organization for Fair and Open Testing (FairTest), the nation's first organization devoted to protecting the interests of millions of consumers of standardized tests.

These uprisings against standardized testing fueled suspicions that such tests played a key role in a rigged game, one that favored the society's well-educated elites under the guise of merit. The Nader report focused its attack on the Educational Testing Service. "An independent analysis of the dominant testing culture is now coming on the scene," the report's author, Allan Nairn, enthusiastically observed. "There will be no turning back this time. The shallowness of the ideology and depth of ETS's political power to preserve its way of testing are apparent to increasing numbers of students, parents, educators, administrators, and most refreshingly, to those deprived people who never made it through the first multiple-choice gate." (1)

Since 1980, the antitesting movement, if one exists, has occasionally lurched forward, even gaining a certain popular cachet. One might even be persuaded to conclude that the Nader report hit the bull's-eye by anticipating the ultimate demise of standardized testing as we know it. But to do so would underestimate the near magical power that quantification, standardization, and the measuring of minds continues to have over Americans.

A Glimpse at the Evidence

To be sure, independent research by academics in recent years, particularly those who aren't employed by the testing industry, has further bolstered the claims of the antitesting movement. Much of this recent research—which upcoming chapters will elaborate on—confirms suspicions that such tests have thwarted rather than helped educational reform and that they continue to be remarkably biased and inaccurate assessments of the abilities of many Americans. From this recent work, we know that:

- *Standardized tests generally have questionable ability to predicts one's academic success.*

Take, for instance, what's known as the Graduate Record Exam, a speeded, multiple-choice test that most of the nation's graduate programs require for admission or financial aid. University graduate departments have shown unwavering reliance on the GRE to predict a candidate's chances of success. This, despite reams of studies showing just the opposite: One's scores on the exam have almost no relationship whatsoever to his or her performance in graduate school.

What about the validity of the SAT, which is required for admission to many undergraduate colleges and universities? Numerous studies show that SAT scores explain just about 16 percent of the variation in actual freshman grades. A student's high school record alone is the best predictor of performance in the first year of college; further, the SAT, when combined with high school grades, adds only modestly to the predictive power of high school grades alone.

What is more, standardized tests like the SAT and GRE tend to especially penalize women and many minority students. Females tend to do worse than males on standardized tests but consistently earn better grades than males. Researchers consistently find that adding test scores to the admissions equation results in fewer women and minorities being accepted than if their academic records alone were considered.

Although the testing arena and the stakes involved might vary from university admissions testing, researchers have reached similar conclusions about the validity of standardized testing in the public schools. Teresa A. Dais of the University of Illinois has commented: "Minorities and students with disabilities, in particular, are suffering as a result of traditional assessment practices, which have proven to be inaccurate and inconsistent, yet continue to be used in prediction, decision-making, and inferences about student performance and lifelong success." (2)

Perhaps a more fundamental point about the relationship of test scores and academic success is often lost in many studies of their validity. It's worth remembering, for instance, that the SAT isn't designed to predict one's ability to succeed at four years of college study, merely freshman grades. When researchers have asked the larger question of how test scores correlate to broader measures of college success or to a student's performance beyond the freshman year, the case for the SAT becomes weak indeed.

"Can a college effectively recruit and enroll students whom it is likely to regard as most successful four years later by evaluating applicants only on the basis of school rank and test scores?" William W. Willingham asked in a 1985 study, *Success in College,* published by the SAT's sponsor, the College Board. "If the institution defines success broadly . . . the answer is no."

When researchers have asked the even more basic question of how well standardized test scores predict one's eventual success in the workplace, correlations all but disappear. At best, high test scores are pretty good indicators of *participation* in professions such as law, medicine, or university teaching, for which one must make certain standardized test cutoffs to enter a required academic program. But test scores tell us little about someone's real-world capabilities in medicine, law, or teaching. In short, scoring high on standardized tests is a good predictor of one's ability to score high on standardized tests.

- *Standardized tests scores tend to be highly correlated with socioeconomic class.*

Although standardized tests have a relatively bleak record of predicting success in school and work, we know that they do tend to correlate exceedingly well with the income and education of one's parents. Call it the "Volvo Effect." The data is so strong in this regard that one could make a good guess about a child's standardized test scores by simply looking at how many degrees her parents have and what kind of car they drive.

For now, consider some evidence from just the SAT. Recent data show that someone taking the SAT can expect to score an extra thirty test points for every $10,000 in his parents' yearly income. In a study of California high school students, parent education alone explained more than 50 percent of the variation in SAT scores. (3) And, according to recent U.S. Department of Education examinations of the backgrounds of students who made the SAT cut (a minimum score of 1,100) for highly selective colleges, fully one-third of these high scorers came from the upper-income brackets; that's compared to well under a tenth of high SAT scorers who emerge from the lower economic rungs.

- *Standardized tests reward passive, superficial learning, drive instruction in undesirable directions, and thwart meaningful educational reform.*

Teachers, researchers, and other educators have expressed widespread disenchantment with the results of several decades of standardized testing in American public schools. Evidence strongly suggests that standardized testing flies in the face of recent advances in our understanding of how people learn to think and reason. Repeatedly in the research over the past few years, especially in the grade school arena (K–12), one finds evidence that traditional tests reinforce passive, rote learning of facts and formulas, quite contrary to the active, critical thinking skills many educators now believe schools should be encouraging. Many suspect that the speeded, multiple-choice tests are themselves powerful incentives for compartmentalized and superficial learning.

At the K–12 level, teachers often don't believe the tests accurately measure their students' abilities, and do believe that widespread practice of "teaching to the test" renders test scores virtually meaningless. In 1994, the journal *Educational Policy* published a study on teachers' views of standardized tests. Just 3 percent of teachers in one sample agreed that such tests are generally good, "whereas 77 percent felt that tests are bad and not worth the time and money spent on them." According to the study, about eight in ten teachers believe their colleagues teach to the tests. (4)

Preoccupied with winning the standardized testing game for the sake of kudos from parents, principals, and state legislators, schools have often neglected reforms that would promote deeper and more active ways of thinking and learning than multiple-choice tests typically capture. The Office of Technology Assessment concluded in its report, *Testing in American Schools:* "It now appears that the use of these tests misled policymakers and the public about the progress of students, and in many places hindered the implementation of genuine school reforms."

A widespread tendency of teachers to "teach to tests" might be harmless if the tests were adequate indicators of the skills and abilities that would well serve pupils in their later academic and life endeavors. But that's doubtful. Listen to educational researcher Bruce C. Bowers:

> However, the main purpose of standardized testing is to sort large numbers of students in as efficient a manner as possible. This limited goal, quite naturally, gives rise to short-answer, multiple-choice questions. When tests are constructed in this manner, active skills, such as writing, speaking, acting, drawing, constructing, repairing, or any of a number of other skills that can and should be taught in schools are automatically relegated to second-class status. (5)

The Shifting Policy Landscape Since 1980

To be sure, concerns over the validity, fairness, and efficacy of standardized testing's role in the meritocracy unquestionably have wrought some notable changes in how our society chooses to measure the merit of American citizens.

As many educators have become disillusioned with standardized testing, some reformers have managed to implement different ways to evaluate students and educational progress. In the schools, these alternatives frequently fall under the rubric of authentic assessment, the notion that students ought to be judged on the basis of what they can actually *do*, not how well they take tests. Also called performance assessment, these methods can mean anything from evaluating portfolios of student work or writing samples to art and science projects.

By fall 1996, as many as thirty-six states had begun to include open-ended, performance-oriented questions on their statewide student tests. But it would be an overstatement to conclude that states had embraced performance assessment and abandoned traditional tests. Indeed, fully forty-one states continued to rely on the garden-variety multiple-choice tests to measure educational progress of their students. (6) Only a tiny handful of states, such as Kentucky, Vermont, and California, took steps to eliminate traditional multiple-choice tests—but in almost all cases even those moves proved to be short-lived.

What is more, a relatively small but increasing number of undergraduate colleges and universities have made standardized admissions tests optional in the past few years. By 1995, the National Center for Fair and Open Testing (FairTest) in Cambridge counted 236 such institutions, an increase of 40 in just a year. In 1998, 281 institutions either eliminated or significantly curtailed the use of admissions tests. Many of these colleges are small, private, and not particularly choosy, but there have been several selective ones as well, such as Bates College in Maine, Wheaton College in Massachusetts, and a handful of colleges in Pennsylvania. Probably the largest is the California state university system. But like others on FairTest's list, such as Kentucky State, Golden Gate University, and the University of Kansas, the SAT is still required at Cal State campuses if a student's grades fall below a certain cutoff.

Entrenched or on the Wane?

What, then, are we to conclude from these recent developments? Is standardized testing in America's schools on the wane? By the end of the 1990s, a new movement of parents and educators was gaining momentum against the use of "high-stakes" testing in the public schools. But it would be naive to underestimate the seemingly magical power that the standardized measurement of minds has on the American psyche. In fact, antitesting trends have been counterbalanced by a backlash that promises to reinforce standardized testing's continued domination of the American meritocracy.

It's worth noting that the mental-measurement culture has certainly withstood similar attacks in the past, as when the journalist Walter Lippmann wrote a series of articles in *The New Republic* in the early 1920s, warning that the prevalent use of IQ tests of the time "could . . . lead to an intellectual caste system in which the task of education had given way to the doctrine of predestination and infant damnation."

Some seventy years after Lippmann's warning, we got *The Bell Curve,* the 1994 book by Charles Murray and Richard Herrnstein arguing that inequality in America was largely the result of people born with different endowments of "intelligence." Tests such as the SAT, the roots of which go back to the very same intelligence tests Lippmann and others condemned, continue to flourish; indeed, they remain the centerpiece, the given in "meritocratic" views of who has "merit" and who does not.

The hegemony of testing to measure academic talent in our culture became especially evident amid assaults on affirmative action in the late 1990s in American education. These included new legal precedents and ballot measures in California, Texas, Mississippi, and the state of Washington. Critics of affirmative action have argued that people ought to be judged on "merit," not on gender or race. For them, the indisputable, unbiased criteria are grades and (especially) test scores. Abolishing affirmative action has often meant a renewed vigor in the decisive role that test scores have played in the "merit" system.

Similarly, under the banner of higher academic standards, the National Collegiate Athletic Association (NCAA) gave new prominence to the already huge role standardized test scores played in determining which athletes would receive scholarships to attend college. Despite strong opposition from civil rights organizations, the NCAA recently *raised* the standardized test scores required for an athlete's eligibility. The NCAA changed its policy contrary to compelling evidence that the real effect of the new rules would be to exclude many minorities from scholarships who would nevertheless have succeeded in college.

Similarly, consider what happened when college leaders convened in a closed-door meeting at Harvard in May 1996 to mull over their affirmative action strategy in the wake of *Hopwood v. State of Texas.* The Hopwood court, aligning itself with the "test scores equals merit" faithful, had simply assumed that different test scores for different races was proof of wrongdoing. That decision, ominous for affirmative action policies, prompted the president of one elite institution at the Harvard meeting to suggest that the SAT be eliminated from the admissions process. But other presidents at the meeting promptly dismissed the suggestion, arguing that quitting the SAT would be unwise in the current political climate. The public, long accustomed to the sanctity of standardized tests as a measurement of merit, would believe colleges were going lax on standards.

Moreover, in the name of education reform and higher academic standards, a conservatively rooted backlash in the 1990s resulted in several states shelving efforts at alternative forms of assessment in public schools. In California, former governor Pete Wilson, under pressure from conservatives, vetoed the reauthorization of the California Learning Assessment System, largely a performance-based assessment. Similarly inspired, conservatives in Arizona forced the state to shelve its performance assessment program. Kentucky, once a leader in performance assessment, brought back multiple-choice standardized tests because parents demanded a return to individual test scores for children in order to compare them on a national basis. The Indiana legislature too defeated proposals to replace multiple-choice tests with essays and open-ended questions.

When one adds up these shifting, often contradictory trends in policy, the net result suggests the standardized testing establishment is stronger than ever. Indeed, the standardized testing industry has assumed an even greater dominance in Americans' lives since the Ralph Nader report in 1980. And as Chapter 10,

"The Big Business of Testing," explores, the testing industry is poised to dig itself even deeper.

In 1980, just about half of the states had mandatory testing programs; by 1998, says a recent study by *Education Week* and the Pew Charitable Trusts, all but two did. By 1997, Americans were spending close to $200 million annually just on testing in the public schools, almost double the outlays of ten years earlier, according to the *Bowker Annual*. Between 1982 and 1994, standardized test sales grew faster than sales for school and college textbooks, mass market paperbacks, book clubs, and other segments of publishing. According to one recent estimate, Americans are taking as many as 600 million standardized tests each year in schools, colleges and universities, and the workplace. (7)

What Are the True Costs?

Why has standardized mental testing managed to continue to explode in this fashion and remain entrenched in American life despite what we know about its dubious validity?

For their part, the educational institutions that continue to buy the tests—costs of which are borne by test takers or taxpayers—would argue that standardized tests are a cost-effective way to evaluate people. It's obvious: Standardized testing is cheap.

But how cheap are the tests, really? Research findings about the utility of test scores raise profound questions about the social and economic costs and benefits of a de facto national policy that has institutionalized the use of standardized tests for college and university admissions as well as the educational progress of individual children, schools, and states. Although the tests might be cheap to individual academic institutions, in many cases these institutions bear neither the direct costs of the tests nor the indirect social costs of testing.

It seems reasonable to question whether the marginal benefits of standardized tests in terms of their predictive validity are worth the hundreds of millions of dollars test takers and taxpayers spend annually on the exams. Also, a true economic analysis of the nation's de facto testing policy would have to estimate the "opportunity cost" of testing: What is forgone when teachers spend inordinate amounts of time teaching to tests that might have a minimal connection to what students really need to learn? In one typical urban school district, the Office of Technology Assessment valued such lost opportunities in 1992 at as high as *$15 million* per test, or $110 per pupil. Compare these true costs to the apparently cheap $6 a student in direct outlays the district normally reports as the "cost" of the test. (8)

When such opportunity costs are factored in, Americans' annual expenditure on state and local accountability testing programs is staggering. Indeed, in a 1993 study devoted precisely to that question, Walter Haney, George Madaus, and Robert Lyons estimated the nation's taxpayers are devoting as much as *$20 billion* annually in direct payments to testing companies and indirect expenditures of time and resources devoted to taking tests and teaching to tests. (9)

The question remains: Have we gotten our money's worth from the vast amount of money Americans spend to test, track, and sort their schools and schoolchildren? I would argue not, and in the chapters that follow, I will try to show why not.

We *do* need to account for the indirect social and economic costs of erroneous decisions about people as they enter higher education and go on to careers in the American workplace. What are the true economic losses to society of such exclusion? Obviously, that's a huge question. In the following chapters, I offer anecdotal evidence as well as evidence from research studies that suggests the social and economic damage of America's flawed gatekeeping system may be considerable.

To offer just one example, consider one university that chose to let in virtually anyone who wanted in, irrespective of a standardized test score: City University of New York, where "arguably," David Lavin and David Hyllegard tell us, occurred "the nation's most ambitious attempt to expand college access to minorities."

Lavin and Hyllegard's 1996 study of the economic benefits of CUNY's open-admissions experiment found that open admissions boosted the economic gain for all races and for both males and females, over and above what they would have earned in the economy without open admissions. But the economic payoff for minorities was especially pronounced. Minority men who entered CUNY through open admissions and obtained either an associate's degree or higher earned $4,600 more a year than if open admissions had not existed. Yearly incomes for minority women were almost $4,000 greater.

All told, for everyone who entered CUNY through open gates between 1970 and 1972, and were working full time a decade later, the additional economic benefit from open admissions summed up to some $67 million, and it is fairly split down the middle between benefits to minorities and whites. That's $67 million that wouldn't exist in the economy without CUNY's open gates. (10)

It's worth noting that that estimate reflects one point in time, 1984, and measures only the CUNY graduates' extra earning power just for that year; the economic gain to society would be many times larger over the entire working lives of the CUNY graduates. What's more, even the greater figure would be multiplied several times if one were to factor in the indirect benefits of the CUNY graduates' extra earning power, when those extra dollars circulate through the economy, spent on everything from movie tickets and groceries to college educations for their sons and daughters.

Taking such forgone benefits into account must occur before it can be concluded that, indeed, standardized testing and its effects are "cheap."

Why Standardized Testing Remains Entrenched

Even if one were to conclude that standardized testing is the best policy to maximize social welfare versus costs—an empirical question that hasn't been fully answered in American society—there are deeper reasons than cheapness for the continued entrenchment of standardized mental testing in the United States.

First, Americans are fascinated with mental measurement to a degree that is rare in other countries. In contrast to what Europeans call "American tests," the examinations for college or university admission in other industrial countries are typically essay tests, in which students demonstrate knowledge of various subjects they've learned in the classroom. These tests are not unlike what American educators call performance assessment. Compared to other countries, Americans appear to be far more obsessed with IQ, the notion that intelligence—most often defined narrowly as logical-analytical ability—is both inborn and representable as a single numerical score.

Indeed, a stroll through any Barnes and Noble superstore speaks volumes about how our culture really views intelligence and how to measure it. For $3.95, one can buy *Self-Scoring IQ Tests* or *Self-Scoring IQ Tests for Children,* both written by an official from Mensa, the so-called genius club; or there is *Puzzles for Pleasure: Test Your Intelligence with 102 Mind-Stretching Exercises in Logic, Mathematics, and Precise Reasoning;* then, take a look at Barnes and Noble's Study Guides section with its dozens of titles on preparing for numerous standardized school and employment exams. My personal favorite, *Can You Pass These Tests?* includes practice mental tests for getting jobs as Bible scholars, baseball umpires, and even wine tasters.

Similarly, our culture places an exceedingly high value on the notion of *potential* to achieve, rather than achievement itself. For most Americans, a "gifted" student is one who scores off the charts on aptitude tests, not one who demonstrates practical knowledge on worthwhile endeavors. "We are one of the few societies that place so much emphasis on intelligence tests," Yale psychologist Robert Sternberg told *Skeptic* magazine. "In most societies there is more emphasis on what people accomplish." (11)

Consider, for instance, the mainly poor and black students at Northampton East High School in rural North Carolina. They took their physics and chemistry lessons and built an electric car that in national competitions bested entries from many of the country's elite high schools, whose students typically score far higher on standardized mental tests. Although Northampton East made the best car, their competitors, who might score a perfect 1,600 on their SATs, are deemed by cultural norms to have won the meritocratic contest that really counts.

Indeed, the notion that merit and achievement equal high test scores, or that higher standards means requiring higher test scores, is repeated constantly in the popular culture. This reinforces the widely accepted legitimacy of standardized tests to rate students, teachers, schools, and colleges.

When New York City schools went shopping for a new chancellor several years ago, they hired Rudolph Crew, largely because he engineered a staggering increase in standardized test scores in Tacoma, Washington, in the early 1990s. Each year, the College Board trots out its list of average SAT scores by state, and the press dutifully reports the rankings as the be-all and end-all of educational quality. Rarely mentioned are the huge gaps in economic advantage the scores really represent. When a local school district reports on educational progress in its quarterly newsletter, SAT or ACT scores top the charts. Test scores have become so politically charged that some teachers, in addition to spending huge amounts of time teaching to tests, have resorted to cheating to make their numbers look good.

What's more, standardized tests serve the perceived economic interests of colleges and universities, particularly their need for prestige, which is often the main asset they have to market to potential "customers." Pick up any of the numerous commercially published guides to colleges, universities, and graduate schools: High among the factors the guides use to rate institutions are average standardized test scores of students admitted. In a sense, Harvard would not be Harvard if those math or verbal SAT scores averaging 750 or so didn't leap from the page at readers of *U.S. News and World Report.* Test scores have become so important to institutions that some have resorted to fudging their numbers to jack up their averages, feeding the public mythology that high scores are a true measure of the quality of its students and therefore the quality of the institution.

Perhaps most responsible for the grip that mental testing holds on America is that it is a highly effective means of social control, predominately serving the interests of the nation's elites. Most people would agree that, in a democracy, merit is a good basis for deciding who gets ahead. The rub is how you define merit. We have settled on a system that defines merit in large part as the potential to achieve according to test results. It turns out that the lion's share of the "potential" in our society goes to those with well-to-do, highly educated parents. The aristocracy also used to perpetuate itself on the basis of birth and parentage. But the nation's elites now perpetuate their class privilege with rules of their own making that have persisted for several decades, rules legitimated and protected by a pseudoscientific objectivity.

The "beauty part," as Ross Perot might say, is that Americans largely buy into the rules of this rigged game. With the small exception of the National Organization for Fair and Open Testing, there is little organized opposition to the mental measurement establishment. Besides a few studies over the years, the federal government, which is the only entity with sufficient power to regulate the testing business, has either remained quiet on the subject or lent its tacit approval, preferring to let private enterprise take its toll.

At the peak of America's antitesting rebellion in 1978, Sidney P. Marland, a former College Board president and ETS trustee, captured well the notion of the mental test as social control device when he said, "I think that we will continue to have something like the Scholastic Aptitude Test (as it was then called) to help millions of young people know something about where they stand in the universe of their peers in terms of intellectual aptitudes and readiness for continued learning." (12)

Judging by trends in the years since his prognosis, Marland has proven to be right so far. I can only hope that more talented people, like the students at Northampton East High and all of America's "overachievers," will have the chance to prove him wrong.

2

Inventing Intelligence: The Origins of Mental Measurement

IT'S IMPERATIVE TO REMIND OURSELVES of how mental testing got its start in the United States. Modern mental testing, and its principal prescription to allocate opportunity based on the designation of the cognitively deserving and undeserving, is hardly a recent invention.

Recall the eugenics movement earlier this century, when state and national policymakers passed laws to stem the flow of such intellectually and morally "inferior breeds" as Italians, Jews, Poles, and other foreigners who came to America during the waves of European immigration. The nation's pioneers of intelligence testing provided lawmakers with the scientific rationale they needed for policies that are now roundly condemned as cruel and misguided: Tens of thousands of army recruits, including recent immigrants, were subjected to IQ tests; bizarre but supposedly scientific conclusions about the natural laws of intelligence were drawn; and eugenically appropriate public policies were enacted in several states.

"An accurate measurement of everyone's intelligence would seem to herald the feasibility of selecting the better endowed persons for admission into citizenship—and even for the right of having offspring," wrote Charles Spearman, among the fathers of modern intelligence testing, in his 1927 treatise, *The Abilities of Man*. So allocating individuals to their proper role in society, based on their intelligence, would render "perfect justice" with "maximum efficiency," Spearman told us. (1)

Gone, of course, are the unenlightened days when influential scholars and policymakers referred to people as social defectives, calling them "idiots," "morons," "imbeciles," or "degenerates" because of an intelligence test. Or are they? In 1998, when a number of prospective teachers didn't pass a controversial new teacher certification test in Massachusetts, a leading state politician labeled the teachers "idiots." Too, intelligence tests and their ilk continue to be used widely in the United States as a sorting and screening device. Although the eugenics movement as such is defunct and roundly condemned, its spirit persists in powerfully subtle ways that most Americans would barely blink an eye at. The eugenics movement may have faltered, but it nevertheless formed certain habits of mind that have been institutionalized in the American belief system.

Well represented on the fast tracks of academic ability are children of the well educated and well off, whereas children designated to the slow tracks are often poor, members of a minority group, or both. Clearly, the continued use of standardized mental tests in both public and private schools to screen the fast and slow, the bright and not bright, exacerbate already disturbing differences in wealth and opportunity in the United States.

No, it is not called eugenics any more; that's a bad word. Nowadays, except for the politicians' occasional misspoken word or two, people are rather more progressive and urbane about such matters, preferring to call this state of affairs a "meritocracy." That's a good word, one that few Americans would take issue at.

To be sure, the roots of modern mental testing are far more complex than what this chapter shows. But the aim of this chapter is to present a distillation of the main ideas of the paradigm's principal thinkers and show how their ideas remain intimately connected to the standardized mental testing of schoolchildren and adults nowadays, practices that are plagued by the same old mystifications and popular confusions. At bottom is confusion about the most basic of questions: Exactly what is intelligence, and what is it that intelligence tests really measure?

British Roots

The British mental measurement duo of Francis Galton and Charles Spearman are good people to begin with. Galton may well be considered the father of modern mental measurement. Having an obsessive tendency to count things, he invented many of the statistical techniques mental testers routinely employ to measure cognitive ability. Profoundly influenced by Charles Darwin and the role that natural selection of superior genes played in the evolution of species, Galton was an early advocate of the modern meritocratic view that the finest genetic material be permitted to rise to the top of the human heap. He was a rabid-eugenicist.

Like virtually all of Britain's most influential mental measurement pioneers, Galton was born into the upper social crust in 1822. His maternal grandfather was Erasmus Darwin, a well-known biologist and poet; Galton's cousin was Charles Darwin himself. When Galton's father died, Francis was provided with a fortune that permitted him a lifelong supply of independent wealth, world travel, and the means to pursue his compulsion to quantify the human mind.

Galton was an inveterate measurer and counter. His favorite saying was, "Wherever you can, count," and he applied that motto to the study of meteorology and psychology. In fact, one finds in the early mental measurement theorists like Galton, himself so influenced by Darwin, a blinding desire to place the study of human behavior into the constellation of the rigorous natural sciences. Measurement, sorting, and counting alone for Galton and his successors gave any endeavor the imprimatur of a hard science, whatever it might lack in other attributes that distinguishes real science from pseudo-science.

Galton invented many pathbreaking statistical methods for measuring intelligence, but his most indelible legacy to the way moderns think about intelligence was conceptual and ideological. After studying abilities in twins raised apart, Galton posited that intelligence is constituted by an overarching, general mental ability, as opposed to a quite distinct set of various special abilities. Also, individual differences in general mental ability were naturally selected, in a Darwinian sense. In other words, intelligence was largely an inherited trait. Galton coined the "eugenics" term, and founded the Eugenics Society (recently renamed the politically corrected Galton Institute). Galton once said: "The most merciful form of what I ventured to call 'eugenics' would consist in natality for the indications of superior strains or races, and in so favouring them that their progeny shall outnumber and gradually replace that of the old one." (2)

It would be too easy to dismiss Galton because of views that sound so similar to Nazi Germany's genocidal project to achieve racial purity. More important for our purpose is to recognize the significant connection Galton made between eugenics and meritocracy.

In Galton, the spheres of meritocracy, mental measurement, and eugenics converged into a single, simple narrative. This member of the British aristocracy might, indeed, be considered the father of modern views of meritocracy, in which one succeeds (or not) on the basis of intelligence and wit rather than one's inheritance. Society's role, therefore, was to promote policies and methods that would provide enlightened assistance to nature for selecting the best and brightest for society's most important roles.

For all Galton's influence on modern IQ mythology, Charles Spearman may have been the more important of the British mental testers in terms of setting the stage for the practical applications and interpretations of intelligence testing. Spearman gave quantitative precision to Galton's hypothesis that human intelligence was governed by a general ability that connected the dots among all other specific intellectual abilities. In doing so, Spearman harbored the conceit that his discovery of the universal principles of intelligence was akin to the monumental discoveries of the natural sciences, such as Newton's laws of motion or the laws of thermodynamics.

A fellow member of the British upper class, Spearman was a great admirer of Galton, particularly Galton's concept of "a general mental ability," passed on from generation to generation as part of an evolutionary process of natural selection of the fittest. "The notion of a general ability," says Spearman admirer Arthur Jensen, "seemed far more compelling to Spearman" than the view that humans might be "intelligent" in one or more of several ways, such as creativity, perception, memory, and so on. (3)

In his landmark 1904 paper in the *American Journal of Psychology,* "'General Intelligence,' Objectively Determined and Measured," Spearman reported his discovery of the "general factor" of intelligence that he simply called "*g*." He likened the discovery to the grand theoretical breakthroughs of astronomy and physics, thereby providing experimental psychology with the "missing link in its theoretical justification," and produced "a practical fruit of almost illimitable promise." (4)

Spearman provided the missing link with a series of experiments involving children at a village school in Berkshire, taking measurements of their abilities in the classics, French, English, mathematics, sensory discrimination (responsiveness to light, sound, and so on), and music. Spearman analyzed his data by means of the recently invented statistical techniques of correlation analysis to determine how the schoolchildren's different abilities varied with each other. He also determined the statistical association between various abilities and several independent measures of intelligence, as indicated by rank in school, teachers' ratings, the opinion of the school rector's wife, and so on.

Before proceeding, a brief note about correlation analysis is in order for nonstatisticians, because it is a topic that will come up frequently in this book. A zero correlation suggests no relationship between one variable and another, whereas a correlation of one (1.0) means that a variable rises or falls in perfect proportion to another. Generally, correlations of greater than 0.5 are considered fairly substantial degrees of association. Another thing to keep in mind: A correlation is typically designated simply as "*r*," and is calculated from a fairly arcane mathematical formula. Nonspecialists, however, might well be advised to routinely square that simple correlation to arrive at what's known as the "*r-squared,*" which gives a truer picture of the proportion of change in one variable that's associated with independent changes in another variable. Thus, a simple *r* of 0.5 squares to 0.25, meaning that 25 percent of the variance in one factor is associated with change in another one. Thus, nonstatisticians should beware that unsquared correlations leave the impression of a greater association between variables than actually exists.

Now, back to Spearman. As it turned out, most of the abilities he measured at the village school were not just highly associated with one another but also with his independent measures of intelligence. Achievement in the classics, for instance, was strongly associated with performance in French ($r = .83$) and English (.78); lesser relationships held between classics and mathematics (.70), classics and sensory discrimination (.66), and classics and music (.63). Oddly, Spearman found the lowest correlations between music and sensory discrimination and mathematics and musical talent (.40).

Based on these correlations, Spearman ranked the abilities into a hierarchy with the classics at the top, followed by French, English, mathematics, sensory discrimination, and music at the bottom. These relationships prompted Spearman to forge his grand theorem, "The Universal Unity of the Intellective Function," which stated that some "general factor," or *g*, was the engine driving the high association among the abilities. The classics were "loaded" with a lot of this *g*, French and English somewhat less, and music less still. His theorem was seemingly proven beyond doubt when he showed correlations between his measures of intelligence and the several abilities. Greek and Latin classics, being most highly saturated with the common factor *g*, were almost perfectly correlated with intelligence at 0.99.

Spearman was clearly enthused with this discovery of his law of Universal Unity of the Intellective Function, common to all cognitive abilities—based as it was upon on a small study of a few dozen schoolchildren. Spearman liked to believe his law was "both theoretically and practically" a "momentous" occasion for psychology. His cautions about what the finding might portend for the measurement of minds were of the boilerplate variety, as he suggested in an afterthought that further collaboration of his result would, of course, be needed. (5)

Still, Spearman's dutiful cautions about his general law didn't dissuade him from suggesting that public examinations on school subjects would be a useful proxy for objectively measuring one's overall intelligence, and therefore determine one's place in the social hierarchy. "Here would seem to lie the long wanted rational basis for public examinations," he wrote, objecting to protests that high test scores on, say, Greek syntax were surely not indicative of the "capacity of men to command troops or to administer provinces." At long last, Spearman told us, "precise accuracy" of measuring human intelligence was at hand. (6) In what's considered his greatest work, Spearman's *Abilities of Man* further refined and qualified the contours of *g*, and he proclaimed the scientific import of the discovery of "a system of ultimate mental laws" as being equivalent to the "Copernican Revolution." (7)

There's No There There

That Spearman elevated his finding to that of a universal natural law remains all the more startling considering the flimsy methodological foundation on which his grand theory stood—flaws that would not pass muster in genuine modern science.

What was the explanatory science behind Spearman's *g*? What he gave us was a quite particular statistical pattern that he fairly arbitrarily characterized as being imbued with a profound scientific meaning, when in fact, *there's no there there*. Other than speculating that some kind of mental energy explained the existence of *g*, Spearman's *g* lacked then and continues to endure without having the most fundamental element of science: a plausible explanation of cause and effect that might account for the observed data.

Harvard astronomer David Layzer took to task Spearman and his mental measurement progeny of recent times, including Arthur Jensen, on this point. The view that the discovery of *g* was a product of real science, simply because it appeared supported by statistical evidence, Layzer observed, is unfounded. "The first and most crucial step toward an understanding of any natural phenomenon is not measurement," he says. "One must begin by deciding which aspects of the phenomenon are worth examining. To do this intelligently, one needs to have, at the very onset, some kind of explanatory or interpretive framework." (8)

Behind the seemingly elegant statistics, the most glaring problem with Spearman's experiments on abilities was this: His independent measures of intelligence were in fact proxies for the very same abilities he was assessing. In other words, his intelligence measures—tied as they were to performance in the school subjects and teachers' opinions—were by definition dependent on changes in his chosen abilities. They amounted to the very same thing, and so of course, they would seem to correlate highly with each other.

That problem alone would suggest that Spearman's seemingly profound results were trivial and spurious. At best, one might conclude that his data demonstrated some relationship between a specific verbal or language ability and performance in Greek, Latin, French, and English. As British observers Brian Evans and Bernard Waites suggest, Spearman built his tests of *g* with "scrupulous selection of the items," rendering *g* meaningless beyond the simple arithmetical correlation that arose among Spearman's craftily engineered choice of test items. (9)

Spearman's legacy, then, is forging the indelible interpretation that persists to this day, that intelligence and performance in certain academic subjects are virtually synonymous. The entire edifice of *g* was constructed on the basis of performance on particular school subjects.

Hence, one arrives on the central flaw of Spearman's *g* that continues to plague mental testing's entire house of cards. Spearman's *g* is a general factor of what, exactly? By whose set of cultural rules are test items that capture this *g* included? Is *g* really a general ability or a spurious result of the common characteristics of very similar, specific abilities?

Alfred Binet's Pragmatism

Although Spearman was developing his pseudo-scientific explanation around his empirical observations of the intelligence of schoolchildren, Alfred Binet of France was actually creating the first practical intelligence test. Under marching orders from the French minister of public instruction in 1904 to create a reliable means for identifying mentally "defective" children, a test that would justify their being kept out of regular classrooms, Binet and his young collaborator, a physician named Simon, developed their so-called Binet-Simon Scale. That test established many of the principles and practices that continue to serve as the model for contemporary IQ testing of young children. Indeed, the Binet-Simon Scale is the original version of an intelligence test known nowadays as the Stanford-Binet Intelligence Scale, a commercially produced test that continues to be among the most popular IQ tests in the United States.

The name of the Binet-Simon Scale itself suggests its creators' principal innovation. With a series of small tests progressing from easy tasks to difficult ones, the Binet-Simon measured a child's level of intelligence according to the most difficult items he or she was able to perform. In turn, the highest level performed was equivalent to the child's so-called mental age. Thus, for instance, a four-year old who successfully performed the tasks of which most six-year-olds were capable, and no more, was said to have a mental age of six.

Binet's original, 1905 scale consisted of thirty tasks, or subtests, including many items that we might find familiar on present-day intelligence tests, such as naming objects in pictures, repeating number sequences and sentences, and comparing two weights. Children were examined individually, in a quiet room, in about forty minutes. The quiet room scenario, one-on-one with the examiner, persists as well with the modern Stanford-Binet, although the latest version now takes more than an hour to administer.

According to a series of updates of the Binet-Simon Scale published in the United States in 1916, its creators appeared to grapple from the onset over exactly what their scale measured, influenced as it was by cultural effects such as the social and economic backgrounds of the children. There's much to suggest in the scales themselves that they were powerfully influenced by such cultural factors and that differences in background culture, in turn, were associated with significant differences in children's performances. When one examines the cultural sensitivity of the Binet-Simon Scale in detail it is evident that the very problems Binet encountered continue to plague modern uses of IQ tests.

In addition to the Binet-Simon Scale being heavily slanted toward verbal and language skills, the "right" answers preferred by Binet and Simon were suggestive of the culturally arbitrary nature of the scale itself. For instance, one question asked, *When the house is on fire, what must one do?* Binet and Simon provided the following three sets of answers given by the children:

* Set 1: *Call the fireman.—Telephone.*
* Set 2: *Save oneself.—Run into the street—One must run so as not to be burned.*
* Set 3: *One must get away.—One must put out the fire.* (10)

I invite readers to guess how Binet and Simon ranked the three sets in terms of the "right" and "wrong" answers. If you replied, as I did, that one should, first and foremost, get out of a burning house, you'd be wrong, according to Simon and Binet. The best answer, in their view, was to call the fireman. But their answer appears to be completely subjective, depending on one's background and experiences. Several questions come to mind: Would children from all the various social classes in Paris of the early 1900s have a telephone in the home? Would children of landowners be more likely than those of the poor to place high value on real property during a fire? Are firefighting services equally distributed between wealthy and poor neighborhoods, such that all children would even consider calling the fireman? Are the poor who live without reliable firefighting services more likely to attempt to douse the fire on their own?

Each of Simon and Binet's "right" and "wrong" answers to the twenty-five abstract questions can be dissected the same way. Consider question 8, which asks: *When one finds that one's copy book has been stolen, what must one do?* I asked my wife, Kathleen, who's a physician, what her answer might be. "I'd try to find the thief," she answered. Wrong answer. In general, Simon and Binet preferred answers that a child first tell his teacher. The test makers clearly frowned on replies that one either try to find the copybook, try to replace it, or try to find the thief on one's own.

Again, the valued replies appear to have nothing to do with intelligence—however that might be defined—and almost everything to do with subjective cultural values of the test makers and distinct cultural attitudes of their own upper-middle-class social milieu, one that perhaps rewards deference to authority figures such as teachers. On the other hand, a tattletale going to the teacher first over a lost copybook might well be considered taboo for other children.

Simon and Binet had little to say on these questions of cultural context and "right" and "wrong" answers. In trying to account for some startling differences in children's performance on the scale, depending on their social and economic class, the authors acknowledged that much of the scale was laden with language and vocabulary skills learned at home in early childhood.

"Consequently," they write, "we have felt justified in supposing that language played an important part in a good many of the tests. . . . Many others seem to us to depend upon home training. It is not at school that the children are taught the days of the week, the months or colors; it is at home, or at least, it seems to us." The authors conceded, too, that their language-intensive tests provided many advantages to the highly verbal children from the upper social classes. "This verbal superiority must certainly come from the family life; the children of the rich are in a superior environment from the point of view of language; they hear a more correct language and one that is more expressive." (11)

Indeed, Binet and Simon observed that children of well-to-do parents performed consistently better on their scale than children from poor families. The authors cite the work of two independent researchers, Decroly and Degand, who administered the scale to the children of an upper-class private school in Brussels, later publishing their results in the *Archives de Psychologie* in 1910. Binet and Simon compared those results with their public school pupils in Paris's Tenth Ward, whom they describe as generally "poor without being indigent." On average, the Brussels children were measured on the scale as a year and a half advanced over those in Paris. "It is to be supposed," Binet and Simon tell us:

> that the school conducted by M. Decroly and Mlle. Degand is differently recruited. At our request M. Decroly and Mlle. Degand informed us that their pupils belong to a social class in easy circumstances; they have parents who are particularly gifted and understand education in a broad sense; they are renowned physicians, university professors, well known lawyers, etc. (12)

Despite the cultural influences on the Binet-Simon Scale, which the authors themselves more or less acknowledge, they ultimately did not deviate from their contention that the scale was a measure of general intelligence and was independent of whatever abilities a child might acquire at home or school. Their notion of untrained ability, a "natural intelligence," as they called it, was at the philosophical core of the Binet-Simon method, and it continues to hold sway in the intelligence testing of young children.

In the end, Binet and Simon's development of their pathbreaking scale had come from a far different purpose and perspective than Spearman's search for a general factor for intelligence. Still, their end result was reminiscent of Spearman's "*g*," that unseen and unaccounted-for force of general intelligence that mathematically titrated out of Spearman's tests on academic subjects. Like Spearman, Binet and Simon remained rather mystical about exactly what they were measuring, variously involving the abilities of "judgment, otherwise called good sense, practical sense, initiative, the faculty of adapting one's self to circumstances." (13)

Whatever their version of intelligence might be or however the Binet-Simon Scale accounted for it, what really mattered in their view was having as many tests as possible by which to discover it. "One might also say, 'It matters very little what the tests are so long as they are numerous,'" Binet famously intoned.

Further, Binet and Simon did virtually nothing to clear up the fundamental question in Spearman's work: whether, in fact, it's possible in practice to achieve such a clear conceptual separation between trained and untrained mental power, untainted by cultural forces. Such conceptual difficulties, however, were of no hindrance to the American promoters of intelligence testing, who steamrolled their version of the Binet-Simon Scale onto the American landscape.

Importing the IQ Test to America

For all the uncertainty surrounding what the Binet-Simon Scale was actually measuring—whether it was intelligence as such or some artifact of the authors' own upper-middle-class culture—observers have since speculated that Binet would have been horrified at the way his scale has been used since its importation to the United States.

Binet intended the scales as no more than a diagnostic tool for assessing the developmental progress of children, and he refrained from interpreting the scores on the examinations as the result of some fixed and unchangeable quantity of mental ability endowed at birth. In fact, he believed that one's intelligence measured with his scale could be improved, and he prescribed certain "mental orthopedics" for doing so. To those "recent philosophers" who were arguing otherwise, Binet replied, "We must protest and react against this brutal pessimism." (14)

"Binet would have resisted vigorously the hereditary-environment controversy of the next research generation," says Joseph D. Matarazzo, in a biographical sketch, "considering it as a pseudo-problem, born of an incomplete understanding of the nature of psychosocial assessment, on the one hand, and the crudity of his early test forms, on the other." (15)

We'll never know exactly how Binet would have reacted to the use of his scale in the United States. He died in 1911, five years before his creation was imported and Americanized by Lewis M. Terman of Stanford University in 1916. Under Terman's guidance and promotional skills, his Stanford-Binet Scales would become a commercial star as well as the standard for all intelligence tests to come.

Considering the human toll that ensued from mass intelligence testing of Americans after the Stanford-Binet's arrival, one could say that Binet's simple creation would become to the measurement of human minds what Einstein's famous expression about energy, matter, and the speed of light would become to human warfare. In both cases, the technology itself far outstripped larger understandings and the requisite social institutions needed to control the technology. In the case of IQ testing, the technology itself and its enthusiastic promotion often seemed to create its own set of social needs and justifications. In essence, promoters of testing in the United States had announced their magic bullet, a simple test that once and for all would measure the intelligence of human beings. Terman and his followers invited Americans to partake in all the various and wonderful ways to which the new technology could be put to use.

Indeed, one might speculate that quintessentially American commercial motivations may have driven interest and growth of the early Stanford-Binet as much as any social or scholarly motivations of its promoters. In Terman's 1916 book that unveiled Stanford-Binet to the public, *The Measurement of Intelligence*, his first task was to enumerate dozens of potential uses for the tests. The "feeble-minded," delinquents, criminals, schoolchildren, and job-seekers would all be ideal subjects for intelligence tests. Like a simple blood test, Terman's editor, Elwood P. Cubberly predicted, the intelligence test's stamp of scientific precision would unambiguously confirm any suspected defects in a person.

Although Terman's Stanford-Binet retained its predecessor's fundamental ambiguities about the nature of intelligence, Terman was not hesitant to attach exceedingly high stakes to these "blood tests." Of the "feeble-minded," Terman wrote: "It is safe to predict that in the near future intelligence tests will bring tens of thousands of these high-grade defectives under the surveillance and protection of society. This will ultimately result in curtailing the reproduction of feeble-mindedness and the elimination of an enormous amount of crime, pauperism, and industrial inefficiency." (16)

To be sure, those eugenicist views can be seen as historically interesting and unfortunate but, one might object, Terman's views then have little relevance to Americans now. Whether that's true or not, however, is irrelevant to a more important point: Besides his role in creating several new uses for intelligence tests, Terman can be credited as the inventor of a certain lingua franca, a philosophical structure for thinking about intelligence that continues to thrive in meritocratic culture today, however one might feel about the eugenics wrapper that covered his views.

Among his practical innovations, Terman may deserve substantial credit for linking intelligence and early achievement tests with the modern practice of tracking young children into various academic streams. Although educators typically no longer call the practice "tracking" per se, its essence lives on routinely and largely unchallenged as schoolchildren are segregated into various levels of classes, often depending on test scores. Chapter 3 discusses how the various groupings have fallen out principally along race and class lines. Says Terman, "We are beginning to realize that school must take into account, more seriously than it has yet done, the existence and significance of these differences in (mental) endowment" which naturally lead to different courses of study. (17)

Another of Terman's gifts to our testing culture is the very American notion of "potential" ability—measured via intelligence and aptitude tests—versus actual performance or achievement as indicated in course grades, years of schooling attained, and other indicators of real-life accomplishments. Terman and other promoters of the IQ test succeeded in convincing policymakers and the public that the intelligence test amounted to a final, indisputable measuring stick of human performance. Mysteriously, such tests of innate ability came to be viewed as a better indicator of human potential than actual performance on the very sorts of things IQ tests were supposed to predict for in the first place.

Indeed, this mode of thinking has become institutionalized in the United States. As just one example, consider Public Law 94-142, the Individuals with Disabilities Education Act. Under that law, a child cannot be designated as having a specific learning disability unless his or her IQ scores are significantly higher than his scores on reading tests. Interestingly, children having this gap between IQ-measured potential and reading scores are eligible for special education services; those children having no such discrepancy are simply considered slow learners, and are not eligible for special services. According to a recent National Research Council report, there's little empirical evidence to support this longtime practice of preferential treatment of those whose potential exceeds their actual performance. (18)

The Great Equalizer

Terman graded one's intelligence according to an intelligence quotient classification system, consisting of the following categories:

* IQ above 140: "Near genius or genius."
* 120–140: "Very superior intelligence."
* 110–120: "Superior intelligence."
* 90–110: "Normal or average intelligence."
* 80–90: "Dullness, rarely classifiable as feeble-mindedness."
* 70–80: "Border-line deficiency, sometimes classifiable as dullness, often as feeble-mindedness."
* Below 70: "Definite feeble-mindedness."

To estimate the number of American children who fell into each category, Terman had to establish American norms, based on the results of giving the revised test to 2,300 subjects, including: 1,700 "normal" children, 200 "defective and superior" children, and more than 400 adults. In addition, he performed various types of analysis on 1,000 IQ scores.

Just as Binet had found on his intelligence test given to schoolchildren in Paris and Brussels, Terman discovered in his data a strong positive association between IQ scores and social class. Of the children, some 492 were categorized by their teachers as belonging to one of five social classes that Terman labeled *very inferior, inferior, average, superior, and very superior.*

Terman's data showed that a child's social class conveyed either significant IQ advantages or disadvantages, depending on whether his family was rich or poor. Belonging to the "superior" social class gave a child a full seven-point advantage in IQ score over the average of all children, whereas being from the "inferior" class provided a child with a seven-point *disadvantage.* (19)

The higher Terman climbed up the IQ scale, the more children he found in the upper rungs of the social and economic ladder. In his "superior" intelligence range of 110 to 120 IQ, Terman found children of well-to-do backgrounds at a rate five times that of children from poorer circumstances: 24 percent of this "superior" IQ group were the wealthier kids—children "of the fairly successful mercantile or professional classes," while just 5 percent of that IQ group consisted of poor children. (20) What's more, at the highest levels of measured intelligence, the numbers of poor and even moderately poor children fell to zero in Terman's data.

Among the intellectually superior, the frequency of university professor dads in Terman's examples was startling. In fact, among fathers of children having "very superior intelligence," there were five university or college professors; a lawyer; a school principal; two whose occupations were not identified; and one house painter—who so happened to be related to John Wesley. (21)

And what model children! Typical of Terman's descriptions was that of a twelve-year-old girl he called J. R., with a "mental age" of sixteen, who was the daughter of a university professor. J. R., says Terman, "was a wonderfully charming, delightful girl in every respect."

How, then, to account for this amazingly strong association between a child's social class and her performance on a mental test? Wasn't the very credibility of his newly imported and revised test of intelligence rendered highly questionable given these results? Not in the least, Terman responded to such questions. Interpreting his results through the hereditarian lens, Terman discounted the differences of home and school environments among social classes as merely run of the mill and inconsequential. Findings from his study on the new intelligence scale, Terman observed, "agree in supporting the conclusion that the children of successful and cultured parents test higher than children from wretched and ignorant homes for the simple reason that their heredity is better." (22)

The public school system, Terman suggested, was the Great Equalizer of the social classes, obviating the influences of family class background and home environment, leaving, for Terman, the cause of IQ differences almost strictly dependent on heredity. He tells us:

> It would, of course, be going too far to deny all possibility of environmental conditions affecting the result of an intelligence test. Clearly no one would expect that a child reared in a cage and denied all intercourse with other human beings could by any system of mental measurement test up to the level of normal children. There is, however, no reason to believe that ordinary differences in social environment (apart from heredity), differences such as those obtaining among (randomly selected) children attending approximately the same general type of school in a civilized community, affects to any great extent the validity of the scale. (23)

The Army Tests

And so Terman's Stanford-Binet Scale would stand, unaffected by yawning differences in economic and social opportunity. Before long, Terman's new device would be detonated among the ranks of U.S. Army recruits during World War I, in an unprecedented, massive application of standardized intelligence tests.

Working under the rather reluctant direction of Robert M. Yerkes, whom the army had appointed as head psychologist, was Carl C. Brigham, a Princeton professor who gave us the most complete public account of those infamous tests of army recruits in his 1923 book, *A Study of American Intelligence*. It is worth reexamining some of Brigham's more absurd conclusions, as perhaps the most historically vivid and explosive example of the cultural dependency of all IQ testing that persists to this day.

Brigham described the army tests as "a national inventory of our own mental capacity." The testing was massive indeed, including 81,000 "native born" Americans, 12,000 foreign-born immigrants, and 23,000 black Americans. Three mental tests were given: American-born recruits competent in English took a paper-and-pencil "Alpha" test; immigrants who didn't speak English were given the so-called "Beta" test, consisting of items thought not to depend on language skills; and each recruit was individually tested either on the Stanford-Binet Scale or on a different "performance scale," depending on competence in English.

Cut to Brigham's notorious conclusions about the intelligence of the foreign-born versus native-born Americans. Virtually all his conclusions were based on the simple comparison of the intelligence scores of the native-born white draftees relative to those of foreign-born white draftees. At high levels of intelligence, Brigham found, were higher proportions of native-borns; and at lower levels of intelligence, according to his combined measures, were greater percentages of foreign immigrants. His results "show clearly that the foreign born are intellectually inferior to the native born," Brigham pronounced. (24)

Although American-born whites were the smartest, according to Brigham, the results also demonstrated a hierarchy of intelligence among the foreign-borns. Draftees from England were easily the most intelligent of the immigrants, as some two in three were more intelligent than the average native-born American.

In terms of the percentage who scored higher than the average American, England was followed by (25):

Scotland	58.8 percent	Belgium	35.3 percent
Holland	58.1 percent	Austria	28.0 percent
Germany	48.7 percent	Ireland	26.2 percent
Denmark	47.8 percent	Turkey	25.3 percent
Canada	47.3 percent	Greece	21.3 percent
Sweden	41.7 percent	Russia	18.9 percent
Norway	37.3 percent	Italy	14.4 percent
		Poland	12.2 percent

Following Brigham's analytical logic, he first noted the rather remarkable fact that measured intelligence was significantly related to the number of years one had lived in the United States. Among the foreign-born, scores on the intelligence scale rose sharply with time lived in the States—and indeed, at about twenty years' residence, measured intelligence of the foreign-born draftees were virtually identical to the natives.

The simplest and far more scientifically elegant hypothesis from these data would be that the army mental exams may have been culturally loaded to a profound degree. Therefore, immigrants with more time spent in American culture would clearly be in a position to outperform more recent arrivals to the United States.

Although a complete content analysis of the army mental exams is not my purpose, a few examples from the supposedly culture-free Beta test are illustrative. Like its Alpha counterpart, the Beta version consisted of tightly timed tests of mental gymnastics on meaningless tasks. The boredom factor alone would be enough to nix one's prospects of performing well. Beyond that, the Beta version's supposed culture-blindness was dubious, even laughable in some instances. For example, consider Beta Test 6, the picture completion test, in which examinees were shown twenty pictures, each having some flaw or element left out. According to Brigham's description, the test proctor would point to each picture and instruct the examinees to "fix it." Remember, these recruits didn't understand English; they had three minutes to finish the test.

Presuming the draftees understood the directions, some items were straightforward enough, like putting a nose on a noseless face. But other implicit cultural assumptions in the Beta test are eye-opening. One picture, for instance, shows an envelope with a postmark and the address of the recipient. The picture's supposed flaw, whether it's the lack of a stamp or even the absence of a return address, is ambiguous at best. Immigrants not accustomed to U.S. postal rules would certainly be hard-pressed to know the answer. Another drawing shows two bowlers at a bowling alley, but a test taker would have to know that—and know what bowling is—in order to see that each bowler has no bowling ball. Still another frame is of two tennis players playing on a court—without a net. This, at the turn of the century when tennis was still a sport for elites. One can only speculate how many poor immigrants from Czarist Russia had ever seen a tennis court.

For his part, Brigham did not seriously entertain the possibility that cultural factors could simply account for differences in measured intelligence among the immigrant groups. Indeed, if the tests were representative of the "typically American" experience, all the better. "It is sometimes stated," he snapped, "that the examining methods stressed too much the hurry-up attitude frequently called typically American. . . . If the tests used included some mysterious type of situation that was 'typically American,' we are indeed fortunate, for this is America, and the purpose of our inquiry is that of obtaining a measure of the character of our immigration. Inability to respond to a 'typically American' situation is obviously an undesirable trait." (26)

Thus while the army tests probably were every bit as much culturally loaded as they were stacked with Spearman's mystical *g* factor of general intelligence, Brigham preferred to interpret the measured differences among the immigrants as reflecting superior or inferior breeds of people. He went on to "prove" the race theory by means of a rather bizarre analysis of the supposed blood content of the foreign-born whites. Specifically, he tried to estimate the relative quantities of allegedly superior "Nordic blood" relative to "Alpine blood" and "Mediterranean blood" among the immigrants.

Alas, Brigham tells us, the percentage of "Nordic blood" coming into the United States had declined from 40.5 percent for the decade ending in 1850 to just 22.6 percent for the decade ending in 1920. That immigrants from countries such as England, Germany and Denmark had the highest percentages of "Nordic blood" is testament to their superior results on the intelligence scale.

Further, there was the matter of intelligence and the Jews. Although saying it was "unfortunate" that the army test data didn't provide finer grains of ethnicity among the immigrant countries, Brigham noted that many Jews had immigrated to America from the largely feeble-minded country of Russia. That, for Brigham, amounted to scientific proof in the inferior intelligence of the Jews, contrary to "popular belief." Wrote Brigham: "The able Jew is popularly recognized not only because of his ability, but because he is able and a Jew." (27)

Brigham hammers home his conclusions about race and IQ by defeating yet another straw man, one he called the "typically Nordic" hypothesis. Doing so, he continued to discount the most simple explanation—mere exposure to American culture and language—as the most likely cause of the "intelligence" differences among immigrants. Brigham tells us the only "possible escape" from the conclusion of Nordic god-given intellectual superiority is that the Alpha and Beta tests were biased in their favor, or "typically Nordic." But, refusing to go down the path of a possible cultural explanation for the score differences, Brigham simply states, dismissively, "Perhaps it would be easier to say that the Nordic is intelligent." (28)

Like Terman's Stanford-Binet Scale before, then, the army intelligence tests stood as an unassailable Rock of Gibraltar. Critics of the army tests should abandon their "feeble hypotheses," he said, and "recognize the fact that we are dealing with real differences in the intelligence of immigrants coming to our shores." (29)

Before going on, a final note about Brigham: If Terman had the vision of the widespread and remunerative applications for the new intelligence tests, Brigham had the practical genius to actually make it happen on an unprecedented scale. After Brigham's stint as an army psychologist, he returned to Princeton University, working in the admissions office, where he extended his work on intelligence tests to the sorting and selection of young men for college. That, in turn, resulted in his creation of the Scholastic Aptitude Test, the first large-scale college standardized admission exam, and he became secretary of the College Entrance Examination Board. That test, of course, lives on, known to everybody as the SAT. The chapters ahead have much more to say about the SAT.

Same As It Ever Was

In one form or another, we can hear echoes of Brigham's arguments even today. Whether an intelligence test, an aptitude test for college admissions, or achievement tests on school subjects, the refrain begins to sound familiar. Don't blame the messenger, proponents of mental testing have been telling Americans for decades now. Standardized tests of academic or mental ability are merely snapshots of the often unpleasant, sometimes brutal realities in real differences in human potential, firmly grounded in scientific understandings.

It's worth remembering that the eugenics practices earlier this century were products of their times, ill-considered results of unprecedented social and economic conflict that came with the expansion of industrial capitalism in the early twentieth century. As Charles Spearman suggested, Western capitalism's holy grail was to achieve maximum efficiency with perfect justice. It is still looking, and it is still using standardized tests as the answer.

With the rise of middle-class professionals, bureaucrats, shop owners, and others who shared the worldviews of the emerging bourgeoisie, Western societies at the turn of the century were in search of new rules for allocating opportunity based on merit and ability instead of blood lines. At the same time, these nations were growing enamored with science and modern technology as the answers to difficult public problems. Measuring minds to determine one's intellectual capacity and therefore one's place in a new kind of society appeared to be the perfect technological solution.

Though the science backing it up was woefully lacking, prompting many legitimate scientists to condemn the early mental testers as practitioners of a pseudoscience, mental testing was embraced by a society that saw it as a socially necessary tool of enlightened public policy. Intelligence testing had all the outward appearances of genuine science, and, more important, it provided cannon fodder for beliefs in the genetic inferiority of immigrants who would desire their own piece of the American Dream.

After World War II, economic and social conditions dramatically improved over those at century's turn, and the fortunes of the American middle class rose to unprecedented levels. Class conflict among owners of capital and workers was ameliorated by an evolving industrial capitalism tempered by government programs designed to even out its inherent inequalities, including unemployment compensation, labor protections, and efforts to democratize access to higher education.

However, that smooth postwar narrative has been shattered in recent years with the onset of several profound changes in the structure of the U.S. economy. Basic manufacturing has withered in influence and as a source of jobs, giving way to an economy increasingly driven by consumer services, high technology, and information. This "new" economy has provided exceedingly rich rewards to the highly educated and skilled and has punished scores of others who are without skills and education. As a result, the United States maintains the most highly skewed distribution of wealth between the rich and the poor of any industrial society, rivaling that of many developing nations. Thus, with the increasingly high value the new economy has placed on educational attainment and job skills, the American public has put its education system under unprecedented pressure to remain "accountable," and ensure that their children know what they need to know to survive and thrive in this brave new economy.

Further, the new economy has been accompanied by new ideology. Recent decades have wrought a sustained neoconservative movement of politicians, educational reformers, Washington think-tanks, and others who have succeeded in mounting a rear-guard action questioning the scope of federal programs. There has been a resurgence in the classical belief in the "natural order" of things, a belief grounded in a new sort of social Darwinism. Like the eugenics movement of the past, proponents of this new natural order are in need of new theories of inequality, properly updated to the sensibilities of polite society, to justify vastly unequal allocation of the nation's economic spoils.

These powerful ideological and economic trends have laid a fresh foundation for a resurgence of mental measurement in the United States. Just as the technology of mental testing performed its desired social function in the past to legitimize beliefs in genetic inferiority and exclude the new immigrants from U.S. enterprise, Americans are witnessing a reinvigorated role for mental measurement as the gatekeeper to the new economy, including testing for intelligence and ability, personality, academic achievement, and scores of other traits.

Indeed, the arguments contained in the infamous work, *The Bell Curve* by Richard Herrnstein and Charles Murray, are nothing new. The work was merely the most recent installment of a long intellectual tradition begun by the eugenicists and their mental measurement brethren. The Murray-Herrnstein book touched a nerve with an increasingly neoconservative audience receptive to its basic message: Inequality of class and race in America was simply the result of the natural order of things, arising from profound, heritable differences in the cognitive abilities of individuals. By now, that pessimistic refrain should sound familiar to readers.

And so, in this new struggle for opportunity and privilege, the nature of "defective" persons has changed from the days of Spearman, Terman, and Brigham. But the basic principle and means by which to identify these new defective persons has not changed. Polite society nowadays has its own "defectives" who don't measure up on standardized tests of so-called intelligence. Once upon a time, they were Italian and Jewish immigrants. Now, they are the poor, the uneducated, African Americans, American Indians, people with learning "disabilities," those for whom English is a second language, and others.

In the past, the designated defectives were said to be genetically inferior. Now it is simply said that, according to this snapshot on this objective test, they lack requisite abilities, cognitive development, or aptitude. Curiously, the outcome has remained eerily similar in both eras, punishing those not born to the right parents and attending the right schools, while propping open the doors of opportunity for the well-to-do. You could call it "perfect justice."

Indeed, the very same kinds of measures that sorted individuals by some correlate of intelligence in America's past remain a steady fact of institutional and social policy today, however abhorrent one may find eugenics views of history. Chapter 3 jumps forward in time, to some snapshots from the present-day workings of America's mental measurement machine, where the testing, sorting, and tracking begins at a tender age.

3

Babes in Test Land: The Sorting Begins

WHEN IT COMES TO INTELLIGENCE TESTING of young children, the fast-paced cultural capital of the nation, Manhattan, may be the "testocracy's" epicenter, a case study of the American brand of meritocracy in action. For many highly educated Manhattan parents of a certain economic means and professional status, the drive to get their toddlers selected for the most selective nursery schools or kindergartens means applying for admission to one or more private schools and even some public schools, including one exceptional school called Hunter College Elementary.

Whichever route parents choose, they must submit their three-year-olds or four-year-olds to one of two intelligence tests: The Weschler Preschool and Primary Scale of Intelligence in the case of the private schools and the latest version of the Stanford-Binet for the publicly-funded Hunter Elementary. In fact, you might call either of them "the Baby Boards."

Certainly, this is not intelligence testing on the same massive scale as the early testing for mental "defectives" we encountered in Chapter 2. But the Baby Boards for this elite segment of the nation's children, as well as similar sorts of testing of young children in many public schools, may be tantamount to the continuing radioactive fallout from the IQ testing bomb's first detonatation many decades ago. With fallout, there's no blast, no overpowering winds, and no flashes of blinding light. This fallout, like the radioactive kind, is far more subtle, more insidious, but equally damaging.

Of course, intelligence tests, used as a screening device to sort the gifted and ungifted and the talented from the merely ordinary, come with requisite warnings from schools, psychologists, and educators to keep the tests in perspective and not let the results color perceptions about children. Schools themselves strive not to label or stigmatize children on the basis of the tests, the experts say, and neither should parents.

Despite all that sage advice, the intrinsic power of ratings, rankings, and percentiles in American culture may well alter parents' perceptions of their own children—particularly on tests of so-called intelligence, perceived to be so fundamental to a child's prospects in life.

The "Wippsie-R"

Carol Weston, a Manhattan parent and author of books about teenagers, listened to the experts' advice about the intelligence test that for many years has been required for admission to private nursery schools and kindergartens in New York City. It's called the Weschler Preschool and Primary Scale of Intelligence—Revised. The test is commonly referred to by its acronym, WPPSI-R, or the "Wippsie-R."

Weston's first experience with the Wippsie-R as a parent came when her oldest daughter was about to enter kindergarten. Weston, who grew up attending public schools, says she immediately resented her child having to take an intelligence test for school. But the poor conditions of many public schools, she says, offered the family little choice. "Everybody I know has had experience with their young children having to take this test; to send your child to private school, you have to get them tested," Weston told me. "It was more important to us that, rather than having a new car, we preferred to spend our money on education for our kids."

"I resented this," she says. "I didn't want to spend several hundred dollars and come away with a number that would influence her chance of success at these expensive private schools."

Weston shared her concerns with officials at the school to which the family was applying, and was told, "Not to worry."

Against her better judgment, Weston had her daughter tested. The first time, the girl sat in the test examiner's room for all of five minutes, and then just got up and left, uninterested and uncomfortable with the situation. Indeed, that's not unheard-of behavior for four- and five-year-olds first exposed to the odd situation of being alone in a room with a stranger asking them all manner of strange questions.

Weston describes her oldest daughter as a "dogged perfectionist and a real hardworking, self-starting, striving kid," and she showed indications of this even at a young age. Nevertheless, when the girl was retested a week later, she scored in the ninth percentile on the "block design" part of the exam—that is, below 91 percent of a nationally representative sample of children who took the Wippsie-R. The kindergarten chose not to admit her.

The Wippsie, originally developed by David Weschler in 1967 as one of a series of popular tests of intelligence for toddlers, teens, and adults, takes more than an hour to administer in a one-on-one encounter between an examiner and the child. The exam is aimed at preschoolers ages four to six and a half years old.

Compared to the first version of the Wippsie, the revised one that came out in 1989 contained mostly cosmetic changes to make it more colorful and appealing, because the original test was criticized as overly long and tedious for young children. Now there are ten subtests on the Wippsie-R, including five verbal tests and five performance tests, yielding two separate verbal and performance scores as well as a full-blown IQ.

Inspecting the sorts of items on the Wippsie-R, one is struck immediately by the intensity of verbal skills and knowledge required for high performance. An information test of two dozen items assesses knowledge of facts and general information; a vocabulary test asks children to define a few dozen words. Also, children are tested on their ability to find similarities in words and concepts; on how they respond to hypothetical situations; and skill at repeating sentences read to them.

The "performance" tests include asking children to complete missing parts of pictures (not unlike Brigham's IQ tests of army recruits during World War I); to solve maze puzzles; to copy geometrical designs and assemble objects. The "block design" subtest, on which Weston's young daughter had difficulty, asks children to reproduce patterns of flat blocks, first from models and then from pictures. The test's performance items are weighted heavily on time of completion—which probably did Weston's young "dogged perfectionist" little good.

What made the exercise so surprising for Weston is that her daughter had demonstrated a remarkable skill at constructing her own designs with her own raw materials, usually of maple wood, at home. "My kid could build Eiffel Towers," says Weston. "She was this phenomenal block builder. She built cities, even. . . . Her preschool teacher was stunned by the test score. 'I don't know what happened,' she said. She was very apologetic." But test results complicated matters considerably for Weston and her daughter, as doors to nearby schools began to shut owing to the test score. "If your kid tests poorly, you have a much tougher time getting into your favorite neighborhood school," Weston says.

Officially, at least, the private schools say they don't use the Wippsie to "weed out" children, claiming that the test carries no more weight than other information about children they get from teacher evaluations and direct observation. The schools formed the Independent School Admission Association of Greater New York almost three decades ago to alleviate the testing burden on families and use a common IQ test in their admissions process. Before the association was formed, children had to take a separate test for each school. The schools have all now been using the Wippsie for some twenty-five years. Additionally, the schools agreed not to set cutoff scores on the Wippsie-R. In other words, children aren't required to have a minimum score to get full consideration to any school.

"Schools don't use it as a competitive exam," Lucille Porter, the associate director of the Educational Records Bureau (ERB) in New York, told me. The ERB is a nonprofit organization under contract with the city's private schools to administer, score, and report the results of the exam. "They use it to get another piece of information, in a standard setting common to all children, and combine that information with interviews, evaluations from a child's current schools on how this child is developing," Porter says. "The test is just one piece of the pie."

In terms of test results, the schools and ERB have also agreed not to report overall IQ scores or percentiles but only scores on the exam's verbal and performance subtests. "The I.Q. number in itself is something schools don't want," Porter says. "Schools don't want to label a child at the age of 4 and don't want to use it as a competitive type of test . . . I think they use it in a very fair way."

"We would never label a child," says Zelda Warner, director of admissions and financial aid at the Grace Church School for eleven years. "I'm telling you the test is just one part of the picture. It's no more important than the visit and the school report. When I look at the three things in the folder, I look at what a child can do and what the child's strengths are, recognizing the fact that a child can have an off day (on a test), any time. If a child had an off day and the school report is much stronger than the test result, then that (test result) goes to the bottom of the pile, and the other two go to the top."

Given the apparent fair-mindedness with which schools use the Wippsie-R results, would Grace Church School's enrollment profile look significantly different without the test? Warner had recently discussed that very question with the head of the school's kindergarten. "I asked her, 'Why do we test? Your report always says the same thing,'" despite the test, Warner told me. "She says, 'The test score is not for the children we take, it's for the children we turn down. I don't want to feel that so much is based on my reaction to that child. I wanted something else to substantiate what I saw. Maybe the chemistry wasn't right. For the children we have to turn down, I look to have this impartial, objective analysis.'"

For her part, Weston says she's skeptical of any suggestion that the intelligence test isn't determinative. The test, she believes, carries more weight than school officials would like parents to believe. "When you look at it from the school's point of view, they have so few spaces. . . . They're looking for any reason to eliminate a child from further consideration," she says. "So if a child's test scores are sub-par, that's one fewer applicant they have to consider, no matter what they tell you."

Five years later, Weston's voice still rises when she talks about having her children's intelligence tested in order that they might attend kindergarten. She's now had two children go through the admissions process to New York private schools. She knows that her sentiments might sound like "sour grapes" because her daughter's test score was lower than she had hoped for.

Still, though both children are now performing well in school, Weston says she's convinced that intelligence testing of children for admission to school does little good. She believes the tests provide parents with almost no useful information and are sources of potentially great psychic damage to young ones. "The damaging thing about testing is that it can color a parent's attitude toward their own child," she says.

Indeed, Nancy Schulman, the director of the 92nd Street Y nursery school in New York, told me that most of the potentially dangerous labeling she's seen has come, not from educators at the schools, but from parents, behaving just as Weston described. "The most disturbing thing about this is that a parent looks at a child's test scores and then reevaluates the child in light of that as either brighter or not as bright as they thought. Therefore expectations change because of this. It's a potentially dangerous thing that can happen."

Schulman has also seen it happen on a personal level in the intensely competitive world of kindergarten admissions in Manhattan. She told me about a friend's son who is now a high school senior. He tested moderately on his ERBs, to parental consternation, but nevertheless has been a remarkable achiever throughout his years at school—to the ongoing amazement of his mother. "His mother has continually expressed surprise at the level of achievement and success of her son," Schulman says. "I don't think the child is aware of that, but I am; and it can be a dangerous practice."

For Weston, the IQ test of four-year-olds also had dubious predictive usefulness. Her youngest daughter did significantly better on the test but had to repeat first grade, whereas the eldest, who flunked block design, has sailed through school. She says the whole ordeal has left her with a bitter taste about the validity of IQ testing. Now, she counsels parents to trust their instincts about their children, and take the test results with a healthy grain of salt.

"I'm a mother with a trustworthy gut," says Weston. "A lot of experts try to undermine that and you end up with the risk of losing your own judgment. You lose confidence in your child's brain. I finally said, 'Screw this.' I'm a sensible mother, and I know what I'm doing."

Hunter College Elementary and the Stanford-Binet

It would, perhaps, be understated to suggest that Dr. Kami Kim and her husband, Dr. Thomas V. McDonald, well fit the demographic profile of parents who vie for slots in the intensely competitive world of elite elementary school admissions. The daughter of a university physics professor, Kim is a research physician specializing in infectious diseases at the Albert Einstein College of Medicine in New York. After graduating from Harvard, she obtained fellowships at the University of California San Francisco medical school and did her medical residency at Stanford. There she met McDonald, who also had been a resident at Stanford. He, too, works at Albert Einstein, as a cardiologist and medical researcher.

In their particular social circle of highly-educated professionals, Kim and McDonald knew well how the meritocracy works and how the testing game is played. It seemed pretty much a matter of course that the couple would try to get their son, Clayton, into the Hunter College Elementary School's kindergarten. Compared with the private schools that charged tuition of $15,000 and up, Hunter Elementary was an amazing bargain for parents like herself, she says, who want academic excellence for their children. As a public school—operated by the City University (CUNY) system rather than the New York City Board of Education, Hunter Elementary costs parents nothing.

Also, having friends who had gone through the admissions process, Kim says the couple generally knew what to expect. The first and foremost hurdle, they knew, was the Stanford-Binet Intelligence Scale, on which Clayton would have to obtain a very high score to even merit further consideration. As for the contents of the test itself, Kim, like most other parents, knew very little, other than it was an intelligence test that placed a high premium on well-developed verbal abilities.

Moreover, Kim and her husband figured young Clayton would simply be a good candidate for Hunter Elementary, owing to its emphasis on the teaching of what the school itself calls "intellectually gifted" children. "Our son is quite verbal," Kim told me, "and showed an interest in books, language, and so on at a young age, and so he seemed like the type of kid who would do well in an academically oriented setting."

Despite all that, however, Kim says she and her husband remained ambivalent about the whole thing, particularly the appropriateness of subjecting their three-year-old to a testing and admissions process that is comparable to highly selective college admissions procedures like one would find at elite universities like Harvard or Yale.

Indeed, the frenzy among Manhattanites to get their kids into the "right" kindergarten or preschool seemed a bit over the top, even when compared to similarly situated parents whom Kim and McDonald knew in the Bay Area. "Manhattan is much more crazed about this stuff than other places," Kim told me. "We came from San Francisco where everyone in our situation sends their kids to private school, and it seemed much calmer. Here, everyone with young children seems to obsess about it."

Kim's description of the lengths to which some parents will go to seek special consideration parallels an installment of the TV show, *Frasier,* in which Frasier and his ex-wife had gone so far as to bake a Thanksgiving turkey in order to insinuate themselves with the haughty, and thankless, headmaster of the private school to which their child was applying. Similarly, Kim says she's seen parents lobbying a school's director, lobbying parents of currently enrolled children, and even asking professional colleagues to write letters of recommendation for their child. "They will also indicate willingness to donate time or money or both."

So why all the fuss over nursery school? Whether justified or not, Kim says, many New York parents of her social class believe that the well-connected elementary school could profoundly influence the eventual lives and careers of their four-year-olds. "There seems to be a lot of concern here in New York about doing and being set up in the 'right' way," Kim says, "and concern by a lot of people about being in the right preschool, so that you get in the right ongoing school, so you get into the right college, and that you know all the right people."

That parents must have their young children admitted to the best schools from the get-go, in order to establish lifelong elite connections, might seem a bit neurotic, but the perception has some validity, Kim believes, at least judging from her experience at Harvard. "Although I have doubts about it so young, there is some truth in that it is easier to go to the next step from the 'right place,'" she says. "I think that my husband, who went to a state university which was not particularly well known, had to work a lot harder to get to medical school and a good residency than I did graduating from Harvard."

Whether it's the "right" elite preschool or the "right" upper-tier university, the game parents perceive is the same, Kim says. "I think that there is more opportunity coming out of these kinds of schools and invariably it's those with the connections and money that foster the opportunities. Then it turns into a self-perpetuating cycle in which successful people come out of place X, others hear that place X was where someone came from and that attracts more people. And although the school doesn't necessarily make you anything different from what you were, the association may give you a certain luster."

A few observations are in order about Hunter Elementary itself. Any parent, regardless of economic status, would surely desire such a wonderful school for his or her child. There's little doubt that it's an educationally exciting place for young children. The school was formed in 1870 as part of Hunter College's teacher education program. Hunter Elementary took its present form in 1941, after its organizers saw the chance to start a school for intellectually gifted children after New York public schools closed an experimental school for gifted education. Admission is restricted to Manhattan residents only.

In terms of teaching philosophy, Hunter College Elementary is clearly a progressive and enlightened place, on the cutting-edge of the latest thinking in educational pedagogy for children. In nursery school and kindergarten, these bright children develop even further intellectual capacity, not fed with trivial, unrelated facts and merely entertaining games, but encouraged to develop specific and powerful cognitive skills.

In short, these young children are taught how to think in ways that schooling rewards. "Teaching strategies highlight the skills of classification and identification of relationships," school officials say. "Teachers introduce the idea that solutions to one situation can serve as sources of new ideas, leading to even more complex goals." It's not until third grade that Hunter Elementary pupils tackle academic subjects as such, learning to translate the thinking skills acquired at the beginning to "the specific content language of different curriculum areas."

Academics are integrated with art, music, foreign languages, chess, and physical education. The school emphasizes a "hands-on," project-centered approach to learning, eschewing the often-fragmented, fact-laden approach found in many American public schools. The learning-by-doing approach is clearly evident in the school's math and science labs. In a K–3 science lab, for instance, children work with bubbles, rocks, minerals, foods, and plants to learn about the physical world, and they construct actual models of dinosaurs, fossils, volcanoes, and the like. In the school's technology lab, kindergarteners make computer-generated graphs, and they actually program a computer with simple software. One recent class wrote poems accompanied by crayon drawings that they scanned into the computer. Fourth-graders helped the younger ones put their work on the Internet.

How does Hunter Elementary ensure students are learning? Whenever possible, the school uses "performance assessment," testing pupils' knowledge by the quality of real-life demonstrations, projects, portfolios, and the like, as opposed to relying exclusively on the standardized achievement tests so common in American education. Indeed, the school espouses such progressive educational philosophies as the notion of "multiple intelligences," Howard Gardner's term for the idea that people can be "smart" in several ways—creatively, intuitively, practically, and so on—ways of being smart that most standardized tests of academic ability don't capture. Besides diversity of minds, diversity of people is another of Hunter's progressive values.

But for all its progressive educational methods and beliefs in the diversity of people and kinds of intelligences, the taxpayer-funded school relies on an IQ test as the principal barrier to get through the doors of this wonderful place.

That test is the Stanford-Binet Intelligence Scale, Fourth Edition, which is the updated, modernized version of the very same Stanford-Binet of Lewis Terman and the Stanford-Binet of the Army Intelligence Tests we encountered in the previous chapter. The modern version of the Stanford-Binet, last updated in 1986, is published by Riverside Publishing Company, the same publishing concern that produced Terman's original exposition of the Americanized test in 1916. (Riverside is now a major supplier of all types of standardized tests.) Until 1986, the most recent full revision of the test was in 1960, and before that in 1937 by Terman himself.

Tellingly, except for its name—the Stanford-Binet Intelligence Scale—documentation for the latest version has eschewed the term "intelligence" for the more fashionable test of "cognitive development," and has replaced the use of IQ scores with something called the Standard Age Score. The changes may be no more than semantic; whether it is called "intelligence" or the more politically correct "cognitive development," the scale's definition of "intelligence" is very much in the same spirit of Spearman's notorious *g* factor.

In contrast to the private schools' use of the Wippsie-R, Hunter Elementary does employ the "cut-score" method. Children who don't score above the cutoff level on the Stanford-Binet are automatically rejected, while those who do score above the cut—usually set at the ninety-eighth percentile—are able to pass on to "Round 2." That phase consists of educational experts' direct observations of the toddlers in small groups. The experts watch the children at play and see how the children perform individually and cooperatively with other children. "We try to look at behaviors that are not assessed by the Stanford-Binet," such as social ability, creativity, initiative, and the like, says Polly Smith Breland, the admissions director at the Hunter College primary and secondary schools.

Clearly, however, scores on the intelligence exam are the biggest barrier for admission, compared, that is, to the school's "Round 2" process. Hunter College Elementary's cut-score process for sorting the supposedly gifted from the ungifted makes it about three times more selective than the most elite universities in the country. Smith Breland told me that some 2,000 Manhattan parents in recent years have requested the school application packet for the kindergarten and nursery school, and that about 60 percent of those families actually apply for admission.

Of those 1,200 applications, the school's designated ninety-eighth percentile cutoff score results in a total of 300 children who receive further consideration for both grades. Breland Smith says about 200 of the 600 children vying for the kindergarten class typically make the first cut, or about a third. Some 100 nursery school applicants, roughly 17 percent of the some 600 applicants, score at the ninety-eighth percentile.

A total of just 48 of the 1,200 children are finally accepted, equaling an acceptance rate of 4 percent. By way of comparison, Harvard's rate of acceptance for the freshman class beginning fall of 1998 was 13 percent; Yale's was 18 percent.

What's the ninety-eighth percentile mean? Like all so-called "norm-referenced" standardized tests, the Stanford-Binet is "normed" based on initial testing of a national sample of some 5,000 individuals. A score in the ninety-eighth percentile means a child scored better than 98 percent of similarly aged children in the norming group. But as a statistical estimate, the score is subject to measurement error, and so a child's true score could actually be several points above or below the measured one. That means the school would certainly miss some intellectually gifted children, even according to its definition of giftedness.

It's test day, and Thomas McDonald is outside the room where the clinical psychologist is administering the Stanford-Binet to his son, Clayton. Until now, the test has been cloaked in mystery. Like most parents, Kim and McDonald didn't have the Stanford-Binet test manual documenting such features as test items, norming sample, nor any information about the reliability and predictive validity of the scores. "The school gave no information whatsoever," Kim says. "I think we thought of the test as a somewhat arbitrary hoop to jump through," representing for Hunter, she adds, "some easy, supposedly reputable way of weeding through hundreds of applications."

Kim says she doesn't recall much about test day, except her recurring feelings of ambivalence about the whole thing. Of course, she wanted Clayton to do well. At the same time, though, Kim was wary of branding young children with a single test, labeling a child as either gifted or simply ordinary. In Manhattan, where few parents would ever admit to a score below the ninetieth percentile, being ordinary would be the unwelcome kiss of mediocrity. "I don't really think a test at such a young age can have a whole lot of predictive value, yet I wanted him to do well enough for the Hunter cutoff," Kim says. "I have problems labeling kids at such a young age."

Outside the psychologist's room, McDonald could hear Clayton laughing and talking with the examiner, a scene not unlike Alfred Binet giving the original exam to his fledglings in Paris at the turn of the century. First came the vocabulary test of forty-six questions, including fourteen pictures of common objects and thirty-two words Clayton was asked to define.

Based on his answers to those questions, the examiner determined his "entry level" for the rest of the test; that is, say, whether Clayton would be started with items appropriate for a four-year-old or an eight-year-old. Next, came the "bead memory" test, where Clayton was shown a pattern of beads for five seconds and then was asked to re-create the pattern. A quantitative test called for doing arithmetic with counting blocks; a sentence memory test asked Clayton to repeat sentences read by the examiner; and so on, for a total of roughly eight to thirteen such subtests, depending on a child's age and entry level.

When the examination was over in about an hour, the tester asked McDonald a disconcerting question. "Does Clayton speak another language at home? the examiner asked. "I noticed he had some difficulties with some of the words." As a matter of fact, Clayton did speak another language at home. He'd had "daily exposure to Spanish," Kim says, from the age of three months.

It may go without saying that Clayton's difficulties with a few words would be sufficient to drop his score to below the ninety-eighth percentile. In other words, he "flunked," and the family received a terse reply to that effect in the form of a single number. Kim believes the outcome should neither have any practical repercussions on Clayton nor influence her perception of their son's abilities.

She is probably right. Clayton fell short of the Hunter cut for designation as "intellectually gifted," but as the son of two highly-educated professionals, chances are quite good, a powerful body of evidence has demonstrated, that Clayton will do very well in school. This particular family had all the right traits to be Hunter material—indeed, Hunter parents are fairly well stacked with graduate and professional degrees—but for one "defect" in their son: his second language.

At least Clayton had a fighting chance. Indeed, an examination of the characteristics of children and their families, whose chances of making the Hunter Elementary cut are exceedingly and predictably poor, may be far more telling about the nature of intelligence tests and what they really measure.

"Can You Make It So Everyone Can Go?"

Bill Crain was the darling of the Teaneck, New Jersey, school board after he was elected as a trustee in 1988. A professor of developmental psychology at City College of New York across the Hudson River, Crain was perennially the top vote-getter on the Teaneck school board. He was the widely reputed expert, the university professor, who would also rhapsodize about the wonders of all children and how they learn, irrespective of race or social class. Indeed, it was fitting that Crain would be embraced by this small northern New Jersey town, where people still take great pride living in the first city in America to voluntarily end racial segregation of its schools, by a popular vote of citizens in 1965.

But then, in 1993, Crain started raising a stir, putting that romantic talk of his into action. It all started with his impromptu conversation at a local diner with a parent and her daughter in the fifth grade. Her name was Jessica. Unknown to Crain when he'd walked in the door for a cup of coffee, Jessica had just been telling her mom about her school segregating the "smart" from the "dumb" kids by means of its "gifted and talented" program.

Mom introduced Jessica to Crain, and she said, "Dr. Crain is on the board of education. Go ahead and tell him what you were telling me." Jessica told Crain, "I don't think the gifted and talented classes are fair. The kids in the gifted classes get to leave the (regular) class and go off and do interesting things, and all the kids left behind think they're not as smart. They feel bad. I don't feel too bad, because I know I could go too, but it's just not right how they make the kids feel who are left in the class. Can you make it so everyone can go?"

And so began Crain's journey into the structure of what he believes was the "institutional racism" in Teaneck schools. He called into question some basic assumptions about the nation's first willingly desegregated school system's real commitment to equal opportunity for all children.

Although Teaneck schools had been officially desegregated at the school level, there were troubling racial disparities in the classrooms. Like many public school districts throughout the country, Teaneck had quit the old practice of "tracking," shunting some students, mostly white and middle class, into the college prep track, while funneling the rest—mostly minorities and economically disadvantaged—into the less academic path. And so, Teaneck school officials had maintained, "There is no tracking in Teaneck."

That was true, but only in a very narrow sense, Crain believed. The semantics had changed but the effect was the same. It turned out that, in both the honors program and in the gifted and talented program, white children vastly outnumbered African Americans and Latinos; and it was just the opposite in the remedial classes. Further, childrens' scores on state-mandated achievement tests were used to channel them into the various academic designations. In this community of some 37,000 people, just one-quarter of the schoolchildren were African American and 7 percent were Latino, and yet their numbers dominated the remedial academic tracks.

For Crain, the underrepresentation of blacks and Latinos in the talented and gifted courses was tantamount to subtle "institutional racism," just as troubling as the overt segregation along color lines that existed more than thirty years before.

The implications were clear. Just as Jessica had seen for herself, testing into various academic levels resulted in a completely different educational experience for students of color compared to many of their white peers: Rote drill and practice sheets to pump up schools' standardized test scores compared with field trips to museums, doing chemistry experiments, and building dinosaur models; and teachers who think you're smart versus those who think you're not smart.

Indeed, Teaneck's very institutional structure was "compounding the effects of racial segregation," Crain told me. Stacking the "dumber track" with mostly African Americans and Latinos simply reinforces feelings of academic inferiority, and does so "on the basis of standardized tests of questionable validity." And so the vicious circle goes, with children branded as underachievers.

While he was on the school board, Crain tried to ignite a serious discussion about the problem. But school boards are political animals, and this issue spelled troubled relations between the board and white, middle-class parents. Often, their children did well enough on the standardized tests to get onto the faster academic tracks and the more enriching educational opportunities to which their children would be exposed. Crain's efforts got nowhere.

Then, something happened to shift the political balance that was wholly unrelated to the tracking issue. Board member Lloyd Houston, the one African American on the board, abruptly quit coming to meetings, in order to register his protest against what he believed to be the police's unequal treatment of African American students. This inflamed the black community's growing sense of disenfranchisement, reminiscent of a 1990 incident in which a local white police officer shot an African American youth named Phillip Pannell in the back. In court, the officer was exonerated, but the incident left people with a nagging sense of doubt about the state of racial relations in Teaneck.

In order to entice Houston back, the board made a deal. At Crain's urging, the board agreed, with Houston's endorsement, not only to examine the issue of disparate discipline along color lines, but also to form the Committee on Institutional Racism to investigate the issue of academic tracking.

Crain placed the problem of institutional racism squarely in the center of his 1994 bid for a third term of office. At one community forum at Teaneck High School, even before the committee's report was released, the fault lines that would divide people over tracking became clear. Crain's opponents asked, Wasn't placing children of the same grade into different ability levels just the way American society worked? At that public forum, school board president Marie Warnke, a special education teacher also going for a third term, compared tracking to competitive sports.

"In sports as in academics, some kids have abilities and some don't," Warnke said.

"Sports are not creating an underclass in our society the way the tracking system is," Crain countered. (1)

And so there it was. The linguistics had become more politically astute since Terman's and Brigham's day. Children weren't blatantly being labeled as defective because of IQ scores. This wasn't eugenically inspired public policy. Tracking, if you want to call it that, was simply the product of different "abilities" of children. The words had changed, but the underlying belief that public policy should reflect the "natural order" of humans—as measured by standardized tests—apparently had not.

For its part, the Committee on Institutional Racism confirmed what Crain had suspected: Gross racial disparities existed between various academic tracks, in all grades. The "gifted and talented" classes in grades four through eight, for instance, admitted four times as many whites as African Americans. But what would be done about it? Essentially, Crain called on the school district to quit practicing what amounted to the academic lynching of children of color, the stigmatizing, public labeling of "dumb" kids and "smart" ones. In general, this would mean "detracking" the school system, at all grade levels. He further proposed that the "gifted and talented" program be retained—but opened up to any child interested in an enriched educational experience.

When no movement on the issue seemed forthcoming, a group of parents decided to take legal action, filing a formal complaint with the U.S. Department of Education's Office of Civil Rights. But a finding that there was a violation of civil rights would also have to determine that Teaneck schools had deliberately set out to harm minority children. Indeed, after an investigation that lasted more than three years, the Office of Civil Rights in June 1998 announced that it had found no such evidence, but nevertheless put the district on notice that federal authorities would be monitoring the situation closely.

That the Office of Civil Rights did not find intentional discrimination, nor any overt discriminatory behavior by school officials, wasn't surprising. Crain had argued all along that ability grouping wasn't the result of officials' deliberate attempts to provide African Americans and Latinos with separate and unequal schooling.

Indeed, the absence of any evidence of evil motives on the part of school officials reflects the insidious nature of ability grouping. But in the aftermath of the investigation, the facts remained: If you were a child of color your chances of ending up in a remedial class were several times more likely than that of a white child, who in turn was far more likely to be blessed as "gifted."

"I believe it's most productive, therefore, to focus on the institutional structure itself—the use of levels or tracks," says Crain. "It's the institutional structure that academically segregates a large number of African American and Latino students from the white students and perpetuates their inferior status in society. It's this kind of institutional structure—not the behavior of particular individuals—that social scientists have in mind when they speak of institutional racism."

In the end, however, Crain touched a highly sensitive nerve among many parents. In particular, he became the target for white middle-class parents of children in the gifted and talented classes, who saw Crain as something of a threat to their way of life.

One evening, Crain's wife went for a walk in their neighborhood with their dog, and she overheard some neighbors saying, "We have to get Bill Crain." Later, a friend of Crain's called and told him, "Be careful." And there were letters calling him variously a Communist or a Nazi, who wanted to "dumb-down" the kids.

His decade-long run on the Teaneck school board ended when he lost his reelection bid in 1997.

An "Enlightened Reservation"

When *The Bell Curve* was published in 1994, it was marketed adroitly to a somewhat naive general public, creating the popular illusion that Herrnstein's and Murray's incendiary views on intelligence and race were novel, bold, and pathbreaking.

But *The Bell Curve* drew much of its general inspiration from the early mental testers and eugenicists such as Terman, Brigham, and Spearman. In many ways, Murray and Herrnstein were no more than popularizers of the thinking of a modern-day scholar named Arthur Jensen, himself a direct intellectual descendant of the likes of Terman, Brigham, and Spearman.

That connection to the past is especially evident in the policy prescriptions based on *The Bell Curve*'s conclusion that intelligence is a fixed, largely inborn trait, and that American public policy ought to reflect the hard realities of the "cognitive distribution" among the population. For Herrnstein and Murray, this meant—absurdly, it might seem—the need for an "enlightened reservation" in which to keep people with low IQs from causing social disruption, one observer has suggested. (2) Reminiscent of the eugenics movement, the *Bell Curve* authors also imply that the government should encourage "smarter women" to have more babies and "duller women" to stop having so many; that current U.S. immigration law, which "assumes an indifference" to the varying cognitive abilities of newcomers, ought to be modified "to serve America's interests"; and that federal education aid should be redistributed away from programs that serve children of supposedly low intelligence, in order to spend more on "gifted and talented" programs. (3)

The Bell Curve's contention that public policy ought to fit measured differences in IQ was actually a restatement of a position taken by Jensen two decades earlier. In an infamous 1969 article in the *Harvard Educational Review* titled, "How Much Can We Boost I.Q. and Scholastic Achievement?" Jensen answered, in essence, "Why bother?" Further, says Michael J. Feurer, a testing expert at the National Research Council, Jensen "seemed to be recommending a policy of providing different forms of education to black and white Americans" owing to apparently immovable differences in average IQs. (4)

Just as *The Bell Curve* was marginalized and dismissed by many educators, Jensen's controversial positions were roundly attacked by the educational egalitarians of the late 1960s. But, in one of the great and largely unnoticed contradictions of American educational policy over the past few decades, the same educational establishment that attacked *The Bell Curve* and Jensen's thinking of twenty-five years earlier has, in fact, adopted the spirit, if not the fact, of their policy prescriptions.

Largely enforced and legitimated by results on intelligence tests—or their surrogate, academic achievement tests—educational policymakers in recent years have essentially created what amounts to educational reservations for certain races and classes of American children.

The tools of this segregation by race and class include the very tracking and ability grouping programs that school board trustee Bill Crain fought against in Teaneck, New Jersey. But Teaneck is hardly an isolated example. Ability grouping and special programs for children of Herrnstein's and Murray's "cognitive elite" are actually common practice in American schools. At last count, the nation's schools spent some $400 million annually—a figure that doesn't include district-level spending—on gifted and talented programs. (5)

Just as in Teaneck, screening policies at public schools across the country have resulted in African American and other children from poor and moderate economic circumstances being far overrepresented in the lower academic tracks, while white children higher up on the socioeconomic ladder continue to dominate the ranks of the decidedly more enriched and enriching upper academic tracks.

To be sure, the use of intelligence tests, as such, to screen schoolchildren for these different levels has diminished in recent years. That has followed from both scholarly and legal attacks on IQ tests of young children, including the criticism that they don't measure the many ways that children can be smart and talented. Thus, at least in rhetoric, many schools have adopted policies that incorporate "multiple intelligences" theories into their screening processes.

Despite this, IQ scores and achievement test scores have remained, by far, the most commonly used criteria to identify "gifted" children, according to a 1995 survey published in the *Roeper Review*, a highly regarded journal on gifted education. Indeed, fully forty-nine states in the survey used "some form of standardized I.Q. scores and achievement test results in their identification process" for gifted programs.(6)

Of course, one might object that *achievement* tests aren't the same as *intelligence* tests. According to common belief and even official policy at most public schools, IQ tests measure something like a god-given, cognitive ability or potential, while achievement tests assess what a child has actually learned in school. That belief, it would seem, underlies the neat separation between the two that has occurred in educational policy, as educators have come to view standardized achievement tests, unlike IQ scores, as directly attributable to school instruction and therefore educationally and legally defensible.

But the popularly perceived distinction between the two kinds of tests may be illusory. For one reason, so-called aptitude test scores are highly associated with achievement test scores. Also, both kinds of tests have been found to be highly charged with the *g* factor of Spearman fame—whatever it is that *g* really represents. Indeed, intelligence tests may represent a rather specific variety of achievement test. Both are "highly similar and inseparable both theoretically and statistically," suggests Stephen J. Ceci, a human development expert at Cornell. (7)

Further, the standardized achievement test has gained vigorous new momentum in recent years with the rise of the school accountability movement in the United States, which has turned into a national obsession to make public schools more accountable at almost any cost. This trend is critiqued in subsequent chapters, but an important point about it needs to be made here. Despite the warnings of child development experts that standardized testing of any sort is especially damaging to, and not appropriate for, young children, four- and five-year-olds continue to be subjected to such testing in many states—largely the consequence of political motivations and accountability ideology rather than sound educational practice. (8)

Recent years have seen a change in acceptable terminology, with a widespread turning down of noses at the measurement of IQ per se. Even intelligence tests themselves—the Stanford-Binet being the chief example—have eschewed the term "intelligence," replacing it with language that might satisfy publicly accountable institutions that are consumers of the tests.

Nevertheless, an IQ test is an IQ test, and IQ tests continue to be used in many public schools as a gatekeeper to gifted and talented programs. Schools that have eliminated IQ tests for the screening of the academic haves and have-nots have turned to its close cousin, the achievement test.

Scores on these supposedly objective tests, whether they be IQ tests or achievement tests, systematically and predictably tend to benefit some classes and races of children and prove costly to other classes and races of children.

Family Background and IQ

Choosing between the "gifted" and the "ungifted" simply brings to the surface the glaring problems that occur when institutions attach great power and major consequences to test scores.

But wait, some readers will object. Whatever the unfortunate effects of segregated school tracks, such a system is largely unavoidable, owing to undeniable differences in the abilities of children. Like the Teaneck board president once implied, school is like sport. Some kids have "abilities" at running the 100-meter dash, and other children are naturally better at, say, lacrosse.

Similarly, some children have "ability" for schoolwork, and others might do themselves a favor by getting some good job training instead of going to college. If, as it so happens, most of the high-ability children are white and most of the low-ability ones are children of color, that's the way the world works.

It's time to deal head-on with the "ability" issue. If there's a single thread running throughout the controversial history of intelligence testing in the United States, it's the debate over the heritability of "intelligence"—that is, the extent to which genetic factors explain differences in IQ scores.

In modern times, this line of scientific inquiry has been both intensive and highly controversial, and any detailed analysis of that scientific and methodological issue of highly-charged debate is beyond my scope here. Depending on which sets of data you believe, genetic factors either account for practically none of the variation in individual IQ scores—according to Leon J. Kamin's extensive 1974 reanalysis of several IQ heritability studies—or as much as 70 percent or more of the variation—according to Arthur Jensen's studies. Some recent and large-scale studies of families in Hawaii and Colorado—work that continues to receive attention in such publications as *Scientific American*—claim data that compute heritability correlations of about 40 percent to 60 percent, depending on the cognitive trait being tested. (13)

Perhaps it would be useful to take as a given that a child's "intelligence" is roughly a fifty-fifty proposition between genetics and environmental influences. Then focus on the 50 percent that matters, the part of the so-called intelligence equation human institutions might actually have some ability to influence.

~

FOCUS: "ISLANDS OF SEGREGATION" IN NEW YORK PUBLIC SCHOOLS

Just as in Teaneck and scores of other public school systems in the United States, the nation's largest school district has an extensive, de facto system of tracking students into various academic streams. As it turns out, those academic tracks are divided largely on the basis of class and race.

At the pinnacle of the tracking system are two elite high schools, Bronx Science and Stuyvesant, both of which require a competitive, multiple-choice examination in mathematics and language arts for admission. Sounds fair enough. But as it turns out, a very specific set of courses and academic experiences is necessary to do well on the exams, and just a handful of "feeder" schools offer the requisite coursework for success on the tests. In a series of three remarkable reports that resulted in an investigation by the Education Department's Office of Civil Rights, the public-interest group Association of Community Organizations for Reform (ACORN) revealed:

- Just three community school districts plus private and parochial schools supplied more than 50 percent of the children admitted to the two elite high schools.
- The mathematics test essentially covered material taught in one specific course, Sequential Mathematics I—a course available to some children from some schools, and not to others. According to ACORN, the course was taught in just a fifth of the city's middle schools in the 1996–1997 school year.
- The language subtest required a high level of sophistication and experiences with language, beginning in kindergarten, both in and out of school, that were available to a relatively few schoolchildren.

The Education Trust is a nonprofit organization ACORN hired to analyze the entrance test. For example, the Education Trust criticized the too-common, dumbed-down practice of permitting some children to compose simple stories about "magic teddy bears" or allowing them to draw pictures instead of write. Performance on such tasks, the Education Trust said, was hardly sufficient to perform at the verbal level required by the tests.

"The examination requires students to have read books and articles to acquire ideas and facts—and to have read beyond classroom textbooks. Daily newspaper reading with discussion of the meaning of articles would be a good preparation for this examination. The passages are about on the level of the weekly science articles in the *New York Times*." (9)

Moreover, ACORN found huge discrepancies in the racial makeup and economic status of children from the feeder schools versus those which sent few students to the two prestigious high schools.

The top five feeder districts, for instance, had a combined African American and Latino enrollment of 45 percent in 1995–1996. On the other hand, the five districts

(continues)

(continued)

that sent the fewest children to the elite high schools had combined black and Latino enrollment of more than 97 percent. Moreover, fully 86 percent of the children in schools with the least chance of going on to the elite programs were classified as poor; that's compared to 50 percent so classified in the top feeder schools. (10)

Also, many of city's "gifted" programs and federally subsidized magnet schools have for the most part been transformed, intentionally or not, into academic enclaves for white children.

For instance, in District 3, Independent School 54 enrolled some 88 percent of its white children in the gifted classes, leaving just 22 of the school's 980 white children *not* designated as "gifted." "The school has created a privileged island of segregation within its walls," ACORN remarked, noting that the same campus received some $100,000 in federal magnet school funds. (11)

In fourteen gifted programs, ACORN found that from 50 percent to fully 100 percent of their enrollments were composed of white children, often in absurd excess of what would be expected according to relative population.

Beyond the raw numbers, which revealed predictable patterns along race and class lines of participation in the enriched academic experiences versus dumbed-down ones, ACORN documented that non–white parents' ability to get simple information from schools about special programs was like a Kafkaesque nightmare.

Using techniques similar to those used by banking regulators to uncover systematic racial discrimination in mortgage lending, ACORN sent black, white, and Latino "testers" into schools to compare how they were treated.

Findings from these forays ought to be an embarrassment to public schools in New York. Nearly 50 percent of white parents were permitted to speak to a teacher or someone else on the professional staff, compared to just 28 percent of those who weren't white; white testers were more than three times as likely to get a school tour after talking to an educator.

Contrary to Board of Education policy that permits school attendance outside any district in which parents live, at least half the "testers" were quizzed, particularly in predominately white districts, about their place of residence. Testers were told they couldn't attend this or that school because they lived beyond its boundaries. "At PS 72, a tester was told that his address was not in the cachement area and he, therefore, 'would not be able to register here' . . . she didn't volunteer to be of any more help, just left me hanging, so I left," says one ACORN tester. (12)

As in Teaneck, ACORN found no direct evidence of some cynical attempt by New York schools to manipulate enrollments so that blacks are shunted to remedial classes, while middle- and upper-middle-class white children are creamed off to the more advanced and enriching courses.

Still, one can imagine how politically beneficial it would be for New York schools to "compete" with the city's expensive private schools by luring middle-class white families with the virtual promise of a distinctive and mostly segregated academic experience for their children.

But we don't need to presume the existence of a conspiracy to explain these outcomes. Rather, the discrepancies follow inevitably from the blind belief that standardized testing is the most fair and objective way possible to make hard choices about children.

As illustrated in the ballyhoo over publication of *The Bell Curve,* the heritability side of the equation has received the lion's share of recent popular attention. Clearly, this is owing in part to the inflammatory issue of race and so-called intelligence. That much of the American psychological community and society itself seem fascinated with questions of race and intelligence is interesting in itself.

Why is this so? Do books like *The Bell Curve* fulfill some guilt-ridden need in some white Americans to somehow justify their largely superior economic and social positions? Is the fascination about genetic differences in IQ the result of purely scientific truth-seeking or does it reflect the need for powerful ammunition in a political struggle over scarce public resources?

Whatever the cause of this fascination, Americans aren't likely to see equivalent notoriety given to scientific investigations that have focused on "the other 50 percent" any time soon—which, ironically, is the only part of the equation over which policymakers might have some potential control.

It turns out, however, that several studies in recent years, unprecedented in their size and scope, have demonstrated beyond doubt this fact: Regardless of genes, children of parents most likely to apply to places like Hunter College Elementary, working in high-status, high-paid professions, endowed with college and advanced degrees, have a powerful leg up in the IQ "competition."

This body of evidence also suggests that children of low-income or poorly-educated parents hardly stand a chance the way the IQ game is currently rigged.

Look at some recent studies that have investigated the relationships between a young child's family background and cognitive development measured by IQ scores. The most compelling and definitive work to date on this question has come from studies by a handful of researchers who have analyzed raw data provided by two large, nationally representative surveys.

One is the survey known as "Children of the National Longitudinal Study of Youth." Sponsored by the U.S. Bureau of Labor Statistics, the C-NLSY began tracking socioeconomic characteristics of young mothers and their children beginning in 1986, and included an abbreviated IQ test.

These pathbreaking studies also relied on data gathered from the Infant Health Development Project (IFHP), begun in the mid–1980s to annually gather information about some 1,000 infants born in several regional health centers around the nation. The IFHP survey also includes three full IQ tests: the Bayley Scales of Infant Development for two year olds; the Stanford-Binet Fourth for three- and four-year-olds, and the Wippsie-R for five-year-olds.

Taken together, these large databases spanning several years have provided researchers with an unprecedented means to assess the effects of such background factors as poverty and family income, neighborhoods, and ethnicity on a young child's cognitive development—measured by the very same intelligence tests on which scores of American institutions rely to make important decisions about children. Let's take up these effects one by one.

Effects of poverty and family income. Much past research on racial differences in child development, the authors of these recent studies suggest, have paid too little attention to differences in poverty and family income measures. Recent work, however, has compared the children of the poor and nonpoor in terms of how they function on intelligence tests and early achievement tests while still very young, from about two to five years old. These studies have looked at various dimensions of poverty, including its extent, duration, and at what ages children were poor. The extent of poverty was defined as the gap between a family's income and the cost of living in an area.

One unassailable conclusion this body of work has is this: When it comes to scores on early IQ and achievement tests, *money matters,* overriding the effects of almost all other pieces of a child's family background.

Consider, first, a 1993 paper titled "Economic Deprivation and Early-Childhood Development," by Greg J. Duncan and other researchers. The team examined a sample of some 900 infants in the IFHP survey, and calculated, among several other relationships, how changes in family income affected scores on the Wippsie-R at age five. The authors were particularly interested in the effects of persistent poverty. The results showed that family income and poverty were "powerful determinants" of cognitive development. Indeed, after controlling for the effects of other family traits, young children in persistently impoverished families had IQ scores fully *9.1 points lower* than children who were never poor.

"There is little doubt," the authors tell us, "that child poverty, which is much higher in the United States than in other Western Countries, as well as higher now than two decades ago, is scarring the (cognitive) development of our nation's children." (14)

That conclusion was bolstered in a 1997 follow-up study, published in a 1997 volume by several scholars, titled, *Consequences of Growing Up Poor*. Researchers Brooks-Gunn, Klebanov, and Judith R. Smith examined, in part, how various aspects of a child's family income during his or her first four years, affected cognitive functioning. Tracking 895 children, this study used a different random sample than the earlier one, resulting in a different set of families and children to follow, but nevertheless reproduced almost exactly the same correlations as the earlier study.

Consider the effects on children of long bouts of being poor. On reading tests of three- and four-year-olds, the negative effect of continuous poverty on achievement was 9.2 points compared with never-poor children; on math tests, it was 5.7 points. Moreover, the detrimental effects of poverty increased with age: Reading scores of continuously poor children, for instance, were a full 9.6 points below the never-poor ones at age five; that's compared to a gap of 7.3 points at age three. Hence, the authors say, the effects of being poor or even near poor are noticeable as early as the onset of a child's learning to speak, count, and reason. (15)

What is more, these family income effects trump nearly all other environmental factors. Consider how the marital status of a child's mother affects her cognitive functioning. In the same 1997 study, the authors discovered that the reading scores of young children living with a single mother declined by some 4.4 points compared with children living with two parents. Interestingly, when these single-parent households faced the disruption of a mom's new marriage, reading scores took an even bigger hit. But when income was added to the equation, such effects of family structure all but disappeared. In other words, material affluence overcomes any detriments in child's cognitive development associated with family structure.

Effects of neighborhoods. Duncan and his coauthors in the 1993 study cited above held constant such factors as family income, mother's education, and so on, to isolate the effects of a child's neighborhood on behavioral traits and intelligence scores. Interestingly, they found that in poor neighborhoods, the effects on behavioral problems were insignificant for IQ. On the other hand, the cognitive benefit imparted to a five-year-old living in affluent neighborhoods was considerable—though still not as great as the family income and poverty effects.

Effects of race. Scholars of intelligence and school achievement, from Carl Brigham to Arthur Jensen to the authors of *The Bell Curve*, have long noted the consistent differences in average standardized test scores between whites and blacks. In virtually any standardized test of cognitive ability, whether the SAT for college admissions or a reading achievement test for third-graders, the differences between blacks and whites are sizable, roughly equal to about fifteen points on the most widely used IQ tests. Moreover, this gap shows up at an early age, as soon as an IQ can be assessed in young children, around the age of three.

These measured differences, along with results of experiments on the heritability of intelligence, have led some observers to suggest that race alone is a powerful predictor of a child's intelligence and later achievement in school. Put in the rude terms of eugenics, these observers would say that, when it comes to cognitive ability, blacks are genetically "inferior" to whites. Therefore, according to this logic, public policy ought to recognize these inherent differences and avoid devoting significant public resources to alleviating a problem that is really not a problem as much as fixture of the natural order.

Although warning against interpreting their results as proof or disproof of the heritability hypothesis, another 1996 study by the research team of Duncan, Brooks-Gunn, and Klebanov offers some startling results that lead to exactly the opposite conclusions of *Bell Curve* enthusiasts.

The team studied yet another large sample of young children in the Infant Health Development Program to investigate, specifically, the differences in IQ scores between white and black children.

Indeed, the initial IQ difference between white and black children in the research team's sample of children was a daunting 17.7 points—certainly enough, for instance, to knock a child out of the running for Hunter College Elementary or virtually any other "gifted and talented" school program. For the fourteen explanatory variables included in the study, racial differences were equally grim. White children, for instance, were about three times more likely to live in relatively comfortable economic circumstances; to have better-educated mothers who provided warmer, more enriching environments for learning; and to live in communities with more neighbors who were affluent and fewer neighbors who were poor. But do any of these factors have a discernible effect on the differences in IQ between young black and white children?

In order to tease out the exact influence of each of the fourteen variables on IQ scores, the team used the techniques of statistical regression analysis. Okay, the team reasoned, there's a 17.7-point gap in the average IQ score of white and black children in this large sample of young children. What if, the research team asked, we add in those fourteen variables to the regression equation, one by one. What effect would each variable, so isolated, have to close, widen, or do nothing to that gap between white and black IQ scores?

In the first "regression," the researchers ran the numbers on the variables of gender, birthweight, and a measure of the extent of neonatal care. But the addition of these factors had no observable effect on the 17.7-point gap. Next, the team included measures of family and neighborhood income. It turned out that family income alone decimated the gap by a full 52 percent, *knocking down the IQ difference between white and black children to just 8.5 points.* Interestingly, lots of affluent neighbors had little effect on the IQ gap at age five, but neighborhood affluence did narrow the difference for three-year-olds. Then, the researchers considered the effects of family structure as well as mothers' educational attainment. None had much effect, swamped by the more fundamental differences in family income and poverty.

The final regression teased out effects of the home learning environment on the IQ gap. Did parents read aloud to children and how often? Did parents use toys and play to challenge children to build new skills? Did parents provide a loving home that nurtured intellectual development? The inclusion of these home measures, it turned out, further *reduced the IQ gap by an additional 28 percent, trimming the original 17.7-point difference to just 3.4 points,* when combined with the family-income effect.

"What our analyses do show," the authors of this remarkable study conclude, "is that age–five I.Q. differences between black and white children are almost completely eliminated by adjusting for differences in neighborhood economic conditions, family poverty, maternal education, and learning experiences." (16)

Their conclusion, of course, begs one question: What is it about intelligence tests that make them so sensitive to factors that, when all wrapped up, virtually all are profoundly associated with one's social and economic class? Part of the answer, it would seem, is that a young child's cognitive ability, as commonly measured, depends on a fairly particular set of experiences that are either formally or informally related to what one learns in school.

"School" in this case could mean a formal academic setting, or more likely in the case of young children, school-like experiences that some children from some families get in bucketfuls, while other children receive just a smidgen. Whether a child has access to these early school-like experiences largely depends on the class status of his parents. Well-paid, highly-educated professionals tend to reproduce their cultural habits and attitudes in the experiences they provide young children.

I asked Hunter College Elementary's Polly Smith Breland about the influence of family background on the school's sorting process, and she acknowledged that stark differences in the early learning experiences of young children either help or severely hurt a child's chances of making the IQ cut score. Remarkably, some Manhattan three- and four-year-olds have their own computers and even their own libraries stocked with books and reading matter in their rooms. On the other hand, Breland Smith told me, "children who come from homes with not a lot of books, are not read to on a regular basis, with parents who don't talk to children a lot, and are not exposed to a variety of things, that's a serious problem."

Thus, to suggest that IQ tests and the like are measures of general intelligence, an overarching cognitive ability, which can sort the intellectually gifted from the nongifted and the merely ordinary from the truly talented, would seem to attach far more weighty significance to the tests than is justified.

From the earliest days of intelligence testing, measures of intelligence have inhabited the specific cultural space of certain economic and social classes, and have been far more culturally arbitrary in their contents and their judgments than commonly believed. We are left with the question: What is it really that intelligence tests measure?

Intelligence and Culture

Clues for answers to that question are provided in evidence about the relationship between schooling and IQ. Is cognitive ability impervious to experience, training, and improvement, or does school matter in making children smarter than they would be otherwise?

As it turns out, among the most striking aspects of measured intelligence is that IQ scores *are* highly associated with the sheer quantity of schooling and school-like experiences, whether the schools are good, bad, or in-between; whether people live in the hollows of the Blue Ridge Mountains or on canal boats in London.

In a 1991 paper remarkable for its analytical depth, Stephen J. Ceci, a human development psychologist at Cornell, surveyed and summarized the results of some 200 empirical studies that investigated the association between years of schooling and IQ scores. One of the earliest such studies examined children raised in the cultural isolation of London canal boats in the 1920s. Low IQs were common among these unschooled children, and the longer they lived in the canal boat environment, the lower their IQs dropped. Indeed, while the young children ages four to six had average IQ's in the 90s, average IQs of the older ones aged twelve to twenty-two had declined to around 60, which would put them in Lewis Terman's category of "definite feeble-mindedness." Thus, "'without the opportunity for mental activity of the kind provided by the school—though not restricted to it—intellectual development will be seriously limited or aborted,'" says the study's author. (17)

Many similar studies have examined such relationships between measured intelligence and schooling, not just between IQ and years of schooling, but also the effects of intermittent school attendance, school vacations, delayed onset of schooling, early termination of schooling, and so on. One conclusion rises to the surface from Ceci's examination of this body of work. Schooling counts. Indeed, Ceci believes that schooling and schoolinglike experiences overwhelm the effects of genetics.

"When one considers the entire corpus of correlations that have been reported this century," says Ceci, "the high correlations between IQ and schooling are difficult to account for on the basis of genetic selection or any other explanation." Ceci adds that "the most parsimonious account" for the strong correlations between schooling and IQ would be that there's a direct causal relationship between schooling—and the values and modes of thinking schooling indirectly inculcates—and performance on standardized tests. (18)

Could, then, "intelligence," as it's measured on common IQ tests, be largely a culturally acquired trait, say, not unlike the taste for fine wine? Examining the contents of intelligence tests themselves, and how the tests' scoring systems evaluate children's responses to specific test items, suggest that supposedly objective IQ tests do in fact reflect certain culturally acquired habits of mind.

Consider the Stanford-Binet, fourth edition. Test Six of the exam, the subtest of comprehension, asks children several questions to explain what are assumed to be commonly understood events and objects. One item asks, for instance, "*Where do people buy books?*" Clearly, a three-year-old born into the home of highly-educated parents—who read often and talk about books and book culture in the home—will be in a far better position to give the examiner a reasonable response compared with a child whose parents aren't regular consumers of books and lattes at Barnes and Noble.

Another item on the Stanford-Binet asks children, "*Why do people read newspapers?*" In order of preference, the best answers listed in the scoring guide are: 1. "*To find out what the news is*"; 2. "*Because it's fun*"; 3. "*To see what's on TV.*" (19)

Full credit is given to any one of those answers. But should a child answer that one reads a newspaper "*Because the TV is broken,*" her cognitive functioning is deemed less well developed than the child who answers one of the above, according to the Stanford-Binet scoring system. No matter that children born to homes with poorly-educated parents might well watch their mothers and fathers turn to a newspaper or other sources of news only when the TV is broken.

What's more, intelligence tests "inculcate," to borrow Stephen Ceci's description, certain styles of thinking that are taught in school. Consider the Weschler Intelligence Scale for Children—Revised, (WISC-R). This widely used IQ test for ages six to seventeen contains an implicit hierarchy of scoring rules that gives bonus points for some very specific thinking strategies that, at bottom, reflect the values and preferences of test designers.

For instance, the test rewards responses that tend toward the most general or abstract ways to classify or describe something, and punishes more particular or even more descriptive responses. The WISC-R asks, "How are an apple and an orange alike? If a child answers that both are fruits, she receives two points. But if another child responds that both are round, contain seeds, can be eaten, or any number of specific—even creative—observations, she would receive less than full credit. (20)

Exposing children to abstract thinking skills are exactly what schools do. Further, it's likely that some schools, such as Hunter College Elementary, which provide supercharged learning experiences to young children that help them learn how to think, perform this acculturation process much more explicitly and probably more effectively than less enriching schools. Additionally, there's little reason to believe this inculcation begins and ends with formal education, but more likely finds root in home environments that are intellectually stimulating.

Further evidence about what IQ tests really measure comes from recent findings about massive increases over time in IQ scores, not just in the United States, but throughout the industrial world. Among the foremost authorities on this area of research is James R. Flynn of New Zealand. Analyzing IQ scores over several decades in fourteen countries, including the Netherlands, France, Norway, Canada, and the United States, Flynn found average IQ gains as high as twenty-five points in a single generation.

In France, for instance, IQ gains of twenty points in a generation were such that a quarter of French schoolchildren could be classified as "gifted," and in the Netherlands, the number of "potential geniuses," having measured IQs of 150 or more, exploded. Comparing average IQ scores of eighteen-year-old Dutch military recruits between 1952 and 1982, Flynn found a surge of twenty IQ points in just one generation. "It is also something quite unique in the literature, a measure of IQ gains over a real generation, a comparison of a generation of fathers with their own sons, " Flynn says. (21)

A strictly psychometric interpretation of such findings would be that people's general cognitive ability has expanded over time. People are simply smarter, not just since humans evolved from the great apes, but are more intelligent than even people of a single previous generation.

The alternative explanation, however, goes to the nature of IQ scores themselves as a cultural artifact. Rather than tapping the mysterious *g* force of general intelligence, it's more likely that IQ exams tap the culture. That schooling and school-like experiences help a child learn abilities that are rewarded on such tests is entirely consistent with Flynn's findings. As school participation rates have steadily increased worldwide over the past several decades, one would expect large IQ gains to follow.

Such massive gains would also mean a "cultural renaissance too great to be overlooked" in many countries, Flynn says. And yet, in two nations with some of the greatest gains, France and Holland, there's no evidence of any remarkable increase in the rate of mathematical or scientific discoveries. "The Dutch do feel they have achieved a marked superiority in sport," Flynn wryly notes. Yet, the number of patents for new inventions in the 1980s were just 60 percent of what they were in the 1960s. (22)

Instead of overall intellectual capacity—if such a thing really exists—what IQ tests really measure is probably something far more specific, narrow, and significantly less grandiose.

IQ tests don't measure intelligence but rather a "weak correlate" of intelligence that Flynn calls "abstract problem solving ability," by which he refers to the ability to decontextualize problems divorced from real-world subtleties and complexities. One might think of this skill as the ability to solve puzzles and play games.

With our present understanding, that's the most that can be said of intelligence tests. "Until the matter is settled," says Flynn, "psychologists should stop saying that IQ tests measure intelligence. They should say that IQ tests measure abstract problem-solving ability (APSA), a term that accurately conveys our ignorance. We know people solve problems on IQ tests; we suspect those problems are so detached, or so abstracted from reality, that the ability to solve them can diverge over time from the real-world problem solving ability called intelligence; thus far we know little else." (23)

Class Rules

Indeed, "abstract problem solving ability" is a poor substitute for "intellectual giftedness" that institutions such as Hunter College Elementary purport to screen for in their search for gifted children. Using the Stanford-Binet and similar tests as the identifier of intellectual giftedness conveys an inference of weighty universality to their selection exercises that's hardly warranted by the more crude reality.

Although schools, both public and private ones, claim they are sorting the intellectually gifted from the ungifted, or the ordinary student from the slow learner, the *real politic* is an entirely different matter.

The evidence examined so far suggests that it is far more likely schools wind up screening for a particular set of cultural traits, most especially for traits cultivated in middle- and upper-middle-class, white American homes. When it comes to standardized mental tests, whether it's an IQ test, the school's ordinary achievement test, or college admissions tests, *class rules*, trumping all other factors.

That's hardly surprising, given the history of mental testing. From Alfred Binet's first experiments with the Binet-Simon Scale; to Terman's repackaging the test for such American uses as the sorting of World War I army recruits on the basis of IQ scores; to the segregation of academic ability levels in Teaneck, New Jersey; or the competition for gifted and talented slots in New York public schools and elsewhere; the content and scoring of most mental tests have tended to be beneficial to people of certain social classes and harmful to people raised in less privileged environments.

For their part, defenders of mental tests argue that these tools can correctly differentiate individual abilities and potentials of humans. Indeed, the various subtests in IQ tests, as well as academic achievement tests, do show high correlations with one another. Therefore, each subtest, it is claimed, is saturated with an independent "general factor," Spearman's famous *g*, that reflects overall intellectual ability. In other words, a child who scores well on one part of an IQ or achievement test is likely to score well on another. Thus, according to the test creators, the sizable intercorrelations of the subtests scores mean that the test and its subparts tap into general intelligence.

It is more likely that the high correlations among subtests reflect a remarkably narrow content that taps a fairly restricted set of abilities. Of course, these subtests would be highly correlated with each other. However, that may stem from little more than a rich methodological tradition in mental testing: typically, when test creators are piloting test items, they discard items that have low correlations with other items on the test. And test creators like to keep questions with high correlations to other test items. Furthermore, these characteristics of the tests get passed on from one revision to the next, from generation to generation, because a test is considered to be a good test when it shows high correlations with other similar standardized tests.

Ultimately, what are sold to consumers as tests of intelligence or general cognitive ability, are carefully selected items that tap abstract problem solving skills, and little more. What test makers view as general intelligence, says Yale psychologist Robert Sternberg, "may reflect the narrow range of the test content rather than an essential property of human abilities." (24)

I would hasten to add that this restricted range of content of intelligence tests tends to mirror the value systems and learning environments provided children born into middle- and upper-middle-class families.

For the sake of truth in advertising, then, the notorious *g* factor of general intelligence should be renamed, to something like the *c* factor of general cultural exposure. To the extent that test designers are predisposed to making tests that are consistent with their own middle-class backgrounds and inconsistent with the cultural backgrounds of less dominant social classes and ethnicities, then it would indeed be surprising if the various parts of such tests did *not* prove to yield some sort of "general factor."

IQ and Public Policy

What, then, do findings on the relationships between intelligence and ethnicity, poverty and affluence, and the quality of a child's home life mean in the real world of public policy—that world in which adults make lots of important decisions about children according to early results on IQ and achievement tests? There are two dimensions to the policy implications.

First, to the extent that intelligence testing and ability tracking of children may be unwavering owing to political considerations and entrenched ideology, several policy implications are immediately apparent. In sharp contrast to those who might contend that public policy can do little to alter what they see as the naturally occurring, fixed-sum allocation of intelligence among citizens, evidence obtained from several large studies surely suggests that IQs of young children can be directly and significantly improved by policies that attack poverty, raise incomes, and other measures that make for intellectually stimulating home life.

Reading to children does matter. Better-educated parents having good jobs matters. Tax credits for low-income workers count. Reforming welfare policies to make going to college an option would matter for young parents and parents to be. And, it is worth remembering the obvious: Money itself matters, and the lack of it matters even more, for a young child's cognitive development. The constellation of traits that constitutes a growing child's social and economic class—not one's racial identity—matters most in terms of what social policy can do to improve young children's performance on IQ tests.

A second set of policy implications speaks to the tests themselves. Given what is known about the nature of intelligence tests and the specific traits that they really measure, and given the long and troubling history of such tests to inflict unjustified harm, it seems indefensible that American institutions, particularly taxpayer-supported ones, would continue to blindly buy into the tests as unqualified measures of a child's intellectual ability. This does not mean such tests have no place in educational settings, but they ought to be restricted to diagnostic uses and then only to confirm a hypothesis of severely attenuated cognitive development.

The overwhelming ethnic and class disparities that result from ability and aptitude tracking suggest that such notions as "gifted and talented" programs need reexamination. People like Bill Crain in Teaneck say schools should eliminate tracking altogether and that gifted and talented programs should be open to any child who wants such an experience. Of course, doing so would bring on shrill protests from politicians and many parents that schools are "dumbing-down" the kids and going limp on academic standards.

In fact, the real reason many schools might not tolerate Crain's proposal is that they're facing unprecedented political pressure to prove their accountability to the public. Accountability has been interpreted to mean that schools must boost test scores at almost any cost. Meanwhile, many educators know that the enriched educational experiences that so-called gifted programs now offer a select few children ought to be the kind of schooling that every child is entitled to.

As far as the tests themselves, the evidence clearly suggests that common intelligence and aptitude tests are far too narrow in the abilities they actually measure to warrant their continued use as an indicator of general intellectual ability. This misuse, moreover, causes parents, teachers, and schools to make sweeping and stigmatizing judgments about a child's "intelligence."

"The most widely accepted explanation for the low participation of disadvantaged students in programs for the gifted is the ineffectiveness and inappropriateness of the identification and selection procedures that have traditionally been and continue to be used," say A. Harry Passow and Mary M. Frasier in *The Roeper Review*. (26)

There is little question that states in recent years have amended official policy to expand their criteria for separating the gifted from the ungifted. But actual practice and outcomes at the local level tell a different story. "In spite of efforts to address this issue through state policies, the demographics of gifted programs still indicate that the number of gifted students from culturally diverse, economically disadvantaged, and disabled populations remains significantly below their proportion in the general population," say Mary Ruth Coleman and James J. Gallagher. (27)

In fact, if the adult world persists in believing that young children ought to be given standardized tests to measure their intellectual abilities, alternatives to run-of-the-mill IQ achievement tests do exist. As just one example, a Connecticut team led by Robert Sternberg has developed such a test, based on a theory of "triarchic' intelligence, to assess a child's abilities to analyze, create, and apply knowledge and information.

Rather than choosing test items so each of the three parts of the test are highly correlated with each other, this particular IQ alternative, called the Sternberg Triarchic Abilities Test (STAT), was designed to produce exactly the opposite result. Experiments with the test indeed show very low correlations among the three subtests, strongly suggesting that it is measuring three distinctly different cognitive abilities. A child's scoring low on the analytical part, for instance—the part that most IQ tests exclusively tap—does not preclude her from making a high score on the practical or creative parts of the test. In other words, the test is designed to get out of the way, ceasing to be a roadblock to a child's opportunity to demonstrate a more complete array of his or her talents than permitted by traditional tests. (28)

I don't mean to pick on Hunter College Elementary, but I believe it's a highly visible symbol of Americans' entrenched ideology about intelligence and its measurement. The school's skewed demographics along class and ethnic lines, resulting from its own admissions process, are not lost on admissions director Polly Breland Smith. Indeed, she says the school is trying to spread the word about the school to day-care centers in the less tony parts of Manhattan, such as Chinatown, Washington Heights, and Harlem.

Apart from that laudable effort, I asked Breland Smith if the school had any system of accounting for the virtually determinative background factors of a child's home life that impede performance on IQ tests. "It would be easy to say, 'Yes, we do that in Round 2'" of the selection process consisting of direct observations of children, Breland Smith says.

"It's a complicated issue because we use the (Stanford-Binet Fourth Edition) as a screen. A lot of factors eliminate children from further consideration. If you make the (test-score) cut, we can consider all sorts of things, then we can look for other ways to be gifted. But if you don't get past that cut-off, we can't consider you. What I call early exposure or early enrichment (of children) is a serious consideration. On the other hand, we are a very small school in a very big city."

Thus, says Breland Smith, in New York City, at least, the onus of reform is on the city's public schools to create more inclusive methods of determining academic process. "It's our hope and expectation that the New York Board of Education will do more than we can do because of the shackles of time and resources," she says.

But public and policymaker ignorance about such matters continues to sustain many dubious beliefs and claims about intelligence, such that the ghosts of Terman, Brigham, and Spearman still lurk. "Although most researchers understand that 'intelligence' is modifiable, many educators, policymakers, and the public still cling to the notion that human intelligence is largely innate and fixed," the National Research Council reported in 1996. (29)

Public policy based on standardized tests, whose results are closely tied to a child's social and economic circumstances, would be equivalent to permitting only a select group of athletes, whatever their naturally endowed and trained abilities, to have special access to steroid drugs during competition. No legitimate sporting competition would even conceive of condoning such disparate treatment of its athletes.

But of course, the analogy still isn't exact. In the case of competitive mental testing, the tests themselves aren't the performance enhancers. But for any given level of "innate" cognitive ability, the measured performance of some children on intelligence tests will be boosted or worsened, depending on the steroidlike effects of differences in a child's cultural and environmental backgrounds.

Furthermore, the effects of a child's background are so undeniably strong that they should be an embarrassment to the American institutions, particularly taxpayer-supported or subsidized ones, that make important decisions about children according to results on intelligence tests and their surrogates.

As matters stand, many unlucky children will continue to face double jeopardy. Even if there were no standardized testing of any young children, anywhere, those born into less privileged social and economic circumstances are punished at least twice: first, when they start life already behind their more privileged peers; and second, when the testing game's sorting, labeling, and screening of children begins.

4

Crusade: Rise of the Test-Driven Accountability Machine in Our Schools

JASON HADN'T EVEN REACHED HIS TEENS when he'd already achieved the status of minor celebrity at his grade school in Boise, Idaho. His teachers adored him because his scores on the Iowa Test of Basic Skills, a common standardized achievement test used in schools across the country, put him in the ninety-ninth percentile. That meant he scored better than 99 percent of a representative group of test takers at his grade level *nationwide.* "Teachers were mesmerized by the numbers," said his mother, Jackie. "They were in awe of him. Because he did so well on the test, in a way they didn't see *him*. They saw him as his test scores."

Given the privileged status of tests and test scores in American schools, who wouldn't be in awe of a number like this? The ninety-ninth percentile is impressive sounding indeed. But Jackie didn't worship Jason's test scores with the same fervor as his teachers. She was bothered by what the test scores were *not* saying about her son.

"He had these fantastic test scores but he was not learning anything in school. He would come home with his papers and his work was very sloppy. Once he wrote three lines for his entire book report. I didn't see a great deal of tie in between how much he was learning and his test scores. He's a bright kid," Jackie says, and when it comes to standardized tests, "he's a good guesser, a risk-taker. He'll just forge ahead."

I met Jackie over coffee one day hoping to hear a parent's perspective on standardized testing in public schools. It became immediately apparent that she knew more about the inner workings of schools than most parents probably do. She's spent a lot of time inside them as a critical and close observer, both as a parent and as a professional. She's a freelance writer now, but was formerly a newspaper reporter who covered schools for the local newspaper. Jackie's views of the importance commonly placed on standardized tests might be described as jaundiced at best, influenced no doubt by the time she spent observing schools in Idaho, a state that has required the testing of all children once a year, every year. (Jackie asked me not to reveal her or her childrens' real names to protect their privacy.)

When the family moved to the Boise area several years ago, about the time the kids were starting school, they got their first whiff of the test-score imperative many parents of her socioeconomic class keep in mind when choosing a school. A neighbor had warned the couple that their designated grade school was populated by children from economically diverse backgrounds and therefore the school's standardized test scores were middling, at best. "When we moved into our house, I was told, 'You need to know about this grade school; it has lots of low-income kids, and its test scores are low,'" Jackie told me.

The couple ignored the warnings and sent the children to the school anyway. In the fifteen years she's lived in Boise, Jackie says the test-score imperative for middle-class parents has become a part of everyday life, like talking about the weather. "It comes up just in conversations you have with people. . . . Parents say to me, 'I don't want my kid to go to this school or that because their test scores are too low, so we are going to move.'"

During these everyday conversations with other parents, when the subject of school quality would come up, most parents in Jackie's social circle looked for just two readily available pieces of information about a school: test scores and the percent of children receiving subsidized school lunches, an indicator of the number of poor children attending a school. Ignored in the calculus were a plethora of characteristics about schools where the true story lay, such as the amount of small-group work in classes, the nature of school activities, and adherence to curriculum plans.

"These are well educated people with high expectations for their children," Jackie says. "They want to be in schools with the highest standardized test scores. They think the level of teaching will be higher. And it's a class thing. They think, 'My kids will be associated with other kids who will be smart.' These are liberal, socially aware parents . . . but they don't usually think about the reality that test scores are just one data point of quality, especially in an economically diverse school."

I asked Jackie whether she would ever miss not having test scores as one of those indicators of school quality. She told me: "It wouldn't bother me. That's because I know how to get the other information. I would talk to teachers and ask them, 'show me how you have implemented the curriculum guidelines, what are your goals for your classes, how do you actually pass the time.' . . . Standardized tests give you a real limited view."

But this parent's experience with school achievement tests gets more complicated still. Jackie's beliefs about the utility of test scores, owing to her son's contradictory experience with them, turns more ambiguous when she talks about her fourteen-year-old daughter's experience with standardized tests.

Unlike Jason's near-perfect scores, Kara's test results have been simply average on the Iowa Test of Basic Skills. But where Jason's actual performance in grade school has tended to be "shoddy," as Jackie puts it, Kara's has been exactly the opposite: In spite of the test results, her actual performance in school is spectacular. Yet, she has had to fight for every inch of recognition from her teachers.

"My daughter is a high achiever in school but she's real mediocre on standardized tests," says Jackie. "My son just whizzes through and takes risks, and she agonizes over every question. She's a 4.0 student, but in the Iowa Basics she's in the sixtieth percentile."

Kara's test scores in grade school were sufficiently low that the family had to apply for a "special exception" so the junior high school would allow her to take the accelerated English class. Now well into junior high, Kara aced accelerated English and continues to maintain an A average in all her courses. "She's a great little student," says Jackie.

Nevertheless, Kara's poor test results—relative, of course, to her classroom work—have taken a toll on her feelings about her abilities and skills, says her mom. After entering junior high, Kara was denied permission to take the accelerated math class. Like its English counterpart, the advanced class represents an early designation of a young student's achievement level and academic prospects. Like most schools nowadays, Kara's school no longer used the politically charged term "tracking." The practice had been thought to label, categorize, and stigmatize kids, and it often resulted in the creation of different schools within a school—one for the college-bound children of the middle- and upper-middle classes and the other for the low-income and low-achieving students whose life prospects were far more muddled. Although the word was banned in Kara's school, the practical effect hasn't much changed.

"She does tie her self esteem to those test scores," Jackie told me. "They don't call it tracking, but it's tracking. My daughter went into 'regular' seventh grade math and she got her 4.0, and she told me, 'Mom, I'm bored in math, I want to take the accelerated math. But then when we got the results of her Iowa Test of Basic Skills she was in the 50th percentile on the math part. She told me, 'Mom, I guess I'm not good enough for accelerated math. Look at my test scores." Jackie added: "It's partly a girl thing. I'm a fake, I'm really not smart, I'm really not that good."

Jackie believes her daughter will succeed in life because Kara thinks highly enough of herself and her abilities not to be completely discouraged by test numbers that tell a story opposite to her actual experience. But Jackie says she also suspects that her son, Jason, may still have the best chances of success in life given the doors of opportunity that will open to him simply because of the way that ninety-ninth percentile resonates in American society.

"My daughter knows she has to work hard, that she has to go from (step) a to b to c and to keep her nose to the grindstone to be successful, whereas my son gets the message, 'I'm great, just the way I am,'" Jackie says. "My children represent two very different models of success, but at this point I can't help but feel it's my son who will have a better shot at life success."

Of course, Jackie knows she's in a distinct minority among Boise parents on the test-score question. That reality was vividly underscored when her family attended a party given by some friends. Jackie describes their hosts as a high-achieving couple, one of whom was an educator. In the kitchen, surrounded by hors d'oeuvres and drinks and people mingling, Jackie saw the couple's son's test report from the Iowa Test of Basic Skills proudly taped onto the family's refrigerator door.

Jackie wonders what message such parents are giving children about the goals, values, and the very meaning of education and learning. But, I thought, as she was describing this event, that even Jackie wasn't entirely immune to the enticing certainty conveyed by numbers in black and white. "They were fairly high scores," she told me. "Not as high as my son's, though."

The "Reform" Crusade

It may be telling that in the late 1960s Americans were in fact learning how to "just do it," as Nike Inc. would say, actually putting the first man on the moon, while by the end of the millennium Americans were consumed by inventing complex new schemes to create a national standardized test that would, in effect, help determine whether a child might even have the opportunity to go to the moon. Opportunities are readily provided to children such as Jason, but denied to children like Kara—because of an entrenched social ideology that defines merit largely on the basis of test scores.

Over the past twenty years, bands of politicians, policymakers, and other self-described crusaders for educational reform, guided by the mantra of "holding schools accountable," have accomplished a near-complete makeover of American schools. They've done so with the public's acquiescence, exploiting the public's demand for quick fixes of complex social and economic problems and its desire for results that can be boiled down into easily understood, simplistically quantified terms.

The accountability crusade has been dramatic and emotionally wrenching for many, and yet it operates with utter, bureaucratic coldness. Cleverly conceived, designed, and implemented, this reformed way of schooling has all the markings of being rational, scientific, objective, and fair. Its fruits have become the essential landscape of school life for teachers, parents and students, school superintendents and principals. The Pandora's box this crusade opened has fundamentally altered the very nature and meaning of education in America: what it means to teach, to learn, and to achieve.

If you're a parent, you might well interject: "I've been sending kids to school for a long time, and I haven't seen any revolution. In fact, the schools need one. We need all the reform we can get. We need accountability. We need to get back to basics."

Most, if not all, of us are educational experts—or so we think. But our thinking about schools lags severely behind changing and complex reality. Let me break the news: Almost everything you think about the way your school system works or does not work is probably wrong. You've listened to the policymakers, you've read the newspapers, and you know as much about schooling as the next person; you believe you've got a handle on it.

I would suggest, though, that that's precisely part of the problem. Not unlike the constant barrage of news flashes meant to solidify popular consent in Orwell's *1984*, Americans have been subjected to a clear, simple, and unrelenting message emanating from politicians, policymakers, news organizations, business leaders, and other influential people. The essence of that message is that American schools are in crisis, that teachers can't be trusted, and that the public must seize control of the classroom and of virtually all decision-making in it, to ensure that children are being taught. More standards, more reform, more accountability. Above all, more standardized testing to prove to a distrustful public that the schools are working and that children are achieving. Who could disagree?

The modus operandi of this meat factory that America's schools are fast becoming is simple, straightforward, and easy to understand: You test them and they will learn. The truth, after all, is out there, the indisputable truth of a child's or school's level of achievement told in the profound language of a test score. That's the powerful elegance of a single number.

Indeed, this reform crusade has exploited some increasingly problematic traits of American society, including those of public apathy and widespread public cynicism about the leading institutions of American life. In the short run, this reform crusade may have unwittingly created a near-perfect model of accountability for a public that has neither the time nor patience to really understand the inner workings of their neighborhood schools. The reform crusade's highly efficient accountability machine may, in fact, be well deserved by a nation in which political rhetoric and public images count for more than educational substance. Relatively few parents are like Jackie, who knows what besides test scores to ask about, or even cares enough to ask.

The accountability machine has produced severe and educationally irrational consequences for students, teachers, and parents. These impacts have occurred beyond the arena of public discussion, largely ignored in many news organizations' unrelenting coverage of the test-score horse race. The country's long-running experiment with large-scale testing with large-scale consequences raises fundamental questions about what an education system really is and what it ought to be.

The Accountability Machine Is Born

The beginnings of America's love affair with the standardized test in schools can be traced back at least 150 years. From the days of the first standardized exams required by the state of Massachusetts in the mid-1800s to the *A Nation at Risk* report in 1983 to President Bill Clinton's 1999 State of the Union address, American politicians have condemned public schools as sitting on the precipice of failure.

Americans have heard the relentless litany: We need to measure, compare, sort, analyze, and categorize schools and schoolchildren in order to fix them.

One would think that educational considerations would be paramount when it comes to standardized tests, school reform, and school accountability. But that has been far from the case. The lesson from history is that political motivations and the exercise of political power by those in positions of authority, rather than sound educational reasons, have driven the nation's use of standardized tests in schools. Indeed, whatever the perceived problems with the nation's schools, the answer has been almost always the same: more testing.

To suggest that claims to political power and control have largely driven testing in the United States might seem overly cynical. This unavoidable lesson from history—that politics and power rather than strictly educational concerns have driven the use of testing—is exactly what the U.S. Office of Technology Assessment (OTA) suggested in a carefully worded 1992 analysis of testing in American schools. This chapter looks at how political agendas behind government pronouncements about testing and education reform have been commonplace. That is why the OTA report has stood in sharp relief to the proposed laws, press releases, and speeches about failing public schools during the Reagan, Bush, and Clinton years.

The edifice that is the Accountability Machine as we know it was built over a span of several decades. Throughout its history, standardized testing in America has been plagued by many of the same problems and fundamental contradictions the nation continues to struggle with in the use of these tests, and yet the push for still more testing continues.

We can begin with Horace Mann, an early proponent of universal education to serve the rapidly expanding American populace. Mann's educational stewardship in the state of Massachusetts underscored early on the basic contradiction inherent to state-mandated, external examinations of public schoolchildren in a democratic society. On one hand, a free society required an open system of public education for all citizens. Yet, according to Mann's view, such an educational system had to be controlled, efficiently managed, and held properly accountable to the public.

A continuous tension between two competing educational objectives in a democratic society was—and has been ever since—the result. An efficient system of schooling for the masses was one kind of system; that system wasn't necessarily equivalent to a fair and equitable one—nor even an educationally sound one.

Early on, the tension between two opposing objectives of universal education was complicated by the staggering growth of the young nation. Waves of European immigrants entered the United States in the mid–1800s (125,000 newcomers each year for some forty years). The country also saw its fastest rate of urbanization in its history during that period.

America's history with the scientific management of its schools has demonstrated time after time that Americans have tended to side with efficiency over equity in the approach to public education. For the sake of efficiency, the nation has tolerated many egregious misuses of standardized tests, permitting those in political power to exploit the simplicity of a test's numerical summaries for uses they were never designed for. Historical experience also suggests people have chosen to ignore the many negative and unintended effects of standardized tests. These trends began in Mann's Massachusetts with a rudimentary school accountability system that was indeed meager compared to the measurement and control structures that exist today in American schools.

For efficiency's sake, as secretary of the Massachusetts Board of Education, Mann oversaw one of the first standardized written exams of public schoolchildren. Prior to that, most such tests were on a smaller scale and were oral exams given to individual students. Mann's efforts were fueled by complaints from the state school superintendent that the schools needed reform and improvement, a refrain the public would repeat over the years. The answer was, as always: test the children.

Misuse of state-mandated tests began right from the start in Massachusetts. Although the first Massachusetts test was intended to measure individual achievement, it consisted of just thirty questions to cover an entire year's curriculum, severely limiting its use as an indicator of anything.

It's instructive to look at the underlying purpose of that test as a demonstration of the political power of state authorities over school headmasters at the time. The tests, says the OTA, "often focused on a rather narrow set of outcomes, selected principally to put the headmasters in the worst possible light." Those early test takers got barely 30 percent of the test items correct. What's more, the exam's creators knew the test items were often "abstruse and tricky." (1)

Early tests also were quickly exploited for purposes that they were never designed for, rendering invalid any interpretations that were based on those uses. This, too, is a theme that would recur throughout America's historical experience with standardized testing in schools. In Mann's Massachusetts, it turns out, the availability of standardized test results compelled public officials to numerically compare and rank schools, even though the test's purpose was to assess the achievement of individual students. "The fact that the jurisdictions were different in so many fundamental ways as to render the comparisons virtually meaningless," the OTA says, "did not seem to matter." This pattern of using such tests for political ends would become all too familiar in the history of American education. Says the OTA:

> The idea underlying the implementation of written examinations, that they could provide information about student learning, was born in the minds of individuals already convinced that education was substandard in quality. This sequence—perception of failure followed by the collection of data designed to document failure (or success)—offers early evidence of what has become a tradition of school reform and a truism of student testing: tests are often administered not just to discover how well schools or kids are doing, but rather to obtain external confirmation—validation of the hypothesis that they are not doing well at all. (2)

Those inauspicious first steps toward standardizing schools through testing and accountability mechanisms were certainly indicative of where American education was headed. But standardized testing as we know it today probably acquired its central features from the American political economy writ large, when the industrial revolution at the century's turn began to reshape American life.

Think for a minute about the commonly bantered rhetoric about the condition of public schools. Government or corporate leaders will often argue that your neighborhood school ought to function like any good business. In these terms, schools are like any enterprise with raw materials of production—whether they be iron ore, silicon chips, or six-year-olds. There's a product sold into the competitive marketplace, whether it be computers, automobiles, or newly minted high school graduates; and this enterprise must show bottom-line results, whether they be quarterly corporate profits, rates of return on an investment in a new hydroelectric plant, or annual achievement results as measured by a standardized test.

In 1991, for example, the former Chrysler chairman, Lee Iococca, told a gathering of educators, "Your product needs a lot of work, and in the end, it's your job." He dismissed talk of poverty and other social conditions students might encounter outside of school. "Your customers don't want to hear about your raw materials problem—they care about results," Iococca told the educators. (Unmentioned was that Chrysler Corporation had been the beneficiary of a huge bailout at taxpayer expense.) (3)

When you hear that kind of talk, you are listening, in fact, to an ideology about the way the world is supposed to work, one born at the turn of the century during the industrial revolution. Vast technological advances of those times permitted the conversion of raw materials into finished products on a massive scale, transforming regionally based enterprises into companies of national and international scope. Factories employing thousands of workers sprang up. With them emerged similarly vast changes in the way business was organized, managed, and controlled. Corporate hierarchies modeled on armies set rigid, militaristic boundaries between ordinary workers and management. The notion of "scientific" management was born, a method that relied heavily on the precise measurement of the most intricate details of a business's inputs and outputs. These new management techniques permitted managers to sort and classify workers as objectively measured factors of production. Business wasn't alone in adopting this perspective on the measurability, standardization, and classification of individuals. If corporations used these techniques of scientific management in order to ensure the maximization of profits, American schools' role had a somewhat different hue. Schools, of course, had no profits to maximize. Amid the rapidly growing, sprawling young democracy, its growth fueled by more waves of European immigration (who were perceived by the established educational and business hierarchies as inferior human beings), schools became a first-line defense against social disorder. "Just as mass immigration was a symbol for—even the embodiment of—cultural disruption," Paula S. Fass, a professor of history at UC-Berkeley, writes, "education became its dialectical opposite, an instrument of order, or direction, of social consolidation." (4)

In practical terms, education's role as a chief sentinel for social order meant that schools soon became means by which Americans could be categorized along class and ethnic identities. At the turn of the century, these classifications were more overt than the far more subtle ways we see schoolchildren and older students categorized along racial and class lines today.

For example, in 1908, Harvard president Charles Eliot proudly laid out his vision for American schools as a tool for maintaining class distinctions in society. He asserted the existence of a "thin upper" crust of individuals, the "managing, leading, guiding class," who presumably would attend elite universities such as Harvard, followed by a layer of skilled workers, then the commercial class, "and finally the thick fundamental layer engaged in household work, agriculture, mining, quarrying," and so on. Schools, Eliot maintained, should "serve each class . . . to give each layer its own appropriate form of schooling." (5)

This kind of ideology helped lay the foundation for wide use of intelligence tests, which would become a device to sort people on a variety of fronts, such as who would be permitted to attend college and who would go to Europe to fight a war. In 1917, for instance, thousands of schoolchildren in Oakland, California, were given IQ tests as a means to place them into their "proper" slots in the school system. Additionally, as discussed in Chapter 3, many thousands of U.S. Army recruits were tested for intelligence, surely among the largest and most damaging social experiments in U.S. history.

Ideology, then, under the guises of meritocracy and managerial and social efficiency, drove these grand social experiments in the testing of army recruits, schoolchildren, and people aspiring to a college education. Testing became an early tool to try to weed out the intellectually weak from the cognitively strong. What's more, the seemingly innocuous technological creations of the multiple-choice test and the scanning machines that scored them would certainly seal the privileged position of standardized testing in American society. These technologies permitted the full expression of the ideologies behind testing, permitting the social objectives of measurement, classification, and control to be carried out quickly and relatively inexpensively, sweetened by the patina of scientific objectivity.

By 1920, some 500,000 different published tests existed, and one leading achievement test—predecessor of today's well-known Stanford Achievement Test—was selling at a rate of some 2 million tests a year. By the early 1930s, some 1,300 different achievement tests and roughly 400 kinds of mental aptitude tests were being sold in the United States. (6)

Watching in horror, the progressive educational philosopher John Dewey once remarked, "Our mechanical, industrialized civilization is concerned with averages and percents. The mental habit which reflects this social scene subordinates education and social arrangements based on average gross inferiorities and superiorities." (7)

Indeed, the era of testing in American life was well under way.

Politicizing America's Schools

One wonders how sustainable the testing movement might have been if it had been forced to survive on its educational merits alone. However, it flourished from the 1960s onward because policymakers continued to relentlessly ratchet up the stakes so that test performance became a national obsession. Schoolchildrens' test scores—and the comparison and classification of children and schools according to test results—has led Americans to buy into the overly simplistic, reductionist view of the complex endeavors of teaching and learning as little more than adding up all the test scores and dividing by the number of test takers. It is the view that you can put a value on the nation's education system as a summation of its test scores.

The making of the proverbial "federal case" out of test scores began somewhat naively in the 1960s, before educators really understood the effects that large-scale testing had on schools and schoolchildren. Defying the mounting stack of evidence indicating that such testing was probably educationally ruinous, the accountability crusade as such was launched when policymakers at all levels began, absurdly, to equate the nation's hopes and dreams, indeed, its very survival, with the results of standardized test scores.

The ultimate effect of the accountability crusade, driven always by the scary notion that the nation was in a pending state of doom because of falling or stagnant test scores, has been to deeply politicize the educational enterprise. Equally disturbing, the crusade has gradually created what amounts to a quasi-private marketplace of public education, where resources and public accolades flow to schools with the highest rate of return on public investment, measured almost exclusively by achievement scores.

The naive part of the story can be traced to one of the most significant pieces of federal education legislation in U.S. history: Title 1 of the Elementary and Secondary Education Act of 1965. In the spirit of other antipoverty initiatives under Lyndon Johnson's Great Society programs, Title 1 was enacted to help financially strapped schools serving communities with high concentrations of poor children. Title 1 remains the largest source of federal aid to the nation's schools.

This well-intentioned program to improve educational experiences of poor children came with strings attached, to assure policymakers that the federal funds were having a measurable impact on poor children receiving the money. The linchpins of monitoring Title 1 spending were "norm-referenced" standardized tests, such as the Iowa Test of Basic Skills. Such standardized tests permit comparisons of schools' and children's test scores to a national "norm." By requiring that Title 1 schools be evaluated by means of scores, objective measures, and aggregate performance, the law effectively mandated states to employ standardized tests in order to receive several billions of dollars a year in federal funding.

Congress has tweaked Title 1 from time to time when reappropriating funds, in order to keep up with the changing political climate of testing in schools. In 1988, for instance, as the national accountability movement was gaining momentum, Title 1's accountability provisions were given much sharper teeth for enforcement. First, schools failing to meet test score objectives were required to submit "program improvement" plans to federal authorities. Congress told local schools they must develop "desired outcomes" for their Title 1 dollars—with results to be measured from standardized test scores. (8)

The effect of these added teeth, of course, meant substantially increased stakes placed on multiple-choice achievement tests. Moreover, the effective scope of Title 1 began to far exceed its original mission to target federal aid to disadvantaged children and communities, and also encompassed schools' regular testing programs when states decided to extend their mandated Title 1 testing to all students.

"(Title 1) has helped create an enormous system of local testing," the Office of Technology Assessment concluded. "Almost every (Title 1) child is tested every year, and in some cases, twice a year, to meet national evaluation requirements. . . . Sometimes this testing is combined with testing that fulfills state and local needs; other times (Title 1) has caused districts to administer tests more frequently . . . than they would in the absence of a federal requirement." (9)

The Elementary and Secondary Education Act, then, had perhaps an unquantifiable impact on the expansion of standardized testing into American schools. The law became a powerful incentive for states to put in place elaborate testing bureaucracies for standardizing their testing programs and reporting information to the government. This is done by virtually every school and district in the country under the umbrella of something called the Title 1 Evaluation and Reporting System, or TIERS, which permits the government to compare results from various kinds of norm-referenced tests to one another.

As a bureaucratically-driven program built on benign origins, Title 1 has not been a testing program per se, nor even a school accountability program. It has been an *education* program at its heart, through which the federal government has asserted its rightful role as a moderator of economic and education opportunity in a nation with historically sharp racial and class divisions.

However, federal intervention in American schools became increasingly politicized with a 1983 government report called *A Nation at Risk: The Imperative for Education Reform.* As one of the most widely distributed and aggressively marketed policy statements to emerge from the Reagan administration, the landmark report would become a veritable New Testament for the modern-day accountability movement. The document itself, authored by the National Commission on Excellence in Education under the auspices of Education Secretary Terrence H. Bell, was a marvel of alarmist propaganda, setting the stage with these famous words:

> Our nation is at risk. Our once unchallenged preeminence in commerce, industry, science, and technological innovation is being overtaken by competitors from throughout the world. . . . We report to the American people that while we can take justifiable pride in what our schools and colleges have historically accomplished and contributed to the United States and the well-being of its people, the educational foundations of our society are presently being eroded by a rising tide of mediocrity that threatens our very future as a Nation and a people. (10)

It is worth recalling here that *A Nation at Risk* came during a troubled time in American economic and social life. Coming off a period of double-digit inflation and record high interest rates in the late 1970s, the economy of the early 1980s was a wreck, suffering one of the most severe recessions in the postwar period. Government budgets and programs at all levels were being slashed in order to accommodate falling profits and wages, and therefore declining tax revenues to the government. The one exception was an enormous flare-up in military spending, owing, of course, to the Cold War inflamed by evil empires and perceived threats to democracy nearly everywhere.

Ronald Reagan declared a new "morning in America." And the hunt began for magic bullets to cure the nation's economic malaise. Indeed, policymakers found no shortage of such quick fixes and easy scapegoats. The prevailing ideology was the privileged position of free markets, unfettered by government. If too much government was the problem, the way to fix the problem was to diminish government. One of the magic bullets was the mythical supposition of "supply-side" economics, theorizing that morning in America was but a tax- or budget-cut away. What is more, according to the crisis mentality that prevailed, the American way of life was endangered by those smart and aggressive economic machines of South Korea, Germany, and Japan. That notion of the invincibility of foreign and alien forces poised to destroy the American Dream, of course, had much historical precedent, but it found new life in the early 1980s.

Against this backdrop came *A Nation at Risk.* In keeping with the fearful climate during those years, the report contained no shortage of magic bullets and easy scapegoats. Underpinning America's problems, the report suggested, was a crisis in American schools. If our foreign competitors were overtaking America's economic dominance, that's because their schools were superior, producing workers better educated and more highly trained than Americans. "The risk is not only that the Japanese make automobiles more efficiently than Americans and have government subsidies for development and export," the report said. "In order to keep and improve on the slim competitive edge we still retain in world markets, we must dedicate ourselves to the reform of our educational system for the benefit of all."

Laying out the danger ahead, the report pointed to several statistics. It so happens that fully nine of thirteen "indicators of the risk" assembled by the National Commission on Excellence in Education pertained to a standardized test of some sort. These included international comparisons on school achievement tests, state-level achievement tests in science and mathematics, tests for "giftedness," and the College Board's widely distributed Scholastic Aptitude Test, as it was then called. Left unquestioned, of course, was the fundamental assumption behind the report: that outcomes on standardized exams are the one and true indicator of the health of a nation's education system. Indeed, without even blinking or acknowledging the growing doubts among many serious researchers about standardized testing's ill effects and dubious validity—a topic taken up later in this chapter—the charter legislation forming the National Commission on Excellence in Education underscored this unquestioned belief in test results. For instance, one of its main goals was to locate educational programs that were good at preparing "students who consistently attain higher than average scores in college entrance examinations. . . ." (11)

According to the commission's ill-formed logic, higher test scores translated into smarter workers, a growing economy, and superior international competitiveness. By the magic bullet theory of schooling, then, *Risk* recommended several solutions to the looming crisis that directly translated into still more reliance on test scores. *Risk* stated:

> Standardized tests of achievement . . . should be administered at major transition points from one level of schooling to another and particularly from high school to college or work. The purposes of these tests would be to: (a) certify the students' credentials; (b) identify the need for remedial intervention; and (c) identify the opportunity for advanced or accelerated work. The tests should be administered as part of a nationwide (but not federal) system of State and local standardized tests. (12)

A Nation at Risk didn't stop at the recommendation for simply more testing. Doing so was important, of course, to the crusaders. But without big consequences attached to test scores, in order that powerful political points might be made by showing that American children don't measure up to their "foreign competitors," simply requiring more tests wouldn't be sufficient. Therefore, *Risk* recommended, educators and elected officials had to be held responsible for "providing the leadership necessary" to accomplish its reform agenda.

Hence, the accountability movement as a national crusade was born.

What "Risk" Wrought

The impact of *A Nation at Risk,* even nearly twenty years later, on the politics of American schools can't be overstated, given as it was a political communiqué sanctioned and supported by the full weight of the U.S. government.

The document was some two years in the making, authorized by Congress and executed at the highest levels of the Reagan administration. *Risk* was unveiled as a major media event, and its nation-in-crisis tone was well received amid the gloominess all about. *Risk*, according to a *New York Times* account at the time, "brought the issue of education to the forefront of political debate with an urgency not felt since the Soviet satellite shook American confidence in its public schools in 1957."

Schools were an easy scapegoat for falling national incomes and ballooning federal deficits. The widely heralded report provided a national framework with which state officials could assert control and authority over classrooms, teachers, school administrators, and even the learning of children. Learning itself would become a political act in this brave new world.

Indeed, *Risk* galvanized the fledgling accountability movement, transforming it into a national project with purported national security implications. It gave focus, emphasis, and credibility to the movement's disparate manifestations occurring through various state accountability experiments beginning in the 1970s—even as these early accountability devices were proving to be of dubious merit.

The state of Michigan was among the first crucibles for early experiments with school accountability in adopting the Michigan Accountability System in the early 1970s, and statewide mandatory testing was its basic tool.

It was an inauspicious beginning for the accountability movement. According to Jerome Murphy and David Cohen, the Michigan system followed a 1969 report by the state's Citizens Research Council, "a creature of Michigan business interests," which held that taxpayer funding of schools should be preceded by proof of educational effectiveness. State leaders responded to the business community's challenge. Michigan's governor agreed that more state money couldn't go into schools "until we can assure taxpayers that they will be getting full educational value for their money." (13)

It's become almost a truism in the history of educational testing that once the political call to action is issued, the testing itself soon follows, before many messy details about validity, reliability, and purposes of the tests are worked out. The first Michigan tests ensued just five months after the program's conception in 1969. How would the test results be used? The answer to that had a lot to do with the *real politic* behind the program's purpose, which ultimately fed the political hunger for comparing, sorting, and ranking students and schools.

In famous last words, the state education agency had promised local school officials that test results would be released only to the local districts. The agency also vowed not to rank schools by test scores. Initially, the agency's summary reports of the test results were somewhat obscure, prompting little public attention, according to Murphy and Cohen. But the local test reports were a different story, as word got out to local politicians and the media of their existence. After a torrent of requests for the test results, mainly from local legislators, the education agency caved, and released the district test results. "The results were immediately picked up by the press and widely disseminated across the state," Murphy and Cohen say. "The response was a lively mixture of excitement and horror, and a political free-for-all began." (14)

Michigan teachers were among the first groups in the state to express concern about how the accountability system might be hurting rather than helping children learn. The state teacher's union, the Michigan Education Association, commissioned three widely regarded educational researchers—Ernest House of the University of Illinois, Wendell Rivers of the University of Missouri, and Daniel Stufflebeam at Western Michigan—to evaluate Michigan's program and report back. The panel gathered testimony from the governor's office, the state board of education, teachers unions, the Detroit Urban League, and several professional teachers associations.

The news, which came in March 1974, wasn't good. House, Rivers, and Stufflebeam attacked virtually all elements of the Michigan Accountability System. They criticized, first of all, its mandate for "universal" testing of all pupils, when smaller-scale testing would be a far more cost-effective indicator of achievement levels at the state level. But a pragmatic *indication* of the state's educational strengths and weaknesses was never the point of the Michigan accountability system. Control and surveillance of the educational enterprise was its underlying thrust. This was underscored by the test's hasty implementation before issues of reliability and validity were ironed out; by its punishments and awards to schools based on test scores; and publishing test results in a way that permitted the ranking of schools and districts. The ghosts of testing's earliest maladaptation, since the days of Horace Mann in Massachusetts, were now evident more than a century later in Michigan. House and his coauthors tell us:

> Such rankings invariably reveal the socio-economic ordering of the state by school district. It is our opinion that the continuation of such practices could lead to highly detrimental consequences for the Michigan educational system as a whole. Probably the most damaging effect of this practice (of ranking) would be the misinterpretation of this data by those whose motivations are based on factors other than of the improvement of education in the state of Michigan. The scores are largely misinterpreted by the public. Low test scores are taken as a sign of a poor educational system. . . . .Test results are not good measures of what is taught in school, strange as it may seem. They are good indicators of socio-economic class and other variables. But unless one teaches the tests themselves, they are not very sensitive to school learning. (15)

The authors concluded that, despite initiating a healthy public discussion about Michigan schools, the new accountability program had opened a dangerous Pandora's box. Indeed, one state official, concerned about the creature that had been unleashed, said, "Sometimes I wake up at night worried about the direction we're going. It's like a giant snowball rolling downhill." (16)

That snowball kept rolling. Testing and accountability were now on the same shelf as mom and apple pie. Testing and accountability were rendered virtually undebatable, and became the essence of the meaning of school reform. The national crusade that *Risk* helped to unleash legitimated beyond any doubt the path that many states had already begun. They now had to prove to taxpayer and business organizations—with a precision offered only by percentile scores—that schools deserved the funding they sought. Within a year after the report was issued, most states had started new testing programs or were considering the enactment of more tests. Local politicians seized on the new opportunities for demagoguery. In one case, a candidate for a school board simply adopted the entire *Risk* report as his political platform. In another, district officials provided the *Risk* document with the tax bill mailed to property owners.(17)

The Crusade Gathers Steam

The nation's march down the path of turning schools into political pawns—as well as politically-driven enterprises—would be unrelenting through the 1980s and 1990s. In 1989, President Bush convened an Education Summit with the nation's governors in Charlottesville, Virginia (led by then-governor Bill Clinton). The summit adopted six National Education Goals, which were soon given the imprimatur of official federal policy, along with a request for a $690 million federal budget. At least three of the six National Education Goals would be assessed through the results of standardized tests. Bush called the policy *America 2000: An Education Strategy,* and a summary of it was published in 1991. In that report, *America 2000* paid due homage to its precursor, *A Nation at Risk*, and borrowed from *Risk's* tactic of fomenting crisis and fear about the country's future.

At the core of *America 2000* was a fifteen-item Accountability Package, which called for a new national exam known as the American Achievement Tests. The idea of a national test was itself remarkable in a nationwide approach to schooling that always had operated under the belief—if not in actual practice—in locally defined curricula and local control of schools. But *America 2000* didn't stop with just a national standardized exam. Besides keeping a highly public scorecard of test results to compare schools, districts, and states, Bush wanted colleges and universities to use the national exam for admissions. The policy also called on employers to consider individual exam scores in their hiring decisions.

Bush's proposal for a "voluntary" national test ultimately failed in Congress, defeated by opposition from such organizations as the National PTA, NAACP, American Association of School Administrators, the National Center for Fair and Open Testing, and the Center for Women Policy Studies. Still, as the first U.S. president to propose such a national exam, with exceedingly high stakes for individuals and schools, Bush's *America 2000* marked an ominous new chapter in the accountability crusade. George Bush would not be the last to speak as "the education president." Bill Clinton would put his own mark on the national crusade. With his State of the Union speech to Congress in February 1997, Clinton again raised the specter of a national standardized test for every fourth- and eighth-grader in reading and math. He issued a Call to Action for American Education, which would consist of the now-familiar-sounding "national crusade for education standards." These would not be "federal" standards, according to the president's parsing, but "national" ones. "To help schools meet the standards and measure their progress," Clinton said, "we will lead an effort over the next two years to develop national tests of student achievement in reading and math" with the goal to sign up as many states as possible for a first administration of the test by 1999.

When Clinton's own national testing proposal ran into political hurdles in Congress, prospects for a national standardized test were fast dimming as the 1990s were ending. Clinton took a different tack in his accountability crusade with his 1999 State of the Union speech, calling on Congress to approve his proposed Education Accountability Act, which would up the stakes still further for states that wanted to continue to receive some $15 billion annually in federal aid to schools. Whether it was Clinton's proposals to "end social promotion," shut schools that didn't "perform," or hire "quality" teachers, any and all of those unarguably laudable goals would be tied to still more standardized testing of doubtful validity.

The nation's business community continued to play a major role in sustaining the fervor of the reform effort during the Bush and Clinton years. As always, the corporate involvement in education policy has been driven by the belief that their enterprises can't compete on the world economic stage with the allegedly inferior workers U.S. schools are "producing." Related to that is the notion that schools should be just like any other enterprise to which the tools of managerial efficiency and the forces of a competitive market can apply. The formula goes thus: institute a common set of standards; measure with a common test how students, schools, and states stack up; encourage a public spectacle and media feeding-frenzy that reduces the complexity of learning to a set of test scores; and then let market forces do the heavy lifting by punishing "nonperforming" schools and rewarding "high-performing" ones.

In short, according to the political and corporate ideology that the country has endured for two decades, the nation is destined to go the way of ancient Rome unless schoolchildren are subjected to more tests and schools are subjected to more surveillance and control. Hence, in words reminiscent of *A Nation at Risk*'s rhetorical flourishes almost two decades earlier, we hear IBM chairman Louis V. Gerstner informing the audience at the 1996 Education Summit: "So here we are in 1996, being passed away by other countries . . . *and what was once a problem is now a crisis that threatens the entire country*" (emphasis added).

What the Crusaders Believe

There's little doubt that the nation's most recent twenty-year reform crusade has had persuasive popular appeal. It is also true that there is much room for improvement in American schools. But whether the remedies the crusaders have called for will accomplish any meaningful improvement in achievement and learning—or in fact worsen the underlying problems with American schools—is a fundamental question (see Chapter 5) that is almost never debated by ordinary citizens. It is not debated because the crusade has rendered the notions of achievement and learning virtually undebatable. As Jackie, the mother of two schoolchildren in Boise, Idaho, discovered on her own, most of her middle-class neighbors simply do not consider or tolerate the idea that learning cannot be completely captured by test scores.

"So it is no small wonder that many Americans have come to believe that education in our country is now in a deplorable state," write educational researchers David C. Berliner and Bruce J. Biddle. "Indeed, how could they have concluded anything else, given such an energetic and widely reported campaign of criticism, from such prestigious sources, attacking America's public schools? To the best of our knowledge, no campaign of this sort had ever before appeared in American history. Never before had American government been so critical of public schools, and never had so many false claims been made about education in the name of 'evidence.'" (17)

Once the crusade reached a nationwide critical mass, any dissent over the path the country was taking with respect to school reform became marginalized, relegated mostly to concerns expressed by some educators and researchers who were discovering the real effects this crusade was having on education. Indeed, the "group-think" quality to the reform crusade has been made possible by widespread trust in several highly questionable beliefs sustained by the powerful coupling of business and political interests. It's time for us to dissect those beliefs.

Myth Number One: American Schools Are in Peril

Historical hindsight, of course, has its obvious advantages. Looking back through time allows one to see a picture that is missed by dwelling on the details of just one historical moment. When the accountability movement is seen in the best possible light, that's exactly what its proponents have done. In doing so they have failed to exercise a measure of caution that would be warranted before embarking on a mind-boggling social experiment on the nation's schools. At best, the crusade's zealots made many sweeping generalizations about a crisis in American education and allegedly grave risks for the U.S. economy. At worst, however, these crusaders engaged in a major deceit of the American public, what Berliner and Biddle condemned as nothing less than a "disinformation campaign." (18)

A more balanced look at the evidence would lead one to question any conclusion that American schools were in crisis at the time of *A Nation at Risk.* And by the late 1990s, when politicians were still debating whether to install a new national test in schools, when states were aggressively creating elaborate new accountability systems for their schools, the notion of such a national crisis in American schools—or even that there's really a serious problem—remains even more doubtful in light of the evidence.

Consider educational attainment—whether, for example, people stop going to school at high school or go on to college. Among the things the crusaders got right was finding that all high schoolers, whether college-bound or not, should be taking more challenging courses, including four years of English; three years each of math, science, and social studies; and two years of a foreign language. Course rigor has a direct influence on a student's later level of educational attainment, and that, in turn, can have a measurable, though modest, effect on the economy's employment, productivity, and rate of joblessness. Elected officials near and far could wring their hands over test scores till the cows come home, but actual educational attainment is perhaps the single best indicator of the skill level of a country's labor force. So, at least *Risk* and its progeny were on solid ground in advocating more challenging high school courses. In 1982, just 14 percent of high schoolers had taken *Risk*'s "New Basics" set of courses. By 1994, almost 51 percent had done so. (19)

Actual gains in what matters more, attainment itself, have been less dramatic. I do not suggest that gains in attainment are bad, but that attainment was *never low in the first place.* The nation's labor force was already among the world's most skilled when the crusaders issued their call to action, in spite of rising joblessness caused by the economic slump in the early 1980s.

Let's look at some numbers during the era in which the crusaders pointed to supposed evidence of America's educational decline. An actual "crisis" would suggest that pre-*Risk* indicators would have been especially dismal compared to subsequent periods or that we'd see cataclysmic damage from this crisis in the larger economy. That's hardly the case:

- In March 1979, fully 85.6 percent of Americans between twenty-five and twenty-nine had completed high school. By the mid–1990s, that statistic had risen just one percentage point to 86.9 percent. In this historical light, then, there was no crisis in high school completion in the United States before or after the *Risk* report. (20)
- Consider higher education. In 1979, almost three in ten Americans between twenty-five and twenty-nine had obtained a bachelor's degree. Was there a problem here? Indeed, the numbers ought to be higher. Still, by the mid-1990s, the rate of college graduation in the United States hardly budged from its pre-*Risk* days, although the American economy continued to thrive, making an educational crisis all the less likely.

Moreover, consider international comparisons of educational indicators at the time *Risk* came out. For instance, in 1985, the United States was tied with Japan for first in the rate at which adults graduated from college, at 23.2 percent. The nation was equal to Japan on this very important measure of labor force skill level, yet *Risk* still painted Japan's highly skilled work force as a major threat to the American way of life. The former West Germany was another of those supposed sources of economic peril for Americans, and yet that nation had a college graduation rate of just 13.5 percent in 1985, roughly half of U. S. graduations. (21)

If there were deep problems with American educational attainment and skills in the early 1980s, one might expect that by 1994, a decade after *Risk*, that the reforms would have brought about higher educational attainment rates relative to foreign competitors, and the crisis would have passed. But consider: The United States continued to lead the world in high school graduation rates in 1994 with a figure of 85 percent. About 24 percent of American adults held bachelor's degree in 1994, hardly a dramatic increase from the 23.2 percent back in 1985. So, by the logic of the crusaders, the United States was still in a crisis in terms of labor force skills. That would be a difficult conclusion to draw given that the United States led the industrialized world in the mid-1990s in the rate at which adults had received a bachelor's degree. (22)

What, then, about achievement levels? For this we need numbers provided by the National Assessment of Educational Progress (NAEP), commonly known as "the nation's report card." In the parlance of many people who routinely use and analyze the exam, it's simply known as "Nape." The NAEP, a congressionally-mandated program, has been humming along without controversy for more than twenty-five years, taking the pulse of fourth-, eighth-, and twelfth-graders' achievement levels in math, science, reading, and other subjects. Even many critics of multiple-choice, standardized tests view NAEP as about as good as any large-scale standardized exam can be. It is partly multiple-choice and partly open-ended and performance oriented. States choose whether or not to participate. To get more assessment bang for the buck, NAEP does not test all children every year, but is able to get reliable results for states using samples of students in various parts of the country during a given year. And, in assiduous avoidance of anything resembling major consequences attached to the tests, "NAEP is forbidden by law to report results at an individual or school level," say the authors of a recent Department of Education report. (23) Because its stakes are low, schools and teachers and parents aren't engaged in a national horse race over NEAP test scores, which immeasurably enhances the periodic exam's validity and usefulness as an educational barometer. It provides a picture over time of educational achievement for the nation and the states.

In complete contradiction to the reform crusade's crisis-ridden agenda, NAEP tells us that math proficiency for nine, thirteen, and seventeen-year-olds was essentially identical in 1973 and in 1982—just prior to the release of *Risk.* From the mid-1980s until the early 1990s, nine-year-olds boosted their math proficiency some but generally remained at what NAEP designates Level 200, defined as having a beginners' skills and understanding of math. Thirteen-year-olds averaged a 266 level in math in 1973; by 1992, that had barely nudged upward by more than what one would expect from statistical measurement error, to 273, a level at which students are deemed competent at arithmetic and beginning problem-solving. The same story goes for seventeen-year-olds—virtually unchanged levels of math proficiency from 1973 to 1982 to 1992. (24) Moreover, this pattern is the same for science achievement between 1970 and 1992, suggesting, again, that prior to *Risk*, there was not a crisis in U.S. math and science achievement.

But, wait, you say. Perhaps the U.S. education system has been crisis-ridden for several decades. Maybe things were as bad in the early 1970s as they are today. As I suggested earlier, American politicians and policymakers have always found public schools to be at the brink of disaster, whether from too many allegedly intellectually inferior foreign immigrants, supposedly shoddy teaching and unqualified teachers, or low-performing schools that aren't accountable for student performance. A belief in crisis and inferiority has been bred into American schools for nearly 200 years.

There is a still more basic argument for why American schools have not been in peril, either before or after the reform crusade was placed prominently on the national agenda. Consider the ultimate rationale for the crusaders' mission in the first place: economic well-being. Or, as Bill Clinton said in the past and perhaps ought to do so again with respect to American schools, "*It's the economy, stupid.*" Let's examine the crusaders' claim that the nation's economy and the American standard of living is endangered because of supposedly shoddy schools.

Myth Number Two: The U.S. Economy Is in Peril Because of an Inferior Education System

Let's recall those bone-chilling words from *A Nation at Risk*, which told Americans:

> The educational foundations of our society are presently being eroded by a rising tide of mediocrity that threatens our very future as a Nation and a People. . . . If an unfriendly foreign power had attempted to impose on America the mediocre education performance that exists today, we might well have viewed it as an act of war. . . . We have, in effect, been committing an act of unthinking, unilateral education disarmament. . . . If only to keep and improve on the slim competitive edge we still retain in world markets, we must dedicate ourselves to the reform of our educational system for the benefit of all.

That passage from the *Risk* report was so wonderfully quotable, a virtuoso performance in political propaganda. Its breathless warnings of a nation in economic peril explains why *Risk* got so much ongoing attention from a press that loves a good crisis. Of course, it's also true that news organizations reported as fairly and accurately as possible what government officials were doing and saying about education. If the Reagan administration and panels of experts were telling them the nation was on the brink of economic disaster because of a crumbling education system, then editors and reporters had to pay serious attention.

But now, Americans are owed a page-one correction and apology regarding the claims asserted by *Risk* and its hyperbolic progeny, considering what has actually happened to the U.S. economy relative to its competitors abroad. If their claims had been even remotely true, then we would be seeing hard evidence of sustained economic problems in the United States over the long term. That has been far from the case.

Consider that feared economic tiger of Japan. By 1998, Japan's economy, with its heralded education system, was foundering badly. Indeed, Japan was being wracked by financial instability, an overextended banking system with too many bad loans, and other blunders of economic policy, the International Monetary Fund reported in April 1998. In spring 1998, Japanese officials had approved a staggering $125 billion package of public works projects and tax cuts to stimulate the economy—the grandest economic stimulus initiative in the country's history.

In what amounted to a stern reprimand of the international investors who had once worshiped at the altar of the Japanese economy, the IMF said in its *World Economic Outlook Report*:

> That this region might become embroiled in one of the worst financial crises in the postwar period was hardly ever considered—within or outside the region—a realistic possibility. What went wrong? Part of the answer seems to be that these countries became victims of their own success. This success had led domestic and foreign investors to underestimate the countries' economic weaknesses. (25)

Meanwhile, the U.S. economy was, by all accounts, nothing less than spectacular by the late 1990s, achieving that rarefied combination of high employment and low inflation reminiscent of the 1950s and 1960s. In 1997, the nation's total economic activity measured by the inflation-adjusted gross domestic product (GDP) grew a stunning 3.8 percent. (Economists are more than pleased when the economy grows by 2 percent.) By April 1998, the U.S. jobless rate had fallen to just 4.3 percent of the labor force. Consumer prices were inching up by just 2 percent annually, and confidence of consumers in their economic prospects was the highest since the 1960s. The federal deficit, widely blamed for a long-term decline in national savings and stagnant productivity, was all but eliminated, with a federal budget in balance for the first time since 1969. "We keep expecting a slowdown and it never comes," Jeffrey A. Frankel of the Council of Economic Advisers told the *New York Times*. "We're returning to the economy of the '50s and '60s—a remarkable combination of strong growth without inflation." (26)

These developments placed the United States at the top of the heap in terms of economic competitiveness, according to a 1998 analysis of world competitiveness by the International Institute for Management Development in Lausanne, Switzerland. Out of forty-six countries rated for overall competitiveness in the institute's annual *World Competitiveness Yearbook*, the U.S. economy ranked first with a score of 100. Observing that U.S. economic performance has been "historically exceptional," the international management institute's Stephanie Garelli said when releasing the report: "The U.S. is strongly installed in its position as the most competitive nation in the world. Privatization, deregulation, flexibility in the labor market, and especially massive investment in new technology has worked." (27)

Hence, contrary to the logic of the American school bashers, the U.S. economy is hardly at the brink of ruination because of a dysfunctional education system. Moreover, I know of no economist who would attribute the current vigor in the U.S. economy to any "reforms" brought forth by the school accountability movement. Does all this mean that educational health ultimately doesn't matter for economic health? Of course not. Perhaps the best thing education policymakers can do for the American economy is to promote policies that improve Americans' opportunities to get more education. Educational attainment does have a direct bearing on the knowledge and skills of the workforce.

Nevertheless, the scope of the relationship between education and national economic performance badly needs some perspective. The relationship is not nearly as great as the reform crusaders would like Americans to believe. Indeed, the mainstay assumption of the accountability movement, that the quality of America's schools (measured, of course, by achievement and aptitude tests) leads directly and profoundly to greater economic growth—has been so overstated as to border on a grand political fraud. In 1993, for instance, the RAND Corporation, a nonprofit, nonpartisan, and highly regarded policy analysis organization, surveyed the economic literature on the education-economic performance relationship and found that just 14 percent of U.S. economic growth can be attributed to education and training. (28)

When the U.S. economy began to roll along in the mid–1990s, Stanford education professor Larry Cuban paused to wonder: Why hadn't the school bashers shifted rhetorical gears and started praising American schools? Mustn't schools be as responsible for improved economic conditions in the same way they were culprits of economic peril? The answer, Cuban says, is that the politically charged accountability rhetoric was a complete myth in the first place. "Not even a cheaply framed certificate of merit is in the offing for public schools," Cuban said. "For the myth of better schools as the engine for a leaner, stronger economy was a scam from the very beginning. . . . Even though Presidents Bush and Clinton knew that stimulating economic growth depended far more on fiscal and monetary policies than turning around schools—they pressed for national goals and standards. The bumper sticker was: Better schools, a better economy! Thus the lack of praise for the performance of public schools as the economy has brightened exposes the deceitful political logic of a decade of school reform." (29)

What, then, about the persistent problem of lagging productivity growth? Aren't business leaders like IBM's Louis Gerstner right in saying that U.S. productivity suffers because American schools aren't putting out enough highly skilled workers? It is true that productivity growth in the U.S. economy has declined modestly from about 1972 onward. During the postwar boom from 1948 through 1972, productivity per capita increased 2.2 percent a year. Since 1972, the average productivity gain has declined to slightly less than 2 percent. Yet the same downshift occurred not just in the United States, but throughout industrialized Europe and Japan. The former West Germany, for instance, saw its average productivity gains slip from 5.7 percent prior to 1972 to just 2.2 percent afterward.

If lax American schools were the culprit for the U.S. productivity decline, then it stands to reason that poor schools would also explain the productivity decline in Europe and Japan. But no credible international economist I know of has made this connection. Indeed, says the economist Stanley Fischer in a symposium in *Journal of Economic Perspectives:* "It is generally recognized that because the change happened worldwide, the explanation of the post-1973 slowdown is unlikely to lie in the special circumstances of a single country." (30)

Myth Number Three: Greater School "Accountability" Will Mean Higher Achievement

Lastly, the nation's school accountability movement has believed that if you make teachers, principals, and school boards more accountable for performance, then schoolchildren will inevitably become higher achievers—if not in fact, then at least as measured by higher test scores. The belief, as it turns out, is suspect. Evidence, in fact, suggests that high-stakes accountability programs do not lead to better educational outcomes. Before proceeding to this evidence, some definitions are in order.

Nowadays, "accountability" has come to mean several things. Specifically, states use standardized test scores in order to determine whether to: (1) promote students to higher grades; (2) grant high school diplomas; (3) reward or recognize student performance; (4) publicly report school performance to news organizations, elected officials, and others interested in comparisons and rankings of schools; (5) issue a "skills guarantee" for high schoolers; and (6) accredit schools.

It's worthwhile reemphasizing that all these high-impact purposes all derive from the results of test scores.

Some historical trends give us a flavor for the nation's growing exuberance for creating school testing programs with big consequences. In 1952, for instance, some twenty-four of forty-eight states had testing programs, and most of them were voluntary. That most of the programs were run by non–politically motivated social scientists and guidance counseling experts at state colleges or universities indicated the absence of an accountability emphasis. By 1968, some forty-two states had testing programs, forty of which were run by state education departments. The philosophical thrust of testing was beginning to be transformed from student diagnosis and guidance counseling to an emphasis on school, district, and state test performance. That spirit, then, drove the nation's experiments with minimum competency testing in the late 1970s and early 1980s. By 1980, thirty-eight states had implemented such programs. (31)

More recently, according to the latest figures available from the Council of Chief State School Officers (CCSSO), fully forty-six states had testing programs by 1996. Of these, forty-two of the programs involved mandatory testing of all students in one or more grades; two states permitted testing on a sampling basis—that is, not all students in a given grade are tested each year because state-level achievement trends rather than individual or school performance was the main purpose; two states' programs were voluntary; and four states had no statewide testing programs during that year. Testless states at that time were Colorado, Minnesota, Iowa, and Nebraska. "School accountability" was the purpose of testing in thirty-eight states. (32)

Now back to the main question: Do these high-stakes monitoring tools lead to higher achievement? Using the CCSSO information as a basis, I compiled three lists of states. The first list included eighteen states, which I grouped as having "high stakes" accountability and testing systems, with at least two of the various monitoring tools I noted above. The second list I classified as having "low or moderate stakes" attached to their tests, meaning principally that these states publicly reported schools' test scores, with no other official consequences other than something akin to pinning schools with a scarlet A.

Next, I gathered achievement trend data for the states from the National Assessment of Education Progress (NAEP). As I suggested earlier, experts regard the NAEP as a pretty good assessment of statewide trends in science, math, and reading achievement for the fourth, eighth, and twelfth grades. NAEP's great advantage for my simple analysis is that schools and teachers don't typically emphasize its results so much that the test itself becomes the main object for which instruction is based. Hence, the NAEP isn't subject to "teaching the test." As we shall see in Chapter 5, the practice of drilling students for tests has become one of the more odious results of big-stakes accountability programs.

In the following three tables, I have listed three distinct categories of states. Table 4.1 lists the states with high-stakes systems—the ones that attach a lot of importance to test scores in terms of publicity, awards, and sanctions; Table 4.2 groups the low- and moderate-stakes states—the ones that mostly just publicly

TABLE 4.1 How 'High-Stakes' Accountability States Fared in Achievement Relative to Average Nationwide Achievement.

High-Stakes States (1995–1996)	*Grades Tested*	*8th grade science proficiency relative to nation (1996)*	*8th grade math average compared to national average (1996)*
Alabama	3–12	**Below**	**Below**
Arkansas	4,5,7,10,11	**Below**	**Below**
Florida	4,8,10,11	**Below**	**Below**
Georgia	K,3,5,8,11,12	**Below**	**Below**
Hawaii	3,6,8,10–12	**Below**	**Below**
Indiana	3,6,10	Above	Above
Louisiana	K,3–7,10,11	**Below**	**Below**
Michigan	4,5,7,8,11	Above	Above
Mississippi	4-9,11	**Below**	**Below**
New Mexico	1–6,8,10–12	**Below**	**Below**
New York	3–6,8–12	Equal	Equal
North Carolina	3–10	Equal	**Below**
South Carolina	3–11	**Below**	**Below**
Tennessee	2-9,11	**Below**	**Below**
Texas	3–8,10–12	Equal	Equal
Virginia	4,6–12	Equal	Equal
Washington	4,8,11	Equal	Above
West Virginia	1–11	Average	**Below**
Percent High-Stakes States with Achievement:			
ABOVE National Average		**11%** (2/18)	**17%** (3/18)
EQUAL to National Average		**33%** (6/18)	**17%** (3/18)
BELOW National Average		**56%** (10/18)	**67%** (12/18)

SOURCES: Council of Chief State School Officers, *Annual Survey of State Student Assessment Programs* (Washington, D.C.: CCSSO) Fall 1996; National Education Goals Panel, *Profile of 1994-1995 State Assessments;* National Center for Fair & Open Testing, *Testing Our Children: A Report Card on State Assessment Systems* (Cambridge: Fairtest, Sept. 1997); NAEP *1996 Science Report Card for the Nation and the States;* (Washington, D.C.: U.S. Department of Education); NAEP *1996 Mathematics Report Card for the Nation and the States* (Washington, D.C.: U.S. Department of Education).

TABLE 4.2 States Attaching Low or Moderate Stakes to their Testing Programs 1995–1996

State	*Grades Tested*	*8th grade science proficiency compared to national average (1996)*	*8th grade math proficiency compared to national average (1996)*
Alaska	4,8,11	Above	Above
Arizona	4,7,10	Equal	Below
Delaware	3,5,8,10	Below	Below
Kentucky	4,8,11,12	Equal	Below
Maine	4,8,11	Above	Above
Missouri	3,5,6,8,10,11	Equal	Equal
Montana	4,8,11	Above	Above
North Dakota	3,6,8,11	Above	Above
Oregon	3,5,8,11	Above	Above
Rhode Island	4,8,10	Equal	Equal
Utah	1-12	Above	Above
Vermont	4,8,10	Above	Above
Wisconsin	3,4,8,10	Above	Above
Wyoming	9-12	Above	Above
% of States **ABOVE** National Average		**64.2%** (9/14)	**64.2%** (9/14)
% of States **EQUAL** to National Average		**28.5%** (4/14)	**14.2%** (2/14)
% of States **BELOW** National Average		**7%** (1/14)	**21.4%** (3/14)

SOURCES: Council of Chief State School Officers, *Annual Survey of State Student Assessment Programs* (Washington, D.C.: CCSSO) Fall 1996; National Education Goals Panel, *Profile of 1994–1995 State Assessments;* National Center for Fair & Open Testing, *Testing Our Children: A Report Card on State Assessment Systems* (Cambridge: Fairtest, Sept. 1997); NAEP *1996 Science Report Card for the Nation and the States;* (Washington, D.C.: U.S. Department of Education); NAEP *1996 Mathematics Report Card for the Nation and the States* (Washington, D.C.: U.S. Department of Education).

report test scores; and Table 4.3 lists the states with no mandatory statewide testing programs. For each table, the first column shows whether a state was above, equal to, or below the national average in eighth-grade science proficiency. The second column shows how a state fared to the national average for eighth-grade math achievement. Here are the results from the eighteen "high-stakes" accountability states:

Table 4.1 shows a clear association between states with elaborate testing programs and below-average achievement on the NAEP for math and science. For example, while 17 percent of these states had above-average achievement in eighth-grade math, fully two-thirds (67 percent) were below the national average.

Look at the next set of figures for the states with low and moderate stakes attached to their testing programs:

Similarly, states having fewer consequences attached to test scores actually maintain higher overall math and science achievement. As shown in Table 4.2, in science achievement, for example, more than 64 percent of these states had above-average achievement; 28 percent equaled the nation's average; and just one of fourteen states, or 7 percent, had eighth-grade science achievement below the nation's average.

Table 4.3 shows what happened with the four states that had no testing programs in 1995–1996:

Obviously, all of these states without any testing program or formal accountability system obtained above-average eighth-grade math and science achievement, according to the 1996 NAEP reports. Now, one more table to summarize the results from the three groups of states. In Table 4.4, I've compiled the summary for math scores only, but the same patterns hold for science achievement ,too.

The summary table fairly neatly makes the point: The accountability movement's implicit claim that more testing—and that more and greater consequences associated with tests will lead to greater achievement—hardly seems supportable. In fact, the claim may be pure fantasy, particularly on assessments such as the NAEP that are rarely linked to high stakes and therefore aren't subject to "teaching the test." According to my analysis of data from the National Assessment of Educational Progress:

- A state with a high-stakes testing program is far more likely to obtain below-average achievement (67 percent) than a state with low (27 percent) or no stakes (0 percent).
- A low-stakes state is more likely than a high-stakes state to reach achievement levels above the nation's average.
- And a state without testing and accountability programs at all has the best chance of having above-average achievement levels.

Indeed, a similar analysis by the National Center for Fair and Open Testing found the same pattern. The organization asked whether states that required students to pass a high school graduation test—about as high-stakes as a testing program gets—did favorably on NAEP's fourth- and eighth-grade math and reading

TABLE 4.3 States Having No Statewide Testing Programs 1995–1996

State	*8th grade science achievement compared to national average*	*8th grade math achievement compared to national average*
Colorado	Above	Above
Iowa	Above	Above
Minnesota	Above	Above
Nebraska	Above	Above

SOURCES: Council of Chief State School Officers, *Annual Survey of State Student Assessment Programs* (Washington, D.C.: CCSSO) Fall 1996; National Education Goals Panel, *Profile of 1994–1995 State Assessments;* National Center for Fair & Open Testing, *Testing Our Children: A Report Card on State Assessment Systems* (Cambridge: Fairtest, Sept. 1997); NAEP *1996 Science Report Card for the Nation and the States;* (Washington, D.C.: U.S. Department of Education); NAEP *1996 Mathematics Report Card for the Nation and the States* (Washington, D.C.: U.S. Department of Education).

TABLE 4.4 Percentage of High, Low, and No-Stakes States Compared to the National Average Achievement for 8th Grade Math 1995–1996

8th grade math acheivement	*High-stakes states*	*Low-stakes states*	*States with no testing/ accountability programs*
% ABOVE National Average	17%	64%	100%
% EQUAL to National Average	17%	14%	0%
% BELOW National Average	67%	21%	0%

SOURCES: Council of Chief State School Officers, *Annual Survey of State Student Assessment Programs* (Washington, D.C.: CCSSO) Fall 1996; National Education Goals Panel, *Profile of 1994–1995 State Assessments;* National Center for Fair & Open Testing, *Testing Our Children: A Report Card on State Assessment Systems* (Cambridge: Fairtest, Sept. 1997); NAEP *1996 Science Report Card for the Nation and the States;* (Washington, D.C.: U.S. Department of Education); NAEP *1996 Mathematics Report Card for the Nation and the States* (Washington, D.C.: U.S. Department of Education).

assessments. "NAEP results do not support the claim that having high-stakes tests leads to higher educational quality than does the absence of such tests," the center concluded. "Rather, it appears that proponents have based their rationale for high-stakes testing on ideology, not evidence." (33)

To be sure, dozens of factors can influence any state's relative performance on the NAEP assessments, including population size, its relative income and educational levels, the numbers of residents living in poverty—a whole mix of complex and interrelated variables that constitute the entire milieu in which a state's education system operates.

The larger point is that the reductionist perspective of the reform crusaders in placing so much importance on testing and accountability, as the means to improve education, completely ignores this more complex and difficult reality. Indeed, as the evidence indicates, focusing exclusively on measurement and accountability may have precisely the opposite of the intended outcomes.

As the following two chapters explore, this national obsession with measurement, surveillance, and control of students, teachers, and schools is likely to exacerbate the real problems of America's schools rather than help them.

5

Crime and Punishment: How the Accountability Machine Hurts Schoolchildren

Chuck Lavaroni was a great believer in the value of standardized tests in schools during his forty-eight–year career as a teacher and administrator. But when he remembers Gilbert Medeiros, a seventh-grader in his class some forty years ago, Lavaroni's earlier belief about standardized testing turns sour.

By any measure, Lavaroni has been a highly successful educator. He taught school in Novato, California, a town in northern Marin County, an hour's drive from San Francisco. He served as district superintendent in Sausalito, and, there was a stint as director of teacher education at Dominican College. Later, Lavaroni launched a profitable business of private schools, which he and his partner would later sell for a handsome return. Nowadays, Lavaroni is semi-retired in affluent Marin County, and he continues to occasionally consult on education issues. At seventy-one, Lavaroni now has the distance of time to remember kids like Gil Medeiros.

There had been an important standardized test given to all seventh-graders, and the results, in Lavaroni's view, hadn't been promising for Gilbert's academic future. Gil was the son of first-generation Portuguese parents; his father ran a small trucking company in Novato. Lavaroni liked Gil and wanted to break the bad news softly. "I had nothing but love for him," Lavaroni told me. "I had deep respect for him as a kid, and I just didn't want to hurt him."

One day at school, Lavaroni took Gil aside and broke the news about the test result. "Gilbert, it's important for you to know that you should not have as one of your goals going to college," Lavaroni told him. "These tests show you. . . .," his voice trailed off. "You're a wonderful human being, but the tests don't show it. You should stay in the trucking business with your dad."

Some thirty years later, Lavaroni ran into Gilbert Medeiros at a social function in Marin County. During that unexpected encounter, Lavaroni learned that Gil was living in Walnut Creek, and that he'd graduated from college at the University of San Francisco. Lavaroni learned of Gil's earning a law degree; that he had become a successful trial lawyer in northern California; that he had worked as legal counsel and vice president for large real estate development firms; and that he had owned and run five different companies, including Vita-Stat, the company that makes the ubiquitous blood pressure monitors in drugstores nationwide.

Lavaroni learned these things about Gilbert Medeiros's life after seventh grade, when a test score might have led him to another fate altogether. When I talked to Lavaroni in February 1998, he was still embarrassed at what he told Gil about the meaning of those test scores, especially in light of Gil's later success. "What I'm embarrassed about is that I thought those tests were useful," Lavaroni says.

When I spoke to Medeiros, he told me that even now he had "more than a vague recollection" of that conversation with his seventh-grade teacher. Medeiros recalled his "great respect" for Lavaroni as a teacher but also the anger he felt at the time, when his future could have been defined by a test score. "He (Lavaroni) basically told me not to go to college, that I'd be wasting my time; because of my test scores I'd have a difficult time in college," Medeiros says. "I told him, 'You don't know what you're talking about.' I do remember being told that, being offended by it, and thinking I don't care about their stupid, goddamned test. Whatever the test was it was not related to myself and what I could do."

Indeed, Lavaroni may not have known about Gil's full ability, because the expression of it didn't seem to fit the relatively rigid norms of school. Certainly the achievement test didn't permit its expression. By the seventh grade, Medeiros had read all of Jules Verne as well as Alexander Dumas. "I loved to read, and I read everything," he says. "These weren't school assignments, I just read them. School itself was not exactly . . . well, it was just boring, and so I read whatever I could get my hands on, and it didn't necessarily coincide with how teachers taught social studies, for instance."

When Gil's Portuguese parents moved to California in 1946, his father started the small trucking company, and Gil worked for him from the age of eleven until he left for college. Gil still remembers the basic value his father had instilled in him: "My father basically said to me, 'You do your best at whatever you do. You are known by what you do.' That's how I grew up, judging people by their actions. It's what you *do* that matters, and that's what still matters to me."

His seventh-grade standardized test score, then, had been a wake-up call to another kind of world with different sorts of values than those his father taught him, Medeiros says. "That was my first run-in with that type of environment, where people are judging you on other norms, in this case a test, that you can be judged on a test alone," he told me. "That value ran against what I was taught, and so I have resented testing all my life. I know what I can do."

A Different World

In at least one important respect, not a lot has changed in American schools since Gilbert Medeiros was in seventh grade and Chuck Lavaroni was a schoolteacher. Naive to the limits of technological fixes of education, the emerging technology of testing in schools was largely unquestioned in the 1950s and 1960s. Nowadays, more questions than ever are being asked about the misuses of standardized tests, in large part because more is known about their real effects on schools and schoolchildren.

And yet, in terms of real education policy and the powerful way in which the rhetoric of the testing culture resonates with the American belief in standardization, efficiency, and quantification, the testing culture of the 1980s and 1990s has become one of the most dominant forces in American schools this century.

In that respect, everything has changed since Gilbert was a seventh-grader. Testing in the 1950s and 1960s was often run by universities, well removed from the meddling of elected officials. Schools used the tests mainly to diagnose learning problems of individual students. Certainly, the tests were misused, especially to place students into the proper "track" by depending on an achievement or aptitude test. Worse, kids like Gil Medeiros were informed by teachers and school counselors that, on the basis of test scores, they weren't "college material."

Now, however, testing is managed by state education departments run by political appointees of governors' offices, under the constant scrutiny and harassment of state legislators vying for votes and public popularity. Joined by a public that remains largely ignorant of the real effects of the testing culture on their children and on society at large, officials in most states—sanctioned and supported financially and politically by the federal government—have erected massive systems of management, measurement, and surveillance of public schools and schoolchildren.

Chapter 4 showed how the accountability machine has been built on myth after myth, deceiving the public into believing that more standardized testing will make for better schools and smarter children, when in fact there's ample reason to believe the opposite is occurring. Moreover, the obsessive drive toward school accountability results in many schoolchildren being treated as criminals, with their punishment inflicted by the state. The "crime"? Not passing a standardized test mandated by local or state officials for promotion or graduation, whatever their real achievement in school course work, or however dubious the validity of a given test to demonstrate any meaningful connection to the real world and genuine learning.

So Gilbert Medeiros was fortunate. He believed in himself enough not to take Lavaroni's advice. But then, it was just one test in the seventh grade some forty years ago. Sure, Medeiros had to overcome psychic barriers in himself as well as powerful societal beliefs about the sanctity of a test score to measure one's ability and potential for success in life. But, lucky for him, Medeiros didn't have the entire weight of the education system to overcome, including school officials informing him under the force of state law that he had to repeat the seventh grade because he failed a standardized test, or that regardless of his course grades and other accomplishments, he couldn't graduate from high school.

Indeed, unlike Karen Price of Smithfield, North Carolina, and Kelly Santos of San Antonio, Gil Medeiros didn't have the Johnson County, North Carolina, board of education nor the state of Texas to overcome.

Policy 842

Karen Price had enough experience with school testing in North Carolina to be immediately wary of the rather unusual contract the Johnson County school district sent her one day in fall 1996. Unless Price and other parents agreed to a new rule called Policy 842, their children would be banned from all extracurricular activities, from playing sports to working on the yearbook. And forget about driving a car to school.

Johnson County schools approved Policy 842 in June 1996 and named it "Student Accountability for Academic Achievement." Taking North Carolina's "ABCs" accountability system a bold step further, the district's new rule stipulated that children in kindergarten through eighth grade would be flunked or sent to summer school if they didn't score high enough on the state's end-of-grade standardized tests. Summer school was mandatory for better test scores that nevertheless didn't make the state's minimum cutoff. Johnson County's high schoolers who didn't pass the state's end-of-course tests in several subjects, including algebra, English, and U.S. history, with a score of at least 70, would be given a final grade of no better than a D—regardless of the grade they had earned in class.

Price told me that letter was the first she'd even heard about Policy 842. She asked to meet with the district's assistant superintendent to discuss her concerns with the test-score requirements. Kelly, a sophomore in high school, was Price's last of three children to go through the state's testing programs in Johnson County schools. Throughout, Price says, she struggled with her children being required to pass standardized tests regardless of the quality of their actual work in the classroom. But Johnson County's new Policy 842 was the most blatantly draconian test-score rule she had yet encountered. Price wouldn't sign the contract until she was given an adequate explanation of its purpose.

"I refused to sign it," Price told me. "I couldn't agree to a policy that they never even bothered to explain to me. And I was still very concerned they would rely strictly on a test in order to pass or fail school, while everything else was completely irrelevant."

Price's meeting with the assistant superintendent was frightening, she says. She told him her concerns. What of children with undiagnosed learning disabilities who would "fall through the cracks" of the new policy? What of children who perform well in school but, like her daughter, had trouble on standardized tests?

The official's response, Price says, was chilling.

"'There are no children who do not test well,'" Price says he told her.

"That's just not true!" Price answered. "What about a child who works extremely hard, makes a C in her class, but doesn't pass the test?"

"'I will do everything in my power to make sure that kid never graduates,'" Price recalls the official saying. He added, "'Those children will not be tolerated. . . . This is not about hard work; you've either got it or you don't.'"

Price was stunned. "That's when I started talking to other parents, and they were treated just as rudely as me," she says. "Realizing what I was dealing with, I asked to meet with Jim Causby, the district superintendent." But in her meeting with him, Causby was unwavering. "When I left his office, I was just in tears," Price told me.

Policy 842 went into action as planned, and the cracks into which many children fell were as wide as Price had feared.

At the Wilson Mills School, Eric had been coming home all year with progress reports from the school informing his mother, Catherine, that her son was "doing fine." Indeed, Eric was earning As and Bs in all his third-grade classes. But that performance was meaningless when Eric scored below his grade level on the state test, and he was forced, with virtually no warning, to attend summer school. (1)

When Shannon was a fifth-grader at Cleveland Middle School, her mom, Julia, asked repeatedly to meet with her teacher and the principal, "because I knew she had a reading problem." Julia wanted Shannon tested for a possible reading disorder but was repeatedly refused.

Instead, Shannon was given an IQ test at the start of sixth grade. Throughout the year, Shannon got As, Bs, and Cs in all her classes, except the D she got in English. Her mother says it wasn't until Shannon passed the state's math test but failed the end-of-grade reading test that anyone at the school even acknowledged her reading problem.

When her mother continued to ask for help with Shannon's reading difficulties during her forced summer school attendance, the district provided help, all right—test-preparation materials for retaking the very same end-of-grade exam. "Shannon is very upset that she is going to be retained even though she had passing grades," Julia says in the constrained language of a court affidavit.

On that first test of Johnson County's new accountability policy in May 1997, some 2,700 out of a total 8,300 pupils in grades three through eight failed the state's end-of-grade test. Compared to the former policy under which just 5 percent of children were flunked, fully one-third of Johnson County's pupils were flunked under the new rule. The vast majority were minority children—in all grades, for both the end-of-course and the end-of-grade (EOG) tests. For instance, of seventh-graders failing to make the cutoff score on the EOG tests, some two-thirds were minority children. (2)

Test Misuse, 1990s-Style

Richard M. Jaeger, a professor at the University of North Carolina, is certainly no flaming radical when it comes to standardized testing. He's built a career steeped in the essential values of testing. But one thing is frequently true about people like Jaeger: They become highly annoyed when tests are badly used. And, they say, Johnson County's Policy 842 was a quintessential example of standardized tests badly used.

Besides his teaching and research at the university in Greensboro, Jaeger works as a hired gun. His résumé runs an immodest thirty-two pages. In a thirty-year career of research and teaching about testing, Jaeger has written hundreds of articles and dozens of books. He specializes in what most people would consider arcane matters involving the statistical characteristics of standardized tests. He has served on the editorial boards of the major publications in his field. Organizations from the Law School Admissions Council to the Association of American Medical Colleges have sought his services. He is a member of the National Academy of Sciences and a recipient of the E. F. Lindquist Award for a lifetime of achievement, the psychometric field's highest honor; the award is named for one of the inventors of large-scale multiple-choice testing. (3)

Jaeger and several other expert witnesses testified in a federal lawsuit against Superintendent Causby and the school board on behalf of Shannon, Eric, and the other Johnson County children who were flunked because of their test scores. They concluded that Policy 842 reflected virtually complete ignorance about the nature of standardized tests and their limitations.

When it comes to test misuse, school officials in any nook or cranny of the United States can hardly plead ignorance. True, there are virtually no laws preventing schools from bad uses of standardized tests, nor are there regulatory government agencies to ensure that buyers of published tests use them wisely and appropriately. Testing is a largely self-policed industry, constrained ultimately only by victims of bad testing who seek relief from the American judicial system. Nevertheless, widely accepted standards exist that any testing director at any U.S. school district knows, or should know. Standards for Educational and Psychological Testing is among the most widely respected of these guidelines, created by the American Educational Research Association, the American Psychological Association, and the National Council on Measurement in Education.

The standards cite the misuse of a test for a purpose for which it was never intended or designed its highest crime. In the evolution of North Carolina's ABCs accountability plan (the ABCs and its effects on schools are addressed in Chapter 6), policymakers had targeted schools themselves as the "unit of accountability." Design of the state's end-of-grade and end-of-course tests, then, *were premised on the condition that results would be used to rank and compare schools and districts.* But what happens when a local school board member has the bright idea to take a test that is designed only to rank schools, and instead uses it to classify individual students?

When the ABCs exams were created for North Carolina public schools, the test makers undoubtedly considered what the standards refer to as "content validity." A test meant to rank all North Carolina schools would have content validity if it adequately reflected all the reading and math taught in schools. Design of the tests for that purpose would lead, in turn, to such key parameters as the test questions, the length of exams, and so on. According to a general rule of test design, a test purportedly valid for an entire district needs to have relatively few test questions to get an adequate sample of the topics covered in school. That's because there are large numbers of test takers likely exposed to that content.

But that same, broad-brush test is likely to be a poor indicator for what a given child might know about social studies or algebra. Such a test would be deemed to have very low reliability for the more specific use of categorizing individual children. On any given administration of that broad-brush test, an individual's score is likely to vary considerably. That's because one administration of the test might well cover a child's knowledge and skills, while another version of the test might not. The broad-brush test, fairly reliable in terms of consistency of scores for the entire school, would have a wide margin of uncertainty for individuals. The kicker here is that any major decisions based on individual scores, such as flunking students for an entire grade, would be wholly indefensible, only marginally better than simply throwing dice.

Yet that's exactly what Johnson County schools effectively did, according to Jaeger and other experts. One of the experts, John A. Hattie, is Jaeger's colleague at the Center for Educational Research and Evaluation in Greensboro. Like Jaeger, who studied mathematical statistics at Stanford, Hattie, a New Zealander by birth, is a numbers guy. For twenty-five years, Hattie has specialized in psychometrics, a field devoted to studying the statistical and measurement properties of all types of standardized tests. According to Hattie's analysis, *the North Carolina tests are so imprecise for individuals that schools can't even determine which grade level a student would belong to based on a test score.*

Consider Table 5.1, which contains the average reading scores for grades three through eight on the end-of-grade tests along with the cutoff scores for failing the test, and thereby flunking the entire course. Suppose a Johnson County fifth-grader, call her Sara, scored a 146 on her end-of-grade reading test. With a cutoff score of 148 for the fifth grade, this child would be flunked, according to Policy 842. Nevertheless, her "true" score could be as high as 156 or as low as 136, given the test's rather significant measurement error of plus or minus 10 points for individual students. Sara, then, is given two more chances to pass the different versions of the same test. "Measurement error alone," says Hattie, "would provide this student with a reasonable opportunity for passing the test, regardless of any additional instruction." (4)

Recall that Sara's actual score could be as high as 156 or as low as 136. Then, take a look at the cutoff scores in the table. Sara's school, then, can't even conclude whether she's reading at her own grade level. But it gets worse. According to the test results, *Sara could be reading as low as the third grade or as high as the eighth grade.*

Under these circumstances, should children be held accountable for test scores? Without acknowledging the unknowns of using the tests this way or offering any evidence or justification for doing so in Policy 842—as the standards demand of testers—Johnson County schools obviously determined that important educational decisions could be made about individuals based on the tests.

TABLE 5.1 Average scores, cut-off points, and true score range, for N.C. end-of-grade reading tests

Grade	*Average score*	*Cut-off score*	*Range for average scores (margin of error equals (+/-) 10 points*
3	143	140	133–153
4	147	144	137–154
5	152	148	142–158
6	154	151	144–164
7	157	154	147–167
8	159	155	149–169

SOURCE: Eric V. et al v. Dr. James Causby and the Johnson County Board of Education, Complaint No. 5-97-CV-587, filed July 28, 1997 in U.S. District Court for the Eastern District of North Carolina, Hattie Affadavit, pp. 20–21.

But that's not the conclusion reached by the Durham, North Carolina, school district, which also considered using the tests in a similar way. "These tests provide little information" for individual children, David Holdzkom, Durham's executive director for research and accountability, concluded. "The fact that a set of numbers is generated that is purported to show individual information may hurt more than it helps, since the individual numbers constitute a very rough estimate of any student performance on a given day." (5)

Thus the North Carolina tests, intended to measure achievement of schools and districts, were far too imprecise for school officials to make decisions on individual children based on the test scores. In the parlance of testing, their "reliability" for that purpose was woefully poor.

But Johnson County schools' use of the exam was bad testing for an even more fundamental reason. When test makers—at least, ethical test makers—produce a test and market it for particular purposes, at a minimum they ought to prove and document that test's *validity* for the intended purpose. In other words, when schools infer that Johnny can't read because he failed a reading test, then there ought to be good evidence presented that the test is a sound indicator of overall reading skills. That's called "predictive validity" in the parlance of testing. According to the standards, testers are ethically obligated to show that their use of a test is a good indicator of some meaningful outcome apart from the test itself. Does the test predict anything else worthwhile, such as one's grades in school or performance on a job? As the standards puts it:

> Validity is the most important consideration in test evaluation. The concept refers to the appropriateness, meaningfulness, and usefulness of the specific inferences made from test scores. Test validation is the process of accumulating evidence to support such inferences. . . . Although evidence may be accumulated in many ways, validity always refers to the degree to which that evidence supports the inferences that are made from the scores. The inferences regarding the specific uses of a test are validated, not the test itself.(6)

So the most important question regarding Johnson County's Policy 842 would be, So what? Even if the district's use of the tests yielded completely reliable scores, without any margin of error for individuals—which was decidedly *not* the case—what does the score really mean? What could school officials genuinely infer about a fifth-grader at Wilson Mills School scoring below the mathematics cutoff? To what is that test score correlated in the real world, outside the test's multiple-choice boundaries?

The obvious purpose of Policy 842 was to weed out students who wouldn't be able to succeed in the next grade. But if that were true, the policy contained no evidence whatsoever to support the claim the pupils would not succeed. In fact, based on the classroom performances of children who were flunked based on the test, there's ample evidence of just the opposite—that they would succeed in the later grade, many with As and Bs. Said Jaeger, "Johnson County Public Schools have provided no evidence that the North Carolina End-of-Grade Tests validly predict the ability of students who score at or above (the passing level) to succeed in the following school grade or the inability of students who score below (that level) to succeed in the following school grade." (7)

Does Flunking Work?

Surely, then, there must have been good reasons and sound evidence to support Johnson County's policy to retain schoolchildren based on a test score. After all, the district, like an increasing number of school systems across the nation, was attacking the dreaded "social promotion" of unprepared pupils—what President Clinton had been lobbying so assiduously against in promoting his national testing plan throughout the late 1990s.

But the evidence is overwhelming that the belief in the power of retention to bolster academic standards or to somehow help the children held back is little more than a myth, yet another unproven assumption that's easily sold to an uninformed public harboring a reflexive mistrust of all public institutions, including public schools.

Indeed, documenting the real effects on children of retaining them a grade or more has been among the most heavily researched topics in education over the past thirty years. The collective verdict from hundreds of studies is unusually unambiguous. That body of work, says Jaeger, "firmly indicates that retaining students . . . has negative effects on students' achievement in later grades; has negative effects on students' attitudes toward school; their self-esteem, and their social adjustment; dramatically increases the likelihood that students will drop out of school; is disproportionately applied to racial and ethnic minority students; and is strongly associated with criminality and incarceration during students' adult years." (8)

The magnitude of the deleterious effects of flunking children are enormous, greater than virtually all other conceivable correlations that can be studied in education. The strength of the association suggests that grade retention may cause—rather than simply be associated with—a child's later problems in school. In fact, if any Machiavellian educators wanted to invent the best way of motivating students to drop out of school, they'd be clever to retain students at least one grade level. That alone would double a child's chances of dropping out. Flunked twice and a child's chance of eventually leaving school is virtually guaranteed, the research suggests. To quantify the effects of flunking, scholars have employed a vigorous statistical technique known as meta-analysis, which essentially allows them to measure the overall effects from hundreds or thousands of individual studies. Hattie, who performed one such analysis, says, "In prior research I have synthesized the results of over three-hundred meta-analyses, based on 150,000 plus studies, and among educational interventions at enhancing academic achievement, retention is overwhelmingly disastrous" for individual children. (9)

Again, the ostensible rationale for flunking children a grade based on standardized test scores is to help children succeed in school and in life, and to make students and their families "accountable" for their own success. But given that retention actually punishes children in school and in life, could there be other motivations for schools to connect retention policy to test scores?

What if flunking students were to raise statistical averages on standardized tests *at the school and district level* at the same time they were damaging both social and educational lives of individuals? And what if, as in North Carolina's case, schools and districts were evaluated by state educational regulators for sanctions, takeovers, firings, and bonuses—all based on standardized test scores? Clearly, it would be in school officials' best personal interests to boost average test scores for the entire school, irrespective of the impacts on individual kids.

Indeed, Steven Holmes, a professor and expert on the effects of grade retention at the University of Georgia, says grade retention can actually boost test scores substantially for campuses and districts. "The literature provides ample evidence that one of the best ways of increasing system averages on achievement tests is to retain large numbers of students," Holmes says. How so? As retained students continue to retake standardized tests, they gain the advantage of at least a year's more familiarity with the exams than their younger peers. Also, the retained children are exposed to more practice tests, more drills for tests, and more "instruction" by worksheets that mimic standardized tests. In any case, systemwide test-score averages do go up. (10)

To be sure, there's no direct evidence of a cynical attempt by Johnson County schools to raise test scores by tying them to grade retention rules. But the whole accountability movement (explored further in Chapter 6) has been rife with such distortions of educational quality resulting from people acting in their own best interests, to feed the accountability machine, or else face the consequences. Officially, Johnson County's Policy 842 was not related to the state's ABCs school accountability plan. However, had Johnson County flunked as many children as possible in order to raise scores, to do so would have been entirely rational under the crimes and punishments set by state regulators.

An Educational Activist Is Born

Even after her painful meetings with Johnson County officials, Price would not be dismissed. "In fourteen years of having children in these schools I've learned that if you don't fight for them, they won't make it," Price said.

Joined by eight other parents in the small town of Smithfield, Price tried to raise public awareness of Policy 842 and its effects on the town's schoolchildren. The parents called their group exactly what they demanded from school officials: Educate Our Children, and it was perhaps the first such multiracial organization in the mostly white district. Still, the group found itself marginalized and easily dismissed by the local establishment. The local paper, Price says, largely ignored them and reported their views only as Superintendent Causby himself related them to local reporters.

Nevertheless, some 2,100 parents in this rural region of 80,000 people petitioned the district to reconsider Policy 842. Without success, they eventually got legal representation, including that of the NAACP Legal Defense Fund, based in New York City. Under threat of the federal lawsuit, Johnson County ultimately modified Policy 842 to make it less onerous on schoolchildren who were succeeding in school despite relatively poor test performances. Educate Our Children had achieved its goal, and the suit was settled without going to trial.

Still, anger over the failings of a dysfunctional, test-obsessed school system has turned these parents into educational activists, fighting for schools to pay attention to individual children, not how school officials look to state bureaucrats and legislators.

"Unless you live through it you can't believe it's really happening," Price told me. "I was so appalled they were willing to just turn their backs on a big majority of children."

TAASing Texas

With hope and reluctance on a summer of day in 1997, Kelly Santos drove alone from her comfortable, middle-class neighborhood in north San Antonio to the city's east side. Kelly rarely had reason to go to the east side, but now she had a life-changing reason.

Kelly was reluctant, even grimly depressed, because this would be her *seventh* attempt over the course of some three years to pass the Texas Assessment of Academic Skills. For most Texans, the series of mandatory standardized tests covering third grade through high school is simply known by its acronym, TAAS; locals pronounce it "toss." Kelly's failure to pass it kept her from graduating with her classmates, getting her diploma, and going to college, the way she'd always planned. But now, she was hopeful. Maybe this would be the day she'd finally score above the magic number needed to pass. She'd been so close, within one to three points, so many times.

The east side of San Antonio is home to the Texas Education Agency's Region 20 service center, where thousands of San Antonio kids like Kelly go to retake the TAAS exam—one, two, even five years or more after they were supposed to graduate. Kelly's first attempt to pass the TAAS came during her sophomore year, as is the case for all Texas tenth-graders. The Texas test consists of three subtests in reading, writing, and math, and Texas high schoolers must pass all three with a score of 70 in order to get a high school diploma. Kelly had missed the cut by just a point or two on each of her previous attempts on the math section.

By then, Kelly's seventh attempt to pass the TAAS, it took all her mother's persuasive powers to convince Kelly to sign up for the summer administration of the test. Her mom, Mary, a teacher at Kelly's high school, convinced Kelly to work with a math tutor this time, a colleague who taught math at the school. The teacher worked with Kelly for several weeks, and before the test she told Mary with some confidence, "She's ready." Mary told me, "All her teachers would say that to me, that she's ready for that test, she knows the concepts." And so, with Kelly still in limbo several weeks after she was supposed to graduate, in summer 1997, Mary was confident that her daughter could now get on with her life. (At the request of Kelly and her parents, I've agreed not to reveal their real last name.)

Originally from Butte, Montana, Mary came to San Antonio with her parents when she was eighteen, just about Kelly's age. Both of Mary's parents were born in Mexico, and they moved from Montana to Texas to be closer to family in Mexico. Mary's grandfather still lives near Acapulco, and her grandmother lives just across the Texas border. Mary went to college and became a Spanish teacher, first at the inner-city schools on San Antonio's south side and later at the more economically advantaged Northside Independent Schools, in the community where Mary lives with her two children and her husband.

She's worked at Northside Independent Schools for some fourteen years and describes herself as "well known in the district." Her husband works as a human resources director at a large company. Altogether, Mary has been teaching twenty-four years, has experienced public education from both ends of the economic spectrum, and deeply appreciates being able to send her children to the good schools on the north end. "When I taught on the south side, everybody, including students and teachers, always wanted to be on the north side," she told me.

It wasn't supposed to turn out this way for their daughter, Kelly, being in limbo, that is, unable to graduate from high school. She'd grown up with the advantages of good schools and a secure, middle-class life. Certainly, Kelly didn't start school life in a bad way. As a youngster, she had high aspirations, and wanted to be a doctor. (The couple's youngest child wants to be a lawyer.) Kelly was always a "beautiful child," well liked by teachers and peers, says Mary. And she was always a good student.

Indeed, Kelly remembers always liking school, and was hardly unusual in her likes and dislikes about school. "In middle school, I enjoyed science and learned a lot in that class," Kelly says. "I didn't like history at all, math at the time was OK, English was good, and band and P.E. were fun." Kelly earned "mostly As and Bs" in middle school, says her mother. "In middle school, Kelly was so cute and gregarious and this wonderful little student. . . . .They just pushed her along, and when kids get to high school they forget about them. It's like they're telling Kelly, 'We haven't prepared you and now it's a sink or swim situation.'"

But on that summer day in 1997, Kelly believed she'd swim this time. She told me a year later, "When I took the TAAS at the regional place, I was worried more about getting lost than the test. I really wasn't all that into taking it again. . . . I went in there for a reason and that reason was to pass that stupid test."

When Kelly arrived at the Region 20 test room, she looked around at the other kids retaking the test, and she was chilled at the sight. Virtually all were African American or Mexican American, and many looked as old as twenty-two or twenty-three years old. Later that day when Kelly returned home, she would tell Mary, "Momma, I was appalled at how many minorities there were. . . . I don't want to be that old and still taking the TAAS." But, then, this time would be different, Kelly believed. She also told Mary, "Mom, I feel good about this test. I think I passed."

The Texas Accountability Machine

A new era of school accountability and high-stakes, large-scale testing of Texas schoolchildren began in 1983, just as the crusade for school reform and accountability was beginning to spread across the country. Headed by Ross Perot, the rich Texas businessman, the Select Committee on Education recommended a statewide system of basic skills testing, and the state legislature promptly adopted the proposal. The result was the Texas Assessment of Basic Skills, known as TABS.

"Texans like Perot," says James Parsons, the assessment and evaluation director at the Humble, Texas, school district, "just didn't trust the system. They saw one way of checking to see if students were learning was to give them a test—hire an outside auditor," in essence. "TABS would do two things: See if teachers were doing their jobs and prove that any kid anywhere in Texas, from Plano or Highland Park to Edgewood ISD, was getting the same education. TABS begat TEAMS (another version of statewide testing called Texas Educational Assessment of Minimum Skills), which begat TAAS" in fall 1990.

According to the Texas Education Agency, "the implementation of TAAS shifted the focus of assessment in Texas from minimum skills to academic skills. . . . Moreover, the TAAS tests higher-order thinking skills and problem solving ability," the agency says. (11)

Although school accountability in Texas assumed these various incarnations, one eye-opening factor remained constant—a continuous increase in public resources devoted to testing and accountability. In fiscal 1998, the state allocated $19 million just for testing plus $7.5 million for its accountability and accreditation program. Thus, the Texas Education Agency spent about $26.5 million that year on accountability and testing. Roughly 38 percent of the agency's entire budget of $70.9 million was devoted to testing and accountability. (12)

By a staggering amount, Texas spent more money on testing and accountability than any state. According to the Council of Chief State School Officers' most recent comparisons, Texas's assessment budget for 1996 of $24 million was twice that of the next highest spender, Indiana, which allotted $12.2 million for testing. The next highest was Ohio at $10 million, followed by California ($9 million), Florida ($8.2 million), Maryland ($6.8 million), and North Carolina ($6 million). (13)

Testing and accountability in Texas has become as big and consequential as any state testing program can possibly be. Besides the exit test required for a high school diploma, Texas also requires all students to pass TAAS exams at the end of grades three, four, five, six, seven, eight, and nine to advance to the next grade. Moreover, end-of-course tests are given in algebra and biology, and eighth-graders must take a science and social studies TAAS exam in addition to the test for promotion to the next grade.

In addition to the consequences of failing a standardized test for children themselves, Texas has perhaps the most elaborate and complete systems of rewards and sanctions to schools, teachers, and administrators of any state. Indeed, the Texas Education Agency has become something very close to a regulatory agency in monitoring the state's schools, similar to public utility commissions, banking agencies, and departments of labor. Under state law, the agency is essentially responsible for regulating learning, teaching, and achievement, largely by means of TAAS exam results.

Schools receive financial rewards and official kudos, largely for improvements in high test scores. School bonuses in Texas have ranged from a total of $20 million in the 1992–1993 school year to $5 million in 1994–1995. (14) The Texas legislature earmarked some $5 million for the 1997–1998 school year for such school bonuses.

On the other hand, the state can yank a school's accreditation and put it on probation or on a "watch list," not unlike the way federal or state banking regulators monitor banking institutions that have many bad loans on the books. Texas schools also face monetary penalties for poor test performance and the threat of a state takeover and dissolution—again, similar to the sorts of sanctions regulators typically impose on insolvent banks.

According to the Texas Education Code, annual evaluations of teachers to determine their continued employment are based on just two general criteria: a teachers' implementation of "discipline management procedures" and the performance of a teachers' students on the various statewide tests. School principal job ratings are based largely on test results, specifically a "statistical analysis comparing current campus performance to previous performance." Like CEOs at large corporations, principals receive "performance incentives," also tied to test scores. A principal ranked in the top 25 percent of such "performance" gains will receive a $5,000 bonus; one ranking in the next highest group will get $2,500 in incentive pay.

In short, TAAS rules in Texas schools, and it's no small wonder that all eyes, including those of parents, teachers, principals, and students are focused on whether children do well on the various TAAS exams. As the sophomore year approaches for all Texas high schoolers, the TAAS "exit" test looms ahead, and much of what transpires in Texas high schools, especially in classes like English and math, are oriented toward that test.

It also should come as no surprise that the great attention paid to test scores and the high stakes attached to them has produced huge effects on the state's education enterprise. The Texas accountability model, not unlike many other states, has transformed the very notion of achievement and learning. Instead of a complex and not easily measured human behavior, the Texas version of "achievement" purportedly is captured by several dozen multiple-choice questions. The accountability system has fundamentally changed the meaning of teaching and the jobs of teachers as well. Instead of being professionals who make informed judgments about what is taught and how it's taught, Texas teachers are fast becoming technical functionaries of a state-run regulatory body, drilling students with worksheets and practice tests so that they might pass the next TAAS exam.

The Two Texases

At the inner-city Sidney Lanier High School in San Antonio, the TAAS obsession is repeated, with a vengeance. "The pressure of the tests is phenomenal," says Michelle Savage, an instructional guide at Sidney Lanier High. "Accountability is the big word in our state right now."

Savage consults with teachers to help them be more effective in the classroom, but the rise of TAAS's hegemony over the Texas school system means that much of what she does is to find strategies for teachers to ring up higher test numbers. At Sidney Lanier, the test score imperative is an unending battle because the school seems always in danger of being placed on state regulators' watch lists. In the entire San Antonio Independent School District in 1998, just six of ninety-two schools, according to the state formula based largely on TAAS scores, rated as "exemplary" by state officials, while seventy-eight, including Lanier, merely got "acceptable" ratings.

Being economically and educationally disadvantaged is virtually the norm for children attending San Antonio Independent Schools, and one could make a highly accurate prediction on TAAS results based on those factors alone. Some five low-income housing projects feed into Sidney Lanier High. About one in three people in the district, which is predominately Hispanic, live in poverty. That's about double the poverty rate in Texas and nearly triple that for the United States as a whole. Moreover, about half the children in the San Antonio district are classified as poor. Educational spending per student is some $500 less annually than the Texas average and some $1,200 a year less than the national average. A mere 5 percent of people living in the school district have a bachelor's degree, barely a third the rate of Texas as a whole. (15) Except for Houston Independent Schools' ten low-achieving campuses, San Antonio schools had more "low-performing" schools in 1997 than any other district in the state, according to the Texas Education Agency.

Indeed, the story of TAAS is mostly a tale of two Texases, split along the lines of race and class. State-sanctioned punishment of its poor and minority schoolchildren, flunking them on the basis of a standardized test, begins to sound like a broken record:

- *"Plaintiff 2 is a Mexican American student who attended high school in the San Antonio Independent School District. She would have graduated and received a diploma in 1997 but for one point on one part of the TAAS test. Although she had good grades and was on the honor roll for three years, she did not receive a diploma only because of the TAAS."*
- *"Plaintiff 5 is a Mexican American student who attended high school in the San Antonio Independent School District. He would have graduated and received a diploma but for the TAAS test. He had good grades and was on the honor roll for two years, but failed TAAS and did not graduate."*
- *"Plaintiff 6 is an African American student who attended public schools in Paris, Texas, who should have graduated in May 1993; he continued to take the TAAS test at every available opportunity until within the last two years. Because of his age, he is now denied the opportunity to take the test." Except for TAAS, Plaintiff 6, too, has met all requirements for getting his high school diploma.*

And so it goes for seven plaintiffs who filed a lawsuit in U.S. District Court in San Antonio in October 1997. The plaintiffs were either Mexican American or African American; they typically had good grades in their high school courses, and would have graduated, some with honors, but for failing the TAAS exit exam. The suit was filed on their behalf by the Mexican American Legal Defense Educational Fund (MALDEF). MALDEF claimed the Texas Education Agency had severely punished Texas minorities by flunking them, retaining them, and tracking them into substandard "drill and kill" instructional programs, completely disregarding a students' actual classroom performance. Moreover, the suit charged, Texas policymakers did these things to African Americans and Mexican Americans with virtually no good evidence that TAAS had any real-world meaning beyond its own insular standardized test format.

"As a predictor of future performance in the classroom and the workplace, the TAAS is so inaccurate as to render it invalid. There is no proof that TAAS scores differentiate on the basis of characteristics relevant to the opportunities being allocated. There is no or insufficient evidence to show how well TAAS scores reflect real life and educational or job performance," MALDEF charged. "The limited power of TAAS tests to predict success in either school or work means that using the test results alone to classify people is discriminatory, especially when test performance is highly correlated with race." (16)

Of course, those are simply allegations in a lawsuit. But the Texas Education Agency's own figures support the claim that thousands of Texas schoolchildren have grown up to be TAAS cannon fodder. Differences among races and economic classes in TAAS pass rates—and chances of graduating from high school—are nothing less than staggering, agency figures show. As illustrated in Table 5.2, roughly one-half of African American, Mexican American, and economically disadvantaged tenth-graders passed the TAAS graduation test in spring 1997, compared with eight in ten white tenth-graders who passed. Thus, white students were almost twice as likely to pass the TAAS than the other ethnic and economic groups. Pick a TAAS exam, and the pattern is the same. White tenth-graders passed the TAAS Algebra I end-of-course test at three times the rate of blacks, Hispanics, and students from poor families; whites were one and a half times more likely than the others to pass the Biology I end-of-course test.

Differences in failure rates among racial and class groups are startling. Almost six in ten Mexican American sophomores in 1996, who would otherwise have graduated in 1998, scored below the cutoff point on at least one part of the TAAS exam (39,000 of 68,000 Hispanic test takers); more than six of every ten African American tenth-graders in the class of 1998 failed the TAAS (18,000 of 28,000). By contrast, one-third of white tenth-graders in the class of 1998 failed the TAAS graduation test (33,000 out of 114,000). (17)

Validity Questions

Underlying the Texas Assessment of Academic Skills—and the school accountability movement in general—is the belief that the public, the business community, and elected officials simply can't trust teachers and schools to do their jobs. Despite the state's endorsement of teachers' professionalism through its certification system, according to this belief, teachers still can't be trusted to help students learn, to assess their performance, to make judgments about what and how subjects are taught—the whole mix of elements that have made teaching among the

TABLE 5.2 TAAS pass rates by race and class in Texas

	African American	*Mexican American*	*Economically Disadvantaged*	*White*
TAAS Exit (10th Grade, Spring 1997)	48%	52%	50%	81%
Algebra I End of Course (Spring 1996)	11%	14%	14%	40%
Biology I End of Course (Spring 1996)	59%	61%	59%	90%

SOURCE: Texas Education Agency, Student Performance Results, Passing Results by Ethnicity and Economic Group, at www.tea.state.tx.us.

most complex and challenging of professions. As a result, schools and teachers must be periodically "audited," as James Parsons told me, by means of the TAAS exams. The standardized test purportedly proves to the public that it's buying the standard-issue graduate, who knows all he or she must know for a life and career after high school.

What's more, the Texas system is founded on the notion that a student's performance over three years of high school, in terms of actual classroom work, monitored and assessed individually, one teacher and one student at a time, is virtually without meaning, severely punishing those who don't perform to par on a one-shot test.

Now, should that test prove to measure something meaningful—that is, to be a valid indicator of skills and knowledge necessary for a young person's success beyond high school, then Texas's crime and punishment method to public education would seem rational public policy. All the better if collective performance on the TAAS has some measurable impact on the state's unemployment levels, crime statistics, the demand for Texas goods and services, or any meaningful measure of the quality of public life. But if standardized test scores do correspond to any such significant aspects of Texas life, there's precious little evidence offered to support it.

Consider, for instance, the Texas Education Agency's own published studies of TAAS's validity, in terms of the correlation between TAAS scores and other variables. The TEA has done studies of TAAS's correlation to course grades, and even those tightly constructed studies show that TAAS's predictive validity is questionable. For example, in fall 1994, the agency analyzed data from the 1992–1993 and 1993–1994 TAAS graduation exam and math course grades of more than 176,000 tenth-graders. The study found that TAAS scores could account for only a small variation in student course grades. This result suggests that whatever complex mix of qualities required for someone to succeed in a class spanning one or two semesters is only minimally related to standardized test performance, and vice versa.

As a result of the poor predictive power of the test, nearly one-third of all tenth-graders who failed the TAAS exam had nevertheless passed their high school math courses. The discrepancy is even greater for individual math courses. Fully six in ten sophomores passed pre-algebra but failed TAAS math; 43 percent of algebra I students succeeded in the class but failed the TAAS. Nearly one-fifth of those who had successfully completed geometry still couldn't pass TAAS's eighth-grade math. (18)

Unfortunately, these discrepancies become even more pronounced when white high schoolers are compared to other ethnic groups. The discrepancies between grades and test scores are also evident between the poor and the not-poor. A whole series of TEA studies from 1992 through 1997 underscores the disparate impact of TAAS on Texas minorities and children of low and moderate incomes. For example:

- *Minority and poor kids were twice as likely as whites to fail the TAAS even while succeeding in their math class.* For instance, more than four in ten African American tenth-graders passed their math courses but failed TAAS math; some 37 percent of Hispanics missed the TAAS cut but still passed the class; and four in ten students from poor families of whatever race didn't pass the TAAS, despite succeeding in schoolwork. On the other hand, just two in ten white kids who had failed the math class also failed the TAAS math graduation test.
- *Minorities and poor kids passed their classes at a much greater rate than TAAS scores alone would indicate.* About 75 percent of Mexican American and African American sophomores passed their math class, but only about 40 percent of those kids passed the TAAS math section. "However," the TEA's 1994 study said, "significantly more white students who passed the TAAS mathematics test (72 percent) also passed their mathematics course (66 percent)."
- *Even Texas school children who earned As and Bs in their classes were flunked because of failing part of the TAAS exam.* In one large urban school district, for instance, fully three out of four eighth-graders who couldn't pass the end-of-course TAAS exam nevertheless earned an A or B in their math class during the 1995–1996 school year. Fully 75 percent of these students in that unidentified district were Mexican American and poor.

Compare those results to a large suburban district composed of far more white kids and many fewer minorities and poor children: Some 33 percent of the suburban eighth-graders failed the TAAS math test while earning an A or a B in math class. That this is significantly lower than the discrepancy between grades and test scores for the inner-city district illustrates TAAS's impact on poor and minority kids. But even that discrepancy in the suburban district remains remarkably high. One in three of the suburban kids who got high grades in math (As and Bs) still didn't pass the TAAS math exam.

Of course, there are many possible explanations for the discrepancies between course grades and test scores. Most teachers, administrators, and educational experts will tell you that teachers in the trenches have a far greater and more accurate grasp of a child's school performance, abilities, and need for improvement than is even conceivable with a onetime standardized test. One basic reason for that goes to the very nature and design of all standardized tests. Standardized tests are no more than a statistical sampling of specific skills that are supposedly covered in the curriculum. Say, for instance, there are 200 identifiable and specific skills to be learned in fifth-grade math. Standardized tests simply can't assess the entire array of all the skills because parents and politicians wouldn't tolerate such a lengthy exam for their children. So a sample of items is selected. According to the laws of mathematical probability, any sample—whether it's an NBC–*New York Times* poll of public attitudes toward Saddam Hussein or a Gallup poll of public opinion—will have a built-in measurement error. A test that has relatively small measurement error at a statewide level, in which a small sampling of skills is spread out over hundreds of thousands of students, could be significantly flawed as an indicator of individual skills. Why? Simply because the sample of skills tested may be too narrow to accurately reflect what a child knows and can do.

It turns out that TAAS's measurement error for individual scores is far from trivial. For example, consider TAAS's sixth-grade math subtest given during spring 1997. At the TAAS minimum passing score of 71, a child's "true" score could be as high as 77 or as low as 64. "That's for *all* kids," James Parsons, the testing director in Humble, Texas, told me, noting that TAAS's measurement errors are even larger for minority children. "What you'll find is that TAAS scores are neither sensitive nor precise, even around the cut score," Parsons says. (19)

As the 1990s were coming to an end, Texas was pushing to sharpen TAAS's teeth still further. Governor George W. Bush wanted to extend TAAS's high stakes to the third, fifth, and eighth grades, using test results to flunk children for the entire grade even if they earn passing grades. Schools, Bush asserted in the who-could-disagree rhetoric of all reform crusaders, "cannot pass children through the school system as illiterate." (20)

This sounds entirely reasonable until one reads the Texas Education Agency's documents showing such publicly ignored "technicalities" as correlation coefficients and standard errors of measurement. TAAS's correlation with classroom performance—or with any other meaningful variable in the real world—is questionable. Supporters of expanding TAAS's high stakes, of course, are implying that any third-, fifth-, or eighth-grade child who earns an A, a B, or even a C in his or her classes is illiterate and incapable of functioning in society—unless she scores at least a 70 on a standardized test. And, as we've seen, the test scores themselves are relatively mushy, yet the advocates of more testing would make life-altering decisions based on those numbers—a fact Kelly Santos knew all too well.

"Sometimes, I Feel Like the Dumbest Person Around"

A week before Kelly's high school graduation day in the spring 1997, her mother, Mary Santos, was teaching in her Spanish classroom when Kelly came through the door. Results from Kelly's spring TAAS exam, her final attempt to pass the math section as a regular high school student, had finally arrived. Mary was in the middle of teaching when Kelly broke the news, sobbing. Again, on her sixth attempt, Kelly had failed to meet the requisite cutoff score, the narrow and yet immense dividing line between two very different scenarios for Kelly's young life.

Mary started seeing the effects these repeated failures had on her daughter. Though Kelly had always earned decent grades, even those started to suffer when she started failing the TAAS. After all, Kelly now believed, she was a failure. The TAAS proved it. Mary tried everything to help Kelly get through the crisis. She told inspiring stories of famous people who overcame long odds to succeed. She told her daughter about her own struggles to get her college degree and to maintain her teacher certification by passing a mandatory state teachers' exam. Mary hired a tutor; tried to have Kelly tested for dyslexia; got special tutoring tapes designed for minority TAAS takers. Mary talked to her teacher friends about Kelly's plight. They would always note Kelly's intelligence, unable to reconcile it with her inability to pass the TAAS.

Kelly's self-confidence was in trouble. Friends on the school swim team, often bright, high achievers on their way to college, began to shun her. The word was out among her chatty peers: Kelly couldn't pass the TAAS. She began to do uncharacteristic things: body piercing, climbing out her bedroom window at night, dating a twenty-four-year-old guy. With Mary's encouragement, she went into counseling.

"I could see a change in her. She didn't care about herself any more," Mary says. "Until she started repeatedly taking the math part she did well in school. Then her senior year everything came tumbling down. Failing became a self-fulfilling prophesy. Kelly has the stigma of failure. She says to me, 'I'm stupid, I can't do it . . . I can't even graduate. I can't even walk the stage with my friends. I will never be able to say, 'I graduated.' Her senior year was like a nightmare. Her self-image was destroyed. Peer pressure is tremendous with these students. They ostracize each other, and not just over clothing and fashion, but also over standardized test scores."

By spring 1998, Kelly had been out of school for one year. She was working part time as a lifeguard at Fiesta Texas, a theme park, and also as a hostess at Bennigan's, a local restaurant. Again, Kelly took the TAAS in April and scored a 65 on the math, still not high enough to pass. But there was still the hope of passing and getting her diploma after the upcoming May test. Again, she studied hard, concentrating on the kinds of items she had missed on the exam. She was ready for college, and wanted to study law enforcement at Sam Houston State.

So, Kelly traveled back to the Region 20 testing center in May 1998. On May 22, Mary got a call on her pager at school. It was Kelly. When she returned her call, Kelly was sobbing. Mary heard the number, a 67, just three points shy of a diploma, again, and she heard her daughter say over and over that she was a failure. "My heart sank again realizing that it was going to be a difficult task trying to convince her to take this test again," Mary says. "I'm as desperate as she is, because this test has kept her life in limbo for the past three years. She is so demoralized and depressed that I really don't know what else I can do."

Taking the GED exam seemed to be Kelly's last hope to get her high school diploma. Or perhaps she'd make yet another attempt at the TAAS after going through a new tutoring program offered by the University of Texas. Mary says it's hard not to feel abandoned by the school system, which she believes has abandoned her daughter. Mary and her husband argue about Kelly's situation. He says Kelly should shoulder the blame for not working hard enough in school. Mary says she can't buy that. Too many questions remain unanswered. Was Kelly actually taught all she needed to know for the TAAS? Why should so much weight be put on the test score and classroom performance count for nothing? And then there's the most important question of all. What will happen to Kelly? "Will she be able to overcome this without doubting herself at every turn?" Mary asks.

Kelly remains haunted by her first sight of the other TAAS repeaters when she drove to Region 20 in summer 1997. Like Kelly, they were mostly African American and Mexican American, many over the age of twenty-one. Since that day, Kelly has been frightened that she was looking at her own future, still without a high school diploma, still traveling to the east side to the Region 20 test center, for another vain try at the TAAS.

"I worry that I won't make it in life, that I won't go to college, that I'll be stuck in a dead-end job and I won't become the cop I want to be," Kelly says. "Sometimes, I feel like the dumbest person around because I can't pass this test. It has taken a lot out of me emotionally and mentally. . . . This has not been fun, it has been hell for me. It has made me feel that if I'm not smart enough to pass an eighth-grade test, then what is the point of me going to college? I wish I never had to worry about this test, but it is always there."

6

The Great American Dumb-Down: How the Accountability Machine Harms Schools

NORTHAMPTON COUNTY SCHOOLS' TEST SCORES were nothing less than extraordinary. Stunned observers in this relatively poor and rural North Carolina county recalled the prior year when barely more than a third of pupils at Coates Elementary scored at least their grade level in reading. A year later, on the state's end-of-grade tests, six in ten Coates children were reading at their grade or higher, according to the new test results.

In math, barely half of Coates's kids scored at least their grade level in 1997. But the following year, more than 75 percent did so. The same story was true for Creecy Elementary, where math scores jumped twenty-four percentage points in a single year, so that 74 percent of Creecy pupils scored at grade level. Reading scores also spiked twenty-four points. (1)

From the third through the eighth grades tested in Northampton County in northeastern North Carolina, the story was the same—an unbelievable surge in test scores, in both math and reading. In June 1998, the results were still "unofficial," not yet public. One North Carolina educator who had seen the results told me, "People are a mixture of proud, amazed, questioning, and confused."

For many proponents of the new school accountability, cases like Northampton are dramatic proof of what disadvantaged and minority children are capable of when educators raise the proverbial bar, expecting excellence rather than the litany of educational failures typically associated with the poor and disadvantaged. That schoolchildren in places like Northampton County or Tacoma, Washington, can be pushed to perform so well on standardized tests proves that accountability works.

It's a narrative most Americans would surely want to believe in. But I'm afraid I must be the bearer of some unsettling news. Beneath heartwarming stories of remarkable improvements in test scores in the most unlikely places, the accountability machine's jagged edges and nasty contradictions come into full view. Beneath accountability politics that are State of the Union speeches, inflammatory reports of the looming end of Western civilization as we know it, and newspaper headlines about the test-score horse race in communities across the country, one sees the machine's ugly effects: achievement gains that are delusional and learning that is dumbed-down and distorted to fit questions on a state-issued standardized test.

Beyond what most of the public sees of the new era of school accountability, we find that learning and teaching have been so narrowly constricted as to be reduced entirely to the collective success of schools, districts, and states on standardized tests, so that officials can trot out comparative test scores showing that all the kids are the statistically impossible "above average."

Teachers are poised to become little more than production-line workers, technical functionaries of a political culture who merely feed their students the correct data needed to pass the next test. Schools are fast becoming quasi-profit centers, not unlike a publicly-held corporation accountable to shareholders for quarterly profits and returns on the New York Stock Exchange. But instead of shareholders demanding maximum sales and net profits, states are holding schools accountable for maximizing growth in test scores.

Like the Lee Iococas and Louis Gerstners of the corporate world, school superintendents are becoming coveted stars, commanding high salaries and public adulation by presiding over dramatic rises in achievement scores.

It's time for us to survey the damage.

The Scores They Need

Northampton's test scores were all the more incredible given the district's history. Indeed, Northampton's schools had been accustomed to occupying the very bottom rungs of the state's test-score hierarchy. Compared to, say, Chapel Hill schools, the university town of well-educated, mostly white professionals whose schools perennially topped the state's test-score charts, Northampton's rural, mostly black and poor children had been testing for years at or near the bottom of the state's roughly 120 school districts.

In fact, three of the Northampton schools had been on the state's watch list of low-performing campuses going into the 1997–1998 school year. Under North Carolina's most recent school accountability law, known as the ABCs of Public Education, Squire, Coates, and Creecy were facing state sanctions if they didn't raise test scores. Teachers at those schools were staring at the possibility of a competency test to keep their certificates. Principals were facing possible sus-

TABLE 6.1 Statistical profile of Northhampton County compared to Chapel Hill, N.C.

	Northhampton Co.	*Chapel Hill*
Poverty rate of school children	32%	10%
Average home price	$37,514	$125,634
Total population with Bachelor's or higher	6%	42%
Rank among 119 districts on 6th grade end-of-grade math tests (1995)	119	1
Rank on 8th grade reading	116	1

SOURCE: School District Data Book Profiles, 1989–1990, National Center for Education Statistics; The 1994–1995 North Carolina State Testing Results, Multiple-Choice End of Course Tests.

pension or demotion. In fact, Coates's principal had been demoted that year because the school's writing test scores weren't good enough for state school regulators.

If suspension and possible job loss weren't incentive enough to raise their scores, Northampton's entire professional staff had an added financial incentive provided under the ABCs plan: bonuses of $750 for each staff member if test scores could be boosted more than "expected" growth, and a sweetener of $1,500 each if they could raise scores even higher. Considering the stakes involved, Northampton's teachers did what was, shall we say, necessary. One early beneficiary of those remarkable spring test scores was the Coates principal, who had been demoted to an assistant. After the school's reading scores shot up almost thirty percentage points and math scores by almost twenty points, he got his job back.

One day, not long afterward, John Parker, the superintendent of curriculum and instruction at the neighboring district of Roanoke Rapids, was interviewing a Northampton teacher for a job in his district. Parker, of course, had gotten wind of what had happened in Northampton. In fact, Parker had been born and raised in Northampton County, had taught math and science for sixteen years in its schools, and even served as the district's testing director. During the job interview, Parker asked the teacher what accounted for the dramatic improvement in the achievement scores. "She responded with a five minute dialogue on strategies for drilling for the test," Parker later told me. "She made no mention of anything I consider substantive in regard to improving the way students were taught."

Asked how he would answer the same question he put to the Northampton teacher, Parker replied, "I think the scores mean a combination of things." The emerging industry surrounding school testing in North Carolina, consisting of "instructional management systems" and other test-coaching efforts, played a role. Widespread teaching to tests also boosted scores, including, he told me, "unethical practices, like coaching students during testing or providing students with actual tests prior to testing." Moreover, teachers' learning curves had simply caught up with the tests—they've come to know the North Carolina tests very well and they were teaching accordingly.

And so the troubled Northampton schools were at last obtaining the test scores they needed. But for Northampton and hundreds of similarly situated schools and school systems throughout the country, uncomfortable questions remained, which few parents, editorial writers, and state legislators cared to ask. But Parker was asking them. Were kids really any smarter? Was there a lot of learning going on, or were the impressive test scores a spurious blip, reflective of something else, unrelated to long-term achievement?

A Testing Culture

Watching test-driven education consume North Carolina schools over the past twenty years has been gut-wrenching for John Parker. In 1977, the second year he taught Northampton County, politicians and business interests were complaining that high school graduates couldn't read, cypher, or spell, igniting the frenzy for a minimum-competency test for high school juniors. By 1978, the state began to require the California Achievement Test, a commercial test battery in common use, for grades three, six, eight, nine, and ten.

When unsettling gaps in achievement scores emerged between different races and economic classes—as between Northampton students and Chapel Hill students—the state embarked on an egalitarian endeavor called the Basic Education Plan (BEP) in 1984. The BEP, passed by the state's Democrats, was premised on the commonsensical notion that children in schools such as Northampton were behind from the get-go, and would rarely catch up in academic achievement without adequate access to resources such as school counselors, computer labs, experienced teachers, and so on. But political winds shifted, bringing antispending sentiments to state government. The BEP was never given the funding its vision required, and its budget was cut from year to year.

Indeed, the new political environment and cuts in funding for the original BEP concept represented a profound shift in ideology of education in North Carolina, from one concerned with fairness and equal opportunity to a good education, to one marked by the accountability mandate.

"The emphasis changed from egalitarian legislation to accountability legislation," Parker told me. "The way it came out politically was, 'We'll give you this money, but taxpayers need to know they are getting results from their money. . . .' When I look back, if the political winds had not changed and there had been resources for the Basic Education Plan, education in North Carolina right now would be in a lot better shape. We never got the chance to see what effects that legislation might have had."

Whereas more counselors did not come to Northampton schools, standardized, multiple-choice tests did. In the ten-year period from 1985 to 1995, North Carolina enacted several new major school testing and accountability programs, many of them adding on to the existing structure. In 1985, the California Achievement Test (CAT) was revised to include grades one, two, three, six, and nine, with an additional writing test grades six and nine. In 1986, the first end-of-course multiple-choice test in algebra I was given. From 1988 through 1990, end-of-course tests in algebra II, biology, U.S. history, chemistry, geometry, English, and physics were added.

By 1990, the following tests were in place in North Carolina: The California Achievement Tests (CAT); a minimum skills diagnostic test in grades three, six, and eight (for children who scored below a certain cut on the CAT); the North Carolina social studies test in grades three, six, and eight; the North Carolina Competency Test in reading, writing, and math; and the end-of-course tests in eight subjects. (2)

Yet it was during the following decade that the North Carolina school accountability movement gained full force. First came Senate Bill 2 in 1990, which Parker says included some twenty-seven "performance standards," virtually all based on a multiple-choice standardized test of some variety, including the CAT in several grades; the state end-of-course tests; and a science and social studies exam in grades three, six, and eight.

Although SB 2 required schools to meet three-year goals for test scores and other standards, its teeth were never very sharp. The Performance Based Accountability Program, or P-BAT, changed that in 1992. Not only was testing expanded to grades three through eight, but the state could take over schools that didn't meet test performance goals. Too, fanfare over state test results was inflamed with the mandatory issuance of an annual state report card of all districts.

P-BAT needed some additional tweaking in the eyes of accountability enthusiasts. The district level was too broad to permit a truth or consequences approach for individual schools and their staffs. In 1995, then, the legislature enacted the ABCs plan, sharpening P-BAT's accountability teeth still further with the threat of state takeovers of schools; "assistance teams" sent in to help low-performing schools boost test scores; sanctions against teachers and administrators of the low performers; and hefty bonus checks to a school's professional staff for good test scores. Schools themselves became the "unit of accountability." North Carolina budgeted some $72 million to pay such bonuses in 1997; costs of the program could eventually top $100 million. (3) In 1985, North Carolina spent some $3.1 million annually on testing alone; that figure had barely changed five years later. As of 1996, the state's testing budget had more than doubled to $7.2 million. (4)

Through it all, Parker was dismayed. The state's unmitigated focus on accountability testing as the chief measure of educational quality, he says, was undermining the real qualities of education: learning for understanding and assessing learning in ways that accurately reflect what children know and can do.

Parker watched teaching and learning distorted as schools did whatever was necessary to boost test scores on multiple-choice exams. Teachers were being transformed into test coaches, and their instruction was increasingly dominated by "teaching to tests." Rather than being driven by teachers' professional judgment, classroom decisions were made by computerized instructional management systems, marketed by commercial consultants and test publishers. These systems track individual students' test results in excruciating detail, and probably wouldn't exist but for big-stakes testing.

"The primary basis for my concern is the correlation that is being implied between test scores and 'Quality Assurance,'" Parker told the North Carolina Testing Commission in 1992, when it was considering cutoff scores for the end-of-course tests. "Most of our students will receive a rote presentation of a core curriculum," a result of "intense pressure from over-zealous administrators and the public to improve test scores.

"I suggest to you," Parker told the testing panel, "that education is a distinctly human endeavor. Thus, the relegation of 'Quality Assurance' to numbers from tests is merely a convenient, political fix" that "will have no positive lasting impact." (5)

Again, in 1997, Parker told the State Board of Education that North Carolina's chosen path was not helping North Carolina children to learn and achieve. The board had been considering a proposal to extend the ABCs accountability model to the state's high schools. "The over-abundance of high stakes, standardized testing emanating from the state level is having a negative impact on classroom instruction," he testified. "Our best teachers, who are under-paid and work in professional conditions that do not correspond to their academic preparation, receive the message, 'I am not deemed to be capable of making professional decisions about my students. . . .' Consequently, they either seek other jobs or devote some of their potentially creative time to rote test preparation."

"Our . . . teachers view this as another game they have to play to keep a job for which they are over paid and under prepared," Parker told the state board. "The games include ethical shortcuts and worksheet instruction." (6)

But, steeped as they are in the prevailing political culture, state policymakers seemed to prefer delusion to realism. North Carolina wound up making high schools also comply with the complete accountability package: Bonuses of $1,500 per teacher to schools exceeding their test-score growth targets; $750 to each teacher at schools that meet test-score objectives; and possible state seizure of low-performing schools as well as forced teacher competency exams at these schools.

FOCUS: THE CHANGING ETHICS OF NORTH CAROLINA TESTING

In the accountability-obsessed 1990s, testing and teaching practices condemned as unethical and educationally unsound a decade earlier became de rigueur in North Carolina.

In 1988, the state of North Carolina enacted a Testing Code of Ethics that laid out proper testing procedures for teachers and schools, having adopted national models for testing ethics that were used in many states at the time. Among the most striking features of the document was its vigorous caveat against any attempts by teachers or schools to extensively coach and drill schoolchildren for upcoming standardized exams, known in the parlance of educators as "teaching the test."

Coming in the wake of a surge in testing in the 1980s, the North Carolina ethics code was undoubtedly founded on a heightened awareness among educators of the growing evidence documenting many unwholesome effects of teaching to tests, which are explored in detail later in this chapter. Indeed, the 1988 ethics code provided little room for interpretation, warning that:

> Coaching of students on specific test content or dissemination of test materials (including reproductions or modifications) prior to testing is not permitted. Such procedures will make results invalid. However, it is desirable to teach students general test taking skills in order to make them aware of strategies that could enhance their performance on tests. (7)

Elsewhere in the same document, the code writers also cautioned testers on the proper uses of tests, pointing out that test scores are but one of many indicators of performance. Again, the code's authors were quite explicit, writing that "*test scores should never be used in formal teacher or principal evaluations*" (emphasis added).

The 1988 ethics code didn't stop there. In several instances throughout the document, we find such cautions repeated as many as two or three times:

- *"Instructional content should not be geared solely to preparing students to score well on standardized tests."*
- *"Although students should be told the general content of any upcoming standardized test and taught good test-taking skills, they are not to be drilled or coached on specific test content."*
- *"Scores on standardized tests must not be the sole determinant of whether a student is to be retained or promoted."*
- *"The curriculum is not to be taught simply to raise test scores. The weaknesses of students as revealed by test scores are expected to be considered in curriculum planning."*

By the late 1990s, however, North Carolina's testing code of ethics had been changed dramatically with educators' and politicians' unabated obsession with educational crimes and punishments. Teaching and testing practices once condemned as

(continues)

(continued)

not only unethical but as educational malpractice became routine in many states and school districts, including North Carolina. Nowadays, test-driven educators can blithely justify teaching to tests as simply teaching the state's designated curriculum for math, reading, or science.

Accordingly, the North Carolina 1996 revision to its testing code of ethics contained no mention whatsoever of any ill effects of teaching to tests. In fact, the new ethics code even appeared to encourage the practice, advising that testing should include "*teaching the tested curriculum and test-preparation skills.*"

Test *preparation* skills, of course, is highly ambiguous, but it clearly permits practices that go well beyond general test-*taking* stills. Hence, under the revised North Carolina code of ethics, all manner of test coaching and drilling—short of outright cheating—became not only acceptable, but were strongly encouraged.

Teaching Tests

Common sense dictates that the very behaviors one tries to measure would be altered by the ways chosen to measure that behavior. Say, an executive at an HMO wanted to pay staff physicians strictly on the basis of how much profit they bring the company. For an HMO, which contracts with employers for an annual fee to cover their employees, doctors' pay would be based on the difference between overhead costs of maintaining a physician's clinic, per patient, and the contracted price the HMO receives for each patient.

Thus, a physician knows the more he or she spends on patient care, the less profit to the company, and the less the physician's salary. What are most physicians likely to do under this system of incentives? As has been frequently documented with growing frequency in health care, such managed care companies are more likely to err on the side of less patient care rather than more. Whether that's good or bad for patients and U.S. health care is debatable. But clearly, the HMO's rules profoundly influence, if not govern, the behavior of physicians.

Suppose the federal government wants to mete out funding to schools based on test results. What would happen, say, if the government bolstered financial assistance to schools based entirely on *poor* performance on standardized tests? That is, the lower a school's test scores, the more funding it would receive from the government. Such a policy certainly makes certain sense if achievement is positively related to economic conditions of schools. Economically poor schools, having the worst achievement test scores, would receive the most federal funding under such a rule.

Suppose, further, that schools' test scores were widely published in school report cards and teachers got big bonuses based on how much federal funding schools received. That's not entirely unreasonable either—higher budgets mean more dollars for teacher salaries. What would happen to test scores under this scenario, assuming no other changes in the fundamentals of schooling?

Such a scenario is unlikely indeed, but one could make some educated guesses on what would happen. Firms hawking test-preparation materials and computer software to track a child's performance on certain test items might not get past the front door of most school systems; teachers would spend insignificant amounts of time teaching test-taking skills to students or going over sample tests; school principals would hold staff meetings reminding teachers of educationally sound teaching, threatening to fire any teachers caught teaching subjects via worksheets and drills aligned to specific test items.

Some perverse effects might also be observed, such as teachers discouraging the top-scoring pupils from coming to school on test day. At the extreme, some teachers might even resort to outright cheating by erasing correct answers. Cheating, however, is risky behavior. By far, the most common effect from such substantial incentives for low test results would be very little directed effort on the part of schools aimed at boosting childrens' test scores.

But now, let's get slightly more real. Turn that improbable scenario on its head to get a far more realistic picture of incentives and disincentives placed on schools for standardized test results. In the environment in which most American schools must operate, poor test scores are severely punished and high ones are, of course, rewarded. What, then, are the effects on teaching and learning in such an environment? As opposed to the conscious efforts of schools to assiduously avoid certain kinds of teaching in the hypothetical scenario, one might suppose that the opposite would be true. Teachers would teach in ways specifically designed to boost scores.

In fact, that's exactly what will and what does happen, according to mounting evidence contained in many in-depth studies by dozens of credible researchers.

Beyond the view of most members of the public is the realm of academia and scholarly journals. Although somewhat obscure, they're good places to find dispassionate examinations of the real effects of big-stakes standardized testing in schools. Indeed, the disconnection between the real damage to American schools of such testing and its virtually unmitigated expansion in recent years is nothing less than mindboggling.

The most common effect of big-stakes testing programs, the evidence shows, has been teaching to tests. Teaching to a test often has various manifestations, whether it be teaching math by rote formulas and worksheets that match test items, or teaching writing by coaching students on which workbook line to divide sections of an essay. In all its various incarnations, teaching to big-stakes tests has made our children dumber than they would have otherwise been, the evidence further suggests.

The Evidence

The pervasiveness of teaching to tests in American schools, as they have become more test driven, has been thoroughly documented. Consider a 1991 study by Lorrie Shepard and Katherine Cutts Dougherty of the University of Colorado.

Shepard has extensively examined school testing and is among the nation's authorities on the subject. In this particular study, Shepard and Dougherty surveyed third-, fifth- and sixth-grade teachers in two large urban school districts, one in the Southeast, the other in the Southwest. (The district names were not identified in the study, in order to protect confidentiality.) Both districts had big-stakes testing and relatively high proportions of minority students. The authors presented their findings at the annual meeting of the American Educational Research Association, a body that is known for rigorous and sound research on educational practices in the United States.

Not unexpectedly, the researchers found that some eight in ten of the teachers surveyed "said that they feel 'substantial' or 'great' pressure from the district administration to raise test scores," and two-thirds of the teachers "said they felt such pressure from newspapers and the media." Moreover, according to the authors, 69 percent of teachers frequently drilled their students on item types teachers knew would be on the state's test. The most common negative statement about standardized testing from teachers in the survey: "the complaint that standardized tests lead to 'too much teaching to test content and test format.'"

What is more, Shepard and Dougherty tell us, "The most telling finding, concerning the influence of test preparation on instruction, was that 68 percent of the teachers reported conducting these test preparation activities 'regularly,' that is 'throughout the school year,' rather than limiting them to a few days or weeks before testing." (8)

Such results have been widely duplicated in other rigorous studies. Researchers find that teaching to tests has little to do with outright cheating. Instances of cheating, of course, do occasionally emerge, such as the infamous Stratfield School in Fairfield, Connecticut, where officials discovered the real reason for the school's remarkable, award-winning test scores: erasures of wrong answers and other indicators of "widespread tampering" with standardized tests, as the *New York Times* put it. (9)

Just how prevalent cheating is on achievement testing in American schools is probably impossible to quantify, and it's more likely rare than common. Rather, teaching to tests has become day-to-day practice in test-heavy environments, having in recent years become entirely legitimate in the eyes of many school officials, who officially sanction such practices as a way to boost test scores. "Teaching to the test," says Daniel Koretz, a testing expert at the RAND Corporation, "is in fact a much larger, vastly more important, and much less tractable problem than frank cheating." (10)

As another example, Joan Herman and Shari Golan, in a project for the UCLA Center for Research, Evaluation and Student Testing, looked at nine medium-sized school districts in nine states across the country. Teachers in the study reported feeling "strong pressure from district administrators and the media to improve their students' test scores."

Where significant public and official pressure is placed on the tests, teaching specifically to those tests in some fashion inevitably follows. One might quibble with Herman and Golan over the semantics of "teaching the test," but they nevertheless found that teachers frequently gave students worksheets to drill students on test content as well as practice tests. Overall, these teachers spent about a month of each school year busying students just in test preparation, and even more so if schools' test scores were declining. (11)

A sensible question is, So what? What does it matter that the media and elected officials put great pressure on teachers to spend a lot of time teaching students what's on a standardized test? And so what if they do so? That's what accountability and high standards are all about, after all. Now comes the insidious part of the effects-of-testing story, one often glossed over or ignored by the public, elected officials, and the media, but which has perhaps the most devastating impact on real learning and achievement.

The Narrow-Down

One day in North Carolina's Roanoke Rapids school district, a math teacher was engaging her grade school students in a seminar on graphical analysis as an important application of mathematics. This teacher's give-and-take session with inquisitive students was wonderfully Socratic. In fact, she enjoyed teaching math this way. After the seminar, the teacher was not in a particularly good mood while chatting with Bob Williams, the Roanoke Rapids director of teacher development. It so happened that district officials were requiring teachers to include a couple of seminars per semester in their teaching. But the bigger picture of testing and accountability in the state of North Carolina loomed large for this teacher, whatever the district wanted. With the state's ABCs accountability mandate in mind, the math teacher grimly told Williams, "I am responsible for improving end-of-course test scores, not using seminars in class." (12)

At an innovative Boston elementary school called the Young Achievers Science and Math Pilot School in 1997, school staff and parents who belonged to the school site council met to discuss school uniforms, the hot topic of the hour in the district. But first, the school site council had some "routine" business to take care of, such as the latest results on the "Stanford 9," a version of the Stanford Achievement Test, a widely used standardized test permitting comparisons of kids' and the school's scores to national norms.

Although the latest test results for the school were middling, at best, teachers told the parents not to be concerned about the test scores. After all, the children and the school were doing so well and accomplishing so much with work on interesting projects that were integrating the students' knowledge of science and math; and children were exhibiting their projects and keeping in-depth portfolios of their accomplishments, allowing teachers to keep track of their progress. One class did a project on snakes. They weighed snakes, dissected snakes, made art about snakes, wrote about snakes. Snake facts were posted throughout the room. "We think we're doing better," teachers said, whatever the test scores indicated.

It immediately became apparent that school uniforms would be moved to the back burner that day, for the test results prompted a near hysterical response among a vocal group of parents. According to district policy, scores on the Stanford 9 were used to assign students to advanced-placement classes beginning in the fourth grade. Parents believed the school's inattention to test scores diminished their childrens' chances of gaining those coveted advanced-placement slots and thereby placing kids on the fast track to high achievement and good colleges.

"The bottom line is I want my kid to get into advanced placement, and what are you doing to improve these scores?" parents demanded. "We want evidence you guys are teaching to make sure our kids pass these tests!"

"Those parents put the teachers in a very defensive position," says Karen Hartke, a parent who was at the meeting. "Teachers were saying, 'Not only are we doing better, we don't want to teach to that test.'"

Hartke is critical of parents paying so much attention to the test scores, but says she understood the parents' concerns. "Parents are not dumb. They know what kids have to do to pass, and at some level, I can understand that," Hartke told me. "But there is no processing or stopping and saying, 'Gee, that's not how we really want the system to be.'"

Back to the question: What if teachers face enormous pressure from parents, media, public officials, and school administrators to teach to a test? The answer, in part, is illustrated by what schools have given up in order to drill kids on tests: a Socratic seminar in a North Carolina grade school; or a Boston fifth grade's creating a dinosaur archaeology project, integrating lessons in science, mathematics, writing, and art.

Call it the dumb-down narrow-down. Researchers have found consistently that one of the most damaging effects of large-scale, big-stakes standardized testing in schools has been to: (1) oversimplify what's taught in school; and (2) to severely constrict what is taught to only those items most likely to appear on an upcoming standardized test.

Consider the latter, the matter of a constricted curriculum. One might easily hypothesize that little incentive exists for students, teachers, and schools to experiment, create, and innovate under the constant threat of failure, loss of job security, and other major consequences from test results.

Moreover, one might guess that teachers in such an environment, particularly at the higher grade levels, are more likely to depend on highly traditional and often ineffective teaching practices that include a lot of lecturing, drilling, and practicing on test items; in short, teachers doing a lot of standing in front of a chalkboard. This approach is premised on the notion that the best way to prepare students for an achievement test is the direct way: Give them just what will be on the state accountability test and in the same format as the test. Math seminars and snake projects are so much extra fluff.

Anyone hypothesizing such effects of teaching to tests would be right on target. According to volumes of accumulated research evidence, the effects are nearly universal, a result of the framework of incentives placed before students, teachers, and schools acting in their perceived best interests.

Consider what happened in British Columbia, when the Canadian province reintroduced twelfth-grade science tests to be used for admission to colleges and other postsecondary training. The province reinstated the test after a decade-long suspension. British Columbia's turn toward accountability and testing was aligned closely, of course, with what was happening throughout schools in North America.

Seeing that "a unique opportunity existed for an impact study on the effects of large-scale testing," Thomas O'Shea and Marvin F. Wideen, both of Simon Fraser University in British Columbia, took video cameras into eighth-, tenth-, and twelfth-grade classrooms to observe the behaviors of students and teachers. The scholars wanted especially to see if behavior in twelfth-grade science classes was markedly different from the earlier grades, which were not subjected to the province-wide standardized tests.

The results of their observations were remarkable, indicating that twelfth-grade science teachers were far less likely to engage students in multifaceted approaches to learning, such as laboratory experiments and class discussions—and more likely to employ traditional and rote teaching methods. For instance, whereas lab work constituted an average of 24 percent of class time in eighth-grade science classes, twelfth-graders spent merely 7 percent of their time doing experiments. Eighth-graders spent twice the amount of time in class discussions of science concepts than twelfth-graders. On the other hand, almost a third of twelfth-graders' time was occupied by teachers' lecturing, compared to just 3 percent for eighth-graders and 11 percent for tenth-grade science students.

"We saw a narrowing of the instructional pattern as we moved from Grade 8 to Grade 12," O'Shea and Wideen told members of the National Association for Research in Science Teaching in April 1993 in Atlanta. They continued:

> As observers, it appeared to us that the most vibrant classes took place at the Grade 8 and 10 levels. Grade 12 classes, on the other hand, were marked with a palpable desire to come to grips with the material presented. A sense of fun and enjoyment seemed lacking here. This was work and made to seem so. We sensed a strong need to process a great deal of material very quickly. (13)

When teachers exposed their twelfth-graders to material that wouldn't be on the upcoming standardized test, students became demonstratively impatient. "In contrast," Wideen and O'Shea tell us, "classes in Grades 8 and 10 showed a more leisurely pace with more time to explore and attempt different approaches."

In order to rule out other explanations besides B.C.'s new testing mandate for this narrowing of what was taught in twelfth-grade science, the researchers combined their direct observations with an opinion survey. The typical twelfth-grade science teacher, the authors told their peers in Atlanta, "is influenced almost entirely by the curriculum and (large-scale external) examinations. . . . The impact of large-scale testing has been very strong on his teaching," now offering fewer lab opportunities and fewer science projects.

The Dumb-Down

That's the narrow-down part of the story. Common sense might further tell one that if teachers are teaching a test via rote teaching styles, rushing through lots of drills and worksheets and practice tests—all aimed to boost test scores—then teachers and schools are ignoring substantial content that lies beyond the narrow scope of the standardized tests. Also shortchanged are thinking, analyzing, synthesizing, performing, articulating, and other active modes of in-depth learning.

Call it the dumb-down. When schools teach to a test, the test becomes the nearly exclusive focus of teachers' and students' attention. "Science," and its teaching and learning, for example, therefore becomes a series of test items, usually in the format of multiple-choice questions. The very nature of learning, as an open-ended, somewhat uncertain, spontaneous, creative, and complex process, is turned upside down.

Learning, in a teach-to-tests environment, is fragmented into bite-sized pieces devoid of meaning or connection to a reality beyond the abstraction of an atomistic test item. Emphasis is removed from the complex whole to a focus on parts of the whole. The whole might be considered as simply any real-world application, for which basic skills, such as proper punctuation or adding and subtracting whole numbers, are just the incidental tools needed for success on the whole application. That's when childrens' interest in dinosaurs or asteroids or Titanically large ships is fully engaged. But, then, interest and engagement, the absence of which may be *the* principal obstacle to learning in American schools, appear to be almost irrelevant in a teach-to-tests environment.

In the Shepard and Dougherty study quoted above, for instance, the clear majority of teachers had only negative things to say about the effects of teaching to tests on learning. "Critical thinking skills are basically non-existent in our children because of drill and practice" for various standardized tests, one teacher said. Another said, "Too much time is needed to emphasize test content, test taking skills, practice work-sheets." And another: "We are *constantly* reminded to practice, practice, for the test. The fun and excitement has been taken out. . . ." (14)

To be sure, notions of "basic skills" and "back to basics" resonate to the American ear. Those notions falsely imply, however, something fundamental, deeply seated, elemental, and thus absolutely necessary before any advanced learning beyond the basics can possibly occur.

Over the past several years, scholars have looked closely at how children learn and what incites them to learn, and the researchers have come to question the validity of the traditional model of education that orders learning hierarchically from "basics" to "advanced." "According to the old theories of learning," says Lorrie Shepard, "complex, higher-order skills had to be acquired bit-by-bit by breaking learning down into constitutive, prerequisite skills. It was assumed incorrectly that after basic skills were learned by rote, they could be assembled mechanistically into complex understandings and insight." (15)

Consider, again, the British Columbia experience. In that instance, twelfth-graders faced the hurdle of a government-mandated high school graduation test, while their counterparts in earlier grades did not. And so researchers observed the curious phenomenon in which eighth- and tenth-graders were in some respects doing more *advanced* work than the senior science students. Eighth- and tenth-graders, relatively unaffected by the provincewide test, were exploring subjects in much greater depth than their elders in twelfth grade. For instance, studying the process of chemical change, one eighth-grade science class made peanut butter. In a genetics class, tenth-graders wrote essays from the perspective of a growing fetus to learn about how a fetus develops.

"I think they (the government) are trying to upgrade teaching by providing a really severe exam," one teacher told O'Shea and Wideen in their study, one of many expressing concerns about the new exam. "And, as a result, you have some teachers who maybe aren't that good as teachers but spend the entire year with a bank of exams, going over and over them and the kids maybe haven't learned anything. But, for a certain body of questions they (teachers) are great. But in terms of high level learning and their attitude toward learning and all the other things that education is about, they really aren't good teachers at all."

As long as high-stakes testing dominates the educational landscape, meaningful education reform will be hard to achieve because accountability testing squelches innovation and creative approaches to teaching and learning, the British Columbia researchers concluded. "If you take the view that the high school presently is an institution badly in need of reform and further speculate that teachers require some freedom to experiment and take risks to bring about this reform, then the existence of large-scale testing as currently practiced effectively reduces the chances that such reform will occur."

Mile-Wide Science and Math

On February 23, 1998, Secretary of Education Richard W. Riley stood at the helm of a press briefing in Washington announcing results of an important milestone in America's chosen route to educational reform. His mood was grim, however. According to a new international assessment of mathematics and science achievement, the most complete of its kind, American high school seniors were performing abysmally. Of the half-million students from forty-one countries in the Third International Math and Science Study (TIMSS), a representative sample of U.S. seniors on the math assessment performed significantly worse than those from sixteen other advanced countries, including Canada, Hungary, Norway, and France. American twelfth-graders were ranked equal to students from countries such as Russia, the Czech Republic, and Italy in math. Except for those countries, the Americans scored worse than any other nation except for developing nations like Cyprus and South Africa.

Riley's announcement of the twelfth-grade results was cause for deep concern, especially when compared to American fourth-graders' performance on the same international study the previous year. American fourth-graders were on top of the world in both math and science, scoring sixteen points above the international average in math and forty-one points above the science average. Then, in November 1997, the administration's euphoria over the fourth-graders' scores was shattered by the outcome of eighth-grade results in the international survey. By the eighth grade, the American students were still doing better than the international average in science but their performance had fallen to well below average in mathematics.

The one constant for each of those events was Riley's insistence that the answer to America's educational problems was for Congress to yield to President Clinton's proposal for a national standardized test of schoolchildren. Whether it was fourth-graders doing well or eighth- and twelfth-graders faring poorly on the international comparisons, the politics were on the same spin cycle. "These results are entirely unacceptable," Riley said at the February briefing, "and absolutely confirm our need to raise our standards of achievement, testing, and teaching . . . "

Critics of the TIMSS study of eighth-graders had fits of indignation over the international comparisons. They alleged that the TIMSS methods were flawed and inappropriate—a useless comparison of apples to oranges owing to highly various cultural traits. Some of the criticisms seemed more well founded than others. On occasion, the complaints came off as not a little lame even if there was some anecdotal evidence to support them. Some critics, for instance, suggested that the international comparisons should be completely discounted because American kids can't be expected to perform well in high school, since it's primarily a place for socialization and growing up in the United States; after all, American kids don't get serious about school until they go to college, the TIMMS critics suggested.

Nor had the complaints disappeared with the announcement of the twelfth-grade results. But a close examination of the TIMMS methods and organizers' answers to critics' various objections clearly suggests that the TIMMS had left almost no stone unturned that might damage its credibility on the twelfth-grade exams. (Its organizers in the United States were the National Center for Educational Statistics (NCES) and the National Science Foundation.)

For instance, one bone of contention was the age of test takers. Critics pointed out that the average age of American seniors was below that for many other countries who scored better in math and science. Older students from the better performing countries were more advanced in math and science, critics charged.

Not so, answered Pascal D. Forgione, Jr., the statistics czar at the NCES, in a rare response to the TIMSS critics that NCES posted on the Internet. First, the international average age on the twelfth-grade exam was 18.7 years, only slightly above the 18.1 average age of the American students. Second, many countries start children in school at least a year older than do Americans, Forgione said. He also answered the objection of cultural differences and other environmental differences beyond the control of educators. Is it that American high schoolers watch more TV? No, they watched TV roughly two hours a day, equal to the average of twenty other countries. Do American kids hate math and science more than kids from France or Britain? Not apparently. Twenty-one percent of American twelfth-graders in the TIMSS study reported liking math "a lot," well more than the 15 percent internationally.

"What is remarkable," Forgione said, "is that . . . so few of the factors examined one-by-one could account for our relatively poor performance." (16)

But for all the hullabaloo and media attention over the math and science scores themselves, the most compelling part of the TIMSS studies over three years was a little-noticed videotaped analysis of actual teaching behavior in more than 200 eighth-grade classrooms in Japan, Germany, and the United States.

The startling differences in how students were taught in the three countries' classrooms alone is enough to indict the current accountability movement in the United States. Indeed, the videotaped analysis, done for the TIMSS effort by a team led by James Stigler at UCLA, underscores the unwholesome effects of widespread teaching to tests in the United States. Teaching for the benefit of bureaucrats and bottom-line notions of educational accountability have produced American classrooms that are dumber, narrower, and less thought-provoking than schools in other countries.

Stigler's team compared several aspects of teaching in the three countries' eighth-grade mathematics classes, finding that Japan stood out in various interesting and surprising ways relative to the American and German classes. Indeed, rote, mechanical, and superficial teaching of math was far more evident in the American classrooms than in Japan—in contradiction to the commonly held stereotypes of overly regimented Japanese schools. For example:

- *Thinking versus skills.* Japan's math classes were far more likely to focus on thinking and understanding of mathematical ideas than either Germany or the United States. The learning goal of 73 percent of the Japanese teachers was to develop thinking skills and the understanding of mathematical ideas; that was the goal for just 22 percent of the American teachers and 31 percent of German teachers. On the other hand, 61 percent of American teachers were focused on the procedures and steps in finding an answer to a math problem, compared with 25 percent of Japanese teachers focused on that narrower objective.
- *Creativity.* Focused less on procedures and more on deeper understanding, the Japanese eighth-graders were far more likely to present their own solutions to problems rather than the teacher-provided answers. In Japan, the students generated 42 percent of the solutions in the lessons, compared with just 7 percent their teachers developed; American students came up with just 8 percent of the solutions, compared with 19 percent that teachers generated. Germany's math classes were evenly divided between student- and teacher-generated solutions.

That finding, it appeared, owed partly to differences in the way teachers typically conducted their classes in the three countries. Japan's students began class trying to invent their own solutions to problems, followed by sharing their answers and working with the rest of the class and the teacher in understanding the concepts underlying the answers. In American and German classes, students first acquired a method to solve a type of problem by means of an example provided by the teacher. Then, the Americans did a worksheet for a few moments on a similar problem.

- *A mile wide or a mile deep.* The American math classes rarely sustained an exploration of a particular math concept for very long, leaping rapidly and often incoherently from topic to topic. Quantifying this "mile wide" phenomena, the study found that American classrooms contained more than two topics per lesson, compared to barely more than one per lesson in the Japanese classes. German teachers switched topics slightly more than Japanese teachers but still far less than American teachers. "Japanese teachers were significantly more likely to provide explicit links or connections between different parts of the same lesson," the video study said. "American teachers devoted significantly more time during the lesson to irrelevant diversions" than either Japanese or German teachers.
- *Showing or telling.* An old adage advises young writers to "show, don't tell," and it's also good counsel for promoting deeper understanding of mathematics. But according to the video study, American math teachers were mostly telling math rather than showing it. "Concepts might be simply *stated,* as in 'the Pythagorean Theorem states that *a squared plus b squared equals c squared,*' or they might be *developed* and derived over the course of a lesson," says the study. But in the American eighth-grade math classes, teachers merely stated almost eight in ten topics, and teachers fleshed out and developed just two in ten topics for students. In Japan's classes, it was exactly the opposite relationship—more than eight in ten topics were developed with proofs and deductive reasoning, and just 17 percent were simply stated. In Germany, there was also considerably less "telling" about math than in the United States.

Clearly, the Japanese classes were actually implementing new ideas about math education being touted nowadays in U.S. educational circles. American math teachers have been pushing in recent years for a greater emphasis on understanding mathematical reasoning and understanding rather than mechanical skills. Oddly, the American teachers in the TIMSS study more often believed that their classes represented new teaching ideas to a high degree than teachers in Japan or Germany. The video study's authors disagreed. Japanese lessons "came closer to implementing the spirit of current ideas advanced by American reformers than did American lessons," the authors wrote. (17)

So, yes, for the TIMSS twelfth-grade study, at least, the NCES's Forgione and the rest of the TIMSS American contingent appeared to have answered most of the critics' objections. American math and science scores could be legitimately compared to other countries. Curiously, the American officials failed to address the implications of the study's most important piece of explanatory evidence: the video study comparing actual classroom behavior in Japan, Germany, and the United States. But then, that would be a troublesome topic to pursue when bosses Clinton and Riley were pushing for yet another big piece of accountability legislation like a national test.

Because school testing and accountability have become so pervasive in American classrooms, the TIMMS otherwise thorough analysis appears even more odd. James Ridgeway of Michigan State University, writing for the National Institute for Science Education, estimated that roughly 40 percent of American mathematics classes and 20 percent of science classes "gave heavy emphasis to preparing students for standardized tests, which have been shown to focus on lower-level knowledge and skills." (18)

Chances are, then, many American teachers in the TIMSS study were simply doing what the bureaucrats, politicians, parents, and the media have told them to do: Be accountable for childrens' achievement, and teach them the standardized tests we've designed to measure that achievement. If doing that should result in a narrow focus on the mechanics of math or science rather than deeper understandings, that's the unfortunate bargain we've thus far chosen for our schools.

Back to Lake Wobegon

America's education reform crusade was in full bloom in the late 1980s, when a West Virginia physician named John Jacob Cannell started noticing something rather odd in his medical practice. He was seeing many emotionally disturbed children who were also having trouble in school. But when he questioned school authorities about the children, the officials would invariably tell him not to worry about the academics; based on the children's achievement test scores, they were doing just fine, according to school officials.

Something still seemed askew; maybe there was something wrong with the achievement scores themselves, Cannell hypothesized. How, for instance, could the schools be doing so well when West Virginia was near the bottom of the country on other independent measures of educational and economic health, such as per capita income and the percent of citizens with college degrees? Yet the state's third- and fifth-graders were scoring better than 60 percent of their peers nationwide on the state's standardized achievement tests.

What was happening here? After obtaining test-score data from the thirty-two other states that also administered similar "norm-referenced" standardized exams, Cannell discovered something quite remarkable. All thirty-two states were achieving the mathematically improbable: scoring better than the national average on school achievement. In what would later be dubbed "The Lake Wobegon Report," whose namesake, of course, was Garrison Keillor's storied town where "all the kids are above average," Cannell and his ad-hoc group Friends for Education published a small tract that caught the attention of education researchers. "These tests allow all states to be above average," the report said. "The tests . . .

allow 90 percent of the school districts in the United States to be above average. More than 70 percent of the students tested nationwide are told they are above average. . . . Friends for Education found that these standardized, nationally normed achievement tests give children, parents, school systems, legislatures, and the press misleading reports on achievement tests." (19)

Cannell, of course, is neither a statistician nor an educational expert, and he did err on several technical details in his statistical analysis that his critics jumped on. But the report got the attention of researchers like the RAND Corporation's Daniel Koretz and Colorado's Lorrie Shepard. Their own, more scientifically rigorous, work on the question has established with little question the essential accuracy of Cannell's unsettling conclusion. "In my opinion, there can be no doubt that current norm-referenced tests overstate achievement levels in many schools, districts, and states, often by a large margin," says Koretz. (20)

The problem Cannell first unearthed has since come to be known as test score inflation—that scores could go up without an underlying gain in real achievement. Evidence began to accumulate, strongly suggesting that a good deal of score inflation has been yet another unanticipated effect of teachers and schools teaching to accountability tests. To see why, it's useful to know a bit more about how standardized tests work.

Consider a garden-variety "norm referenced" test, such as the Iowa Test of Basic Skills, Stanford Achievement Test, or the Metropolitan Achievement Test. Contrary to prevailing public opinion and the high-stakes uses for which many states employ such tests, standardized tests *do not* measure achievement. In fact, a test is but a sampling of skills and knowledge covered in say, fourth-grade math. The test covers only a fraction of the whole domain of the hundreds of specific skills covered in that curriculum.

Any test that reflected the entire domain of fourth-grade math would be too costly, time-consuming, and altogether unwieldy, as pointed out in Chapter 5. Even as they are, most standardized achievement tests administered to gradeschoolers are quite long enough. Versions of the California Achievement Tests for kindergarteners, as just one example, are allotted almost three hours over three sessions; a fourth-grade exam requires more than seven hours to complete. (21) And so testers attempt to estimate achievement levels by sampling just a small part of what constitutes "achievement." The process isn't fundamentally different, in a statistical sense, than a manufacturing operation sampling items coming off the production line for quality control.

Thus, by the very nature of statistical sampling, testing to measure achievement struggles with several inherent constraints: being complete enough to accurately reflect a course of study as well as what individual children have actually learned; having an acceptable level of reliability, such that repeated tests produce consistent results; and containing specific test items that have a high degree of validity, that is, some significant connection to a meaningful outcome, such as grades, graduation rates, and educational attainment.

Although those fourth-grade math test scores are merely an estimation of something far more ephemeral that is called "achievement," parents, the press, and politicians appear to believe the test scores actually equate with achievement of fourth-graders; often, they make the further unfounded leap that the scores actually measure the educational health of schools and school systems, and even the entire nation.

The sober counsel of many testing experts, however, is at considerable odds with such exalted attributes of testing. Robert E. Stake, in a recent scholarly book on reform in math education, for instance, utters the heresy that "standardized mathematics test scores are not, however, a sound basis for indicating how well students are becoming educated in mathematics. He adds: "Whether standardized test scores are going up or going down has little to tell us about what is happening to education." (22)

Another useful piece of knowledge about how standardized tests are constructed is the function of the so-called "norming" process. When one reads a fourth-grader's test score as the fiftieth percentile on a norm-referenced test, that means she or he scored at about the national mean, within a band of uncertainty, of fourth-graders on that particular test. But the norm itself is also merely an estimate of national achievement at the fourth grade, drawn from a sample that is purportedly representative of test takers in that grade nationwide.

Technical manuals for various standardized tests—which parents, politicians, and the press rarely, if ever see—often provide details about norms. For instance, if a school happened to use versions "E" or "F" of the California Achievement Tests, published by CTB/McGraw-Hill, a highly unusual parent with access to the test's technical manuals would learn that the norming group consisted of a total of 300,000 students in kindergarten through twelfth grade, who first took the exam in fall 1984 and spring 1985. The sample, according to the test publisher, also included students from different geographic regions; those from urban, suburban, and rural communities; large and small school districts; and rich and poor students. (23)

When a fourth-grader's test results are reported in reference to those norms, the grand assumption undergirding the entire enterprise is that the children took the test under *roughly identical conditions to the original norming group*. But as the North Carolina test ethics code vividly suggests, what constitutes acceptable test practices and legitimate test-taking conditions can vary considerably even within a state from one year to the next, and especially from district to district. Schools under great pressure to improve test scores because they've been put on a state watch list for de-accreditation or other severe sanctions might routinely encourage dubious test-coaching methods inconsistent with the norming process.

One school district might hire highly specialized testing consultants, paying them hundreds of thousands of dollars just to boost test scores. Another school system might buy the *Scoring High* package from a major publisher or any one of several such programs that have little to do with improving real achievement and everything to do with boosting scores. In one analysis of *Scoring High*, for instance, researchers concluded that "the materials were so similar to the test that practice with *Scoring High* is equivalent to giving the parallel form of the test as a practice test and explaining all the answer choices to the students," observes Lorrie Shepard. "Although the latter would be clearly unethical, many educators purchase *Scoring High* without confronting any ethical issues because it is sold as instructional or review material." (24)

One can imagine how even a bit of teaching to a test at one school might produce dramatic results relative to the national norming group. Even seemingly innocuous practices like making copies of an old test and allowing students to practice it under actual testing conditions would result in familiarity with the test not availed to the original norming group. Or if a fourth-grade math teacher knew with some certainty which test item types were considered most difficult on that grade's achievement test, then intensive coaching for just those items could significantly raise a class's percentile ranking. Either practice would render the scores virtually meaningless.

Researchers have quantified the effects of test familiarity on test scores for some commonly used achievement tests. Shepard, for instance, discovered, astoundingly, that children with mid-range scores could boost their percentile ranking by as many as seven points with as few as one more correct answer. On "Form E" of the California Achievement Test, Shepard found that teaching just four vocabulary words to half a class would raise a class's overall reading scores by five percentile points. "This means," according to Shepard, "that teachers could relatively innocently teach to just a few items and raise achievement by several points." (25)

Clearly, then, schools that strictly enforce proper ethics of standardized testing—ensuring that the test items are "covered" only incidentally in the routine exploration of a subject—are at a significant disadvantage compared to heavily coached test takers. Schools that frown on teaching to tests might be singled out as "underperforming," its students and staff subject to all manner of sanctions ranging from de-accreditation to inability to graduate, to loss of a job. This scenario is entirely possible even if the school has explored subjects like math, science, reading, and writing in great depth, even combining them into integrated projects on interesting subjects.

The most disturbing implication of the evidence about the effects of teaching to tests is that one can come to virtually no defensible conclusion about long-term, underlying achievement based on test scores. Say, for instance, that our fourth-grade math students are given a 1985 version of a common K–12 achievement test. From 1985 on, fourth-graders in the district are given the same 1985 test. Given what we know about the teaching-to-tests that occurs in districts with big stakes attached to the scores, we might hypothesize that each subsequent administration of the test garners better and better results compared to the norm. Further, we might predict what would happen if the district went to another brand of test altogether or if the original test was re-normed. The district's fourth-grade test scores would very possibly slip as a result of either change.

One who reasonably hypothesized these effects would be right, the evidence strongly suggests. A study reported at the annual meeting of the American Educational Research Association in Chicago a few years ago confirmed exactly the predicted pattern outlined above. Indeed, any generalizations about real school achievement levels based on a set of test scores would be highly suspect, according to RAND's Daniel Koretz, along with a team of researchers that included Robert Linn at the University of Colorado, Stephen Dunbar of the University of Iowa, and Shepard. They looked at test scores at a large urban school district, characterized as high-poverty, with large numbers of Hispanic and black children. (Given the nature of the project as "politically risky" for participating schools, the study's authors said, the identity of the districts was kept confidential.) Each test was a "conventional, off-the-shelf, multiple-choice" and was characterized as having "high-stakes" consequences for the schools.

The study compared three sets of test scores for third-graders: Test C that the district used through 1986; Test B used from 1987 through 1990 (a revision and re-norming of Test C); and the researchers' experimental readministration of the original Test C to a current sample of some 840 children in thirty-six schools.

Consider what happened on the mathematics part of the three tests:

- Districtwide, average math scores on the original Test C for third-graders in 1986 were equivalent to achievement at three months into the fourth grade (4.25). But as soon as Test B was given in 1987, the average grade achievement level immediately declined by half a year.
- Then, with the continued use of and familiarity with Test B, the predicted pattern played out, as the average grade level, measured by test results, climbed steadily upward to about where it had been back in 1986.
- Even more remarkable was the difference between the researchers' 1990 retest on Test C compared with the same test's results in 1986. The 1990 test takers scored roughly four academic months *lower* than their counterparts on the exact same exam in 1986.

And those are just comparisons of the entire district's *average* scores. Individual schools, comparing the researchers' own readministration of Test C with the last administration of Test B, the greatest decline at one school on the retest was a full three years and three months. Five of thirty-six schools were measured at a year or more lower on the redo of Test C. Just five schools scored better on the redo of Test C than on Test B, gaining no more than a quarter of a school year. The researchers discovered similar patterns on the reading tests.

The meaning of these results is unambiguous. Test familiarity and outdated norms combine to inflate test scores beyond real gains in underlying achievement. Because the main object of instruction in high-stakes accountability environments is often reducible to test scores, because the politics of such environments actually encourage teaching to tests, such "instruction" to a specific test will inevitably "defeat" that test—until another test comes along and the children's scores are back where they started. Then the pattern repeats.

In this test-driven environment, a child's or school's real achievement level is understood only by those who knew it in the first place, without the benefit of a test: the teachers themselves.

The results of their study, Koretz told his peers at that Chicago meeting, "provide a very serious criticism of test-based accountability of the sort used in this site and in many other districts and states throughout the country. Few citizens or policymakers, I suspect, are particularly interested in performance, say, on 'mathematics as tested by Test B but not Test C.' They are presumably much more interested in performance in mathematics, rather broadly defined." (26)

History keeps repeating itself, at least when it comes to standardized testing in schools. The myth-shattering mismatch between real achievement and big-stakes testing continues to play like a broken record. Hard evidence from real experience is ignored for the sake of political expediency and quick fixes.

Indeed, one observer once said in a pithy summary of the problem that big-stakes testing is "a game of mechanical contrivance in which teachers will and must learn to beat us. It is . . . possible by ingenious preparation to get children through the (exams) in reading, writing and ciphering without their really knowing how to read, write or cipher."

That observer was Matthew Arnold, who served as a British school inspector in the nineteenth century. (27)

Rudy Crew Goes Big Time

"*That's a very sensitive issue. We don't like to talk about it.*"

Indeed, test scores—particularly an interesting set of scores on the Comprehensive Test of Basic Skills in spring 1995, remain to this day a touchy subject in Tacoma, Washington, the district's community relations director, Judy Parker, darkly hinted to me in February 1998.

In fact, but for that spontaneous statement, Parker and other district officials apparently preferred to avoid the subject altogether when I repeatedly sought information about Tacoma's miraculous gain in test scores that year. My inquiries included numerous phone calls and e-mail messages to Joe Wilhoft, the district's testing and research director, whom Parker said had all the answers I would need, as well as an unanswered certified letter to Superintendent James F. Shoemake.

It goes without saying that my curiosity was more than aroused, if by nothing else than Parker's mysterious comment. I had recalled a *New York Times* story from October 1995 that New York City schools chancellor Rudy Crew, then Tacoma's school superintendent, had orchestrated a spectacular rise in achievement test scores in Tacoma—a gain on the order of twenty percentile points in a matter of seven months, an extraordinary surge under any circumstances. Soon after those remarkable gains were posted, publicized, and celebrated, to the delight of this working-class town south of Seattle, Crew left Tacoma to become chancellor of New York City schools, the nation's largest school system.

To be sure, the *Times* story raised concerns and questions expressed by a few dissidents in Tacoma about the district's spectacular gains in achievement. Crew was also said to have revolutionized the philosophy of teaching disadvantaged and minority children. Described as a visionary and an inspiring leader, Crew reportedly cajoled teachers to raise their academic expectations of poor and minority children. To carry out his new vision, Crew hired the Efficacy Institute, a consulting and training organization based in Lexington, Massachusetts. Founded by Jeff Howard, a Harvard-trained social psychologist, the institute's guiding principle was that academic achievement boiled down to a matter of childrens' self-esteem and confidence in their intellectual abilities, regardless of their social and economic backgrounds. By the time Crew left, the district had spent some $750,000 on Efficacy training of its teaching staff.

So that was it? Tacoma's test scores surged twenty percentile points because teachers raised their expectations of pupils? These children performed so well on the tests because they had higher self-esteem? Were these remarkable gains in achievement sustainable? Did they reflect long-term gains in learning and understanding? In my letter to Shoemake, I wrote: "The news clippings I've seen don't sufficiently explain what exactly caused the surge in test scores. I'm left with some basic questions that I'm hoping your office might be able to assist me with. Basically, I'm interested in knowing whether it's the district's conclusion that the test-score surge in 1995 reflected a substantive and sustainable increase in underlying academic achievement. And, if not, I'm interested in knowing to what the district did attribute the sharp spike in test scores."

So what did happen in Tacoma, Washington? More important, did those test-score gains reflect a sustainable increase in the children's actual achievement, or were they, in the final analysis, little more than a spurious blip? Was the Tacoma miracle a result of raising the self-esteem in the city's schoolchildren, or the product of blatant teaching to a test?

What follows is my own dissection of the events that unfolded between 1992—a year before Crew came to Tacoma—and 1996, the year after he'd left. Many of the facts that follow were recorded in press accounts, particularly the Tacoma *News-Tribune*. Indeed, as Crew's chief cheerleader for higher test scores, the editorial pages of the local newspaper turned out to be a key player in the infamous Tacoma miracle. In addition, a relatively obscure report on the Tacoma experience helps demystify what happened. The Tacoma Report, prepared by the Bethesda, Maryland, office of Abt Associates, a consulting firm, was paid for by the U.S. Department of Education and the Efficacy Institute itself. They, too, were wondering what could account for the same remarkable phenomenon that Judy Parker didn't want to talk about.

~

In this blue-collar city, the state's second largest, widely viewed in the Northwest as the homely sister to the emerald city of Seattle some thirty minutes north on Interstate 5, Tacoma schools for years struggled simply for a distant view of Lake Wobegon.

Some 15 percent of the city's schoolchildren in 1990 were black, roughly the national average but about five times that for the state as a whole. Sixty-six percent of schoolchildren were white, and almost a quarter were poor, considerably above both the state and national poverty rates. At one time, the city was better known for its forest products, shipping ports, the Point Defiance Zoo, and the pungent smell of paper manufacturing. It was known as a gritty but solid union town and no-nonsense working folks. In the 1980s, the city struggled with drug-related crime, as gangs arrived from California and set up shop.

Despite problems of poverty, crime, unemployment, and all the rest of the big world unfolding beyond the control of schools, those perennially below-average test scores simply couldn't wash in the minds of some in local political and media establishment. The *News-Tribune*, for instance, applied relentless editorial pressure to get test scores up. The newspaper reported local test scores as if they were election results. Its editorial pages commented on a point or two change in annual fall test scores as if they were harbingers of educational disaster or academic nirvana, depending on whether scores were up or down a few points.

In fall 1992, Tacoma fourth-graders scored at the forty-fifth percentile on one national achievement test. That was slightly down from the forty-seventh percentile a year earlier. "Lackluster. Mediocre. Disappointing. Frustrating," remarked the paper's editorial under the headline, "TACOMA TEST SCORES DISAPPOINT—AGAIN." Of course, academic achievement is a complex endeavor and can't be improved overnight, the newspaper conceded. "But there's simply no hiding the fact that the district is making little progress toward achieving its goal for student achievement." To be fair, the newspaper was simply holding school officials to the goal they'd set for themselves, which had been to raise the district's average to at least the fiftieth percentile. "The district has been facing subpar scores for years and knows it must do better." (28)

In July 1993, Rudy Crew came to Tacoma after spending four years as chief of Sacramento schools, where he'd implemented Efficacy Training as well. A native of Poughkeepsie, New York, Crew had also been deputy superintendent in Boston in the 1980s. That's where he first hooked up with Howard and the Efficacy Institute, working together on Boston's desegregation plan.

Within months of arriving in Tacoma, Crew was sounding like George Bush in Kuwait, drawing lines in the sand on test scores, bringing with him the Efficacy Institute's philosophy about disadvantaged children and achievement. In fact, a member of his transition team in Tacoma had been an Efficacy Institute official.

From the beginning of Crew's two-year tenure, he cleverly framed the issue of school achievement in a neoconservative populism that was exceedingly difficult for anyone to openly doubt. Daring to question just how much schools can fix the fundamental social and economic factors that lead to academic success would be tantamount to suggesting that poor and minority children "aren't capable" of high achievement, given the manner in which Crew couched the subject.

Critics of Crew's philosophy, of course, would open themselves to such attacks even if they believed that Tacoma children, in fact, were fully capable of high achievement given the same opportunities to learn as children from, say, Mercer Island schools. That's Washington State's richest—and highest scoring—school district, located on an island of the same name surrounded by Lake Washington in Seattle. In Crew's view, poverty, unemployment, and crime might well be related to low achievement in schools like Tacoma, but they can't be used as an "excuse" for low test scores. Crew told the Tacoma *News-Tribune* editorial board, "I refuse to accept as an explanation that students are not capable of doing the work." To raise academic expectations, he said, "is a case of being far more strategic, far more focused, far more attentive . . . than perhaps we've been before." (29)

At a school board meeting in December 1993, Crew put down the rhetorical hammer. He did so after fresh standardized test scores showed fourth-graders up "by only one point," said the *News-Tribune*'s editorial board, to the forty-sixth percentile, and eighth-graders' scores were unchanged, still four points below the national average. All "bad news," the Tacoma paper editorialized.

But "there was one bright spot" at the school board meeting, the editors said. "And that was Crew's own response to the disappointing numbers. Instead of citing Tacoma's high proportion of poor, minority, and immigrant students as an excuse, Crew bluntly declared the results were not acceptable under any circumstances. In a steely tone, he told board members, principals, and parents, 'I will not preside over a district which fails to expect more, both from its students and its staff.'" (30)

With the path to academic achievement so framed, Crew was able to convince the school board in early 1994 to commit to spend $2 million over four years to train teachers in Efficacy techniques and philosophy, summed up by the motto: "Think You Can. Work Hard. Get Smart." Teachers' "basic" Efficacy training, consisting of one four-day workshop, began in March of that year.

Then came the fall 1994 scores on the Comprehensive Test of Basic Skills (CTBS). Both fourth- and eighth-grade scores were down four points and one point, respectively. Again, meeting with the *News-Tribune*'s editorial board, Crew attacked the results as "unconscionable." Reporting on the meeting, the *News-Tribune* quoted Crew, "'Let this be both a wake-up call and a last line in the sand,' he said, slapping the table lightly. 'This goes no further. This goes no further.'" (31)

Indeed, in response to the latest test results, Crew announced to the editorial board that he would send school principals and his top aides into the classrooms. He also announced a highly unusual move to arrange a special retest of Tacoma's fourth- and eighth-graders the following spring.

The Tacoma Miracle

Results from the unusual spring retest were beyond extraordinary, surpassing, I would venture, even Crew's bold promises to the *News-Tribune*'s editorial board. In the fourth grade, the average score jumped twenty-one points, from the forty-second percentile in the fall to the sixty-third percentile. Eighth-graders' scores spiked thirteen points, from the forty-fifth percentile to the fifty-eighth percentile.

Gains of just half those would typically bear scrutiny for signs of cheating or other inappropriate testing practices that would damage the test's validity. Exactly what happened inside Tacoma classrooms, between fall 1994 and spring 1995, remains somewhat murky given the reluctance of Tacoma's staff to discuss the matter. But three independent sources provide some interesting clues. They include a fourth-grade teacher named Leon Horn, who agreed to talk; a memo by testing director Joe Wilhoft; and the Abt Associates investigation.

According to the 1997 Abt Associates report, the district had embarked on a test-score improvement "campaign" after the district's poor test results in fall 1994. The Abt report, titled, "Evaluation of the Efficacy Initiative: A Retrospective Look at the Tacoma School District," says the district's test-preparation efforts intensified considerably as the spring retest approached. (32)

In fact, Tacoma's test-score campaign was in addition to the Efficacy training that teachers and staff were already receiving, the report says. The district's spring 1995 campaign aimed just at improving test scores involved the Department of Planning, Research and Evaluation; the Department of Curriculum, Instruction and Staff Development; and the Elementary and Secondary Education Department.

These departments orchestrated districtwide training workshops showing school administrators and teachers how to "practice test-taking skills with students," according to the Abt report. The training sessions were targeted specifically at math and language teachers and grades subject to the state tests. Further, school principals organized campus "test-taking teams," consisting of a testing coordinator, parents, fourth- and eighth-grade language and math teachers, and the principal. These teams were to ensure, in part, that "teachers participated in the training workshops."

Beyond that, the Abt report becomes a bit vague as to how the campaign's efforts were actually implemented in the classrooms, except to say that the district created lesson plans on "various test-taking skills" as well as a "test-taking handbook" of "reminders" to principals and teachers about how to prepare the students for testing.

Leon Horn's account is generally consistent with the Abt report, and it amplifies many of the report's more general descriptions of Tacoma's test-prep campaign. When I spoke to him in early 1998, Horn was a fourth-grade teacher at Reed Elementary, and was active in the teachers' union, serving on the board of the National Education Association. During my conversation with him, I judged Horn to be forthright and generally supportive of Crew's controversial leadership and the value of the Efficacy training. Too, Horn was descriptive and nonjudgmental about techniques the schools had adopted specifically aimed at raising test scores.

Horn described the approach teachers undertook following Crew's veritable mandate to get scores up. First, they emphasized specific test-taking skills. "We took a look at that kind of test and said (to pupils), 'When you are asked questions on a test, this is what you need to do; read through the questions first, then read the passage, and then read the questions again,'" Horn told me.

All well and good. But Horn says schools went well beyond just teaching testing skills, which brings one to the more murky and troublesome realm of teaching specifically to the upcoming exam. As we've seen, such "teaching the test" practices not only border on the unethical but their effects often prove to be short-lived in terms of genuine learning and achievement.

In many cases, Horn says, teachers created practice tests and drilled students on them. "The staff got together and decided to write questions similar to the questions that were on the test, the same kind of style, so the kids were pretty familiar with the kinds of questions, the style of questioning they would be asked. It really helped the kids," Horn told me.

What is more, some schools went so far as to actually "change curriculum," in order to suit "the same style of questions that kids would be tested on." (33)

Concerns about the legitimacy of the spring 1995 test results prompted Joe Wilhoft, the district's testing director, to circulate an unusual memo in which he defended the integrity of the scores. In that memo, Wilhoft purportedly addressed this question on the minds of skeptics. Rhetorically, he asked: "Couldn't our gains have come from sort of non-standard, or improper, testing procedures, like allowing students more time, or giving them practice on the test?" he asked. Wilhoft's answer: "No," and then he proceeded pretty much to avoid the question.

That question, of course, went to the issue of teaching to the test. Tacoma's scores would be highly suspicious if teachers went so far as to alter curriculum to match specific test items, or drilled children on specific test items. But Wilhoft didn't really address that issue, instead speaking to whether the test was properly *administered,* which speaks to such issues as the proper amount of time provided, clean scoring, and appropriate sorts of assistance given students during the exam. "We have looked very hard and have absolutely no evidence that the tests were administered improperly," he said.

So what did account for the improvement, in Wilhoft's view? His memo cited the Efficacy approach. "Staff and students . . . spent a lot of time this year on the 'Think you can' and the 'Work hard' sides of the model with the target being the spring testing. Our results reflect, I think, the 'Get smart' part of the equation."

Besides that, Wilhoft maintained, the district's sharp focus on the spring test, and teaching pupils better test-taking skills, paid off. "There is no question that students across the district were encouraged to do well this spring to a greater extent than ever before," he said. "In school after school we find instances of very creative ways that the school staff have found to motivate their students to work hard and do well." (34)

Did those "very creative ways" include the sorts of practices that teacher Leon Horn told me had occurred, such as changing curriculum to match test items and drilling students on practice tests? In his memo, which the *News-Tribune* published as a guest editorial, Wilhoft sidestepped that touchy subject.

Did the Efficacy Training itself contribute to the test-score spike, as Wilhoft suggested in his memo? That was a central question of the Abt report, sponsored as it was in part by the Efficacy Institute, looking for evidence that training teachers to have higher expectations of students actually paid off in terms of hard test-score numbers.

Employing some fairly rigorous statistical techniques, the Abt investigators tracked test-score changes comparing two groups: students whose teachers had received Efficacy Training and pupils whose teachers had not. The results had to be disappointing for advocates of the Efficacy approach. First, the analysis confirmed that the fall to spring gains in both grades tested were significantly greater than what would be expected as a result of pupils having mastered more material in the natural progression of the school year.

Still, the researchers found, these gains couldn't be attributed to the Efficacy training, as there was no significant difference between gains in comparative groups. If not the Efficacy training, then what? The Abt report concludes: "In our view, the test-score gains are most likely a result of the one-time efforts in March 1995 . . . to increase students' test-taking skills."

A senior vice president at the testing company, CTB/McGraw-Hill, was nevertheless baffled by the Tacoma results. "I really can't begin to explain what exactly occurred in Tacoma," Michael Kean told the *News-Tribune* in June 1995. "If everything was on the up and up, it's just a remarkable increase." (35)

But Tacoma, it seemed, wasn't in the mood to question the good news about its schools. Yes, there were concerns about the integrity of the spring test scores, but surely the district had laid those doubts to rest. Wilhoft said everything was on the up and up. Teachers, parents, and others were excited that their children's hard work was paying off. In July, the Tacoma school board voted to renew Crew's contract and up his annual salary by $10,000.

Crew's Star Rises

Autumn had been a tumultuous period for Tacoma's schools and a heady time for Dr. Crew. Headhunters had reportedly called Crew from the day he arrived in Tacoma, because districts nationwide hoped to entice the turnaround artist to their schools. Clearly, Crew was the man of the hour. He'd already spurned an interview for the top job in Boston in July. He'd signed up then–Deputy Education Secretary Madeleine Kunin to see the Tacoma miracle for herself. Kunin praised Tacoma's amazing rise in test scores.

New York came calling in early September. At September's end, Crew resolutely announced his withdrawal as a candidate for the job. "I really feel an obligation to getting on with business here," he said. "I don't think you can do it and walk away from it in two years. I've really opted to see this one through. It's not a flash-in-the-pan thing that happens in fifteen to eighteen months." (36)

After continuing to deny that he was a candidate until a day before he took the chancellorship's job, in early October Crew accepted New York's offer of a $195,000 salary and use of a $1 million home. He'd leaped from a medium-size school district of some 31,000 students to the largest in the country, with 1.1 million students, more than 1,000 schools, and a budget of $8 billion.

When the school board received Crew's two-sentence fax announcing his resignation, they promptly evicted him from his office and briefly mulled a lawsuit compelling Crew to honor his employment contract with the district. The anger and sense of betrayal in Tacoma was palpable. The *News-Tribune* even invited readers to submit comments to the paper about their opinions of Crew in light of his abrupt departure. Their comments were not kind.

The "Crew Effect"

Jump forward to fall 1996. Crew had been gone a year, and his replacement, James Shoemake, had been on board only since July. The fall CTBS scores for fourth- and eighth-graders had been released, and the scores were disappointing, especially after the heady days of the previous year.

The *News-Tribune*'s editorial board showed brief hints of souring at Crew's earlier enterprise. Lamented the editors: "After all the attention focused on student achievement in Tacoma's schools during the last few years—particularly by Shoemake's predecessor, Rudy Crew—the district doesn't have much to show for it." (37)

A year later, the fall 1997 tests again proved to be lackluster for eighth-graders and troubling for Tacoma's fourth-graders, as twenty-six of thirty-six schools posted declines in their CTBS scores. "Baffling," even "disturbing," wrote the *News-Tribune*'s editors.

By then, it would seem the *News-Tribune*'s editorial board, having seen the achievement gains evanesce, might have finally gone deeper into the test-score question, and begun to ask the tough questions about the score spike; about the nature of standardized tests; teaching to tests; and how a total emphasis on test scores alone can distort teaching and even harm real learning and sustainable achievement. Perhaps the editors and the Tacoma school board might have finally drawn their own lines in the sand, and once and for all put a stop to this silly game.

But the numbers game was relentless. Challenging current notions of accountability would have amounted to an admission of not caring about academic standards, as those standards were defined in the minds of a largely deluded public and their political figures. Indeed, Shoemake's honeymoon was over, and it was high time to get test scores back up. "Tacoma's taxpayers and parents shouldn't have to wait . . . to see more progress," the *News-Tribune* editorialized. "Something went wrong, and it needs fixing."

~

By the end of the "Crew effect," if I might coin a term for the short-lived spike in Tacoma's CTBS scores, test scores had generally fallen back to their 1993 level. A glance at the following table of percentile scores from 1993 through 1997 illustrates that achievement for fourth-graders had pretty much settled into its long-term level by the end of the period, irrespective of Crew's intensive efforts. For comparison purposes, I've included the Mercer Island district, the enclave of wealth and privi-

TABLE 6.2 CTBS percentile scores in Tacoma, Auburn, Mercer Island 1993–1997

Fourth Grade	*Tacoma*	*Auburn*	*Mercer Island*
1993	46	57	84
1994	42	54	83
1995	49	54	83
1996	48	56	84
1997	45	56	82

SOURCE: Washington State Office of the Superintendent of Public Instruction, Reading, Language and Math combined

TABLE 6.3 Test Scores and Economics in Tacoma, Auburn and Mercer Island, Washington

	Tacoma	*Auburn*	*Mercer Island*
Poverty rate of school children	22%	11%	2.6%
Average house value	$67,000	$97,700	$332,457
Bachelor's degree or higher	11%	9%	43%
Average 4th grade percentile score CTBS 1993–1997	46	55	83
Average 8th grade percentile score on CTBS 1993–1997	49	56	83

SOURCES: School District Date Book Profiles 1989–1990, National Center for Education Statistics; Washington State Office of the Superintendent of Public Instruction

lege in Seattle. Also shown is the Auburn school district, a small middle-class city between Seattle and Tacoma toward the foothills of the Cascade Mountains.

In each of these school districts, the CTBS districtwide scores settled into a long-term pattern: Tacoma scores remained somewhat below the national average of the fiftieth percentile; Auburn's were near the national norm; and Mercer Island's settled significantly above the national average.

If the post-Crew scores on the Comprehensive Test of Basic Skills had cast serious doubt on whether the Tacoma miracle reflected real achievement gains or instead was a fairly predictable outcome of intensive coaching for the test, then the results of Washington State's transition to a different achievement test altogether appears to have been the final nail in the coffin.

In spring 1997, the state of Washington staged a trial run of its new Assessment of Student Learning for fourth-graders. The CTBS is a "norm-referenced" test, with results reported in percentiles comparable to a national norm, a method that permits comparisons of individual schoolchildren. Washington's new assessment was, instead, a "criterion-referenced" standardized test. Such tests are designed to match up closely with what's supposed to be taught in a given locality and state.

The new state test, then, attempted to measure how well a child mastered the taught curriculum. Too, the new Washington assessment was more varied in format than the multiple-choice CTBS, requiring pupils to explain answers in somewhat more open-ended, performance-oriented tasks in math, reading, writing, and listening.

Results of the new exam were discouraging for Tacoma. Except for listening, fewer than one-half of Tacoma's fourth-grade children had met the performance standards on the four skills. In math, just 14 percent of the children met the standard. Compared to the earlier statewide test that was virtually all multiple-choice, the new assessment required more thoughtful answers, Leon Horn told me. "When everyone took it, it was kind of a shock to everybody's system," he says. "I think the thinking behind the development of the test is they wanted kids to be able to do something, to test greater skills and greater understanding, that they really knew what they were doing and not just guessing at taking a test."

To be sure, in districts across the state, the vast majority of children didn't meet the standard for math, in particular. In only the highest achieving districts did even half the children meet the math standard. In Mercer Island, the state's richest district, nearly 60 percent met the standard for math; 76 percent did so in reading; 71 percent did so in writing; and fully 84 percent met the listening standard. (38)

The implication seems evident. Test scores in Tacoma, as in Auburn and Mercer Island, settled into a long-term pattern that was profoundly affected by social and economic forces not easily overcome with quick fixes.

"Buying" Achievement

In retrospect, it appears that the Tacoma miracle is easily explained, after all. Between fall 1994 and the remarkable spring 1995 retest, Dr. Crew and Tacoma schools were on a mission to get test scores up. An intensive test-preparation campaign was launched, and their mission was, briefly, accomplished. After Crew left, and that brief jolt of that spring's stimulus had played out, Tacoma's achievement scores settled back to their long-term pattern.

Moreover, Efficacy training—which was continued even after Crew's departure from Tacoma—appeared ineffective to change the district's long-term achievement-score pattern. Abt's investigation concluded, "These one-year gains were also found not to be sustained over the ensuing two years, and again there is no evident relationship between Efficacy staff training and temporal changes in student test scores."

Tacoma's experience shows that schools can stress the test and the numbers will improve—to a point and, unfortunately, all too briefly. It remains highly doubtful that Tacoma's efforts to boost test scores were aimed at genuine learning for understanding; rather, teachers, principals, and administrators did what they thought necessary simply to effect higher test scores. Schools under severe accountability pressures, like Northampton, or those like Tacoma that serve as stepping-stones for politically astute and ambitious chief executives, certainly can "buy" brief gains in "achievement" with intensive, short-term initiatives.

But at what cost? In the end, taxpayers are fooled to believe that year-to-year changes in average test scores really mean anything; and when scores settle back to their historical pattern, taxpayers are frustrated thinking that schools are lousy and teachers aren't doing their jobs.

"It's a numbers game," veteran Tacoma teacher Dick Kinnaman said when he was asked about the dramatic spike in Tacoma's test scores. "Because the public sees the higher scores, they make an assumption there's better teaching going on. But there's always been good teaching going on. I think we're playing the game now. If that satisfies taxpayers, that's good." (39)

In a very real sense, public schools playing the test-score game is something of an educational fraud hoisted on taxpayers. True and lasting achievement is not likely to budge with quick fixes. That truism is often lost when members of the public, politicians, and the media focus on test scores as if schools and schoolchildren were race horses or candidates for political office.

Sadly, children pay the worst price. Ultimately, they're cheated when schools live or die by test scores. Playing the test-score game comes with grave risks for children: Evidence is overwhelming that defining achievement by test scores inevitably constricts the range of subjects and the depth in which they are covered. Researchers have discovered that schools can ratchet scores upward on a given test by emphasizing the test in the curriculum—until the test changes and the cycle starts over again. Meanwhile, children are getting short-changed on the teaching and learning they need.

"We spend a lot of time getting ready to take tests," Tacoma teacher Leon Horn told me, even with Crew's departure. "We lose a lot of instructional time, and when kids don't do well on a test people think schools are failing. We get different types of tests and we teach kids how to take these tests and then they change the test. It becomes a real back-and-forth game. Everyone is so concerned about testing that we spend a heck of a lot of time on it. . . . You're taking time away from what they should be learning."

Horn adds: "The public doesn't know how in trying to be accountable to the public we are giving up instructional time to make sure kids know what they're supposed to know" for standardized tests.

Thus, a case can be made that Tacoma's achievement gains were phony in at least a couple of senses. The sharp rise in achievement was the result of an intense effort ranging from instruction on innocent testing skills to the more dubious practice of teaching the test itself. The district's commitment was unprecedented in devoting instructional time and resources to relatively superficial efforts aimed at boosting the politically charged test scores. Those gains were phony as well, because they didn't last.

In my view, the Tacoma story wasn't about student achievement. This was political theater, featuring an ambitious and dynamic Rudy Crew and a school board hungry to prove to citizens that schools weren't a mess. What's more, the local press, particularly the *News-Tribune*, played a significant part in shaping the outcome of this story. Its coverage largely framed childrens' achievement in terms of test scores alone, and its editorial board continually upped the pressure on local school officials for higher test scores. Further, the efforts of these well-intentioned people did not pay off in terms of real learning and long-term gains in achievement. In the end, the children wound up as pawns in a political game.

7

Do No Harm: Stopping the Damage to American Schools

OUR INAUSPICIOUS ERA OF EDUCATIONAL crimes and punishments shows no signs of waning. Young people like Kelly Santos, whom we met earlier, aren't isolated examples of the fallout from the national crusade for more "accountable" schools. Texas is among some nineteen states that require high school "exit" tests, and more are in the offing. Dozens of states hold schools, students, teachers, and principals "accountable" on the basis of standardized test scores. "We have been, frankly, inundated with calls from states that are looking at their accountability laws and want to strengthen them," says one official at the Education Commission of the States. (1)

Indeed, states are engaged in an elaborate round of musical acronyms, replacing one testing system for another one, more often than not with one that has significantly higher stakes for all people involved. Some states have abandoned their efforts to try alternatives to standardized tests, such as performance assessments, which strive to permit children to think and perform in deeper and more creative terms than allowed by multiple-choice sound bites, worksheets, and test drills. But such new approaches—promising as they might be to refocus attention on learning instead of scoring—aren't easily fitted into the politically driven objective of school accountability. That objective? Apparently to compare test scores of individual children across the state or the nation and show the public that policymakers are tough on academic standards by punishing those who don't measure up. Some examples:

- In a Hawthornesque variant to the scarlet *A*, Louisiana's accountability law requires school districts to identify and publish the names of all schools scoring in the bottom fifth on the state's standardized test. All

Louisiana school districts but New Orleans comply with the 1997 law, pending the outcome of a lawsuit. One of the plaintiffs, a local state representative, ridicules the mandate as tantamount to requiring a public declaration of "Here are the dummy schools." (2)

- In a case of school achievement levels determined simply by which test one chooses to use, school officials in Idaho wring their hands over reading scores of fourth-graders when one exam finds that 60 percent of the children can't read at grade level, while another test indicates just 18 percent cannot. A battle of name-calling, disavowals, and insults ensues over which test was right. (3)
- Illustrative of the newfound lack of concern among some school officials over the educationally dubious practice of "teaching the test," Milwaukee public schools in Wisconsin agree to pay an Arizona consulting firm almost $400,000 for a program called TargetTeach. The firm specializes in getting test scores up in schools "with a problem." The firm, Evans-Newton Inc., promises a 20 to 200 percent surge in test scores in just a year. (4)
- In Chicago, 1 in 10 of Chicago schools' 424,000 students are sent to summer school on the basis of standardized test scores. Thousands of others are forced to repeat a grade even after summer school because of poor showings on a retest. Under the hammer, students at Amundson High School in Chicago spend six weeks of class time on intensive test preparation and coaching for the upcoming test. (5)
- In California, funding for a performance-based assessment system known as CLAS, which had been in place to assess learning without reliance on standardized testing, is vetoed by Governor Pete Wilson. In its place, the state legislature invents STAR, the Standardized Testing and Reporting program, which requires all children in the second through eleventh grades to take a commercial multiple-choice test. A group of several school superintendents from major California cities condemn the plan as educationally regressive, one that "wastes taxpayer dollars and will impede, rather than support, our statewide push toward higher performance." (6)

Adding the Damage

Without a doubt, crackdowns such as these on public schools, as well as tales of amazing turnarounds in test results in such locales as Tacoma, Washington, and Northampton County, North Carolina, reflect the good news of American schools for many elected officials, corporate executives, parents, newspaper editorial writers, and others working under the mantle of school reform.

Tales of higher academic standards and achievement test scores beyond expectations sustain popular belief in the reform crusade's holy trinity: standards, accountability, and testing. For many, such stories show that the accountability movement is indeed having the reformers' desired effects: reinforcing high academic standards, forcing teachers and principals to do their jobs, and providing meaningful incentives for students to achieve.

The evidence from the previous three chapters shows just how empty those beliefs are. In fact, while the rhetoric is highly effective, remarkably little good evidence exists that there's *any* educational substance behind the accountability and testing movement. In fact, when one adds up the real costs of the uniquely American model of school accountability and compares them to the minimal or nonexistent benefits, the inescapable conclusion is that the nation's fifteen-year experiment has been an unmitigated failure. Let's sum up the damage:

One: Educational considerations have been subordinate to the political and ideological motivations of politicians, educational bureaucrats, and business leaders. These interests have wielded political power over schools in order to assert their control and to demonstrate preconceived failures of the school system as the means to sustain that power. This was as true at the beginning of the American testing movement in Horace Mann's Massachusetts as it was in Johnson County, North Carolina, in the 1990s.

Two: Blatant and harmful misappropriations of standardized tests for fallacious uses have been a constant of America's historical experience with standardized testing in schools. Zealots, for instance, have taken tests intended to broadly assess achievement at the school, district, or state level, to instead rank and sort individual children. The opposite has also been true: tests intended to evaluate individual achievement have been used to base unfounded conclusions of the educational quality of entire school systems.

Three: In the ongoing struggle between educational equity among social classes and an efficiently managed school system, public policy toward schools has historically tended to side with the latter. Public schools have borrowed the management, surveillance, measurement, and control techniques of American business in order to achieve this efficiency.

Four: The notion of "accountability" itself has been defined in terms analogous to the corporate model, such as profits and returns to shareholders. In practice and in public belief, the educational product of schools has come to be judged almost exclusively by test scores. Borrowing, too, the market-driven ideology of the corporate world, policymakers have created pseudo-market systems of rewards and punishments to schools. Test scores are the currency of these incentives.

Five: The modern accountability movement became "federalized," in some decidedly tangible and pervasive ways. The federal government's markings on the accountability movement occurred, not insignificantly, as a result of the federal Title 1 law that has meted out many billions of dollars in federal funding to schools using test scores as a key part of the calculus. Further, prominent national leaders, including three recent American presidents, have ratcheted up the stakes for public schools to that of a national crusade for educational reform, with accountability testing as its linchpin.

Six: The underlying belief in the school reform crusade of the past few decades is that the American way of life was at grave risk because of lax standards and poorly educated schoolchildren. Evidence has proven this belief to be politically convenient mythology, wrong on at least three counts: First, academic achievement was never as horrible as the crusaders made it out to be; next, in the aftermath of an alleged deterioration of American schools, the U.S. economy continued to remain the most productive in the world; and finally, contrary to the implicit assumption that more testing and greater accountability will produce higher academic achievement, states with the most testing and the highest consequences of testing have fared worse on independent measures of achievement than states with no or low stakes to their testing programs.

Seven: Focused on test scores and the means to effect higher scores, the accountability movement has been curiously oblivious to the unintended damage to the learning environment. The movement has ignored the distortions to teaching and learning resulting from teachers, students, and others in the system acting in their own perceived best interest.

Schools and teachers, under intense pressure to boost achievement scores, have discovered the educationally dubious practice of teaching to tests. That, in turn, has narrowed what's taught to material that closely matches items on multiple-choice, standardized tests. Too, teaching to tests has had a dumbing effect on teaching and learning, as worksheets, drills, practice tests, and similar rote practices consume greater amounts of teaching time.

The greater the consequences attached to the test, the more severe these distortions are on teaching and learning. Indeed, a widely discussed international study of math and science performance of twelfth-graders suggests American students' relatively poor performance can be traced to the superficiality of their classroom experiences, which in turn can be linked to the rise of accountability testing.

Eight: Schools have also discovered they can boost test scores by drilling students on practice test items, but gains won in this fashion prove to be ephemeral in the long run. In the short run, schools can jack up scores on one standardized test, only to see scores go back down when a new test comes along. Similarly, achievement that is apparently high on the test for which schools have prepared and drilled turns mediocre with a different test for which there was little or no specific preparation.

Nine: An important element of the calculus of school reform, as defined by the modern accountability movement, has been a heavy emphasis on state regulation of schools, similar to other regulatory agencies. State utility regulators, for instance, have historically monitored electric companies to ensure that rates are kept to a reasonable level. Similarly, the new school regulators have tried to ensure the academic integrity of schools through rules on educational "infractions" and punishments to schools and schoolchildren. "Violators," in this sense, have been the children, schools, teachers, and others that perform poorly on standardized achievement tests. Punishments for these "violators" have been severe.

But that seemingly attractive analogy collapses in the end. Whereas determining reasonable rates of profit for electric companies is a relatively straightforward exercise in measurement, assessing educational quality is exceedingly problematic. Is educational quality measured by results on standardized tests? Is it measured by how well students perform on tasks that require them to integrate skills and knowledge from several subjects, such as writing an essay or creating a multimedia presentation? Or does educational quality boil down to the success of graduates in college or in jobs after they leave the school system?

Educational quality may be all these. Even a modicum of justice to this complex, ephemeral concept—and especially for the sake of people whose lives are affected by decisions about what constitutes educational quality—would undoubtedly require an equally complex measurement system. Such a system would have to assess educational quality from a variety of perspectives to be fair, complete, and accurate. But, again, choosing efficiency over equity, Americans through their elected officials have largely chosen to assess quality of schools in exceedingly narrow and often inaccurate terms.

Beyond these social and economic costs of current notions of school accountability, however, is one costly and pernicious piece of damage that framers of the accountability movement have virtually ignored over the past twenty-five years. Obsessed with test results and holding schools accountable for those results, the entire accountability enterprise has studiously avoided confronting the real problems of American schools. I've alluded to the powerful correlations between socioeconomic factors and test scores, taking note, for instance, of the huge economic gaps between communities like Tacoma and Mercer Island, or Northampton County and Chapel Hill. Quite simply, one can't write a book about standardized testing in American schools without confronting the effects of poverty, race, and class on test scores.

From *A Nation at Risk* to Bill Clinton's Goals 2000, the accountability crusaders have given no more than lip service to the uncomfortable schism in the American school system between rich and poor, one that in recent years has increasingly resembled the economic and social stratification in the larger society. The accountability movement has sustained, and been sustained by, a big but comfortable lie: that schools themselves are the agent for social and economic change, rather than a reflection and reinforcer of existing social and economic divisions. In practice, this illusion has implied that "fixing" schools—via gains in achievement test scores—will also fix unemployment, crime, and poverty as well as racial and economic inequality. The entire accountability project in the United States over the past two decades has been based on a refusal to even acknowledge the far more difficult prospect that the causal relationships between schools and the larger society might in fact work largely in exactly the opposite direction to that wishful thinking.

As a result of this denial, the accountability machine's damage to children from families that aren't economically comfortable and highly educated or who are African American or Mexican American, has been inestimable, as we saw specifically in Texas, North Carolina, and in Tacoma. In those places and in hundreds more like them across the country, poor and minority schoolchildren have borne the brunt of the accountability machine's punishments.

Indeed, if social engineers had set out to invent a virtually perfect inequality machine, designed to perpetuate class and race divisions, and that appeared to abide by all requisite state and federal laws and regulations, those engineers could do no better than the present-day accountability systems already put to use in American schools.

Inequality in the larger society bleeds through the education system. Rich schools and poor schools match the income levels and occupational status of parents. Compared to rich schools, poor schools, whose children come from homes with incomes of less than $20,000 a year, are more likely to have relatively poorly paid teachers who are also teaching out of their fields of expertise and have less access to special learning tools like the Internet. Quite simply, compared to a rich school district, such as Mercer Island, a relatively poor one like Tacoma is likely to spend significantly less money on each of its students. In one recent year, for example, the nation's richest school districts spent almost 60 percent more per student than the country's poorest schools. (7)

Class Is Paramount

To be sure, inequality may not be on the minds of a lot of parents, except to steer as far away from it as possible when choosing a school. Recall from Chapter 4 how many parents in Boise, Idaho, were known to choose schools for their children based on test scores and child poverty rates; the higher the scores and the lower the poverty, the better the school in the eyes of many parents. Those parents might have been behaving quite rationally—but only up to a point. As it turns out, the economic class of individual children and their parents bears decisively on a child's chances of success in the school system, regardless of a particular school's test scores.

Let's digress momentarily to Chuck Lavaroni, the former teacher and school superintendent in Marin County, California, a community of high-achieving, well-paid professionals and schools boasting exceedingly high test scores. At the end of our two-session conversation, Lavaroni somewhat reluctantly confided his hypothesis concerning his Marin County students, which he'd arrived at after years of rumination about his experiences.

"You could take kids (in Marin County) who have grown up in that environment and not send them to school at all and they'd still pass the (standardized) test," Lavaroni told me. "If one of those schools drops below the ninety eighth percentile, they worry."

That was Lavaroni's highly educated guess, after years of experience in education. But he may in fact be close to the sober reality about the powerful relationship of class background and a child's success in test-driven school systems. We can go back to a sweeping 1972 study for some enlightening discoveries along these lines that should still give parents and educators on the edge of the millennium reason to pause. That study suggests Lavaroni's guess is hardly a novel idea nor an unproven supposition. Titled *Inequality: A Reassessment of the*

Effect of Family and Schooling in America, the three-year project was led by the sociologist Christopher Jencks and several other coauthors at the Center for Educational Policy Research at Harvard. The researchers examined how educational "attainment"—whether one obtains, for instance, a high school diploma or a medical degree—is related to such factors as class background, IQ scores, and average test scores of schools attended. As we've already seen, educational attainment is perhaps the most powerful of all indicators of educational quality, because attainment bears most directly on one's economic prospects and well-being.

Contrary to popular belief in the power of a school's average test scores as an indicator of a child's future academic success, the study found that "school quality" measured by scores has in fact a small effect on how much schooling a given child who attends that school will eventually obtain. "We can be almost certain," Jencks wrote, "that a child's going to a grade school with top-drawer test scores will add less than a year to his or her total years of schooling—and probably far less than even that." (8)

Absent any significant effects of schools' average achievement scores on one's years of educational attainment, that leaves such individual characteristics as cognitive abilities, behavioral traits, and the class background a child is born into as possible explanations.

As it turns out, the class background of a child's parents, combined with the behavioral traits about school which that class background imparts to children, appear to explain most of the variation in how much schooling someone eventually obtains. According to the Jencks study, a child's social and economic origins, measured by her father's occupational status and income, alone accounts for some 55 percent of her eventual educational attainment. Put another way, upper-middle-class children will obtain a total of four more years of schooling than lower-class kids, simply by virtue of the families they were born into. Further, so-called cognitive abilities, measured by IQ scores, account for less than 10 percent of the variation in the child's educational attainment.

On the other hand, the far more subtle behavioral traits often found in high-achieving households that "nurture the cognitive skills that schools value" have a far more substantial effect—something on the order of 25 percent—than IQ scores in explaining a child's educational achievement. Even then, the authors say, it's not clear that academic aptitude is that important to how much schooling one gets. Rather, attainment could be more related to "coming from the right family." Comparing, for instance, people with significantly different aptitude test scores raised in the same household, the study found that people who were more capable on the tests only attained less than a year of additional schooling. Again, class rules.

"Overall, the data lead us to three general conclusions," Jencks writes. "First, economic origins have a substantial influence on the amount of schooling people get. Second, the differences between rich and poor children is partly a matter of academic aptitude and partly a matter of money. Third, cultural attitudes, values, and taste for schooling play an even larger role than aptitude and money." (9)

Income and Poverty

Thus, the effects of social and economic class on how much schooling people get are immense, as most parents of schoolchildren implicitly know and understand. Where many parents often get it wrong is in believing that by associating their children with other high-scoring children in top schools, parents can do sort of an end-run around the powerful effects of *family* socioeconomic background. Tragically, this belief in the power of test scores by association sustains the beliefs that schools can either make or break a middle-class child's academic prospects in school or fix the horrendous problems of underachievement in the nation's poor and minority communities. The belief fuels the nation's unhealthy obsession with test scores, while we avoid the underlying problems and inequities.

The uncomfortable truth, however, is that the accountability movement that many states have embraced for their schools has, in fact, accomplished nothing to address the real problems with American schools. Instead of alleviating the problems of schools, which are clearly associated with the vast differences in wealth and privilege, the accountability machine's hard-core system of crimes and punishments has merely stiffened barriers to academic success for many.

Indeed, states have erected these barriers with virtually no firmly grounded evidence that they work to anyone's benefit except to those politicians, educators, and policy elites who professionally benefit from the bombardment of bad news about schools and from the engineering of high test numbers.

Besides the high correlation of class background to levels of attainment in the American school system, the relationship between poverty and achievement test scores has been firmly established in various field studies. Consider the Cleveland City School District, where fully 80 percent of schoolchildren are poor, as measured by their eligibility for school lunch programs. In 1990, the Ohio legislature told schools to administer a standardized test to ninth-graders to determine whether students might receive a full-fledged diploma or a downgraded "certificate" at their high school graduation. Students would have to pass all four parts of the test to receive a diploma, and they'd get two chances. James Lanese, of the Cleveland school district, looked into the question that had been troubling some skeptics: Would the state's testing program further punish schoolchildren in places like Cleveland, whose schools and families were already damaged by poverty?

Examining thirty-one school districts of various socioeconomic classes in Cuyahoga County, including Cleveland, Lanese applied the techniques of statistical correlation analysis to find out. Indeed, correlations between poverty levels of a district and success on the statewide tests were considerable. Lanese later told his peers at a meeting of the American Educational Research Association in San Francisco, "The comparison of district level performance on the Ohio Proficiency Test as a function of each district's poverty rates indicates a strong positive relationship exists between the economic status of the district's pupils and their performance on the test." (10)

Perhaps it comes as no surprise, then, that in the initial stages of the new testing program, just one-third of Cleveland students had passed the proficiency test by their junior year in high school. That's compared to three out of four students who had passed statewide. A year after the Lanese report, Michael Gallagher, also of the Cleveland school district, confirmed Lanese's results with slightly greater precision, accounting for more variables that might explain differences in pass rates. Specifically, Gallagher controlled for the confounding effects that occur between school districts, such as curriculum, racial makeup, and per-pupil spending. He looked at both income and poverty rates of the neighborhoods that surround individual schools within the Cleveland school district.

Even then, Gallagher found both household income and poverty were significantly correlated with the chances of passing the Ohio proficiency test. In fact, for every 10 percent drop in the number of pupils eligible for free lunches, a school would produce a 4 percent gain in its passing rate on the standardized test. He also discovered that, as a school approached having almost no pupils eligible for free lunches, the closer to the state average in the rate at which its students passed the test. (11)

Hold it a minute, some readers might interject: "But most studies have shown that differences in the *actual funding* of schools don't come close to explaining the yawning gaps of achievement between rich schools and poor ones." Indeed, there have been at least 100 such studies, and few have demonstrated any significant relationship between school funding levels—unequal as they are—and test scores.

And all of those studies may be seriously flawed, taken as a whole. In fact, virtually none have been based on nationwide samples of schools. In perhaps the first study to remedy this shortcoming and investigate the effects on achievement of school funding *on a national basis*, a team led by Bruce Biddle at the University of Missouri compared test scores on three national and/or international studies against the variables of poverty and school funding. Even when controlling for such variables as race and curriculum, the team found the combined effect of poverty and school funding was "mammoth," accounting for the lion's share of differences among average achievement scores in states.

Further, the Biddle team came to a startling conclusion when applying their analysis to the entire pool of nations participating in a recent international comparison of mathematics achievement, on which the American students generally fared poorly (see Chapter 6). When accounting for economics, the Biddle team estimated that math scores in "advantaged" American schools (those with high funding and low poverty rates) would beat *all* European counterparts and come in second only to Japan. On the other hand, scores for typically disadvantaged American schools would be below all European nations and approach those of many developing countries.

Evidence like this is why the accountability crusade's push for more and more testing persists in going off into left field while the real action is at home plate. Summing up his research team's remarkable findings in *Phi Delta Kappan*, the highly regarded magazine about education, Biddle says:

> The effects I report here help us understand why setting higher standards will have so little impact on achievement. If many, many schools in America are poorly funded and must contend with high levels of child poverty, then their problems stem not from confusion or lack of will on the part of educators but rather from lack of badly needed resources. In fact, setting higher standards for those disadvantaged schools can even make things worse. If they are told that they now must meet higher standards, or—worse—if they are chastised because they cannot do so, then they will have been punished for events beyond their control. (12)

Adding fuel to the flames that hurt rather than help children from poorer backgrounds, schools in poor neighborhoods bear the greatest brunt of public and official pressure to raise test scores. At these schools, teachers are most pressured to turn teaching and learning into a rote exercise of practice and drill for the next standardized test. We saw evidence of this disparate burden placed on the poor in Tacoma, Washington, in Northampton County, North Carolina, and in San Antonio, Texas. But further quantitative evidence on a wider scale underscores the observations from those case studies.

For example, investigators Joan Herman and Shari Golan examined eleven medium and large school districts in nine states to quantify the effects of big-stakes testing programs. Most noteworthy, the authors said, were the disproportionate effects of such testing on schools with lots of poor children and high numbers of minorities. The poorer the children attending the schools, the more pressure schools place on teachers to raise test scores, and the greater chance that the teachers will focus on the tests in their instruction rather than on deeper understanding.

And to what benefit? In the Herman study, teachers were asked whether the testing programs helped their schools to improve. On a scale of one to five (one corresponding to definite agreement, three to a neutral opinion, and five to definite disagreement), teachers in both wealthy and poor areas were inclined to rate standardized testing as more harmful than helpful for school improvement. Teachers in the poorer areas were least sanguine. "In the minds of teachers," the researchers conclude, "test results are of uncertain meaning and of uncertain value in school improvement." (13)

A Proposal

Judging by the evidence compiled in the previous three chapters, there's abundant reason to believe that the clearest route to raising the achievement levels of schoolchildren, in a real and lasting sense, may be—quite contrary to popular belief—to diminish reliance on standardized testing and high-stakes accountability systems. Instead of helping minority children and children of low and moderate incomes get past already stiff barriers to academic success, the accountability machine has given us bad teaching and perpetuated rather than dampened a powerful structure of economically segregated and unequal schools.

To be sure, that's not the sort of message that flies well in these times, when efforts to attack the problems of schools at the fountainheads of poverty and wealth are frowned on as failed strategies of a bygone era of liberal ideology. Above all, the accountability movement has been incredibly successful at framing the debate about school reform and improvement in the United States, persuading a largely uninformed public that more testing, more standards, and greater accountability for schools and teachers are the panaceas for whatever ails schools. Indeed, a 1997 public opinion poll conducted for Phi Delta Kappa International, the educational organization, showed that two in three Americans highly favored a national standardized test; that well more than half favored Bill Clinton's proposal for a national exam; and that most Americans are content to believe that the massive quantities of standardized testing in their schools is "about right." (14)

Perhaps the public is right in believing that government programs cannot rectify the social and economic inequalities that reproduce more inequality in public schools. But Americans fail to engage a genuine debate over the real problems with their schools at their collective peril. To continue to avoid that debate, to remain out of touch to the hard problems of American schools, means taxpayers will keep throwing good money after bad. They will continue to erroneously believe that more testing and higher consequences for poor test results, enforced by the power of the state, will fix what is wrong with American schools. The public will also be led down a particularly troublesome slippery slope: The nation remains at risk because the standards, testing, and accountability movement never went far enough. Repeating the age-old pattern that the fix for American schools lies in some new technological solution, Americans are likely to be told by the next generation of crusaders about the imperative for *national* standards and a *national* test to measure student performance against those world class standards.

Indeed, the next generation was already coming on the scene as I was writing this. About the time of the fifteenth anniversary of the 1983 *A Nation at Risk* report, a prominent group of school reformers and Washington policy elites, led by Ronald Reagan's former education secretary, William J. Bennett, had come out with just that message, in what might be called *Risk II.* Not surprisingly, they dubbed the sequel, *A Nation Still at Risk: An Education Manifesto.*

To be sure, *Risk* was in dire need of an update. Unfortunately for the movement's followers, it had been eclipsed by reality. The American economy's performance relative to all its international competitors was outright defying crusaders' gloomy predictions. Educational attainment was improving, as was student performance on the National Assessment of Educational Progress.

Addressing those difficulties for its message, *Risk II* pleaded that Americans had lapsed into a state of complacency about their schools, and it labeled critiques of the schools-in-crisis mentality as mere "fantasy." Recent poor international showing of American high schoolers on math and science (the so-called TIMSS study dissected in Chapter 6) was a key piece of new cannon fodder for the movement. Also, *Risk II* trotted out the tried-and-true straw men, including my favorite, supposedly held by "many educators" that "some boys and girls—especially those from 'the other side of the tracks'—just can't be expected to learn much." Demonstrating such concern for America's downtrodden provided much needed modernization for the crusaders' message.

Still, the take-home message of *Risk II* was the same as always: The nation's in peril because American schools are in a state of crisis. And the way to fix the problem was also essentially the same, but with some updated wrinkles. Yes, more standards, testing, and accountability—but make them national ones. Additionally, give parents and students more school "choice," permitting "public dollars to . . . follow individual children to the schools they select." (15)

All such solutions, in my view, will do little to address the root causes of the achievement gaps between rich and poor. In fact, these solutions constitute highly flammable rocket fuel that will make the underlying problems all the more severe, wasteful, and tragic.

Stopping the Damage

The lesson for parents, taxpayers, and policymakers seems clear. Addressing the real problems with American schools means coming to grips with the relationships between academic success and the pervasive influences of class, poverty, and race. I don't mean to be glib, but perhaps the very best way a parent can ensure their children's success in the school system, in terms of achievement and attainment, would be to obtain as much education for oneself as possible. But to do so, parents need the help of policymakers. If politicians are really interested in promoting equality, improving schools, and helping the American economy, they would, at a minimum, tear down false barriers to educational attainment that have been erected in the era of school accountability, barriers that have no proven benefit.

Indeed, if government can't feasibly "buy" equality in the schools owing to the political infeasibility of doing so in these neoconservative times, policymakers could try an alternatively novel approach, one of a genuinely conservative bent. How about just *get out* of the nation's classrooms? I'd like to stipulate for policymakers a maxim from the medical profession: First and foremost, *DO NO HARM.* In other words, if policymakers' endless tinkering, controlling, measuring, punishing, and manipulating of schools has failed children, the best thing they could do would be to stop hurting them.

To do that, state legislatures must go back to basics about the role of schools in a democratic society. In a larger society that tends to produce great inequalities between socioeconomic classes and ethnic groups, public schools have little place being a regulatory or credentialing agency that places the Good Housekeeping Seal of Approval on a school system's graduates. Schools should not be handmaidens to American business interests, which demand cheap and easy—and publicly subsidized—certification of alleged competency through achievement scores. *Public schools ought to have one overarching purpose in a free society: Provide citizens an opportunity to learn and ensure that those opportunities are equal across the lines of class and race.* American citizens ought to begin to question any public policy that does harm to that simple purpose. The public should apply their well-honed skepticism of modern institutions to hold accountable the accountability machine itself.

But a few affirmative, practical steps are in order as well. I would not go so far as to suggest that standardized tests have no legitimate purpose in American schools. In fact, they do; and that purpose is to periodically take the pulse of achievement but do so in a way that doesn't interfere with what should be the real business of schools: teaching and learning for understanding and long-term, sustainable achievement.

That means policymakers need to defang standardized testing programs, exorcizing the punishing consequences of poor test scores for students, teachers, and schools. Schools should compile and report testing data only for broad educational jurisdictions, and do so in terms of running averages over several years. That alone would discourage public and media obsession with meaningless, short-term changes in test results. States should reduce the economic drain of testing programs by rotating schools through the assessment system on a sampling basis. Doing this would also ensure that the test is broad in content, so results are sufficiently reliable and are an adequate indication of broad levels of student achievement. In short, such a test would by guided by the maxim that educational policymakers, first and foremost, *Do no harm.*

Alas, it might surprise some readers to learn that such a "test" already exists. In fact, it's been functioning remarkably well as America's educational barometer for some thirty years, and it's called the National Assessment of Educational Progress. Indeed, the NAEP isn't even really a test, in the sense standardized tests have come to mean in the accountability era. In a very real sense, NAEP, known as America's "report card," is simply a regularly conducted national survey of educational achievement in reading, writing, math, science, geography, and U.S. history, of Americans in grade school, middle school, and high school.

A report by the U.S. Office of Technology Assessment reminds us of the beauty of NAEP. "The designers of the NAEP project took extreme care and built in many safeguards to ensure that a national assessment would not, in the worst fears of its critics, become any of the following: a stepping stone to a national individual testing program, a tool for Federal control of curriculum, a weapon to 'blast' the schools, a deterrent to curricular change, or a vehicle for student selection or funds allocation decisions." (16)

Between the politically sensitive lines of that OTA report is a grave and prescient concern over any attempt to tinker with the NAEP that transforms it into a national standardized test along the lines of the Clinton and Bush administrations' proposals, a national test complete with individual scores and the horse-race mentality that invariably accompanies such an approach. Commenting on the safeguards built into the NAEP that recent national testing proposals had threatened to undermine, the University of North Carolina's Lyle Jones, one of the original technical advisers on NAEP's development, says, "Were these features not to have been maintained, I believe that NAEP would have become so controversial that it would not have survived to be the useful indicator of educational progress that it is today." (17)

The NAEP should be left alone, and it should remain the nation's report card. It's the only report card America really needs.

As anybody who's gone to school knows, there's a certain beauty in a report card, that periodic summary boys and girls have taken home to moms and dads since the beginnings of formal public education in the United States. Whether they're compiled in terms of As, Bs, or Cs, in the precise terms of decimal points, or even in narrative form in a teachers' handwriting, a report card is a meaningful thing.

A report card is a simple summation of a teacher's intimate and expert knowledge of a child's progress in school to that point. It is a simple answer to simple questions: *How am I doing? How's my child doing?*

And we all know this truth: A teacher knows. Teachers, working day in and day out with a child, who sees, hears, and reads the real work that child has actually accomplished at school, know. When parents really want to know the answer to the question, *How is my child doing?* they also know this: They go to the teacher, and they ask.

Teachers write down what they know about schoolwork of boys and girls in the report card. Parents have always put good report cards on the refrigerator door, and they have always known what a good report card meant. It meant keep up the good work. And they have always known what a bad report card meant. It meant there was room for improvement. It meant "work harder," "study more." Teachers and moms and dads did not need a standardized test or an accountability system to tell them what they already knew. They did not need to put the standardized test scores on the refrigerator door.

8

Unnatural Selection: Testing in the American Workplace

The Journalist

DAVID J. MORROW WRITES FOR THE *NEW YORK TIMES*, and he's been a hard-driving journalist at similarly prestigious publications for almost two decades. So it's not farfetched to suggest that Morrow has a certain aptitude and capability for journalism. After all, he's proven his worth as a reporter, rising to the pinnacle of the profession at the nation's best newspaper.

But it's a good thing for Morrow that, when he was hired in 1996, the *Times* didn't require job candidates to pass a preemployment aptitude test to qualify as a staff writer. It was probably a good thing for the newspaper, as well, that it relied on Morrow's proven track record in the field. Otherwise, the newspaper would have missed out on Morrow's obvious talents as a writer and reporter. Indeed, had the *Times* taken aptitude tests seriously, it would have discovered that journalism was decidedly not Morrow's best choice of careers. In fact, journalism was a rather poor choice, according to his abysmal test results on the job aptitude test Morrow took in 1996.

It all started when Morrow, a business reporter for the *Times*, saw the advertisements for the Johnson O'Conner Research Foundation in Manhattan. The organization's battery of aptitude tests was supposed to guide people to careers that matched their true talents and abilities. Additionally, Morrow says, the business desk at the paper had been getting numerous calls from readers seeking information about the exam. Readers wanted to know if the test was worthwhile. Morrow decided to find out by taking the tests himself and writing about his experience for the paper. The *Times* agreed to foot the $480 bill for the service, allowing Morrow free rein to describe his experience as he saw fit.

In a sense, Morrow's signing up for the test was the "ultimate setup," he told me, owing to the fact that he's usually bombed on standardized tests. He recalls taking the SAT in the late 1970s and scoring a mediocre 1,000 on the combined verbal and math tests. He defied that test's prognostications by graduating with Phi Beta Kappa honors in journalism and economics at the University of South Carolina in 1983.

"On standardized tests, I usually score in the single-digit percentiles," Morrow told readers of the *Times*, "a feat that once prompted a test administrator to call the home office to see if there had been a mistake in the scoring." But, Morrow says, he learned over the years to take his test scores with a healthy dose of skepticism. "I wasn't going to make the tests into something bigger than they should be," he told me.

The Johnson O'Conner test battery, consisting of several subtests, lasted almost three days, administered in the organization's luxuriously appointed headquarters in the Upper East Side, in a stately old home not unlike the Von Trapp's estate in *The Sound of Music,* as Morrow described it. (Indeed, it had been the home of a granddaughter of the railroad baron William H. Vanderbilt.)

Morrow's first two days of testing at Johnson O'Conner's testing center revealed few surprises: He was lousy at matching patterns of holes punched in paper—a test physicians and architects routinely ace. Morrow was remarkably good at recalling observed details, pointing him in the direction of detective work. As he expected, Morrow was less than stellar with math puzzles.

But on the last day, Morrow confidently figured, he'd prove his worth as a journalist on the language tests. The first of these would be the 100-word vocabulary exam, on which he had to pick the right meaning out of five often closely related alternatives. "You'd think that a reporter for *The New York Times* would have no trouble with words like rancor, obtuse, acrid and indigent," Morrow told his readers. "And you'd be right—for the most part. "But when I encountered gems like tyro, salubrious and effrontery, I waffled. This was not going to turn out as expected."

According to the aptitude test, Morrow's vocabulary skills fell short of what would be expected for a journalist. He was ranked at just the twenty-fifth percentile of all test takers on the vocabulary exam. But perhaps he'd save himself from any newsroom sneers and snickers on the "ideaphoria" test. On this subtest, the examiner asked Morrow to spew forth as many thoughts as he could on a given topic in six minutes. Figuring that's something journalists do routinely when writing news on deadline, Morrow expected to score highly on this test. Again, though, he figured wrong, scoring in just the tenth percentile on ideaphoria—among his worst performance in three days of testing.

How about analytical reasoning, then? Surely, as a business writer at the *Times*, where reporters must constantly survey and sift through the business environment for interesting and complex connections, trends, and contradictions on their respective beats, the ability to think critically and analytically was virtually a job requirement. Nevertheless, Morrow's analytical abilities were in the disabled range according to the aptitude test, which placed him at the fifth percentile. That meant 95 percent of the test takers on whom the test was standardized scored better than this *New York Times* business reporter.

What did the three days of aptitude testing all add up to for Morrow? Had an exceedingly productive journalism career, including jobs at *Time, Fortune,* the *Detroit Free Press,* and *Smart Money*, been a monumental fifteen-year mistake? Apparently so, according to the aptitude test, which concluded he'd do well at administrative tasks not so heavily dependent on top-notch language and reasoning skills.

I asked Morrow what he made of the whole exercise. "You have to be a little suspect," he says. "If I wasn't supposed to have been in journalism, I wouldn't have made it this far."

By the way, Morrow also visited a psychic in his search for career advice. She cost him just $60 and told him he was smart and creative. Sure, she was "way off base several times," Morrow says, regarding some personal and romantic matters. As for careers, the psychic was no less astute than the aptitude test costing $480. Says Morrow, "She told me to stay at the *Times.*"

Bible Scholars to Pro Football

Morrow's experience with job testing is sort of funny, ironic, and on the whole a fairly innocuous exercise in self-exploration. His journalistic ego appears to have survived intact, and he was never in any danger of losing his job at the *Times* because of a test score.

Still, Morrow is lucky. As a journalist, a line of work that puts great weight on what you can actually do, not how well you test, Morrow is among the increasingly few Americans whose working lives have not been profoundly touched by the testing game. Tens of thousands of other employers, on the other hand, require people to pass tests to get a job, keep a job, or be promoted to a better job.

Consider a few recent illustrations of the grip that standardized job testing has on the American workplace: In 1996, 43 percent of employers in one large sample tested job applicants for so-called "basic" literacy and math skills, up from 33 percent in 1990, according to the annual survey by the American Management Association. Other studies have shown that about half of American employers "rely on some form of testing as part of their employment process," drawing on an estimated 8,000 published mental tests by hundreds of test manufacturers. (1) But those estimates don't show the frequency with which tests are required for some types of jobs. The Bureau of National Affairs, for instance, in a survey of 245 companies, reported that fully nine of ten required preemployment exams for certain jobs, primarily clerical and office workers. (2)

Taking a standardized test to get a job is equally pervasive in the public sector. To match the supposed aptitudes of candidates to various jobs, the U.S. military gives the Armed Services Vocational Aptitude Battery to some 1 million recruits annually and the Office of Personnel Management tests hundreds of thousands of college graduates every year for professional jobs in the federal government—and tests some half million more each year for clerical jobs. Then there's the General Aptitude Test Battery (GATB), which states have adopted to screen government job applicants at the local level. By the mid–1990s, some thirty states were using the GATB to process 600,000 job applicants a year. (3)

Employment tests range from what you might expect to the just plain weird. Of course, there are the usual civil service exams, such as the Fireman Entrance Aptitude Tests, a paper-and-pencil test of 100 questions "designed to assess [an] applicant's aptitude for firefighting" and the Police Officer Examination, which among other things is supposed to measure "ability to exercise judgment and common sense."

Then, there are standardized tests for jobs that would seem a stretch for any pencil-and-paper exam. For example, many NFL football teams require their annual crop of potential draft picks to take a general intelligence test to ensure they've got the academic smarts for professional football (more on this later in the chapter). What is more, a search of one database on standardized tests for athletes yielded thirteen different exams, one devoted specifically to swimmers. The same database included seven exams for ministers.

There are standardized tests for wine tasters, baseball umpires, plumbers, ballroom dancing instructors, Bible scholars, and art collectors. And even writers. The Brand Emotions Scale for Writers, for instance, is supposed to "measure the emotions of writers immediately before writing, immediately after writing, and when writing in general."

One would be hard-pressed to find a line of work that doesn't require a certain score on one or more standardized test somewhere along the pathway to that job. These gatekeepers of occupational opportunity include general aptitude and intelligence tests for a variety of occupations, job knowledge tests, basic literacy skills tests, and personality tests. They also include the aptitude tests required of people seeking entry into the professions, such as the Law School Admissions Test, the Medical College Admissions Test, or even the Graduate Record Exam, which is almost always necessary for admission to graduate programs that lead directly to specific professions, such as economics, psychology, and social work.

Fueling this inexorable expansion of the standardized test into the lives of American workers is the belief held by most employers that such exams can sort the capable from the incapable, and thereby allow employers to select people who will contribute the most to the organization. American institutions arguably have chosen the quick fix in their selection methods, believing that cheap, *indirect* measures of human ability in the form of standardized tests are superior to the real deal—one's actual performance at real work.

But this cheap, standardized solution to selection and admissions decisions, which increasingly relies on indirect evidence of human ability, isn't working. In fact, according to the evidence in this chapter, test scores are decidedly poor predictors of one's job performance or career achievement. As a result, organizations frequently mismeasure the abilities of potential workers and professionals, at untold cost to the society in terms of lost profits and productivity, not to mention damage to American lives.

The Manager

After many years of experience as a civil rights investigator, television producer, and host of a public affairs TV program in Chicago, Carmelo Melendez figured he'd have an excellent chance to land the community relations job at Illinois Bell. The company wanted a fluently bilingual manager who could help it form stronger ties to Chicago's Hispanic community, and Melendez had these skills in boatloads.

Indeed, the company called *him*, several months after receiving his résumé, asking Melendez to come downtown for an interview. After three interviews, including two at the urban affairs department and one with human resources, Melendez was told about the test.

"You've got to take a test," the company's urban affairs manager, John McDermott, told Melendez when the interviews were over.

"I don't understand," Melendez protested. "I have my degree, I have the experience; I'm qualified for the job."

But there was no arguing with company policy, which required a passing score on a general aptitude test to merit further consideration for all entry-level managers at the company. And so in September 1988, Carmelo Melendez was taken into a room on the fourth floor of the company's downtown headquarters. Pencil and test in hand, Melendez sat with about ten other test takers that day, filling in bubbles on an exam known as the BSAT, the Basic Skills Abilities Test.

Welling up inside Melendez was a disturbing sense of déjà vu when he saw the test. He says he felt his mind go blank, unable to focus on the test questions. It was like he was seventeen again in East Chicago, Indiana, facing his very first American standardized test, one of several that would inform Melendez that he wasn't smart enough for his new country. At the age of fifty, after a lifetime of hard work and high achievement, always proving the counselors and testers wrong, here was yet one more test to overcome.

Melendez, now in his late fifties, immigrated to the United States from Puerto Rico with his parents when he was ten. The family landed initially in Utah, where his father got a job as a worker in the ore mines, and they moved to East Chicago in the early 1950s. There, his father found a laborer's job at Inland Steel, the company he would work for until his retirement.

When Melendez started school in East Chicago, he knew no English, and it took him several years just to catch up to his classmates at the Catholic school. These were days, of course, well before bilingual education in American schools. He was told to repeat the fourth grade, which Melendez says was a blow since he and his cousins used to have contests in Puerto Rico over who'd get the most As on their report cards. Carmelo usually won. "I got straight As in Puerto Rico," Melendez told me. "My family has always been very education-oriented."

Melendez's first encounter with an American standardized test came with a battery of aptitude tests he took while in high school. The results, altogether disappointing, prompted his high school counselor to give him the proverbial, "*You're not college material*" speech. He wanted to go to college, recalling an eye-opening trip he had once taken to the Indiana University campus at Bloomington. That's where he really wanted to go. But as fundamental Baptists, his parents wouldn't think of allowing Carmelo to leave the nest so young, and besides, there was no money for college.

So Melendez set his sights on the steel mill, but he aimed higher than just a laborer's job. There was an entry-level program for electricians at the plant, but he'd have to pass an aptitude test to be considered. Again, another test, and again, failure: He missed the cutoff point by a single point. By then, he began to recognize a familiar pattern from taking high-pressured, speeded-up, standardized tests of cognitive ability. "I've always had this aversion to tests," he told me. "When you put a clock in front of me it distracts me so much that I can't focus. It becomes very difficult for me to try to go fast, and the more I try the more difficult it is to concentrate. Taking speed tests, for me, is just a disaster."

Failing the electrician's test, Melendez was offered a laborer's job at the steel plant, but he refused it. "I was so upset and disappointed," he says. "I felt that if they would have hired me, I would have made a damned good electrician."

Melendez took some evening courses at Indiana University's local extension office, but lacking the money for school he wasn't able to continue. The only option at that juncture was the military. At the air force recruiting office, Melendez signed up to enlist, and the recruiters gave him a bus ticket to Chicago for a day of testing. The recruiters had him stay overnight at the YMCA.

He would spend the entire next day with the Armed Services Vocational Aptitude Battery, used to supposedly measure the intelligence of military recruits. "I went through the whole battery, and it was so unpleasant," Melendez says, recalling the time clocks and the examiner's "you've got 10 minutes to complete this test" refrain, and the other men in the room hunched over their desks. "It felt like we were cattle," he says.

At the day's end, an air force examiner approached Melendez. "Do you know how to speak English?" he wondered.

"Yes, I know how to speak English," Melendez answered.

"It's just that your scores. . . . I'm sorry, you didn't make it; you've just got some very low scores here," the examiner said. "You'll need to go back home, I'm sorry."

And there it was. Again, Melendez was informed that, according to this one and true yardstick of mental ability, he was an idiot, lacking the smarts to go to college, or be an electrician at a steel mill, or even a private in the air force. "That was so demoralizing, and I felt so inadequate," says Melendez. "My confidence in myself was just torn apart."

~

A little bit at a time, Melendez built a solid career and a good life, not allowing the tests to dictate what he was capable of doing. For a short while, he worked at a jewelry store. The pastor at his family's church suggested Carmelo might consider a career as an X-ray technician, a promising occupation in the 1960s. He took the pastor's advice, taking a two-year program in X-ray technology, and he quickly got his first job at the South Chicago Community Hospital. Soon, he was teaching other would-be X-ray technicians in addition to doing his own X-ray work at the hospital. "I loved X-ray," says Melendez. "I was very dedicated, and that's why I did well." He worked nine years at the same hospital.

Melendez loved the work but the pay wasn't great, as X-ray techs were among many hospital workers that had yet to be organized to negotiate with employers for better pay and working conditions. He got involved with a new union in Chicago, the Hospital Employees Labor Program, which had been trying to organize hospital workers.

Through his union organizing, Melendez met a member of the Indiana Advisory Committee to the U.S. Commission on Civil Rights, who, he says, had been impressed with Carmelo's skills at community organizing. The commission was becoming increasingly concerned that school desegregation wasn't being properly implemented, and providing for bilingual education was becoming a key piece of the puzzle. Melendez's contact recommended him to the commission's midwestern headquarters in Chicago for a job as a civil rights analyst. Melendez took the job, but was hesitant because the work would entail a lot of report writing, and, he says, "I wasn't a writer."

Yet he learned, not only writing and editing skills, but also investigative skills. Melendez spent about fifteen years at the commission. His job was to perform large-scale investigations on topics of compelling interest to the commission and to various communities in surrounding states. He was an investigator and coauthor of five major projects during his tenure at the commission, including investigations of bilingual education in Wisconsin and school desegregation in Deluth, Minnesota. He investigated the working and social conditions of migrant workers on Indiana farms.

Meanwhile, Melendez had been adding to his résumé in other important ways. For six years, he attended Governor's State University, taking night classes. He eventually obtained his bachelor's degree, graduating in the top half of his class. Also, an executive at a local TV station, whom Melendez had met while at the commission, approached him. Would he be interested in producing and hosting a TV talk show, one devoted to serious discussions of public affairs? Melendez had never done any such thing and was afraid he'd flop, but the executive persuaded him to do a pilot or two and see what happened. Melendez would end up spending several years at Channel 32, working part time to produce, write, and host the weekly program.

By the mid–1980s, Melendez's job at the commission was in danger, as Ronald Reagan was slashing federal programs. The U.S. Commission on Civil Rights wouldn't be spared, and in 1986, Melendez was "riffed," bureaucratese for "reduction in force." In his late forties, having earned a salary of some $40,000 a year, Melendez (who by now had a wife and children) was now without full-time work and benefits.

And so the idea of a "corporate job," with good pay and ample benefits, was looking better and better for a fifty-year-old man with a family. Indeed, the new position that had opened at Illinois Bell seemed the perfect fit. He'd be helping the company better serve the Chicago area's Hispanic community, and he'd be working in the security of a corporate environment. It would be a very good job.

~

Ostensibly because of a scheduling conflict, Illinois Bell deviated from its usual interview procedure with Melendez. Typically, the company required a job candidate to "pass" what was called a "structured interview" with the personnel office, followed by more informal interviews with people in the department doing the hiring. But in Melendez's case, the informal interviews came first.

What happened during those interviews is unclear, owing to the different claims of the people involved. Melendez told me that his interview with McDermott, head of the urban affairs department, struck him as a bit odd. I asked him how the interview went. "Quite frankly, I was relaxed," he says. "This guy has his feet on his desk . . . and the first thing he asks me is what did I think of Jesse Jackson." McDermott followed that question, Melendez says, with inquiries into his views of John Kennedy and affirmative action, none of which seemed to him entirely appropriate for the job as urban affairs manager. "It didn't feel like an interview."

The session lasted about thirty minutes, at the end of which Melendez was handed over to McDermott's assistant, Suzette Broom, for another interview. Under the pressure of litigation, McDermott would claim in court that his session with Melendez went poorly, among the worst he'd ever experienced. By Broom's account, her interview with Melendez went just fine. In any case, it may be telling that McDermott did pass Melendez to the personnel department to complete the structured interview. Sort of like an an oral exam, the interviewer asked Melendez a set of standard questions to assess his managerial and organizational skills. Melendez passed it with flying colors. (4)

As it turned out, the most daunting gatekeeper into the castle that was Illinois Bell was the BSAT. Having passed the gauntlet of three interviews, Melendez was told he still had to take the aptitude test. As for the test itself, AT&T psychologists actually developed the exam in 1979, and the Baby Bells adopted the test in the early 1980s to measure the "learning potential" of candidates for management jobs. The test consisted of 100 multiple-choice questions in math, grammar, reading comprehension, and following instructions. The test was "speeded," meaning job candidates had one hour to complete the 100 items; on the math section alone, test takers were allotted just twenty minutes for fifty questions. (5)

"It scared the living daylights out of me," Melendez recalls of the BSAT. "Here I was, fifty years old, and how long have I been out of school? I didn't remember the rules of grammar, and I wasn't good at that anyway. I was good at doing the work. I could come up with a project that was decent. But to sit there and be tested on the rules of grammar!"

Three days later, Melendez got a call from the Illinois Bell personnel department, informing him that he had not passed the aptitude test. Personnel also told him he could retake the exam in six months. For Melendez, the notion had little appeal. "I told them to stick the test," he says. "I said, 'I'm too old to be going through this again.' I was so demoralized, going through the same experience as I had in high school and the same for the service test. I said, 'I know I can do this job; I've got tons of experience.' It just felt unfair. So, I refused."

Eventually, there was anger, a hot and indignant anger about injustice, as Melendez began to examine his personal qualities that helped him to succeed at virtually all his life's endeavors. Asked how he had succeeded, without hesitation he said, "My hunger. My hunger to succeed. I wanted to find a way to succeed, and I wasn't going to let anyone or any test tell me what I can do and what I can't do. . . . I've proved over and over I can do difficult jobs, and do them well."

Through an acquaintance, Melendez hooked up with Elaine Siegel, a Chicago lawyer specializing in employment cases. At first, Melendez and Siegel tried to reach a settlement with the company, working with the Mexican American Legal Defense and Educational Fund, which had already established some dialogue with Illinois Bell on Hispanic employment matters. The effort failed. Melendez filed a complaint with the Equal Opportunity Employment Commission, alleging that the company's use of the BSAT—and the cut-scores attached to it—systematically discriminated against Hispanics. Indeed, according to the company's records, in 1987 and 1988 almost 90 percent of whites passed the BSAT compared to pass rates of 57 percent and 53 percent for African Americans and Hispanics, respectively. (6)

Again, there was no luck to be had with the EEOC. Its investigator surmised that the company's eventual hiring of a Hispanic, a man named Henry Lara, to fill the urban affairs job indicated on the face of it that the company's hiring practices weren't discriminatory. After losing his EEOC complaint, Melendez filed an employment discrimination suit in U.S. District Court. It was set for a jury trial in Chicago before Judge Brian Barnett Duff in September 1993.

It would be a lengthy legal battle. Melendez charged that Illinois Bell knew its BSAT lacked any meaningful relationship to the actual job duties for which it was supposedly testing. According to federal civil rights protections, an employment test "that causes a disparate impact on the basis of race, color, religion, sex, or national origin" is unlawful if it's not "job related." There seemed little doubt that Melendez had met the "disparate impact" litmus test, given the grossly different pass rates between minorities and whites on the BSAT; but did the disparity flow from a valid test related to the job, and did Illinois Bell intend to create the disparity by using the test?

At the trial, the jury decided in favor of Illinois Bell on the question of intentional discrimination, thus ruling out any possibility of punitive damages. But the district court ruled in favor of Melendez on the test's lack of job relatedness. Illinois Bell appealed that decision. By then, Melendez says, he'd reached the point of no return in the suit, having gone into debt to pay his lawyer's costs. If he didn't prevail in the appeal, he'd face financial calamity.

On March 27, 1996, more than seven years after Melendez was informed he wasn't qualified for the job because of his test score, the federal court of appeals agreed with the district court that Illinois Bell's use of the BSAT violated his civil rights. First, the appellate judges made clear that Melendez's scoring below the cutoff on the aptitude exam was the *only* reason Illinois Bell did not hire him. Indeed, McDermott claimed his interview with Melendez had gone poorly only after the lawsuit was filed, the court noted. Melendez, the Appeals Court wrote, "has sufficiently demonstrated that he was not hired due to his failure of the BSAT . . . "

The court also expressed a dim view of the BSAT's utility as a true test of skills to be an entry-level urban affairs manager. The judges took note of evidence presented at the trial by Dr. Fred Bryant, an expert in social science research methods at Loyola University in Chicago. Bryant found that the BSAT had no predictive power at all for Hispanics, and he discovered little evidence that the aptitude test predicted job performance for either whites or African Americans. Analyzing Illinois Bell's internal data, Bryant also found that what small correlations did exist between test scores and job performance had been inflated because of poor research methodology (see *Focus,* p. 186).

"Even if one uses the inflated overall data," the court wrote, "the BSAT predicts job performance only 3 percent better than chance alone." What is more, when Illinois Bell had hired an outside consulting firm—prior to the lawsuit—to review the BSAT's validity, the consultants concluded that "there is little or no support for the validity of BSAT scores in predicting the core areas of management performance." (7)

In fact, whites may have generally outperformed Hispanics on the pencil-and-paper test, as the figures quoted above indicate, but when it came to *actual job performance*, there were no measurable differences between the ethnic groups. "Importantly," the appeals court observed on this question, "the data from the validation study illustrate that, despite the large and statistically significant differences in test scores between whites and Hispanics, "there is no significant difference in job performance between the two groups."

"That was a glorious day," Melendez told me, recalling the favorable appeals decision. But for all the financial and personal toll that seven years of litigation had taken on Melendez and his family, he was awarded just $20,000 in lost wages plus his attorney's fees.

Still, despite the small compensation, Melendez says he was vindicated in an emotionally more satisfying way. Soon after Illinois Bell told him he couldn't be considered for the urban affairs manager because of his BSAT score, the U.S. Department of Housing and Urban Development hired Melendez as a fair housing investigator in Chicago. He quickly rose through the ranks. He was hired in February 1989, and by 1992 Melendez was promoted to branch chief in Chicago, where he supervised seven other investigators. In 1995 he won yet another promotion to be a division director in Dallas.

Melendez advanced his career at HUD without having to take job tests. "They know who can do the work," Melendez explained. "If I've worked for you for two years and I've closed forty cases and you have other investigators who have closed fifteen or twenty, that's how you measure whether I'm good or not. . . . They didn't have to test us. They already knew what we could do."

Having landed on his feet and proven himself at successively more challenging jobs, it would have been easy for Melendez to forget about the BSAT and Illinois Bell and get on with his life. But there was more at stake. "I wasn't going after money," he told me. "I truly believed, and I still do, that tests do not measure the ability of individuals. I had proven myself and had done everything required by this society, succeeding in college and at work, and I didn't need to prove myself again by passing another test. There should come a point in time when someone's work and reputation should be worth something."

As a final note on the Carmelo Melendez case, it's worth pointing out that Illinois Bell replaced the BSAT with a revised version called the BSAT-R. In fact, the new test was being developed even as the Melendez case ground on—though, in numerous depositions, company officials never admitted the existence of the new test. Illinois Bell has said the BSAT-R would be an improvement on the BSAT as a predictor of job performance. But Melendez, his lawyer Elaine Siegel, and expert Fred Bryant remain skeptical that the new one is any better.

"Thank God it turned out this way," Melendez says. But, for the sake of other job applicants barred from employment over a test score, "I wanted this company to stop using this test," Melendez says. "I'm still very concerned about the company. They're still using the test. They're still giving it to people in spite of all I went through and sacrificed. That really hurts."

A Question of Validity

When Troy Davis finished playing football at Iowa State University, he'd become the first player in college football history to rush for more than 2,000 yards in consecutive seasons. Despite his enviable record of actual job performance, however, red flags about Davis's ability to play football were raised among some NFL coaches and general managers after he scored poorly on a paper-and-pencil IQ test.

Each spring, at what's called the "scouting combine" held by National Football League teams in Indianapolis, prospective players show their stuff, including taking an intelligence test known as the Wonderlic Personnel Test. NFL teams require the exam apparently to ensure that potential players are mentally equipped to handle all those Xs and Os, whatever their strength, speed, agility, and specific knowledge about football acquired after a dozen years of experience of doing it, from the Pop Warner leagues through four years of college ball.

NFL prospects have just twelve minutes to complete fifty questions on verbal literacy, mathematics, analytical reasoning, and clerical speed and accuracy. First published in 1938 by E. F. Wonderlic, the exam continues to be produced by E. F. Wonderlic and Associates of Northfield, Illinois. Wonderlic says its intelligence test can apply to hundreds of occupations, from "warehouseman and custodians to engineers and administrators," according to one observer. (8)

Clearly, employers find a special appeal in tests such as the Wonderlic, primarily for simple reasons of economic efficiency. First, employers love that a twelve-minute test translates into quick and easy information for personnel administrators when they sift through stacks of job applications. Moreover, the test's designers contend the exam applies to all manner of jobs, based on the controversial theory that if somebody is "smart," that is, she scores highly on an intelligence test, then she's capable of high performance in virtually any job.

At the NFL combine, Davis ran the 40-yard dash in less than four and a half seconds, demonstrating partly why he was capable of rushing for 2,000 yards two years in a row. He'd proven over the course of four years of playing Division I college football that he was fully capable of high levels of achievement and performance at the actual job of playing football.

But it was his one-time score of 12 out of 50 on the paper-and-pencil test that raised coaches' eyebrows. Could it be that his accomplishments were a mere fluke? That the test now proved Davis was incompetent at running with a football and breaking tackles?

Indeed, for many employers, test scores have a talismanic quality. Many companies are mesmerized into believing standardized tests are cut-and-dried proof of someone's future job performance. Meanwhile, as we saw in the case of Carmelo Melendez, employers often ignore or discount evidence from one's work history that may be contrary to what they believe the tests prove. In Melendez's case, his impressive work record didn't even matter because he scored below the Illinois Bell cutoff level on an aptitude test.

There's little question that many employers see standardized tests as the be-all and end-all of efficient selection of employees. Listen to Wanda Campbell, manager of personnel research at the Edison Electric Institute, the research arm of a national consortium of electric utility companies: "Testing saves money by streamlining the selection process," Campbell says. "You can test twenty or thirty people in one hour with a pencil-and-paper test, the same time it takes to interview just one." The EEI consortium produces ten batteries of standardized tests for some 100 companies, making it the largest testing consortium of private businesses in the nation. The member companies rely on the tests to pick people for jobs ranging from meter readers to customer service reps to power plant operators. Says Michael Moomaw of Georgia Power, "Tests are the best way we have at our disposal to provide us with the most qualified candidates." (9)

But standardized testing is rife with danger, often inviting organizations to draw completely unfounded conclusions about the abilities of people. Indeed, because many employers rank-order job applicants by test scores, even tiny, statistically insignificant differences in scores prove to be decisive. This danger was underscored when one local government, seeking to fill more jobs with women, picked Diane Joyce for a dispatcher's job, the first woman to fill the position. One Paul Johnson sued the county, alleging he was more qualified for the job than Joyce. Why? Because he scored a 75 on the employment test—1 point more than Joyce's score.

No matter that, according to the laws of statistics, a single-point difference on a standardized test is meaningless because of measurement error (meaning that one can be confident only that a "true" score falls only within a fairly wide range of scores). In fact, no court that considered the Johnson suit ever questioned the assumed perfection of the test as a measure of merit. Michael Selmi, writing in the *UCLA Law Review*, says, "Based on that test score difference, the case reached the (U.S.) Supreme Court, under the apparent assumption that Mr. Johnson was better qualified than Ms. Joyce. Indeed, it appears that no one ever questioned, or even mentioned, that assumption, but it was simply accepted throughout the litigation without debate." (10)

On the Wonderlic, too, the danger of overinterpreting test scores is serious. First, there's the highly speeded nature of the exam. Fifty questions in twelve minutes translates to about fourteen seconds per item, rewarding speediness and penalizing slower or more thoughtful thinkers. As a result, the test may be "overly difficult," says psychology professor Kevin Murphy, writing in *Test Critiques*. He points out that, among the initial comparison group consisting of 370,000 people on whom the Wonderlic was initially tested, fewer than 1 percent answered even forty questions correctly, and less than 15 percent got scores of at least 30.

What is more, users of the Wonderlic tests might draw unfounded conclusions about somebody's cognitive ability based on small differences on the fifty-point scale. For instance, Davis's score of 12 would put him only somewhat below average in terms of other types of IQ tests. But when NFL teams use the Wonderlic, they are led to believe that such a low score renders him almost mentally incapable.

Even scores between 16 and 22 on the Wonderlic, according to the test's technical manuals, "suggests a limited capacity for anything other than routine tasks for elementary training approaches," says Murphy. He notes that such scores fall in the range of 93 to 104 on standard IQ tests, which is right about average. That means employers relying on the Wonderlic guidelines would pass over many job applicants having average intelligence (as measured on IQ tests), who'd be perfectly capable of doing jobs requiring far more than mindless and routine tasks.

How much does the Wonderlic matter for NFL teams? More, perhaps, than the ordinary sports fan might think. "It can turn a first-round pick into a third-round pick if he's got a terrible test score, no question," one NFL personnel director told *Sports Illustrated*'s Richard Hoffer in 1994.

Indeed, actually playing quarterback at the highest levels of intercollegiate competition, and well enough to win a Heisman, was apparently insufficient to overcome a relatively low Wonderlic score for one player. In April 1994, Hoffer says, "the Atlanta Falcons passed on Florida State quarterback and Heisman Trophy winner Charlie Ward, who was rumored to have bombed the Wonderlic (and went undrafted). . . . Judging from the buzz on the talk shows, a lot of Falcon fans wondered if maybe the folks in the front office shouldn't be taking the Wonderlic instead of the kids." (11)

A different question altogether is whether the IQ test actually does much to improve NFL predictions of superior performance on the field. Dave Shula, coach of the Cincinnati Bengals in 1994, had his doubts. "I've seen guys who have scored very, very high on those tests, and then you put them on a football field and they cannot learn," he says. "And then I've seen guys who have poor reading and writing skills, but you put them on the football field and you tell them something, and they do very, very well." (12)

To be sure, many other coaches are true believers in the tests. "A player needs a baseline mental capacity to play this game," San Francisco 49ers president Carmen Policy once said. "When you're talking about quarterbacks and offensive lineman, you need even more intelligence, especially in our system. For us, the Wonderlic test is a way of measuring that intelligence." (13)

By such reasoning, then, Pat McInally, a Harvard graduate who had a ten-year NFL career as punter, ought to have instead made one of the greatest quarterbacks or offensive lineman in NFL history. He's the only player known to have scored a perfect 50 on the Wonderlic.

Test Scores and Job Success

Actually, many employers don't really know what standardized employment tests prove, because they have little evidence that the tests can predict someone's true capability to do the job. According to the Bureau of National Affairs, just 50 percent of employers actually determined the validity of their job tests, following federal guidelines to help employers avoid testing programs that violate antidiscrimination laws. (This doesn't mean those 50 percent of job tests were necessarily valid, only that the employers had done the investigations.)

Such validity studies generally entail gathering evidence of job performance, say supervisor ratings—or even yardage rushed in the case of the NFL—and compare those performance measures with test results of employees. Validity studies show the degree to which test performance is associated with job performance. Were employers to more frequently scrutinize their job tests in this light, there's little doubt many would discover that paper-and-pencil tests simply cannot provide a true and full account of why some people do well at jobs and achieve a high level of success in an occupation, while others do not.

Perhaps a great deal of the stock employers have placed on paper-and-pencil job tests can be traced to John Hunter's work for the U.S. Employment Service (USES). Hunter synthesized the results of some 515 USES validity studies, covering several hundred jobs, between 1945 and 1980. All the studies in Hunter's analysis had examined the predictive validity of the General Aptitude Test Battery. This federally-sponsored cognitive ability test is used by about 1,800 state employment service centers across the country to screen some 19 million people a year for jobs in the public and private sector.

Hunter concluded that the GATB was, on average, fairly predictive of job success across a variety of occupations. In statistical terms, Hunter estimated the GATB's overall correlation coefficient, its *r*, at about 0.5. Recall that the *r* must be squared to get a true sense of a variable's ability to account for changes in another variable. Thus, according to Hunter, scores on the GATB alone could be expected to predict 25 percent of the variation in job performance for potential employees. (14) What's more, Hunter made some startling predictions of the economic benefits of ability testing. He reckoned that more capable and productive workers selected on the basis of a widely expanded role for the GATB would pump an additional $80 billion into the U.S. economy. (15)

With these impressive results for the test in hand, by the late 1980s the USES began to push for a much expanded role for the GATB, arguing it could apply equally well to all of the some 12,000 different jobs in the United States. The notion was reminiscent of the American experience with intelligence testing much earlier in the century, when IQ testing's proponents had argued that *g*—Spearman's shorthand for general intelligence—was about the only human trait that mattered for human mental ability. Since being "smart" was necessary for success in virtually all jobs, the USES's reasoning now went, then a single test for intelligence would predict success in any job. The notion had obvious economic and bureaucratic appeal.

The main hitch, however, as always, was over questions of fairness and accuracy. Given systematic differences in GATB scores that had been observed between whites and most minority groups, what would be the social and economic impact on minorities of such a vastly expanded role for the GATB?

So the USES sought a second opinion, contracting with the National Academy of Sciences and its research arm, the National Research Council (NRC), to evaluate several dimensions of the GATB. Central to the NRC's task was to investigate the power of the exam to predict success at work. In turn, it would take a closer look at the extravagant claims for job testing's ability to add $80 billion to the American economy.

The NRC reanalyzed Hunter's 515 studies as well as an additional 264 validity studies, for a total of 755 empirical studies covering some 38,500 workers who took the GATB over the years. In its report, the NRC took exception to several assumptions in Hunter's work that the committee believed had considerably inflated his estimates of the GATB's validity. Accordingly, the NRC slashed Hunter's estimates nearly in half, estimating the GATB's overall validity coefficient ranged from just 0.2 to 0.4. Squaring the average *r* of 0.3, then, means that scores on GATB could be expected to account for *just 9 percent of the variation in job performance* among workers. (16)

On the question of the economic benefits of employment testing, the NRC report noted that the present state of economic knowledge and technique rendered such an estimate virtually impossible to undertake. Still, the NRC's report concluded that "both the logic and the numbers used in the estimate of $80 billion to be gained from testing are flawed, and that an estimate in the range of $1.5 billion to $10 billion is more plausible." (17)

It's worth pointing out, however, that this quite modest conclusion reflects only the estimated *benefit* side of the economic equation of testing. It says nothing about direct and indirect costs associated with testing, costs that might include, for instance, effects of employers not selecting more productive employees who fail to score above a certain cutoff.

"The claim of omnipotence for the GATB," the National Academy report concluded, "is based in part on the idea that the test measures some attribute that underlies performance in all jobs, an attribute that is usually identified as intelligence, or *g*. There are dangers in promoting intelligence testing to which policy makers should be sensitive. Data from intelligence testing were misused in the early twentieth century in a way that fed the racial and ethnic prejudices of the day, and the potential for generating feelings of superiority in some groups and inferiority in others is equally great today." (18)

~

Although the National Academy report focused on just one test, the GATB, in the journal *Research in Higher Education* Leonard L. Baird examined many different standardized tests in an important 1985 study. At some eighty pages in length, Baird's is among the most wide-ranging and exhaustive literature reviews on the question of standardized tests' ability to predict workplace success.

In Baird's review of this large body of work, one is struck by the paucity of evidence that paper-and-pencil tests have even a modest ability to foretell one's prospects of career achievement.

Finding relatively poor powers of prediction for many standardized tests was by no means novel. For example, in a 1959 study of 10,000 air force cadets, Thorndike and Hagan compared aptitude test scores with the cadets' eventual success in the labor force, measured by income, numbers of employees they supervised, job satisfaction, and so on. The cadets fell into some 100 different occupational groups. Aptitude tests predicted job success no better than if one had flipped a coin.

"This would suggest that we should view the long-range prediction of occupational success by aptitude tests with a good deal of skepticism and take a very restrained view as to how much can be accomplished in this direction," Thorndike and Hagan concluded. (19)

Baird, for his part, focused on studies done between 1966 and 1984, reported in any of nineteen highly-regarded scholarly journals. A look at just a handful of this work illustrates the pattern of consistent weakness in the predictive powers of test scores:

Highly creative people. Several studies of highly creative scientists, teachers, artists, and other people showed that intelligence or aptitude test scores, beyond some threshold level, were virtually meaningless in differentiating their accomplishments. Of decisive importance, however, were other behavioral traits unrelated to cognitive abilities measured on tests. These included a willingness to take risks, a "bohemian" nonconformity, motivation to succeed, and similar personal qualities. (20)

High-level professionals. Baird presented several studies that measured how well test scores predicted career achievement in various professional groups, such as engineers, biologists, and those with doctorates in scientific fields ranging from mathematics to chemistry. Often, the studies compared standardized test scores early in one's career, such as the Graduate Record Exam required for entry into graduate training programs, to his or her eventual career success. Success in these studies was measured variously by publication frequency, income, and job performance reviews.

In study after study and test after test, many of the reported validity coefficients were zero or near zero, and some even showed a *negative* correlation between career success and test scores. For instance:

- One study tracked the career success of National Science Foundation fellows, who had taken the GRE to compete for fellowships several years before. The study compared their test scores to numbers of patents, income, frequency with which the fellow's work was cited in scientific literature, confidential reports by colleagues, an overall productivity rating, and so on. Consider the biologists. The study found their GRE verbal test correlated with productivity and income in the range of 0.06 to 0.08, which for practical purposes is zero. The correlation between the GRE quantitative test and frequency of being cited in the biology literature was an r of 0.29. Squaring that result means the test score could still account for only about 8 percent of the variation in citations among the biologists. (21)
- A huge study of some 6,300 doctorates in math, physics, chemistry, biochemistry, and psychology—the largest one that Baird reviewed—also found essentially zero correlation between academic aptitude and citation counts. (22)
- A study of 239 chemists, 142 historians, and 221 psychologists compared their GRE score with the numbers of articles and book chapters they'd published. GRE verbal and quantitative scores had near-zero correlations. For historians, interestingly, all the correlations between aptitude test scores and publishing record were *negative*. "In fact," says Baird, "*the largest number of publications was reported by the lowest scoring groups in all three fields*" (emphasis added). (23)

Business executives and managers. Baird also provided evidence from several studies of business executives and managers after graduating from MBA and other business or technical training programs. In general, these studies showed weak associations between career achievement and scores on business aptitude tests.

On the other hand, a manager's grades during graduate business training were generally much stronger predictors of career success. Indeed, results of one study prompted the authors to suggest "a second look at the practice of selecting persons for higher education solely or largely on the basis of academic aptitude or achievement." (24)

A decade after Baird's report came another exhaustive review of studies about the validity of employment and aptitude testing. Authors Terry W. Morris and

Edward M. Levinson aimed their 1995 survey in the *Journal of Counseling Development* at school counselors. According to Morris and Levinson, counselors often harbor an uncritical acceptance of intelligence and aptitude tests as predictors of career achievement. However, according to the evidence presented, counselors might do well to reconsider their assumptions.

Like Baird's review, their findings from some fifty years of scholarly literature on the question amounts to pretty thin support for standardized tests to predict workplace success. First, the authors compiled results of several studies that reported IQs for various occupations. The list is enlightening in that the studies often had major inconsistencies about just how smart people in various careers might be. For instance, in one 1984 study, physicians had exceedingly high IQs of 145, but in an earlier study they were grouped with lawyers, librarians, and cops as having IQs of 115, a bit above average. Writers in one study were really smart, with IQs of 122, but hardly better than average in another. Interestingly enough, plasterers had measured IQs at the near-genius level of 130 in one study, comparable to chemists, accountants, and mechanical engineers. College professors in one study had the intelligence of sales clerks and file clerks in another study. (25)

When the results of these many IQ-occupation studies are examined as a whole, any school counselor would see a rather discouraging picture for the predictive ability of aptitude tests when advising their fledglings. Morris and Levinson say the message to be gleaned from these data is "that there is no agreed on score that guarantees potential success in an occupation. It can be said that the higher an individual's I.Q., the greater the probability the individual has the potential to complete the educational requirements necessary to gain employment in high status occupations that require more formal education." (26)

Of course, that reasoning has a discomfiting ring of circularity. One has "potential" to succeed if one has "potential," that is, high aptitude test scores—which happen to be necessary for entry to high-status careers via educational training programs. But to what extent is that potential translated into actual achievement within a career?

For the many studies Morris and Levinson included in their survey, covering all sorts of jobs, the highest reported correlation between test scores and career success was, in fact, that found by Hunter of GATB fame whose estimated r of 0.5 was, of course, subject to much qualification in the National Academy of Science's report. Many reported correlations between IQ scores and various career achievements were zero, some were even negative (machine tenders), and most hovered in the range of about 0.3 or 0.4. The latter range of correlations translates to about 12 percent of the variation in career achievement explained by IQ scores, leaving nearly 90 percent attributable to other factors.

"In most cases," Morris and Levinson conclude, "the relationship between intelligence and occupational and vocational variables is moderate at best. Hence, factors other than intelligence play a major role in influencing occupational and vocational adjustment. . . ."

Even then, with the clear weight of the explanatory evidence coming down on the side of those "other factors" besides IQ scores, the authors, both experts in counseling psychology, appear reluctant to degrade the importance of IQ tests in the work of counselors, invested as they are in intelligence testing as a tool of their trade. Thus, the authors recommend, those other noncognitive factors "must be considered in combination with intelligence when generating vocational recommendations. (27)

The Teachers

"I can tell you who won't be a great teacher, the idiots who took that test and flunked so miserably."

That's Massachusetts Speaker of the House, Thomas Finneran, reacting to news that some 40 to 60 percent of the state's prospective teachers had failed the state's first-ever teacher certification test in April 1998. Finneran took the results of a standardized test hook, line, and sinker, without for a moment stopping to consider whether the pencil-and-paper exam tells us anything useful about the competency of teachers.

The most important distinction between the testing of teachers and other occupations is political. In the obsessive drive to make schools more "accountable" to taxpayers, policymakers at all levels of government, from the White House to local school boards, have pursued a basketful of supposed educational reforms they contend will bring American schools up to "world-class standards." The linchpin of the reforms has been tests: a lot more of them and ever greater stakes attached to them.

The political solution was simple: The route toward better schools, in part, would be paved by better teachers. Well and good. But, according to reformers, the way to ensure teacher competence was to make them pass a competency test. To an unassuming public, which largely has viewed test scores as a black-and-white reflection of competence or incompetence, the politicians' answer has had the clear ring of truth.

Caught up in the hysteria over more accountable schools, elected representatives have tended to gloss over concerns that such teacher tests may not reflect the truth about a given teacher's competence. And Thomas Finneran is hardly alone.

"We all want the best people," says Thomas Fisher, the state of Florida's director of testing. "These tests are to protect the public welfare from incompetents in the classroom. That is what it boils down to." (29)

"The Test Is the Problem"

Meet Julie Gauthier, one of the alleged "idiots" who flunked the Massachusetts teacher test. Amid the political squealing over the test results, Board of Education Chairman John Silber blamed the state's teacher training programs, which "dropped their standards to negligible, risible proportions," he told the *NewsHour with Jim Lehrer*. But Gauthier is one prospective teacher who has never set foot in

FOCUS: SHOE SIZES, SALARIES, AND THE "FALSE CORRELATION PARADOX"

When poring over the various validity studies and reams of statistical evidence supplied by Illinois Bell in Carmelo Melendez's lawsuit against the company over its aptitude test, Elaine Siegel began to notice something rather strange.

Examining Illinois Bell's statistics on the purported validity of the BSAT exam, Siegel noticed that the test's power to predict various aspects of job performance was always higher for the combined samples of minority and white test takers than for each of the ethnic groups individually.

For instance, take the job performance criteria of "written communication" in Illinois Bell's validation studies for entry-level managers. For whites, the "correlation coefficient," known as the *r* value in statistical parlance, was measured at 0.21. Squaring that number means BSAT scores could account for about 4 percent of the variability in the writing skills of whites. The BSAT's *r* value for black test takers' writing skills was found to be about 0.26, slightly more predictive than for whites.

Curiously, however, Siegel noted that the BSAT's predictive validity for the entire group of black and white test takers was reported at 0.28 for writing skills—higher than for either of the subgroups separately. And so it went for some fifteen other measures of job performance. Given that the company was offering the combined, or pooled, correlations as its chief evidence of the BSAT's validity, the anomaly was of crucial importance for her client, Carmelo Melendez.

"I started looking at the data, and it puzzled me, and I became, frankly, suspicious," Siegel told me. "How could you have that pattern? It defied common sense."

What was going on here? Siegel, a lawyer, and her colleague, Dr. Fred Bryant, an expert in psychological statistics at Loyola University in Chicago, believe they've discovered the answer. If they're correct—and there's little reason at this juncture to believe otherwise—several decades' worth of conclusions about even the modest amount of utility for standardized tests in academia and employment may have to be tossed out the window.

It's called Simpson's Paradox, apparently named for the scientist who discovered the problematic nature of statistical correlations pooled from very different sorts of samples, the statistical equivalent of erroneous comparisons of apples to oranges.

The way to see it, Siegel and Bryant say, is to imagine a job interviewer telling an applicant to take off her shoes so he can determine what salary to offer. How so? It turns out that the interviewer would be quite accurate to say that American salaries are fairly well correlated with shoe size, owing to two facts: men tend to earn more than women and they have bigger feet.

Imagine a graph. On the vertical axis is salary and on the horizontal axis is shoe size. Plotting the data on average salary levels for various shoe sizes, one would find a cluster of dots in the lower left part of the graph. Those would be the women: smaller feet, lower pay. In the upper right corner of the graph would be the men, with their bigger feet and average higher salaries.

Now, here's the paradox: The shoe-size and salary correlation for the whole lot of men and women together is represented by a line sloping upward to the right that connects the women's dots on the lower left part of the diagram with the men's dots in the upper right.

Looking at the data this way suggests a rather substantial relationship between shoe size and pay. Indeed, in one realistic data set that Siegel and Bryant compiled, the correlation between shoe size and pay was estimated at 0.78, which means that shoe size alone would "explain" an astounding 60 percent of the variation in salary among all employees!

But when the shoe-size and salary data for men and women are separated, a much different impression of the relationship between pay and shoe size emerges. If one were to draw separate lines that best fit each cluster of data, one line through the men's data and another line through the women's, both lines would be virtually flat. In other words, the "true" relationship between salary and shoe size would be zero. (28) That, Siegel and Bryant say, is a variant of Simpson's Paradox, which they call the "false correlation paradox." If one wants to know the true statistical relationship between salary and shoe size for people in general, the way out of the paradox is to make certain technical adjustments to the shoe size data for both genders to make them comparable.

FIGURE 8.1 The False Correlation Paradox

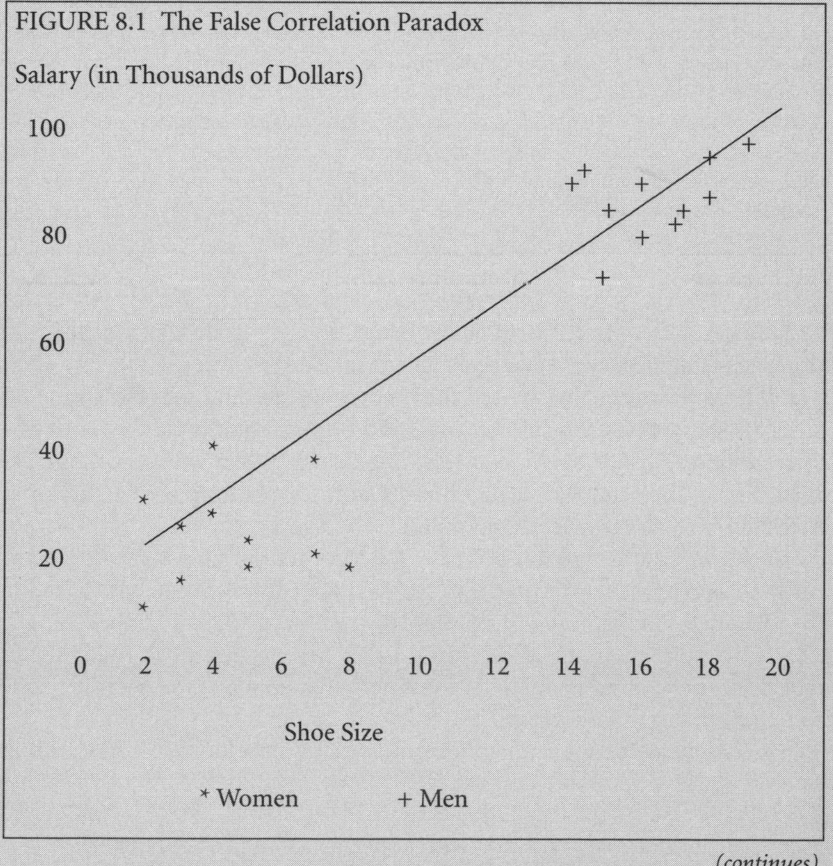

(continues)

(continued)

That's exactly what they did on the Illinois Bell test validity data that Siegel found so puzzling. After making the adjustments for the different sets of data, they found that the predictive validity of the company manager's aptitude test all but disappeared for both whites and minorities.

"If one group scores higher than another on the test and/or higher on the performance criterion, then validity coefficients cannot be trusted if they are based on the data of these two groups simply pooled together," Bryant told me.

In any case, Siegel and Bryant believe, the false correlation paradox has pervaded studies on standardized test validity because most studies have based validity coefficients on combining data from disparate groups of people. Taking the paradox into account has the potential to capsize the entire corpus of validity generalizations compiled by the testing industry and other various researchers over the years.

Their findings are especially troubling for the gigantic "meta-analysis" of the past, such as those conducted by John Hunter for the Department of Labor. In meta-analysis, researchers synthesize results from many studies to derive the power of tests to predict job or academic performance. Hunter, as we saw in the National Research Council's reanalysis of his validity studies on the federally sponsored GATB, claimed, of course, to have found substantial correlations between test scores and performance—results with which the research council took strong exception.

But the National Research Council did not consider Simpson's Paradox. Because many past job-test validity studies are based on pooled data for men, women, blacks, and minorities, Siegel and Bryant say, the resulting correlations between test scores and job performance have been inflated, and the entire job-testing industry may be standing on a housc of cards.

an education school. Indeed, on closer inspection, it's likely that Gauthier was one of many test takers who was too smart for the test itself.

Gauthier, a history major, passed the literacy and reading sections of the new teacher test but missed the cutoff score of 70 by seven points on the exam's history section. As a result, she had at least one firm job offer withdrawn. One administrator at the school that had hired Gauthier, pending the results of the certification test, was clearly disappointed.

"I think our school system's policy will be not to hire unless certified which means she won't get the position with us," said the administrator, who asked not to be identified. Taking note of her impressive academic record and teaching experience, the administrator also said Gauthier had provided "SUPERB recommendations (her emphasis.) "This is absolutely an example of the horrors that are resulting from this testing mania." (30)

What does the academic and work record of an "idiot" look like? In Gauthier's case:

- A bachelor's degree in history, with a specialization in world history, from Fordham University in 1994. She spent her junior year at the Sorbonne in Paris, studying French and French history. At Fordham,

Gauthier was elected to Phi Alpha Theta, the history honor society. Grade point average: 3.2 overall, 3.4 in history.

- A master's degree in the teaching of history from Northeastern University. The program, by the way, was in the history department, not the education school. Grade point average: 3.8.
- A year of intense graduate work at Queens University in Northern Ireland, where she received the Post Graduate Certificate in Education (PGCE), the principal teaching credential in Great Britain.

Rounding out her curriculum vitae, Gauthier spent eight months traveling around the world after college, worked as a legal secretary for about a year before going to graduate school, and landed the first director's position at the newly created World History Resource Center at Northeastern, the first such center in the Northeast.

Gauthier's experience at Queens University in Belfast would prove particularly instructive for Silber and Finneran. Gauthier, the first American ever to be admitted to the program, was one of 200 prospective teachers in a course of study on education and politics, combining coursework on theory and policy with classroom teaching experiences. The program placed a scholarly emphasis on the training of teachers—in the "teachers as scholars" model. Besides her coursework, Gauthier taught at two schools with very different kinds of students and economic circumstances. One was Saint Louise's Comprehensive College, located in the Catholic nationalist area of West Belfast. At the other extreme, Gauthier also taught at the Royal Belfast Academic Institute, where she worked with eighteen-year-olds of "very high ability."

Culminating her achievements at Queens University, Gauthier was awarded the Elizabeth Fulton Prize for teaching and writing, in a competition with her 200 classmates. The annual prize, awarded to the most outstanding teacher-scholar in the program, was based on her performance evaluations as a teacher as well as an outside examiner's assessment of her writing during the yearlong program.

In short, it's probably fair to say Julie Gauthier knew something about history and teaching when she showed up at the Cambridge Rindge and Latin High School in Cambridge, Massachusetts, on July 11, 1998, to take the state's teacher test, which would, purportedly assess her knowledge of verbal and numerical literacy, reading, and her knowledge in her teaching specialty, history.

The first thing Gauthier noticed about the history section of the test was its historically confusing presentation, with multiple-choice questions randomly ordered without any organization according to either historical themes or chronology. As a historian, Gauthier says, it's difficult to shift from theme to theme if one is interested in being thoughtful about history.

"There'd be a question about the Pilgrims and the next second there'd be one about Hinduism and Buddhism. Each question required you to think about that era and what was going on, and it was very difficult for me to switch in and out,"

Gauthier told me. Still, she says, "The test itself was not difficult. I thought it was very easy—easy for the right person right out of school who had prepared for this test with a textbook."

That was the second feature about the history test Gauthier noticed, its particularly textbookish view of history. Indeed, she'd spent the last few years of graduate work trying to go well beyond that approach. For her, the analysis of and reasoning about history were central to being a good teacher of history, not a field that lent itself to black-and-white interpretations. Indeed, genuine scholars and truly academically inclined students view textbook knowledge with a great deal of skepticism. True, most undergraduate textbooks are useful as relatively simple, if often a bit dumbed-down, entry points to a field, but beyond that, memorizing textbook facts provides one with little insight.

Gauthier says, "I kept asking myself, how is this testing whether I'm going to be a good history teacher?"

Indeed, if a test taker has gone beyond the textbook approach to learning, she's in danger of being too smart for the test. Somebody in that situation would be more sophisticated about a field of knowledge than the test is capable of tapping. Gauthier was among the Massachusetts test takers who found herself in exactly that unfortunate circumstance.

One history item on the test, for instance, asked about the Renaissance and its origins. Gauthier found herself wondering what the testers were looking for, and the answer was much more complicated than what the test led one to believe. "The test was so Eurocentric from my perspective, and I'm trying not to be Eurocentric. In talking about the Renaissance, most textbooks will talk about the Renaissance starting in Florence, Italy," says Gauthier. Scholars, meanwhile, have discovered that the Italian Renaissance actually borrowed many ideas of Muslim Spain. "But for this test, the Renaissance started in Italy. I see its roots being much deeper, and that was problematic for me," Gauthier says. "I knew more about the depth and breadth of the Renaissance, but it wasn't the right answer."

For all the teacher test's internal shortcomings, what's irritatingly troublesome about Gauthier's story is that she's *never* done well on standardized tests. Her failings on such tests have forced her to jump through hoops that better test takers would never dream of encountering.

Thinking about going to college, Gauthier had set her sights on Fordham because of its history program. She had been inspired to study history, and study it hard, after an oversees trip as a fifteen-year-old, when she ran into European kids who had embarrassed her with her scant knowledge about the world. In Germany, she recalls, kids had asked if she'd read Proust. When she pleaded ignorance, they'd been curious how she could not know about the famous French writer. "I became so angry with my teachers and parents. I felt completely undereducated because those German kids were so far above my education level," Gauthier says.

But Gauthier literally had to talk and write her way into Fordham because her SAT scores were lacking. "I've never done well on standardized tests," she says. "They've influenced me every step of the way, a hindrance that I have to go out of my way to overcome. I'm an above average student, a hard worker and have talent as a communicator. But people look at my test scores and automatically think the worst. I've had to sell myself on my talents. Even getting into college. I wanted to go to Fordham but I knew my SATs were not up to par. Applying to Fordham, I knew I would have to sell myself to them, so I wrote a million essays. If anyone meets me they know I'm ambitious and enthusiastic."

For Northeastern's master's program, as well, Gauthier's scores on the Graduate Record Exam were below those for the program's typical graduate student. "I had to beg my way into school," she says. "I assured them that if I got in, I'd pull out the grades. And I've proven that I can easily do the work."

Gauthier says the dread of yet another test to overcome worried her when she learned of the state's standardized test for new teachers. "I feel that I have so much more potential than any of the tests say I do," she says. "I've been fighting them all my life, so when I found out I had to take the teacher test, I knew I was going to have a problem."

For people like Gauthier who have had to outmaneuver a test score in order to achieve up to one's potential, it's a particularly galling experience when he or she is more intelligent than the test itself. When Gauthier finally saw the new teacher test, its multiple-choice questions glared back, calling as always for the "one best" answer.

"A multiple-choice question is going to give you three or four various responses, and what if I don't agree with those because I've got three of my own?" she says. "Because of my history education, I'm trained to think critically and analytically about history. There is never one correct answer, especially with history. History is conceptual and theoretical, there are so many different perspectives and viewpoints. That test regarded history as a series of events and facts that didn't allow for any other interpretations."

Not long after Gauthier received her test results from the Department of Education's automated phone system, she was interviewed by Fox News about the teacher test. By then, the high failure rate across the state had elicited a great deal of discussion and controversy. Her sound bites were so pointed—and apparently, so embarrassing to state education officials—that she was invited to the offices of the commissioner of education, Dr. David Driscoll, for a sort of chat. She met first with Driscoll's chief of staff, Alan Safran, and then briefly with Driscoll himself. Gauthier says the experience was "very enlightening." They asked Gauthier, "What can we do to please you," she says, and it seemed clear they meant "her" personally.

Many test takers, meantime, had been expressing concerns about the fairness with the state's procedures in implementing the new test. They said the test was rushed into print, and so there were no study guides available so they might prepare for the exam. Test takers also say they were misled about the importance of the first exam, having been informed that the first administration would be a pilot run and thus wouldn't keep anyone from being certified.

But at her meeting, Gauthier told Driscoll and Safran she wasn't interested in just her own failure to pass the test nor just those logistical problems with the first administration. Her main concern, she told the officials, was the nature of the test itself. "'You can please me by not making this test eighty multiple-choice questions,'" she said. "But they just looked at my test score and kept asking if I thought the test was fairly done."

Gauthier proceeded to give Saffron and Driscoll a small lesson on what made for good teaching. "I said, 'No, that's not the problem. The test is the problem. This is not testing what teachers *do*. If any teacher actually taught the way this teacher test would encourage them to do, with a lot of recall and multiple choice, and if any parent saw their kid reciting events, dates and names, that teacher would be out of there. That's not what teaching is about.'"

~

Anecdotally, at least, there was ample evidence emerging from the Massachusetts teacher test suggesting the new exam, a product of National Evaluation Systems, was troubled with weakness in sorting competent from incompetent teachers.

For instance, there was the case of Nancy Schmeing, who had recently earned her doctorate in physics at the Massachusetts Institute of Technology. Incredibly, Schmeing failed the reading comprehension section of the new teacher test, which required one to quickly read short essays and then choose the one "best" answer among those provided by the test maker. The exam supposedly assessed one's ability to boil down the essential meanings of prose. Schmeing's failing the reading section created a small furor about the test's credibility. After graduating from MIT, Schmeing worked as a technical consultant, translating engineering, science, and business documents for clients around the world. Thus, the very nature of her work necessitated the ability to find essential meanings in written texts, to comprehend a writer's purpose, and so forth.

Moreover, Schmeing was a Fulbright scholar, had graduated magnum cum laude from college, and was fluent in three languages, including German, Spanish, French, and of course, in her native language, English. Schmeing's failure simply defied common sense, fueling concerns over the exam's predictive validity.

Debra Andrake also failed the Massachusetts teacher test, and was told that she wasn't "teaching material." In one form or another, she'd heard it before. Let's consider the course of events that got her to that teacher test, starting out with a working-class background, followed by years of unsatisfactory jobs.

"I always wanted to be something," says Andrake, who grew up in Somerville, near Boston, and now lives in Wenham. "My parents didn't go to college. I always wanted to go to college and find out what that life was like." Then came the SATs and a student guidance counselor at Somerville High. Above both those stood a formidable, interlocking structure of social ideology that would inform Andrake, in no uncertain terms, to stop wanting so much. "I remember it like it was yesterday," Andrake says. "My counselor told me, 'In reality, you're not college material.' I felt stupid. I told him, 'I must be really stupid, then. I guess I'm not college material.' So, I never went."

Actually, Andrake eventually did go to college, graduating magna cum laude at the age of forty-two with a 3.62 grade point average at Salem State College. She specialized in early childhood education. But it would take many years in the workforce, mastering job after job, to finally break through the vast web of cultural ideology about the smart and not smart and the distinguishing features of those who are college material from those who are allegedly not college material.

After high school, Andrake worked as a hairdresser, travel agent, convention planner, and so on, until she met her husband, a middle-school science teacher, who encouraged her to go back to school. He suggested Andrake consider taking some night courses at a local college. Her response startled him. "But I'm not college material," she said. "He looked at me (incredulously) and then said, 'You've got to be kidding.'"

She began her new venture with an intense summer school psychology course at Salem State, its material packed into just eight weeks. Her husband told her, "If you can pass this class, you can pass anything."

She aced the course.

At that juncture, Andrake's heart sank, now coming to the grim and ironic realization that she had wasted so much time at unsatisfying jobs because she'd listened to her school counselor, who had put so much faith in her SAT score. "Oh, my God, I thought, I've wasted my whole life, how could I have done this, how could I have underestimated myself all these years. That guidance counselor poisoned my mind."

And so, in 1992, Deb Andrake went to college, starting out part time with evening classes. Because she couldn't afford full-time school, she took evening classes for nearly four years before being able to take full academic loads the last two and a half years.

Andrake's magna cum laude certainly suggests she's an outstanding student. Beyond that, however, there's good evidence to believe she's an even better teacher. In fact, her favorite parts of Salem State's teacher education program were its junior-year opportunities for real classroom teaching at the Horace Mann Laboratory School next door. She learned about teaching by doing it and learned how to manage various classroom situations with a problem-solving approach. After two weeks of orientation, she took full control of a kindergarten class. "Do what you want," her supervisor told her.

So she did. Andrake's teaching performance evaluations are worth quoting in full. One Salem State College student teaching report dated March 13, 1998, carefully printed by her teaching supervisor, Susan Snyder, reads:

> Debra Andrake successfully completed an eight week practicum in our kindergarten classroom. Debra proved herself to be prompt, reliable and well prepared. She was highly skilled at planning, motivating lessons appropriate to students' attention spans and learning needs. Debra was professional in every sense of the word, working well with teachers and children alike. She treated children with kindness and respect at all times. Prediction of success: excellent. Promise of growth: excellent.

What more, then, could the state of Massachusetts want in a new teacher? To score a 70 on the teacher test, of course. Andrake's first clue that she'd have to take the April 1998 exam came the prior September. Like many others, she decided to fork over $150 for the right to take the first test after being told that it wouldn't count. Andrake felt she had nothing to lose. Then, a week before the test, while still in the throes of a demanding student teaching schedule, she and the other test takers were informed that the test would count after all in order to be certified to teach. "Everyone is by now flipping out," Andrake says. "We were going in cold."

When I last heard from Andrake several months after she failed her first try at the teacher test, she had found what she hoped would be an in-between job as a teacher's assistant, waiting for her next attempt to pass the certification exam a few months down the road. Meantime, Andrake says she'd like to have a few words with Thomas Finneran, the Massachusetts politician who more or less publicly tarred this Salem State graduate as a witch for the 1990s.

"If I could speak to him, I'd ask him to come into my classroom, to sit down and watch me teach. I can guarantee that he would not get up and call me an idiot," says Andrake. "There are so many things in teaching one can't measure in a paper-and-pencil test. And one of those things is compassion, passion for the subject you are teaching and compassion for the children sitting in front of you."

How Valid?

Typically, when a new standardized test comes onto the market, taxpayer-supported test users—in this case the Massachusetts Department of Education—will make public a test publisher's empirical studies on a test's predictive validity. Indeed, members of the testing community, they often claim, generally consider that publishing a test's validity information is part of their ethical responsibility as test users and makers.

Curiously, however, no validity studies on the first Massachusetts teacher test were made public when controversy over the test flared up, even in response to the vocal demands by educators and others for the state and for National Evaluation Systems to come forward with the evidence.

In public testimony before the state legislature, several expert witnesses told lawmakers that the dearth of any publicly available evidence about the test's validity meant they were on thin ice drawing any conclusions about teacher competence, no matter how many prospective teachers failed it.

"National Evaluation Systems has offered no proof whatsoever that its teacher test measures what it is supposed to measure," Clarke Fowler, an early childhood education specialist at Salem State College, testified. "I can tell you that I have heard this past week from some of my students—good students, students who do spell words correctly, who do form cogent and grammatically correct sentences and paragraphs, students whom I know meet and even exceed the state's standards—who have failed this test. It appears that this teacher test may not be doing what it is supposed to do: namely, tell us which candidates do and do not meet minimal standards for literacy and content knowledge." (31)

Thus, nobody really knew whether the Massachusetts teacher test was valid or not. Even if the hard evidence existed, few knew about it because it wasn't made public. Nevertheless, were Massachusetts lawmakers so inclined, they wouldn't have had to search far to see that picking good teachers with a standardized test would probably prove futile. Had lawmakers like Finneran looked at the hard evidence from the American experience with teacher testing, they might well have a far different opinion of people like Julie Gauthier and Deb Andrake.

Research studies on teacher tests reach back a good deal further than what we'll examine here, but a handful of recent investigations will serve the purpose. In 1990, for example, Iris M. Riggs and Matt L. Riggs reported findings on the predictive powers of two widely used teacher tests, the National Teacher's Examination (NTE) and the California Basic Educational Skills Test (CBEST). The researchers looked at the predictive validity of both test scores and undergraduate grades for some 800 students admitted to the teacher education program at one California State University campus. "Success" was assessed with several measures, such as teaching performance reviews and grades in certain core subjects.

Except for the writing part of the CBEST, which showed just a modest relationship with grades in the teacher training program, *none* of the standardized test scores showed *any* association with a teaching student's success. On the other hand, undergraduate grades and a teaching student's performance in one prerequisite reading methods course were highly predictive of success in the program.

"The failure of the standardized test scores (CBEST and NTE) to provide any meaningful information relative to subsequent performance as measured in this study must cause some concern," the scholars say. They continue: "The use of admissions requirements that show no relation to performance creates the potential for just litigation. . . . Validity coefficients must support the expectation that these scores enable programs to select the best applicants, not just randomly reduce the pool. It may be time to give serious consideration to the nature of these tests, and why we should expect their scores to be predictive of subsequent teaching performance." (32)

Standardized tests for teachers have proven to be especially damaging to minority teaching candidates. Searching for explanations of a recent decline in African Americans enrolled in teacher education programs, the American Association of Colleges for Teacher Education commissioned a 1992 study to determine what student characteristics led to success in teacher education programs. The study's sample included 712 teacher education students at various four-year universities. Variables identified as possible predictors of success were high school grades and SAT scores. Success was defined as completing all requirements leading to certification to teach.

Of critical importance, the universities selected for the study put exceedingly high value on entrance examination scores when selecting their new teaching students. But findings from the study showed, again, that SAT scores proved to be a weak predictor of performance in the training programs, while the statistical relationship between success in a program and high school grades was sizable.

As an inexorable result of institutional policy placing great weight on test scores, the study concluded, fully capable African Americans and Hispanics would be systematically barred from careers in teaching owing to persistent gaps in test scores between minorities and whites. The report sums up the problem of overreliance on entrance exams:

> The implication then is that admissions decisions that emphasize SAT scores as opposed to high school or college-level performance . . . may put minorities at a disadvantage in terms of access. . . . There is evidence that once minority students gain access to teacher education programs, their college performance is comparable to that of their white counterparts." (33)

To put the results of the teacher testing validity studies into the broadest, most concrete terms, evidence from some 176 studies compiled by one scholar demonstrated that such teacher tests correlated slightly with job performance. How slight? The *r* value measured from those studies was 0.21, indicating that standardized test scores explained just 4 percent of the variation in job performance among teachers or teachers in training. That means, in turn, that fully 96 percent of the differences in job success *must* be accounted for by other characteristics that teachers bring to their jobs. (34)

"Contrary to what many test takers and test users like to believe," says Terry S. Salinger of the International Reading Association," tests at entry to and exit from teacher education programs do not provide predictive validity. Testing companies do not claim that their tests predict how good a teacher examination will actually be because they recognize that tests cannot measure . . . dedication, empathy, motivation, sensitivity, and so forth." (35)

Job Performance Versus Test Performance

In Maine, licensed outdoor guides relate the tale of the newly minted employee at Don Helstrom's guiding outfit who had recently passed the state's paper-and-pencil test to become a licensed master guide. Helstrom told the guide to come to work one day prepared to set bear baits in the woods. "He showed up in shorts and river sandals," says Don Kleiner, a guide himself and legislative director for the Professional Maine Guides Association.

Any experienced guide would be dumbfounded by the sight of that guy in river sandals. Bear baiting, says Kleiner, requires one to tromp into thorny bushes and tree branches. "He came out of the bushes looking like he'd been in a catfight all day," Kleiner told me. "One would presume that a master guide would have at least that level of expertise."

Kleiner also recalls a rafting trip from his own experience, while working with a new guide who'd passed the state test to be a master guide. A storm came up quickly, and Kleiner asked the guide to get a fire going. "After a couple of minutes, he came up and told me, 'We can't get a fire going; it's raining,'" says Kleiner, who stood flabbergasted. "One of the most basic things you learn as a guide is to light a fire when you need one, and the conditions shouldn't make a difference,"

Kleiner says. "A fire is basic to people being comfortable. In that situation, it's a skill you've just got to have."

Indeed, it seems that the really important things that go into being good at a job aren't even touched by the standardized tests on which employers, school counselors, admissions committees, state legislatures, state fish and game departments, and even the American judicial system have placed so much uncritical faith. We've seen several cases of people informed of their incompetence to do a job even though they've already done the job and done it well. In case after case, one's *actual performance* at the job flatly contradicted what the test foretold.

Such contradictions, in fact, should not be surprising. When you think about it, given the nature of most real jobs, requiring increasingly more sophisticated skills working with technology and with other people, there's actually little reason to believe that paper-and-pencil tests can possibly capture the complex expertise required to succeed at many occupations.

Indeed, according the many validity studies we've examined, any measure that purports to predict job or career success will be more accurate to the extent that it's closely aligned with actually doing the job. That's why, for instance, grades in graduate business studies are far better at predicting career achievement for managers and executives than scores on any aptitude test.

This, too, should not be surprising. In graduate business school, students acquire job-specific knowledge through case studies and projects that attempt to approximate the realities of business. That is particularly so at more progressive business schools that train business leaders through a pedagogy that emphasizes learning by doing.

We can find many examples of the shortcomings of overly generalized and unreal paper-and-pencil tests. Take physician training. Standardized entrance tests that emphasize knowledge in basic sciences, it turns out, are decidedly poor predictors of medical students' success in their clinical training during the final two years of medical school, which is the stuff of real doctoring. Indeed, the further one gets down the path of professional experience and all the expertise that entails, the worse tests become as predictors of anything worthwhile.

To be sure, standardized screening exams have occasionally demonstrated some relationship to success at the job or in professional training programs. They have served employers and other organizations with an undoubted source of bureaucratic efficiency. Indeed, this efficiency underlies employers' unswerving belief in the usefulness of the tests. The belief, however, is largely founded on fantasy; in many cases, employers would be just as well served, in many cases, of interviewing job applicants on the basis of a random lottery.

This book has shown several instances of the unmatched importance of so-called noncognitive factors that go unmeasured on most employment aptitude exams in predicting someone's success in the workplace. It appears highly likely, in fact, that persistence and motivation to succeed at specific jobs or skills are far more important than most employers and academic institutions commonly believe, given their heavy reliance on test scores. Tests were completely inadequate to capture the personal qualities in people like Carmelo Melendez, Julie Gauthier, and Debra Andrake—to be a manager, to do sophisticated historical analysis, or to engage kindergarteners in learning.

Indeed, the role of personal traits that lead one to a successful career may be far more important than most Americans have been led to believe. Beginning with the early promoters of IQ testing whom we encountered in Chapter 2, Americans have put great faith in the power of innate, immutable ability to explain why some of us become great musicians, writers, or athletes, while most of us are relegated by the laws of genetics for ordinary lives. Michael Jordan is the greatest basketball player ever because he was born a great athlete. William Faulkner was simply meant to achieve great eminence as a writer. The widely institutionalized nature of aptitude and ability testing to "predict" success in education and the workplace reflect and reinforce this peculiar American belief about human potential.

But some psychological researchers are beginning to question this widely held view. They are finding good evidence to suggest that old-fashioned hard work, practice, and experience may, in fact, vastly supercede the role played by innate ability in one's achieving high levels of performance.

For example, K. Anders Ericsson of the Institute of Cognitive Science at the University of Colorado and his colleagues at the Max Planck Institute in Berlin investigated the respective roles of "deliberate practice" versus innate ability for expert performance in a variety of fields, from music to chess to athletics. Expert levels of performance in virtually any field, they found, was the result of one's steady, focused attempts to improve performance over at least ten years.

"We reject any important role for innate ability," the researchers conclude. "It is quite plausible, however, that heritable differences might influence processes related to motivation and the original enjoyment of the activities in the domain and, even more important, affect the inevitable differences in the capacity to engage in hard work (deliberate practice). (36)

Believers in the power of intelligence to predict career success, of course, will point to the many studies that have been able to stratify occupations by average intelligence level—more or less, that is. For instance, one frequently cited 1945 investigation of the relationship between intelligence and career status partitioned occupational groups by average IQ scores. The authors of that early study compared the aptitude test scores of some 10,000 military personnel during World War II with their later occupations in civilian life. The study found that accountants had average IQs of 128, mechanics tested on average at 106, and teamsters averaged about 88 IQ points. (37) Such results conform to those of later studies and also feed popular notions that high-status occupations are filled with the most intelligent individuals because high IQs are supposedly necessary to do the jobs.

To conclude that some occupations have more productive and capable people than others, based on such evidence as that contained in the above study, would be scientifically unwarranted. One would have to consider the alternative explanation that the strong association between IQ and occupational status is, in fact, an artifact of the credentialing and gatekeeping role higher education plays in the occupational structure of the United States.

When one complicates the analysis with adjustments for such background factors as the amount of schooling somebody attains, the role of intelligence per se almost evaporates. That is, one's educational attainment becomes paramount to his or her occupational status and achievements. For instance, controlling for social class differences among people in his study, James Crouse discovered that as much as 80 percent of one's career success was attributable to how much schooling he or she obtained, and a relatively small proportion was accounted for by one's IQ. (38)

Given the poor record of aptitude and other sorts of employment tests to predict job performance, a sobering conclusion seems warranted. Differences in occupational status and success reflect not so much one's ability to perform a job as they are artifacts of the structured pathways to success and high-status jobs in American society. In other words, apparent differences in intelligence between occupations follow inexorably from institutional rules that require high test scores for entry into certain restricted occupations, such as medicine, law, or accounting. "Since the social structure enforces the existence of a substantial correlation between educational achievement and occupational success," suggest British writers Bernard Waites and Brian Evans, "it follows that anything else which correlates with educational achievement (like test scores) is also likely to correlate willy-nilly with occupational status." (39)

Indeed, were occupations that are now relatively unrestricted to entry suddenly become otherwise, like journalism, for example, we'd likely find that the average "intelligence" of practitioners in those jobs would leap upward—without the slightest gain in the actual journalistic capabilities of reporters and editors.

The would-be social engineers among us, like Thomas Finneran, Illinois Bell, and John Silber, can continue to legislate through the use of standardized tests the structured pathways to success in the American workplace. Screening for jobs on the basis of aptitude test scores can be almost certain to raise the measured "intelligence" of the practitioners in almost any field one chooses to so structure, from Massachusetts schoolteacher to Maine hunting guide.

In the process, however, the social engineers would discover an increasing sort of standardization of the profiles among people working those jobs. Successful applicants, in this evolution, are more likely *not* to be Hispanic or African American, and more likely *not* to come from homes of modest or poor economic means. They *are* more likely to be white, middle-, and upper-middle-class, with parents who are white, middle-, and upper-middle-class. They are more likely to think alike. And more likely than the rest to test into the structured pathways of success.

9

Standardized Minds: Thinking Styles and the Testing Game

How Objective?

THE STANDARDIZED TESTS IN WHICH Americans have placed so much trust have not proven to be particularly trustworthy indicators of individual human potential. In a word, they've been awful.

Generally, the poor ability of the exams to tell us much about later performance has been true both for people who score well on standardized tests and those who do not. Test scores stratify largely along race, class, and even gender lines, whether it's an IQ test of young children or the SAT for college admission. Pick a multiple-choice test, and one finds that whites tend to score better than blacks; men typically score better than women; and those from middle to upper-middle-class backgrounds are apt to fare considerably better than people from families of low or moderate socioeconomic circumstances.

Further unpeel the layers of this conundrum and one is left with this basic question: Is there something in the nature of standardized tests themselves—particularly the very multiple-choice format that permits high levels of standardization, reproducibility, and ease of scoring—that rewards some kinds of thinking processes and penalizes other types? Also, might a portion of the historical differences in standardized test scores among various groups of Americans be attributable to fundamental differences among them in their common ways of thinking and knowing? Is it possible that somebody might have difficulty on such standardized tests because, in fact, she's in a sense smarter than the test itself?

Standardized testing is far from the objective process that many Americans might believe. In fact, it's rooted in certain epistemological value judgments about knowing and ways of knowing. Commonly, when Americans talk about the "fairness" of a given standardized test with respect to possible ethnic, cultural, or gender biases, for instance, they look no further than the test items themselves, scrutinizing them as if they were magic beads to determine whether they offend, ignore, or marginalize particular groups of people. Indeed, test makers' public accountability to make unbiased tests is achieved by means of just such a process.

Largely unquestioned in both internal examinations and public discussions of test bias, however, is the very structure of timed-constrained, multiple-choice tests and the particular kinds of thinking processes these tests encourage and reward.

Let me be clear. I am not suggesting some New Age, postmodern paradigm in which there's no such thing as objective truth, that anything goes, or that all ways of thinking and knowing are equally valid. I am, however, suggesting that so-called objective tests formatted in the multiple-choice mode are decidedly not objective simply because their bubbled-in answers can be scanned and scored by a computer. They are subjective in the same sense that a historian is subjective when choosing which aspects of a historical era to emphasize as historically decisive, or a newspaper reporters' choices about what's news and what's not news.

For the measurement of human talent, this is by no means a trivial problem, particularly when the sorts of talents and abilities lost in the shuffle, or discouraged from revealing themselves in most standardized testing exercises, may be more valuable than the stuff that actually does get measured.

Debra Andrake, introduced in Chapter 8, is just one woman whose way of thinking and approaching problems in her chosen field, teaching, fell victim to a multiple-choice test. When she saw the test items on the new Massachusetts teacher exam, she suffered an uncomfortable rush of adrenaline, her heart racing and her breathing quickened and labored. Compounding the sense of panic, Andrake told me, was a profound irritation and incredulity at what she was seeing on the exam. Looking at the items on the general reading and literacy sections, Andrake kept asking herself, "What does *this* have to do with what I got my degree in?"

She recalls, for instance, one subtest at the beginning of the exam, when a man stood up in the front of the room to read aloud a passage from a formal document in American history, uttering phrases in a monotonic, slightly pedantic tone of voice. These would-be teachers were supposed to transcribe the orally rendered passage, then go back to punctuate it. The task incensed Andrake. "What does that have to do with teaching?" she says. "Maybe a secretary. I'm saying to myself, 'This is ridiculous.'"

Then there was the reading comprehension section. An irksome but common feature one eventually begins to notice about many commercially produced standardized tests is that test creators seem to adore dry, unimaginative, fact-laden, and abstract reading passages—in other words, simply bad and utterly boring writing. Here's a small sample from one passage on the Massachusetts teacher test that was reprinted in the *Boston Globe:*

> Sociologists would be uncomfortable describing a modern city from only a few interviews and often supplement detailed accounts with broad urban surveys or censuses. For similar reasons, geologists and geographers often combine very specific information gathered from soil probes or individual field studies with the larger scale perspective provided by satellite imagery. Over the last fifty years, archeologists have developed a technique, called a systematic settlement pattern survey, for studying areas larger than one or a few sites. (1)

And so droned on the teacher test, for dozens of paragraphs and several similarly titillating mini-essays. Andrake, for one, wasn't titillated.

"The first four hours of the test were a waste of time," Andrake says. "I had no idea, and I still don't to this day, what they were looking to accomplish on that part of the test. I did very poorly on this part of the test, and I know why. I had little interest in it."

But even on the early-childhood education items, her teaching specialty, the test's multiple-choice, "one best answer" format failed to reflect the complexities of real teaching, says Andrake. She recalls the "Little Jimmy" question, for example, in which a young child named Jimmy was crying, scared because he didn't want to go under a large parachute with his classmates in a physical education class. The multiple-choice item asked test takers to pick the "best" choice of action for dealing with little Jimmy's problem, such as: *A. Take him away; B. Drag him under;* and *C. Yell at him.* As she looked over the possible answers, Andrake found nothing to match her own professional sense of what to do. "Where's the answer? Where is the right answer?"

She explained, "I felt that the answers given (on the test) did not completely coincide with my philosophy of teaching. . . . In the 'real world,' I need to know more about 'little Jimmy.' . . . There could be problems at home, he could have behavioral problems, medical problems, and so on. The list is endless."

Now, suppose the state of Massachusetts, in setting its specifications for a new teacher test, had told the test maker to design a test that could simulate, under carefully controlled conditions, how Andrake and other prospective teachers would actually *perform* as teachers. In that case, one can be sure that the state and its commercial contractor would have come up with a much different exam, one that would allow for less cut-and-dried thinking about teaching than is possible with multiple-choice items, and create opportunities for people like Andrake to show their stuff. Such a test, for instance, might include a ten-minute teaching simulation. Or perhaps roughly similar information about a test takers' classroom skills could be ascertained from a 500-word exposition, say, in the form of a mock memorandum to the school principal.

Such testing formats, where the often-messy complexities of the real job of teaching enter the fray, by their nature elicit a different set of thinking skills than are rewarded by the fast-paced, pressurized atmosphere that characterizes most standardized testing situations. The point is this: When testers make up their exams or buy them off the shelf, they are doing far more than deciding which multiple-choice items to put in the mix. They're making choices, subjective ones at that, about the very structure, pacing, organization, and format of the test. It would be naive, indeed, to believe that the testers' choices on the structure and format of their exams has no effect on the outcome.

Making *choices* and judgments of value about what is worthwhile to measure and what is not renders standardized testing hardly the exercise in objectivity that Americans have been led to believe. Indeed, a growing body of empirical evidence is suggesting that format matters, and it means this: When employers and educational institutions use any of a thousand speeded, multiple-choice tests to sort and classify people, the institutions are implicitly rewarding some kinds of individuals who tend to think in ways that are highly efficient for that format, while punishing other individuals who tend to approach problems and solutions in a manner that's decidedly incompatible with most standardized tests.

Test Format and Performance

Whatever the standardized test, the significant score differences persisting between girls and boys, men and women, and between whites and other American minorities has been a commonly known and much discussed phenomenon. Consider, for instance, 1998 figures from the College Board, the network of colleges and universities that sponsors the SAT college admissions test. The College Board says females scored an average of 998 on the combined verbal and math portions of the SAT (out of 1,600 possible points), which was forty-two points below the average score for male test takers. That gap, according to the National Center for Fair and Open Testing, was the largest between male and female SAT takers since 1995. The gender difference in scores on the math subtest was worse: In percentile terms, the gender gap on the SAT math test proved equally dramatic. The average math score for male SAT takers put them at roughly the fifty-sixth percentile, meaning males scored better than about 56 percent of all test takers nationwide. Women's average math score placed them well down the ladder, at roughly the forty-second percentile.

Although women typically have fared consistently worse on college entrance exams than men, females have invariably outdone men in terms of their actual performance in college. Empirical studies supporting this conclusion are eye-opening. For instance, in one study of grade differences between sexes for more than 68,000 students at forty-one institutions, women earned an average grade point of about 2.7, compared to 2.5 for males. A study of nearly 8,000 seniors at University of California at Berkeley showed women outperforming men by a tenth of a grade point. Among mathematics majors at the University of Michigan, women also bested men, earning grade points of 3.53, compared to 3.38 for men. The litany goes on. Among some 560 calculus students at a handful of universities, women earned grade points of about 2.8, versus 2.3 for males. Another study showed women outperforming men even at the higher levels of math beyond calculus. Name a math course and chances are exceedingly good, according the volumes of empirical work, that women will outdo their male counterparts, despite their dramatically lower SAT scores. (2)

In the search for clues as to why males do better than females on standardized tests but generally fail to keep up with girls and women in the classroom, researchers have turned their gazes on the multiple-choice format itself. Is there something in the nature of the exams and the divergent thinking styles and behavioral traits with which males and females tend to approach the tests that might explain the discrepancy? Indeed, might women and girls outperform males if the testing format were reversed, permitting free responses such as essays and short answers instead of multiple-choice items? The answer is an unqualified yes, a pattern has been replicated in numerous recent studies.

A typical investigation of this type comes to us from Ireland, where researchers Niall Bolger and Thomas Kellaghan sought to determine the likely effects of test format on performance gaps between some 740 fifteen-year-old boys against 750 girls the same age. In particular, the scholars examined gender differences on a common multiple-choice achievement test used in the Republic of Ireland, and compared those scores to another common "free-response" exam, validated for high reliability, that permitted test takers to construct their own responses. The researchers took care to ensure that the subject matter and specific questions were identical on both tests in order to isolate the effects of the different testing formats.

Whether the subject was language or mathematics, the same result held: Boys outscored the girls on the multiple-choice achievement test, and girls outperformed boys on the free-response exams. Bolger and Kellaghan could only speculate as to why this pattern held, but they cautioned that girls shouldn't be educationally punished simply owing to test format.

"Whatever the explanation of our findings, they raise issues for educational policymakers regarding the choice of method of measurement in examinations," the authors say. "This is particularly important if the results of examinations are used, as they are in a number of European countries, including Britain and Ireland, to make important decisions about a student's educational and vocational future." (3)

Another investigation of the effects of test format comes by way of the Educational Testing Service, the concern widely known as the maker of the SAT, whose sponsor is the large network of colleges known as the College Board. In the study, ETS researchers Brent Bridgeman and Rick Moran examined gender differences on the ETS/College Board Advanced Placement (AP) exams that many high school students take for college credit. The researchers exploited the unique features of the AP exams in that they contain both essay and multiple-choice components. Doing so, the investigators were able to compare test performance between males and females, as well as various ethnic groups, on the two test types.

Bridgeman and Moran focused especially on individuals in a sample drawn from thirty-eight colleges who fell into two opposing but revealing categories: those who scored well on the essay part but relatively poorly on the 100 multiple-choice items; and another group of low essay, high multiple-choice individuals. Bridgeman and Moran then compared the later college grades and SAT scores for students in the two categories.

Generally, the ETS investigators discovered that in terms of college grades, there were few differences between the two categories of students. Yet, as one might expect, those who scored highly on the AP's multiple-choice tests had far superior SAT scores—also a multiple-choice exam—than their high essay/low multiple-choice counterparts. For instance, on the AP biology exams, the high essay/low multiple-choice group earned an overall grade point average (GPA) of 2.8, roughly equal to the low essay/high multiple-choice group's average GPA of 2.84. But the latter high multiple-choice bunch well outperformed the former on the SAT verbal test, with an average score of 618 compared to 558, a sixty-point difference.

The gender and ethnic differences were dramatic as well. In relative terms, the AP's multiple-choice tests favored men and Asians in particular; at the same time, the essay portions favored women, blacks, Latinos, Native Americans, and those for whom English was a second language. Some particulars:

- The some 28,000 women in the study were two and a half times as likely to write superior essays as to score highly on the multiple-choice format.
- Blacks were three times more likely to fall in the high-essay/low multiple-choice group.
- And, astoundingly, students whose English wasn't their best language wrote superior essays—in English—two and a half times as often as they scored very well on the multiple-choice items. (4)

With respect especially to the gender discrepancies, there may be several possible explanations. Many scholars believe certain tendencies in thinking styles and behavioral traits of girls and women don't add up to a particularly efficient match for the speeded, pressurized nature of the multiple-choice format found on most achievement and aptitude tests. Girls and women may tend to be more focused on the process of learning rather than scoring points in the gamey context of most tests. Sometimes lacking the "full speed ahead" confidence of many males, females might tend to be more anxious and frustrated in testing situations. Results gleaned from more than 560 studies have lent empirical support to that hypothesis, generally finding that females suffer more test anxiety than males even after controlling for levels of academic achievement. (5) Evidence also suggests that risk-averse girls and women tend to approach standardized tests with a deliberateness and carefulness that makes them less willing than males to guess at multiple-choice questions, which puts them at a disadvantage when incorrect answers are not penalized. Similarly, females taking standardized tests may tend to rely to a greater extent than males on the more methodical techniques and skills acquired in the classroom—organizing, synthesizing, analyzing—instead of shortcuts and tricks that males more frequently use. As Cathy Kessel and Marcia Linn of UC–Berkeley put it regarding standardized tests in mathematics: "Some students view the test as more a measure of trick-detection than a measure of mathematics skill. Females report this as one more reason to conclude that math is frustrating rather than interesting." (6)

Skimming Surfaces

Playing games and using tricks was the last thing on Karina Moltz's mind when it came to her learning.

Born in New York City, Moltz moved with her family to Portland, Maine, as a seventh-grader. She excelled in school, taking all the advanced placement courses through four years at Portland High. She won extra honors for achievements in history, language, and citizenship. Raised by college-educated parents, Moltz "never questioned" that she would get at least a bachelor's degree too. Mom and dad gave Moltz practice application essays to write, held mock interviews for her, and helped her arrange a Northeast tour of such colleges as Brown, Connecticut College, Vassar, and Wesleyan.

Moltz, of course, took her SATs, the rite of passage that would permit her to achieve what she'd been preparing for most of her life. Her test score, however, proved disappointing, particularly on the mathematics section, on which she managed only a modest score on her second try.

Like Andrake's, Moltz's style of thinking and learning often mixed like oil and water with standardized tests. Talking to people like Andrake and Moltz, one finds they are intensely motivated learners and achievers, and at least part of that intensity stems from a few habits of mind. For them, learning can almost never be separated from some meaningful context. They are doers and problem solvers, eschewing overly general abstractions. They are keenly oriented to realistic applications of the skills and information they acquire from textbooks and professors' lectures. Whatever the subject or task, they take care not to get so sidetracked on minutiae that they lose sight of the bigger picture. Listen to Moltz: "I don't really feel like standardized tests reflect my abilities," she told me. "I think the whole format creates a result that has little true importance. . . . I am uncomfortable with the thought that my abilities and worth could be judged on scores of such tests." Even at Bates College (a "test-optional" institution), where Moltz was in her junior year majoring in psychology when I spoke with her, the test-taking abilities required of the SAT and its ilk had rarely, if ever, been useful in doing well in her academic subjects. "I have never been asked to take an exam or complete an assignment that has anything to do with standardized tests, and I really don't think that, while at Bates, I will," Moltz told me.

I asked Moltz to reflect on her own approach to learning and thinking that, though eminently useful for doing well in her classes, proved to hinder her ability to perform well on standardized tests. I gave her some time to think about it, and she responded a few days later in an e-mail. "It's a tough question," she wrote, "but I think that generally my way of looking at things doesn't score well on standardized tests. I tend to look at the broader perspective, and I always feel more comfortable evaluating the effect that one 'thing' has on another. . . .

"When I do work for my classes here, I am able to solve problems by looking at the context and other factors involved. I can create my own answer, which is often the correct one, but if I am presented with three or four set options, I find myself at a loss trying to figure out how any of the options were decided upon." Moltz cited the example of a course she'd been taking, a research methods course required for her psychology major, called Action Research. "The unique aspect of this class is that rather than memorizing facts about (research) methods, each student executes a semester-long study in a local classroom. This applied learning is so much better for me." (7)

Through the Lens of Cognitive Psychology

Depending on the model of intelligence one chooses to use, Moltz might be said to have, say, a certain "practical intelligence," as Yale psychologist Robert Sternberg might phrase it. And in Andrake's deep concern for realism, she may exhibit one of the "multiple intelligences" that Harvard's Howard Gardner has theorized. Whatever term of art is used to describe them, the point to be made here is that Moltz's and Andrake's fundamental approaches to thinking and perceiving would appear to be a disadvantage for them on standardized tests—owing not to a lack of ability but to the the nature of the tests themselves.

It has also been said that most standardized achievement and aptitude tests tap just one of the various kinds of "intelligences," particularly a sort of logical-analytical intelligence, or abstract problem-solving ability, while altogether ignoring other varieties of intelligence. Clearly, one can make a persuasive case for this weakness in most standardized tests by looking at the tests' contents, which focus almost exclusively on verbal and quantitative gymnastics.

Further, the very standardization and format of most tests creates its own unique internal logic that has virtually no relevance to anything beyond the logic of the test itself. This is why the tests have proven to be abjectly poor predictors of achievement in school and success in the workplace. Hence, having well-developed logical and analytical abilities might be *necessary* to perform at high levels on most standardized tests; but having such abilities, by themselves, are insufficient for meaningful success and achievement beyond the confines of the abstract testing exercise.

What's worse, a growing body of evidence suggests, the internal logic of standardized tests appears to engender its own styles of thinking that, more often than not, would probably wind up getting students flunked from Moltz's research methods class, or cause teachers like Andrake to fall flat on their faces in a real teaching situation. Evidence of this generally indicates that the standardized testing format Americans have grown accustomed to appears to promote a sort of superficial *pseudo*-thinking style that probably has little real-world utility beyond doing word games and crosswords puzzles, and of course, taking more tests.

Some evidence has come from the the emerging field of cognitive psychology, which essentially concerns itself with how individuals think and the process by which people learn, create, memorize, and solve problems. This approach stands in sharp contrast to the "psychometric" perspective that for several decades has dominated the study of human intelligence as well as educational practice in the United States, through its abiding focus on individual and group differences in mental measurements.

Viewed through the lens of cognitive psychology, it's clear that people have the capacity to think at different levels or depths of cognition, depending on their individual abilities and the nature of the thinking task at hand. Some researchers have used models of cognitive psychology to bifurcate the thinking process into at least two levels: a "surface" level, calling on one's skills of immediate recall and repetition of factual information; and a deep cognitive level, which involves the synthesis and analysis of a variety of sources of information in order to interpret that information, solve a complicated problem, and possibly even create something interesting and new.

As a result of insights gleaned from cognitive psychology, scholars concerned with the effects of mental testing have naturally attempted to deconstruct standardized tests for clues about which levels of cognition such tests require of test takers. The answer would have enormous implications for policymakers, in particular educators and education reformers. Although surface-level thinking would clearly be needed in many activities, whether to read a bus schedule, remember a phone number, or calculate the per-unit price of a can of squash, such skills would be insufficient for higher, more complex endeavors.

Consider, for example, a recent study that examined the thinking styles of students and their relative performance on the SAT college admission test. The study, presented at the National Association of School Psychologists in Seattle in 1994, analyzed SAT scores for some 530 students at a large university in the Southeast with respect to their thinking and learning styles. Styles were measured by means of a questionnaire to determine whether students used a surface approach to learning, defined as retrieving only essential information through rote memorization; a deep approach, where students were focused on learning for its own sake; or the achieving approach, characteristic of students mostly concerned with getting high grades.

Interestingly, the researchers found that the group that scored highest on the SAT actually tended to use more superficial thinking strategies, relying on surface and achieving approaches more often than those who scored in the low and moderate ranges on the SAT. To their apparent disadvantage with respect to SAT performance, the lowest-scoring students employed the deep approach more often than the higher-scoring students.

The researchers suggest that the high-scoring students relied on surface thinking more often because "the American system fosters this type of learning style." (8) Thus, it would seem that lower-scoring students were not less capable of thinking. Rather, they were less indoctrinated into the more mechanistic thinking styles that the education system has emphasized and rewarded.

A similar study looked at 670 grade-schoolers in a mostly working-class school district in a large metropolitan area in the Midwest. Eric Anderman of the University of Michigan compared the middle schoolers' scores on a standardized reading exam relative to the following schema of individual children's thinking styles: Students were considered "learning focused"—whom I shall dub the "Young Scholars"—if they mostly used "deep level cognitive processing strategies," including reflecting on their understanding of material and thinking about the relationship of new ideas to previously encountered ones.

On the other hand, the students in Anderman's study whose learning goals were "ability focused"—whom I shall call the Top Guns—employed surface level ways of thinking, "such as rushing through assignments, giving up, and writing down the first answer that comes to mind." Among Anderman's remarkable findings:

- Girls tended to fall into the Young Scholar group at a higher rate than boys. That is, girls were more learning focused and used the deep thinking strategies more frequently than did boys, who relied on surface level thinking more often than girls.
- The Young Scholars—again, those who valued writing and reading and were learning-focused—fared worse on the standardized achievement tests as a group than their Top Gun peers, who used more superficial learning strategies. Although Anderman found a positive correlation between Top Gun tendencies and test scores, there was a *negative* association between Young Scholar attributes and scores.

The apparent contradiction between the demands of standardized testing against the deeper and more taxing kinds of thinking more valuable to schoolchildren in the long run was not lost on Anderman. He concluded that "these data suggest that there may indeed be a mismatch between the purposes of standardized testing in literacy skills, and students' emotional/motivational orientations toward reading and writing activities." (9)

A Finnish Experiment

Indeed, mismatch between the sorts of superficial thinking encouraged by most standardized tests and more sophisticated thinking styles required for lasting, meaningful achievement carries well beyond grade school and even college. Consider the field of medicine. Medical educators in both the United States and Europe have long been aware that widely-used standardized tests of basic science and medical knowledge, such as the Medical College Admissions Test (MCAT) universally used by American medical schools to judge applicants, have severe limitations as an indicator of success in medical school. Although the MCAT has been shown to have limited proficiency to predict achievement in the first year or two of studies in basic medical sciences, the MCAT and similar tests in other nations have been notoriously poor predictors of later performance in clinical rotations, internships and residencies, and ultimately how one performs as a physician.

In recognition of this drawback, the Helsinki University medical faculty in Finland began to experiment in the 1990s with an alternative entrance exam to complement the multiple-choice science exams the university had relied on in the past. As the research team headed by Sari Lindbloom-Ylanne reported in the journal *Higher Education,* the medical faculty drew from the theories of cognitive psychology to develop the new exam that it called the Learning From Text test or LFT.

In contrast to its multiple-choice entrance exams in physics, chemistry, and biology, the LFT was an essay exam calling for applicants to read texts of material for about ninety minutes, and then respond to the articles by writing three essays, each of which would demonstrate a particular kind of cognitive skill. One recent examination piece, for instance, had been written by Finnish philosopher G. H. von Wright, from a 4,000-word chapter of his book, *Science and Human Reasoning.*

In the first examination essay, the medical applicants were asked to explain two concepts (chosen by the examiners) from the von Wright article to an audience assumed to have no previous knowledge of the philosopher's complex ideas. This aspect of the LFT was called the "detailed learning task," which called on the test takers' comprehension of basic ideas in the text. In the second essay, the applicants completed the "synthesis task," which asked them to explain the piece's title, again to nonexperts. That essay called on the test takers' skills to sift through secondary and extraneous details and forge a coherent statement of von Wright's ideas. Third, the test takers were required to complete two "critique tasks," by using their general, beyond the text knowledge to evaluate von Wright's piece.

In designing the LFT, the Helsinki medical faculty wanted a test that would draw on more sophisticated cognitive abilities than were required by the multiple-choice science exams. As the study's research team explains it, the faculty hypothesized that the standardized science exams primarily tapped into medical school applicants' book learning or surface level reproduction, which would explain why the tests became increasingly insignificant the further students went in their medical studies. At later stages of training in genuine clinical situations, developing physicians faced more complex and challenging tasks, requiring what the study's authors called "deep-level construction," involving "active constructive processing, elaboration, and efforts to understand."

In order to determine whether the LFT exam would function as intended, the researchers collected data from the usual standardized entrance tests for 503 applicants to the Helsinki University Medical School and compared scores on those multiple-choice exams with the applicants' performance on the three LFT essays. To perform as intended, the LFT would have to correlate very weakly, if at all, with the three multiple-choice exams in biology, chemistry, and physics.

Indeed, applicants' scores on the multiple-choice entrance tests correlated highly with each other—as frequently happens with correlations of standardized test scores—but the standardized tests proved to be entirely unrelated to one's performance on the LFT. In turn, the three LFT results were powerfully correlated with one another.

That scores on the two divergent testing formats were wholly unrelated suggests the exams drew on distinctly different kinds of thinking processes, consistent with the deep versus surface-level strategies predicted by the cognitive psychology model. (10) The larger question, whether the LFT exam predicted medical school performance any better than the traditional standardized tests, remained for another study. Still, as Chapter 13 shows, there's ample reason to believe that institutions can actually enhance academic standards by using alternatives like the LFT when they choose candidates.

Ability Versus Speed

If standardized tests are anything, they are speeded. With speed comes the conventional wisdom that being smart and being fast on tests are one and the same thing.

A good example of a speeded test is the SAT, the common standardized test for college admissions. When the Educational Testing Service creates new forms of its so-called SAT I exam, one of its foremost considerations is to ensure that just a percentage of those who take the multiple-choice reasoning test will even finish it. Because a score on such norm-referenced tests has meaning only as a percentile comparison to nationwide averages, the ETS strives to make the test yield a wide range of test scores. Doing so results in the bulk of scores falling around the middle and fewer numbers distributed at the "tails" of the proverbial "bell curve."

Indeed, the ETS considers a given form of the SAT I appropriate if test takers, on average, get about half the questions right. In order to engineer these outcomes, ETS must make the SAT sufficiently difficult, and an important element of that difficulty is to make the SAT a speeded test, which means that, for a given level of item difficulty, there are considerably more questions on the test than test takers have time to answer.

Take the verbal section of the SAT I, for instance, which the ETS and the test's sponsor, the College Board, claim with a straight face is a test of critical thinking abilities. On the SAT I, test takers are given seventy-five minutes to answer seventy-eight multiple-choice questions, or less than sixty seconds per item. The verbal subtest is broken down into two thirty-minute sections and another fifteen-minute subtest. On a few recent thirty-minute portions, for instance, as many as 29 percent of test takers had insufficient time to complete it. But completion rates on the SAT I's mathematics subtest, where test takers are given seventy-five minutes to do sixty questions, are even worse. On a recent thirty-minute section of math items, as many as 55 percent of test takers were unable to finish. Nevertheless, with national sorting as the principal design objective built into the

SAT I, the ETS claims the exam's severe speededness is appropriate as long as virtually all students have time to complete just three-quarters of the test's questions. (11)

Rapidity is the sine qua non of most standardized tests, on which sizable proportions of the variation in abilities among test takers are derived from mere differences in the number of test items attempted and completed. The nature of such tests begs some important questions: Do test scores reflect real differences in abilities among test takers or rather differences in the speed at which people take tests? Can such tests do justice to careful reasoning, thoughtful analysis, and the sort of genuine critical thinking the ETS claims to assess, when so much emphasis is placed on speed?

Evidence and examples from a variety of standardized testing settings suggests that, in our mad rush to sort one human from another, American institutions have indeed sacrificed broader and more meaningful measures of human ability (such as the LFT exam at the University of Helsinki) on the altar of speed and efficiency.

Indeed, this premium on rapid response occurs as soon as young children are tested for their intelligence, in order, for instance, to gain admission into many American preschools and kindergartens. Readers may recall the discussion in Chapter 3 about the sorting of young children on the basis of IQ to qualify them for admission to both public and private schools. I argued that it's wrong for institutions of any stripe to sort young children on the basis of IQ, because doing so often simply reflects and reinforces built-in advantages provided to children of privileged backgrounds, and in essence denies access to other children largely on the basis of being born to less educated and well-to-do parents. Sorting with IQ tests provides enormous advantages to children raised in highly verbal, stimulating households. When children are raised by highly educated and articulate parents, they are provided with lots of practice with words, sentences, and ideas; with practice comes speed; and with speed, it turns out, comes higher scores on IQ tests that place a premium on speed of response.

Consider one commonly used IQ test for young children, the Weschler Preschool and Primary Scale of Intelligence—Revised (WPPSI-R), produced by the Psychological Corporation. The "Wippsie R," as it is often called, is aimed at children ages three to seven years, and is the benchmark intelligence test used for admission to most of New York City's private preschools and kindergartens. The Wippsie R contains about a dozen subtests, including several verbal tasks, some arithmetic items, and several performance tasks, such as object assembly, geometric design, and mazes. At the end of the test, children are given three scores: a verbal IQ, performance IQ, and a resulting overall or full-scale IQ.

The Wippsie R is built for speed. Owing to initial problems in statistical reliability (a measure of test scores' consistency after repeated administrations of the test) of the object assembly subtest, the Psychological Corporation that makes the test added bonus points for speed on the object assembly subtest. Doing so increased the test's reliability but also called into question whether the Wippsie R was becoming more a test of speed than underlying ability. Alan S. Kaufman, an

IQ testing expert at the University of Alabama, had this to say about the Wippsie R's profound emphasis on speed: "I feel guilty being forced to say 'Now HURRY!' to a preschool child who 'dawdles or seems merely to be playing with the pieces' and feel ridiculous rewarding a little person with 3 bonus points if he or she assembles a car puzzle in 5 seconds or less." So great is the Wippsie R's speeded nature, a child could get every "object assembly" puzzle right but would still score in just the ninth percentile on the subtest if he or she had received no bonus points for quick answers. (12)

Similarly dramatic results occur on another widely used IQ test for slightly older children and adolescents, the third edition of Weschler Intelligence Scale for Children (WISC-III). According to Kaufman, fully 40 percent of the total points awarded on four WISC-III subtests come from bonus points for quick responses, while 60 percent of the points are given for correct solutions. On either IQ test, says Kaufman, "many will rise to the occasion, and earn loads of bonus points. But what about the immature, reflective, insecure, or poorly coordinated child who is quite gifted? That child's I.Q. will suffer . . . because of the age-inappropriate stress on solving problems with exceptional speed." (13)

Investigators like Kaufman have based such observations on giving lots of IQ tests to children and analyzing the scoring structure of the exams themselves. However, one can also find empirical support to the claim that speeded tests are apt to reward fast, reflexive thinking and punish more reflective cognitive styles. One example is a 1996 study of the WISC-III on 141 children ages six to twelve from throughout the state of West Virginia. In the study, Ann S. Fishkin and John J. Kampsnider of the West Virginia Graduate College wondered whether IQ testing's speededness could cause educators to overlook genuinely gifted children who scored relatively poorly on the exams because they were slower, more reflective thinkers.

To answer this question, the researchers analyzed the relationship between speedy test taking and overall performance for children scoring at three levels on the WISC-III test: bright children scoring between 115 and 123; superior children with IQ scores of 124 to 131; and gifted children with WISC-III scores of 132 to 148.

As it turned out, winning bonus points for speed—answering problems in five to fifteen seconds, versus, say, forty-five seconds—is what separated the "gifted" from the merely "bright." That such dramatic differences on IQ scores could be based on a few seconds of variation in problem-solving time would seem absurd, given the potential stakes involved: being declared eligible for entry into a school's gifted program, or not. "The possibility of overemphasis on speeded performance on the WISC-III subtests," Fishkin and Kampsnider conclude, "may preclude adequate identification of some children who are abstract, reflective thinkers but are not as highly able in speed of their visual motor abilities." (14)

Evidence can also be found that speeded tests may be mismeasuring the mathematical abilities of women. This chapter already noted that females do worse than males on standardized mathematics tests and yet outperform males in the classroom, and examined a number of possible reasons for this. In addition to principally behavioral reasons, some researchers have suggested, for instance, that men do better on the SAT math test because they have superior ability to think in spatial terms. One common indicator of spacial prowess is the ability to imagine the appearance and position of a geometric object after mentally rotating it. Because males typically outdo females on mental rotation tests, and because such tests are correlated with mathematics performance, researchers have figured males' superior spatial ability might explain their superior SAT performance compared with females.

Case closed, one might then conclude: Males may tend to simply have more efficient mathematical minds than females, and it's well and good that they should have better test scores too; the tests are doing what they are supposed to do. But before jumping to that conclusion, consider this: Just like the SAT mathematics subtest, spatial tests are often themselves speeded multiple-choice exams. Rather than a natural reflection of males' mathematical prowess, could speededness itself be causing males to outperform females on both tests? What if one designed an experiment to completely remove the element of speed from a pure test of spatial ability? If, under those carefully controlled conditions, males continued to outperform women on the exams, then the theory of male math superiority might be credible.

That is precisely the kind of experiment that two mathematics educators performed on some 239 high school students attending the North Carolina School of Science and Mathematics. In their experiment, Shelagh A. Gallagher and Edward S. Johnson gave mental rotation tests consisting of thirty-two pairs of cubes to the students. The 114 males and 117 females were instructed to determine whether the cube pairs were rotated forms of the same cube or different versions. The subjects were given two trials, one timed at two minutes and the other untimed.

The results were astonishing. On the timed version of the mental rotation test, males on average attempted significantly more questions than females (22.3 versus 14.7) and thus got far more items correct than the females (20.3 compared with 12.9). But the pattern reversed itself completely when test takers worked at their own speed. Females attempted more than twice as many items (17.3 compared to 8.7) as males, and they got almost twice as many correct (13.3 versus 7.5). What's more, when the timed and untimed results were combined to form a composite score on the mental rotation test, male and female performance was virtually identical: both groups attempted all thirty-two test items and both males and females got an average of about twenty-seven items correct. Therefore, familiar gender differences were sharp on the speeded test but disappeared when test takers worked at their own pace. (15)

Standardized Minds

Gender differences in thinking styles can bear heavily on standardized test performance, but it is important to keep in mind that such differences also cut across

FOCUS: HOW THE WRONG ANSWER MAY BE THE RIGHT ONE

It is a truism that standard-issue, multiple-choice tests thrive in a black-and-white world, where there are decidedly right answers and wrong ones. This house of testing is erected upon several basic assumptions about how people, children especially, learn.

One of these assumptions is that schoolkids' mastery of a subject proceeds in a linear pattern directly proportional to the amount of instruction they receive. Another is that the choice of bubbles children scratch in on their test forms indicates their degree of conceptual understanding. Related to those two assumptions is a third one that says children who pick wrong answers have less understanding of a concept than those who pick right ones. Indeed, *understanding* must be assumed of superior test performance, because the entire ethical and philosophical basis of standardized testing would collapse without the belief that the tests were more than mere mechanical exercises.

These fundamental assumptions about standardized tests may be deeply flawed. Wrong answers may indeed be right answers if one examines schoolchildren's performance by looking at how conceptual understanding of complex ideas evolves naturally over years of schooling. Take the example of astronomy and the deceivingly simple topics like the cause of seasonal changes, the reasons for night and day, and so forth. If the answers to those questions were simple, it surely wouldn't have taken the best minds on the planet several hundred years to develop the solutions that we accept as fact nowadays.

Indeed, the facts are simple enough. A typical multiple-choice standardized test would list the one right answer and several clearly wrong distractors that don't match textbook definitions, which one can merely memorize in order to answer the test item correctly. Day changes to night because Earth spins on its axis, of course. It is written down in black and white, and you could look it up. But what if a test question tossed in some highly desirable alternatives, like one that says "the Earth moves around the sun?"

Test takers who have learned the textbook definitions in a relatively brief period of time would very likely mark the item correctly. But what if the schoolkids were exposed to a deeper study of planetary behavior in which they developed real understanding of the concepts behind the one correct answer? What if they were permitted the chance to test out their own theories of day and night using scientific method, rejecting wrong theories on their own and revising their ideas? When deeper understanding is the objective instead of the superficially correct answer, it turns out, developing minds are very well apt to pick wrong but nevertheless attractive answers, depending on their stage of conceptual understanding.

A Harvard specialist in science education, Philip M. Sadler, is among the researchers who have demonstrated this "wrong is right" phenomenon experimentally. As part of Project STAR, an experimental curriculum designed to develop conceptual understandings of astronomy and earth sciences, Sadler devised a unique multiple-choice astronomy survey built on alternative conceptions of astronomical phenomena. He gleaned these wrong, but attractive ideas from research literature about what kids believed about various natural phenomena at various stages of learning, rooting out how they think and why they might choose answers incorrectly. One question on the forty-seven-item survey, for instance, asked subjects about the reason for warmer temperatures during the summer. The correct answer is that the sun is higher in the sky, but the survey item also included attractive alternatives, such as one suggesting the temperature difference between winter and summer was owing to variable distances between the sun and Earth.

Sadler reported the five-year scoring pattern on the survey taken by about 1,250 kids in eighth through twelfth grade at a few dozen schools across the country, who were taking the STAR curriculum. Some unusual things happened. Sadler calculated the probabilities of kids' choosing the various alternative answers, including correct ones and attractive alternatives, as their abilities expanded over time. In graphical terms, he found that for almost all forty-seven items, the chance of picking the right answer (vertical axis) formed a J-shaped curve as ability levels rose (horizontal axis). This meant that as the students' understanding of astronomical concepts developed over the years, the kids were more likely to pick incorrect answers for a period of time, until they reached a point later when they fully understood a concept and therefore were more likely to pick right answers.

Indeed, standardized test makers have occasionally noticed this phenomenon, but have tended to chalk it up to oddities of testing, such as incidents of cheating or poor test building. In any case, testing companies have endeavored to design multiple-choice questions that eliminate the chance of more skilled students possibly choosing wrong answers.

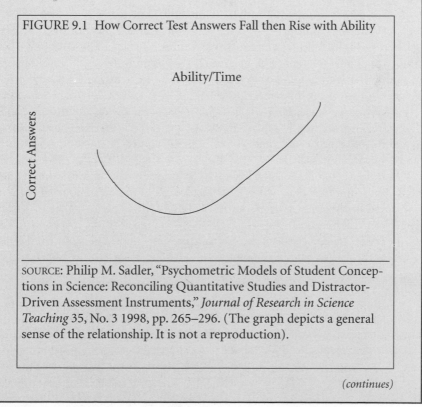

FIGURE 9.1 How Correct Test Answers Fall then Rise with Ability

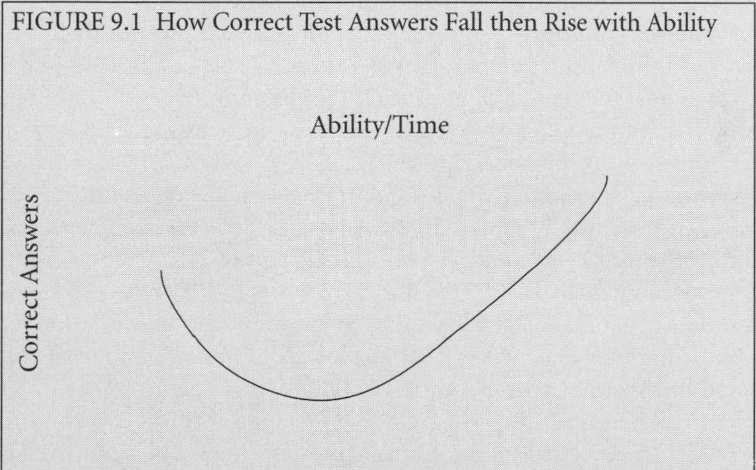

SOURCE: Philip M. Sadler, "Psychometric Models of Student Conceptions in Science: Reconciling Quantitative Studies and Distractor-Driven Assessment Instruments," *Journal of Research in Science Teaching* 35, No. 3 1998, pp. 265–296. (The graph depicts a general sense of the relationship. It is not a reproduction).

(continues)

(continued)

Sadler contends that children picking incorrect answers is not just okay, but reflects the natural process of learning and mastering highly difficult ideas that often take one years to fully understand. Only after *seeing* how wrong ideas are wrong, by experimenting, playing, and trying out their own alternative theories, do people eventually master complex ideas. Misconceptions are part and parcel of learning science, deeply and truly. The upshot, says Sadler, is for educators to devise new science assessments that monitor schoolkids' growth of conceptual understanding over time, information that isn't captured by most cookie-cutter tests that merely provide snapshots of the percentage of kids who pick right answers. (16)

That's why wrong answers on standardized tests can often be right.

gender lines. Ultimately, deep-level versus surface-level thinking, high-paced, reactive thinking versus more deliberate, reflective thinking, and so on reflect individual traits that both males and females share to greater or lesser degrees. Thus it would be foolish to assume that only females are punished by our prevailing testing methods that promote certain cognitive styles. The larger point is that the choice of test format is fully loaded with value judgments that determine individual winners and losers in the testing game.

In fact, there's reason to believe individual differences may be shared by members of different ethnic groups as well as genders, which suggests that persistent gaps in average test scores among ethnic groups have less to do with underlying ability than how that ability is measured. For instance, Jerome Schiele has suggested in the *Journal of Black Psychology* that the epistemological perspective of African Americans is fundamentally different from that of dominant white society. African Americans, Schiele tells us, have ways of knowing and thinking about the world that are largely reliant on right-brain functions, characterized by the holistic processing of information that is rarely tapped by intelligence, aptitude, and achievement tests.

On the other hand, so-called left-brain functions process information sequentially and computer-like, which is in fact virtually the only mode of thinking measured in America's testing culture. "Though lower performance of African American children on I.Q. tests is said to be the result of the disproportionate numbers of African Americans found in poverty, more attention needs to be given to the role of culture differences, of which epistemology is a part, and the extent to which design of intelligence tests reflects these differences," says Schiele. (17)

What's more, studies of brain assymetry and cognitive styles of American Indians indicate that, like African Americans, they may rely on right-brain, simultaneous mental processing more often than whites. Studies of this type have often referred to American Indians' relatively superior performance on tests of spacial and visual skill, considered a right-brain strength dependent on the ability to process information through simultaneous, parallel channels. For example, one study of schoolchildren in Hardin, Montana, compared fifty-seven Native American and sixty white children in terms of their relative strengths at sequential and simultaneous mental processing, using the Kaufman Assessment Battery for Children, which was developed to measure just such relative cognitive styles. As expected, the Native American children as a group proved to be significantly more skilled at the simultaneous processing tasks involving such spacial and visual abilities. White children, however, were better as a group at the sequential mental tasks. (18)

The implications of such findings bear not only on how kids are taught. Teaching in ways consistent with their cognitive strengths would be meaningless if school systems were then to give the same old standardized tests to all children as a universal measure of what they have learned. The speeded, multiple-choice structure of most standardized tests is historically rooted in a particular paradigm of education that largely has defined learning and teaching as rote memorization of facts and formulas; the hegemony of abstract knowledge over real-world application and performance; and rigid, militaristic hierarchies placing students in the role of passive observers. In such a paradigm, learning is artificially constructed for schoolchildren rather than something children construct for themselves by their own initiative and desire. Speeded, multiple-choice tests well serve the entrenched system of passive learning.

Indeed, when learning becomes passive, it is easily standardized. The ecology of the American merit system places most value on people with particular thinking styles that shine on fast-paced, logical, and reflexive tasks. The merit system devalues individuals who strive to deeply understand and who prefer to create something new rather than repeat something already told them. Like the process of natural selection, some individual traits thrive while others are threatened with extinction. But unlike a natural system, the American merit system has artificially decided on selection rules that ultimately determine which traits win out.

Improbable? Perhaps this paints too dim a picture. But one can find examples of just such a standardization of minds occurring in contemporary America. Again, take the medical profession as a particular example of how the merit system's selection rules have promoted a certain conformity in thinking styles. Medical educators have long been troubled by the restricted range of abilities, talents, and interests of medical students who are chosen to become doctors, based on exceedingly narrow selection rules on merit and accomplishment, which are based on test scores and science grades. Selection rules have engendered a sort of standardized medical student, a trend that medical schools have seemed helpless to counteract. Norman Anderson, as admissions dean at Johns Hopkins School of Medicine, once remarked that the very "educational independence of medical schools is eroding as psychometricians and statistical theory gain an even greater influence in determining who is fit to study medicine and how they will be trained."(19)

When thinking becomes standardized, people are easily objectified, their skills and talents translated into the language and mechanisms of commercial enterprise. "Testing," remarks Wolff-Michael Roth of Simon Frazier University, "is part of a network that turns students into commodities." (20) When deconstructed to its elemental features and placed into its broadest context, mental testing boils down to a political and economic act of rule making that implies winners and losers—hardly the enlightened tool for the wise use of human capabilities that is often claimed by the testing establishment.

So the argument for diversity in schools and the workplace takes on a new light. When examined through the lens of cognitive styles, people can be diverse in a number of ways besides ethnic origins, having differences in ways of thinking, knowing, and solving problems, differences that could actually improve the quality of American schools and workplaces if they were to be included in the merit system's gatekeeping rules.

Indeed, one possible solution to the nation's conundrum over racial preferences in affirmative action policies would be for institutions to take a color-blind view of diversity. Institutions might encourage differences in ways people learn and think, shedding the one-size-fits-all view of merit which pervades higher education. Even conservatives and psychometricians who have trouble buying into this perspective on diversity would do well to recall the writings of their own Arthur Jensen, the scholar noted for his controversial views on intelligence and race, whose work inspired the publication of *The Bell Curve*.

"An education system that puts inordinate emphasis on only one mode or style of learning will obtain meager results from the children who do not fit this pattern," Jensen wrote in a much discussed 1969 article in the *Harvard Education Review*. "Diversity rather than uniformity of approaches and aims would seem to be the key to making education rewarding for children of different patterns of ability. The reality of individual differences thus need not mean educational rewards for some children and frustration or defeat for others." (21)

In upcoming chapters, I will show how schools as well as colleges and universities in both the United States and elsewhere are being compelled to reexamine their views on diversity and the measurement of human talent. The revolution beginning to unfold is redefining the tattered and crooked rules of the American meritocracy, in favor of measures that have a far broader perspective on what people in all walks of life are capable of achieving.

10

The Big Business of Testing

A CHILD IN CALIFORNIA ENTERING THE STATE'S SCHOOLS in 1998 could expect to take at least ten standardized tests by the time she graduates from high school. Another child in the Chicago school system would take some two dozen standardized tests just from the middle of the third grade to the end of the fourth. All told, Americans take anywhere from 143 million to nearly 400 million standardized tests yearly for *education alone*, according to one careful estimate. Americans take another 50 million to nearly 200 million job tests for business and industry, and several million more for government and military jobs.

If you think somebody, somewhere is getting rich off all this testing, you'd be right. The amount Americans spend taking tests, preparing for tests, scoring tests, and running magnificently elaborate testing programs in schools, colleges, and the workplace is stunning, probably running in the billions of dollars each year. Indeed, it is possible that Americans may be taking as many as *600 million* standardized tests annually, or more than two tests per year for every man, woman, and child in the United States. (1)

The previous chapters surveyed the damage that America's test culture has inflicted on schoolchildren, schools, and adults. The question remains: who benefits from all this testing?

Of course, many politicians, parents, and institutions might believe they're better off as a result of the sorting, classifying, and measuring of schoolchildren, college aspirants, and job applicants. People who obtain the numerical credentials and test scores necessary for being placed on the fast tracks to achievement and success might be counted among the individual beneficiaries. Even these winners are counterbalanced by the losers in the testing game. So much depends on the ability of the tests themselves to predict anything meaningful, such as achievement in school or success on the job. But even that is doubtful. Who wins, really?

However you slice it, the unambiguous beneficiaries of all this testing have been business enterprises themselves, which have invested heavily in the nation's testing obsession and reaped its financial rewards. Indeed, if one wants to understand the driving forces behind the unmitigated expansion of standardized testing in the United States, then it behooves one to obey the simple adage: Follow the money.

Again, Technology Rules

Nobody really knows just how big America's testing industry is. It is a highly fragmented industry, with dozens of testing companies, both commercial and tax-exempt ones, vying for one or more of several niches in the testing market. Some companies design tests and sell them; some simply distribute and administer tests produced by others; other companies specialize in scoring tests and managing massive amounts of test data; and still other concerns fill in the margins of the testing industry, offering test consumers whole libraries of test preparation materials, from practice tests to courses intended to improve test takers' testing skills and boost their scores.

The testing of American minds has become big business, and is poised to become an even bigger business in coming years. By 1997, standardized achievement test sales in the K–12 market *alone* had reached more than $191 million, and that was up more than 21 percent in real, inflation-adjusted dollars in five years. (2) Americans are spending hundreds of millions more each year on college and university admissions tests plus job licensing and screening exams.

New testing technology has driven the industry from its inception, seeming to create and justify its own demand and uses. New methods of measuring intelligence provided its own rationale for massive IQ testing in the early 1900s. Later, standardized testing as a commercial enterprise was provided fuel for growth in the 1950s and 1960s, with the advent of technologies that permitted automated scanning and scoring of multiple-choice tests.

A half century later, the industry is on the verge of even more explosive growth, again the result of new methods of testing people that will no doubt create even greater "needs" for tests in employment and education. This time, companies are moving to exploit recent technological advances in computer and information technologies, in order to replace old pencil-and-paper tests with computerized versions of tests.

Indeed, both established testing companies, some backed by major American corporations, as well as relative upstarts, have set their sights on a potentially huge worldwide market for electronic testing. Companies see portentous growth of computerized testing in education, and they are salivating over potentially huge numbers of such standardized tests for the workplace.

As one indication of what's at stake here, consider what Nader F. Darehshori, chief executive at Houghton Mifflin Company, one sizable testing company, told Wall Street analysts in July 1998. The worldwide market for preemployment testing delivered via computers, he told analysts, represented a *$3 billion market*, some 40 percent of that in the United States. And, while computer-based testing currently made up just 10 percent of the U.S. testing market, the business was growing at a yearly clip of almost 35 percent. (3)

The Players

American companies banking on the long-term viability of the mental testing industry both in the United States and abroad include major public corporations as well as closely held, tax-exempt organizations. Some are compelled by the federal Securities and Exchange Commission (SEC) to file reams of financial data, but even these firms' operations may be masked as divisions of larger corporate concerns that choose to veil detailed information about their testing enterprises.

Others testing companies are so-called "nonprofit" ones, meaning they don't pay federal income taxes. Nevertheless, they can look like any private company whose operations are closely held. Such companies also do not file detailed reports to the SEC, but instead are required to provide somewhat more sketchy yearly reports to the Internal Revenue Service. Here are the major players:

Harcourt General Incorporated. Formerly known as the General Cinema Corporation, this nearly $4 billion-a-year company based in Chestnut Hill, Massachusetts, was once a chain of movie theaters. In 1991, General Cinema, desiring a piece of the huge market for educational publishing and testing, bought the old-line book publisher Harcourt Brace in a $1.5 billion deal.

Through its Harcourt Brace subsidiary, the company now runs several interrelated testing businesses through its Learning and Assessment Group. These include the Psychological Corporation, a testing firm founded by three well-known psychologists (James Cattell, Robert Woolworth, and Edward Thorndike) in New York City in the 1920s. Since then, the Psychological Corporation, which operates out of San Antonio, has evolved into a major supplier of standardized tests, such as Stanford Achievement Test, the Metropolitan Achievement Tests, the Weschler Intelligence Scale for Children, and the Weschler Adult Intelligence Scales.

When states adopt new testing mandates, companies such as Harcourt are first in line to reap the rewards. After Governor Pete Wilson in California nixed the innovative CLAS system of performance assessments in the late 1990s and retreated to a system based exclusively on multiple-choice, standardized testing, Harcourt Brace was there, landing a four-year contract to provide its Stanford 9 achievement tests to more than 4 million California schoolchildren. In 1998 alone, the deal yielded revenues of some $30 million to Harcourt Brace.

Although school testing remains its bread and butter, Harcourt has exceedingly high hopes for its Assessment Systems Incorporated (ASI), the company's entry into coveted market for electronically delivered employment tests. Harcourt purchased ASI in 1995, and then watched its revenues double to $50 million in just three years. ASI administers computerized versions of its standardized tests for real estate and insurance brokerage licensing in about three dozen states, in addition to electronic tests for various health occupations. George E. Simon, ASI's president, told Wall Street investors and stock analysts that ASI planned to have opened well more than 200 company-owned testing centers across the nation by the end of 1999, so that almost three-quarters of Americans would be able to travel less than 100 miles to take one of its computerized tests.

All told, testing and related businesses have been very good for Harcourt Brace in recent years. Sales of tests alone surged to $171 million by the end of 1997, an 84 percent gain from five years earlier when revenues from its standardized tests were about $93 million, company financial reports indicate. In 1998, company's Lifelong Learning and Assessment Group had revenues of some $619 million. (4)

Houghton Mifflin Company. This Boston-based company has a noble pedigree indeed when it comes to standardized testing, having published psychologist Lewis Terman's 1916 tract, *The Measurement of Intelligence,* which ushered in the dubious era of widespread and indiscriminate IQ testing in the United States.

With sales of nearly $800 million in 1997, this publishing firm owns the Riverside Publishing Company, its principal testing subsidiary. Riverside's 1998 product manual runs more than 200 pages, listing such standard-bearers as the Iowa Test of Basic Skills, a popular standardized achievement test for grade schools; and the Stanford-Binet Intelligence Scale, a commonly used intelligence test. A search on "Riverside" in one large database of published tests yielded some 240 tests, including the various forms of all Riverside's testing product line.

As mentioned, Houghton Mifflin has targeted electronic testing as the fountainhead of growth in the testing business. In 1998, the company acquired Computer Adaptive Technologies, an Evanston, Illinois, concern specializing in delivering tests to computer desktops. The deal was valued at just $16 million, but Houghton executives believe the acquisition puts them in position to compete in an estimated $1.6 billion domestic market in computerized job tests.

Meanwhile, Riverside's tried and true pencil-and-paper tests have shown few signs of weakness, company financial reports indicate. In recent years, Houghton executives have frequently cited Riverside—part of the company's educational publishing group—as among the stars of Houghton's various subsidiaries. Year after year in the 1990s, percentage sales gains in the double digits were common for Riverside. Even during years when the rest of Houghton's educational publishing business was lackluster, Riverside watched testing sales expand, rising as much as 20 percent in one twelve-month period alone. By the end of 1997, led by Riverside, the educational publishing group (Houghton does not routinely break down sales figures for individual subsidiaries) recorded revenues of $709 million, an increase of nearly 12 percent from the previous year.

Houghton's fortunes soared with a resurgence of national interest in education and standardized testing in the late 1990s. "Riverside's efforts were timed perfectly to take advantage of the renewed interest in testing which has swept through American schools in 1997," company chairman Darehshori said in January 1998. "Riverside's products won wide acceptance, and revenue growth reached double-digits." Indeed, reports filed with the Securities and Exchange Commission indicate Riverside's sales increased 17 percent that year. (5)

National Computer Systems Incorporated. When the state of California chose Harcourt Brace to supply achievement tests to 4 million students a year, testing each child each year from the second through the eleventh grades, this Minneapolis-based company's fortunes also rose: The deal was worth $12 million a year to NCS over several years.

Unlike the Harcourts and the Houghtons and other producers and publishers of tests, NCS has built a $400 million-plus enterprise in the nuts and bolts of managing massive amounts of data that comes with standardized testing of schoolchildren on a large scale. The company estimated the "test administration" segment of the testing industry alone was worth more than $1 billion in the late 1990s. NCS, for its part, has extracted a sizable chunk of that billion, watching its sales climb 23 percent in 1997 alone. Between January 1994 and January 1998, NCS revenues had increased nearly 60 percent.

Often, NCS works as a subcontractor to testing companies that win multiyear contracts with state testing agencies. In other cases, NCS contracts directly with the state. For instance, NCS has had a long-standing relationship with the Michigan Department of Education to administer its standardized tests. In 1998, that tie was reinforced when the department gave NCS another three-year deal to print, package, distribute, and score some 1.4 million state-mandated tests per year, a deal worth $13 million to NCS coffers. (6)

Indeed, in NCS's 1997 annual report to shareholders, the company prominently cited the school accountability movement—the crusadelike efforts of states to hold schools accountable by giving more tests—as economic nirvana for companies in the testing business. By the late 1990s, NCS was doing test processing for forty states. In 1997 alone, NCS processed more than 50 million tests, mostly in the United States, but also for education agencies in Australia, Canada, Japan, Latin America, and the Middle East.

Again, an even faster growing market for electronic testing, company officials say, provided impetus for NCS's April 1997 purchase, for $14.6 million, of a company known as Virtual University Enterprises. VUE was launched in 1979 to develop computerized testing for the National Association of Securities Dealers—that is, VUE made licensing tests for stockbrokers.

From the VUE platform, which focuses on the delivery and scoring of tests on the Internet, NCS executives say they're well positioned for the on-line testing workplace testing market. Indeed, its 1998 acquisition of London House and a separate software supplier from McGraw-Hill suggests NCS's business rhetoric isn't just talk. London House had been market leader in all sorts of personnel tests, and NCS's $29 million cash payment for the two McGraw-Hill divisions suddenly gave NCS and VUE an entire product line of dozens of job tests. These included personality tests for executives; tests for sales and customer service jobs; tests for office and clerical workers; mental abilities exams; and many others.

By summer 1998, VUE had persuaded Microsoft Corporation to use VUE testing centers worldwide to deliver computerized versions of the software giant's exam to become a Microsoft Certified Professional, or a technician who troubleshoots the company's software products. In announcing that deal, VUE also said it had opened 185 testing centers and was on track to have 600 centers running by year's end. The company's long-range business plan calls for opening some 2,100 testing centers worldwide.

CTB/McGraw-Hill. Formerly known as the California Test Bureau, which was founded in 1926, this Monterey, California, company boasts that it is the nation's largest publisher of "norm-referenced" exams. These are standardized tests often used in schools and college admissions that yield scores that are comparable to national averages. Most standardized tests are norm-referenced, but a growing number of tests in many states are known as criterion-referenced, in which scores have meaning only relative to the subject matter, and don't provide national comparisons.

In any case, CTB is big by any measure, mainly as a result of school achievement testing. A subsidiary of the McGraw-Hill Companies, CTB/McGraw-Hill employs 600 people and publishes sixty-five different tests, including the ever-popular California Achievement Tests, the Comprehensive Test of Basic Skills, and the National Educational Development Test—a test that claims to predict performance on various college admissions tests, such as the SAT. Besides making and selling tests, CTB processes tests and administers testing programs.

Although McGraw-Hill doesn't report CTB revenues separately, public SEC filings show that CTB is part of the company's Educational and Professional Publishing Group that contributed almost half of McGraw-Hill's $3.5 billion in 1997 sales. The publishing group's revenues increased more than 23 percent that year, climbing to $1.6 billion, while profits were up almost 13 percent. (7)

Educational Testing Service. Let us not forget the granddaddy of the mental testers, ETS, which produces and manages the SAT, PSAT, GRE, and dozens more standardized job and school testing programs. Over the course of more than fifty years since its founding by a triad of prestigious organizations in 1947, ETS has gotten rich by nearly cornering the market for college and university admissions tests.

The company's SAT was and remains ETS's real star, which will be discussed more in the chapters ahead. Suffice it to say here that the SAT was born a close cousin to the intelligence tests Americans had become enamored with in the early part of the twentieth century; that the test has always been sponsored by one of ETS's nonprofit progenitors, the College Board and its member institutions; and that the SAT has gone through various revisions, changes, and names over the years to maintain ETS's public image as a progressive and enlightened not-for-profit organization.

For years, the SAT was known as the Scholastic Aptitude Test. However, when criticisms began to mount in the late 1970s and 1980s of standardized testing's effects on America's underclasses, anything that smelled of testing for aptitude became bad public relations for testers. So the SAT became the Scholastic Assessment Test, nicely in tune with mental testers' turn to the more civilized sounding term, "assessment," which had come into vogue as the lingua franca in education circles. Instead of an aptitude test, the SAT was now, in ETS parlance, simply an "assessment of developed abilities."

Perhaps realizing an SAT name revision would be inevitable every few years, ETS later simply settled on the acronym, SAT, meaningful of nothing in particular, and eminently adaptable to changing times.

Unlike the companies highlighted above, ETS is a "not-for-profit" 501(c)(3) corporation, meaning that it pays no federal income taxes, and further, is not required to report financial information to the U.S. Securities and Exchange Commission.

Nevertheless, limited financial reports ETS files with the Internal Revenue each year show that the firm's testing business has exploded over the years. Indeed, ETS's meteoric rise in power and influence through the years has been the concrete result of one nation's unyielding fascination with the measurement of minds.

When ETS got its initial cash infusion of $750,000 from the Carnegie Foundation along with several dozen employees provided by the College Board, the company had just seventeen testing programs and a total budget of $1.7 million. By its fiftieth anniversary in 1998, ETS had 100 testing programs, a budget of $460 million, and employed some 2,400 people, with field offices across the country.

To the extent that educators and consumer advocates were expressing some serious concerns about the role of standardized testing in the 1970s and 1980s, ETS seems to have barely felt it. ETS's total sales surged 256 percent from 1980 through 1995, from $106 million to $378 million—nearly quadruple the 68 percent rise in consumer prices over the period.

Sales on ETS's main product, the SAT, were relatively weak among the company's product line: up "just" 93 percent. That's compared to a 187 percent rise in sales for graduate and professional tests; and a more than 300 percent spike in revenues for standardized tests aimed at teachers and others in academia.

That's not to say that ETS has been blind to the shifting policy and rhetorical landscape of standardized testing. In the early 1980s, the company's annual reports show, ETS embarked on a significant public relations campaign to counter the public flack it was taking over its standardized tests. ETS's theme of change and openness is repeated throughout the 1980s, until the 1993 annual report in which ETS began to talk up performance assessment, which by then had become something of a new buzzword in education.

ETS, of course, was hedging its bets: "Performance Assessment is increasingly viewed as a valuable asset for learning by educators at all levels," Gregory R. Anrig, then ETS's president, told the public in 1993. The same report went on to suggest that "new approaches to assessment transcend the limits of traditional multiple-choice, paper-and-pencil tests. In effect, assessment at ETS has moved from multiple choice to multiple choices."

Although that's nice-sounding public relations, standardized testing, not performance assessment, remains ETS's bread and butter. Most of the time, there is nothing optional about the mental measurement game. Whether taken to apply for admission to college, law school, graduate school, a New York City kindergarten, or to get hired as a professional guide in Maine, a standardized mental test is most often *mandatory*—a fact that testing companies can go to the bank with.

Except for the academic patina surrounding the ETS empire, with its universitylike atmosphere on its 360-acre campus outside of Princeton, New Jersey, complete with swimming pool, hotel, tennis facilities, and employees considered members of a faculty, one would be hard-pressed to distinguish the "not-for-profit" company from any number of profit-maximizing commercial testing ventures. Employing the familiar symbols of corporate America, many of the firm's tests and related products are registered trademarks. By June 30, 1997, the company was sitting on cash reserves of some $42 million, even after spending tens of millions on new property, buildings, and equipment over the past few years.

Rich nonprofits that sell in the commercial marketplace, competing both with other firms that pay federal taxes and those that do not, will from time to time invite scrutiny of their nonprofit status. That has been the case for ETS as well. The company passed tax-exempt muster after a three-year IRS investigation in the 1950s, but questions have risen anew in recent years. "ETS is standing on the cusp of deciding whether it is an education institution or a commercial institution," Winton Manning, a recently retired ETS executive, told the *New York Times* in 1997. "I'm disappointed in the direction they have taken away from education and public service." (8)

For its part, ETS officials believe its nonprofit designation is safe and well deserved because the company doesn't compete head-to-head with commercial firms like CTB/McGraw-Hill or Houghton Mifflin in the markets for which ETS earns the lion's share of its revenues—college and university admissions testing. Indeed, its one principal rival in that business is another nonprofit, ACT Incorporated, the Iowa City company that makes the ACT college admissions exam and that has grown into a sizable concern itself since its founding in 1959. ACT employs some 1,100 people and boasts having a product line of more than 100 tests and related services. Its ACT test, in fact, has gained market share at the expense of the SAT, with nearly one million high-schoolers now signing up to take the ACT each year.

Something of a competitive truce appears to have settled over the testing industry, at least for educational testing. The commercial companies have carved up the vast market for grade school and high school testing, apparently leaving two nonprofits, ETS and ACT Incorporated, to vie for admissions testing in higher education.

When it comes to doing what it takes to make money, there may be little real difference between ETS and its profit-seeking competitors. In order to keep the IRS at bay, ETS must continually emphasize its educational mission and notions of research for the common good, which hard-nosed economists may well view as little more than good corporate PR and tax-free R&D, the latter of which is eventually reflected in the ETS product line. ETS must play up its altruistic side, expressing its concern for American minorities, the poor, and others who have seen doors of opportunity shut to them over standardized test scores. Traces of this corporate culture are found all over ETS's public statements, particularly in its annual reports of recent years.

Beyond educational testing, however, a commercial brawl involving all the major players in the testing industry is unfolding. The chances of mergers and business failures in the years ahead seems more probable as companies duke it out for a piece of what portends to be a multibillion market in computerized testing for hundreds of occupations.

Fully recognizing the implications for its tax-exempt status were it to aggressively go after this market, ETS made a pivotal and crafty move in January 1996, spinning off a for-profit subsidiary known as the Chauncey Group to be the testing giant's designated competitor in personnel testing. ETS provided Chauncey (named for ETS's founding president, Henry Chauncey) with $18 million in cash and gave it job testing contracts worth nearly another $2 million. (9) ETS designated itself as the sole owner of Chauncey shares, but describes the relationship between them as one of "arm's length."

The pieces have fallen quickly into place for Chauncey. The ETS subsidiary made its first major acquisition in July 1997, paying $20 million for the Insurance Testing Corporation, a provider of standardized licensing tests for real-estate agents and insurance brokers. Further, Chauncey was positioned to exploit ETS's new relationship with a once-sleepy little company called Sylvan Learning Systems. In 1993, ETS signed a multimillion-dollar contract with Sylvan to be ETS's exclusive provider of electronic tests at Sylvan's learning centers in North America—a relationship that ACT Incorporated has contested in federal district court as a possible violation of antitrust laws.

Nevertheless, in July 1998, Baltimore-based Sylvan announced the renewal of its agreement with ETS, extending through 2005, to electronically deliver ETS's academic admissions tests, particularly the GRE and the Graduate Management Admissions Test, as well as Chauncey's personnel exams. That agreement was in addition to a separate, ten-year deal for Sylvan to deliver ETS and Chauncey tests outside North America. By September 1998, Sylvan was operating 174 permanent testing centers and eighty-eight temporary ones in more than 100 countries, delivering electronic versions of ETS's tests.

The ETS-Sylvan marriage has proven to be of considerable value to Sylvan, transforming it almost overnight into an important player in the testing industry. Sylvan's rise has been nothing less than meteoric. In 1993, Sylvan was a small company by most standards, with sales of $51.5 million, according its SEC filings. By the end of 1997, Sylvan's revenues had climbed to $246.2 million, a staggering 378 percent increase.

That pace has shown no signs of slowing. Sylvan's 1997 sales were up 35 percent from the prior year's; and through just the first nine months of 1998, revenues had climbed to $295 million, running a full 47 percent ahead of sales for the same nine months a year earlier.

The Periphery

Prior to joining forces with ETS, Sylvan Learning Systems was a good example of smaller companies that have risen on the periphery of the testing industry, whose very existence has depended on mandatory standardized testing. These firms include hundreds of small test-prep shops across the country, employing a handful of people each, who coach people for college and university admissions tests.

Mostly, however, these subsidiary enterprises include the Coke and Pepsi of the test-prep industry: the Princeton Review and Stanley H. Kaplan, a subsidiary of the Washington Post Company. Kaplan won't specify its sales figures, but its parent's SEC reports show that Kaplan enrolled some 125,000 customers in its test-prep courses in 1997. Owning some 1,200 coaching centers worldwide, Kaplan is a major part of the Washington Post Company's nonpublishing businesses, which racked up $157.4 million in sales in 1997, up 7 percent in a year. Kaplan's sales, however, contributed half the gain, advancing 21 percent, a not-unusual occurrence for the firm in the 1990s, as hundreds of thousands of students have sought any possible edge in the competition for admission to good colleges and graduate programs.

For its part, the Princeton Review assumes a no-holds-barred, test-bashing marketing persona, but nevertheless was posting sales of about $60 million annually in the late 1990s, a spokeswoman told me. That was double the company's 1992 sales, which were also up 25 percent in a year.

Nowadays, like Kaplan, Princeton Review's sales growth is closely guarded in the feverish competition between the two big coaching services. "We don't release our revenues, but I can tell you that in 1998 we worked with nearly 80,000 students in Princeton Review courses for tests at the high school, grad school, and professional level," company spokesman Kevin McMullin told me. As an independent concern, Princeton Review says it maintains some 700 test-coaching sites in sixty U.S. and foreign cities.

Test coaching firms also exploit public school testing. For example, when the state of Texas launched its new Texas Assessment of Academic Skills exams, a cottage industry soon ensued as entrepreneurs started selling practice TAAS tests for pupils and teachers. When states' accountability programs require schools to post certain test scores gains in order to avoid educational damnation, still more educational consultants pop up, promising schools huge gains in student achievement test scores.

Pick up any issue of *Education Week*, a leading trade publication for public schools, and see the advertised promises. For instance, one September 1998 advertisement by American Guidance Service (AGS), was headlined: TEST SCORES INCREASE BY OVER 300% AT GEORGIA ELEMENTARY SCHOOL. The Minnesota firm tells prospective customers that its program can take the "(T)error out of the Iowa Test of Basic Skills (ITBS)."

In the very same issue of *Education Week* (September 9), another company called Lightspan boasted that its test-prep program won schools in New York, Iowa, and Arizona double-digit gains on such widely used standardized tests as the California Tests of Basic Skills, ITBS, and the Stanford Achievement Tests.

Lightspan perhaps speaks for the entire testing industry, and in more ways than one, when it says, "There is no limit."

11

Authentic Achievement: Assessing Performance in American Schools

"Swimming Upstream"

A longtime teacher and school administrator, John Parker had grown accustomed to running up against the standardized testing culture of North Carolina. Chiefly, there were the North Carolina state bureaucrats to please and the ubiquitous presence of the ABCs of Public Education, the state's massive system of do-or-die testing of children in his school district. Parker and his progressive educational ideals mixed like oil and water with the Skinnerian world of the ABCs.

To be sure, the politicians had stocked the ABCs with all the right tools: multiple-choice reading and math tests in grades three through eight; end-of-course high school exams in several subjects ranging from algebra to biology to economics; competency exams to get a high school diploma; and boatloads of stick-or-carrot incentives intended to push teachers, schools, and pupils to achieve the coveted bottom-line results. All eyes were on test score gains.

Even Parker's modest plan to have teachers quit thinking about the ABCs occasionally by holding Socratic-like seminars with their students was met with resistance by teachers. Parker figured the Socratic dialogues would give teachers a chance to explore subjects and ideas in depth with pupils, to do what most teachers had entered the profession for in the first place—in short, to really *teach.* But some of Parker's teachers couldn't do it, didn't have time to do it, weren't interested in doing it, and, most important of all, told Parker there was no point in doing it. If Socratic seminars didn't immediately, directly, and incontrovertibly lead to higher ABCs results, why bother?

If higher test scores were what the General Assembly, parents, and taxpayers demanded, that's what they'd get from the state's teaching force. And, they *would* get them. Almost overnight, some of the poorest-performing schools in the state were making extraordinary test-score gains on their ABCs. No matter that their impressive boosts were wrought from rather dubious teaching methods that had mutated many North Carolina classrooms into test-item drill sessions, conducted by teachers turned technical functionaries. Teaching to the test? That bugaboo was now an old-fashioned, needless fear of educational fuddy-duddies. Hardly anybody cared about how you got there so long as you got there.

In short, there were dozens of reasons for people like Parker, the assistant superintendent for curriculum and instruction in Roanoke Rapids Schools near the Virginia border, to just go along and play the state's test-score game. Yet he couldn't ignore this educational disaster in the making.

Despite all the legal and monetary incentives to focus on test scores, an educational rebellion of sorts has occurred in recent years in North Carolina. Some of the state's educators have seen the damage to teaching and learning that the test-score obsession has wrought, and they've chosen a different path to school reform.

These North Carolina upstarts aren't alone. People in the trenches of teaching and learning in schools across the country are choosing to defy the test-score imperative. Instead of dwelling on what schoolchildren *can't* do, as defined by abstract standardized tests with dubious connection to reality, these educators are trying to get a firmer grasp of what pupils *can* do, on tasks that do have some meaningful connection to the real world. Doing so, these educational rebels are discovering that when schoolchildren are permitted to show their stuff for genuine purposes, through writing, speaking, presenting, building, drawing, solving, synthesizing, and analyzing, then going to school suddenly becomes a lot more interesting.

Call it authentic assessment, performance-based assessment, or any number of terms educators have invented to describe these alternatives to standardized-test driven schools. Whatever you call it, students and teachers have discovered that learning *and* teaching aren't only harder, but a lot more fun when everybody involved turns their eyes on the real prize, that of *learning* itself.

This chapter looks at some exemplary educators and schoolchildren in North Carolina, as well as states like Kentucky and Washington, who, despite officialdom's standardized test score mandates, are falling in love again. They're falling in love with learning and teaching, and they're rediscovering what school should be all about.

Parker's Hope

Even before the ABCs came along, North Carolina schoolchildren had been among the most tested in the nation. Year after year, the General Assembly kept ratcheting up the accountability machinery in a continuously evolving alphabet soup of new testing programs. One important ally for change came from the governor's office. James B. Hunt, a Democrat, had given his blessing to arguments being forcefully advanced by Parker and others that the state's sole dependence on the standardized testing model as a measure of school quality could mean big trouble in the long run.

Sure, the state could artificially jack up test scores and threaten students, teachers, and schools with all manner of sanctions for nonperformance. But such short-term test-score boosts would be ill-gotten, and would last as long as the current version of whatever standardized test was in use. Then test scores would invariably recede until teachers had, again, reworked testlike items into their drilling-and-killing machine. Is that what the state's taxpayers *really* wanted?

Parker's hope for modifying the General Assembly's perspectives on school reform came with the creation of a new commission the assembly had formed to do a top-to-bottom examination of the state's academic standards for public schoolchildren. Launched in 1993, the Education Standards and Accountability Commission was charged with figuring out just what North Carolina pupils ought to know and be able to do—the proverbial setting of standards many states had recently been embarking upon. The commission also needed to figure out how to determine whether children were meeting the standards. The commission would be chaired by E. K. Fretwell, a former school superintendent from Charlotte, while Sam Houston, a well-connected lobbyist from Raleigh, would direct the commission's day-to-day affairs.

Meanwhile, seeds for the ABCs had also been planted, and its development continued along separate tracks in the state bureaucracy. Eventually, the two tracks would have to merge into a single plan for North Carolina school reform. As it happened, the commission came up with a proposal that wound up placing considerably less emphasis on standardized testing than North Carolinians had been accustomed to. The commission was careful in its public statements not to appear eager to scrap standardized testing altogether, occasionally describing, for instance, its developing model as ABCs Plus. Still, the commission's written reports, at the very least, suggested that school reform driven by standardized tests was an idea whose time had passed if North Carolina wanted top-notch public schools.

In its first year of existence, the commission held dozens of public meetings throughout the state, listening to ideas from parents, business, and education leaders and others about what North Carolina graduates should know and be able to do after graduation. It became clear what the public wanted. Of course, people wanted graduates who could read, write, do math problems, and possess a modicum of computer literacy. But state residents also wanted young graduates who could speak and listen well, work happily in teams, and apply their knowledge and skills to real-world problems and situations. The public wanted lifelong learners and graduates who cared about doing work of quality, no matter what the task. With the public's input, the commission boiled down these public sentiments to six competency areas in which North Carolina's young people had to demonstrate proficiency in order to leave its schools with a high school diploma: communication, using numbers and data, problem solving, processing information, teamwork, and using technology.

With a list of competencies as broad as those, it became immediately apparent that the usual multiple-choice, standardized tests North Carolina had been so fond of for so many years wouldn't be up to the job. The old standardized tests were simply too blunt a tool to assess the complexities and nuances of student learning.

If one wanted to determine whether students really were learning at high levels—as the public apparently wanted—pupils would take their knowledge in math, reading, and science and apply it to the ill-structured messiness the real world usually presents. Not only that, the commission realized, standardized tests have one particular shortcoming antithetical to what it was trying to accomplish. The old tests promoted a kind of superficial, rudimentary teaching and learning completely at odds with the high standards the public insisted it wanted.

What to do? The commission, without reservations, embraced a relatively recent development in the annals of educational testing and assessment in the United States, a sort of "test" variously known among educators as performance assessment, authentic assessment, or alternative assessment. Authentic assessment ideas had been bubbling up through the educational system for several years by then, chiefly the result of educators like Parker across the country becoming disenchanted with high-stakes testing as virtually the only widely recognized yardstick of educational quality and merit. Besides that, evidence emerging from the research community about the unwholesome effects on teaching and learning from the nation's test dependency was becoming crystal clear: large-

scale, big-stakes testing was doing more harm than good. However, getting parents, policymakers, and others to recognize that was a different question.

The idea of performance assessment certainly had natural appeal for progressives like Parker. If parents, teachers, and taxpayers must determine how children are doing in school, then make the assessment real. A chief complaint about standardized testing in schools was that it forced students to de-contextualize their knowledge and skills. That is, the often-abstract, superficial nature of most multiple-choice tests neither permitted students to think deeply and creatively, nor to engage with problems at a level of abstraction closer to real problems and situations. Developments in cognitive psychology had shown that learning context was not simply a matter of the 1960s refrain that school must be "relevant," but in fact reflected the way people think and learn.

If the tests themselves were real, then, to the extent that teachers were faced with institutional incentives to teach the test, at least they'd be teaching to something worthwhile. That is, they'd be teaching knowledge and skills necessary to perform on tasks that had some connection to real-life problems and situations. Authentic, or performance assessment could take many forms. At a minimum, performance assessment could mean open-ended test items on which correct answers may not be as educationally important as determining how well a child actually *understands* a concept. Performance assessment could mean teachers

compiling portfolios of student work so that detailed comparisons could be made to assess a child's progress and understanding over time. Authentic assessment might mean children tackling big projects, lasting several months or weeks, where they bring together knowledge and skills in several subjects, such as math, science, and writing. In the end, the children present their findings on, say, the environmental and political issues of a local proposal to build a new coal mine, in concrete terms, from essays to artwork to scale models to multimedia presentations.

In its recommendations to the governor and to the General Assembly, the commission drew directly from the performance assessment playbook advocated by reformers. That was owing, in no small measure, to the commission's 1994 decision to hire the Center on Learning Assessment, and School Structure out of Princeton, New Jersey, headed by Grant Wiggins. Indeed, Wiggins was widely known in education circles as one of the nation's foremost authentic assessment gurus, having written widely and passionately on the subject for many years.

The commission stated with a certain bravado that an assessment is real-world if it, for instance, "replicates or simulates the ways in which a person's knowledge and abilities are tested in real-world situations"; if it "asks the student to 'do' the subject—to *do* science or history, not just recite or replicate"; or "simulates the *contexts*" that adults encounter in jobs and life, complete with the "constraints, messiness and murkiness so common to life's challenges—but so typically absent from neat-and-clean school tests." (1)

With those ideals, the commission proposed what it called the Next Century Assessment for North Carolina, or NCANC. Truth be told, the final plan proved to be relatively conservative in its call for a balanced system for evaluating the academic achievements of North Carolina's schoolchildren. The NCANC would consist of some standardized testing, some performance assessments, and what it called an anthology of materials marking student progress over time.

What's more, the commission called on the state's schools, by the year 2000, to launch the granddaddy of all performance tasks, a high school project for seniors, culminating in an oral presentation to a panel of local educators and community members. Seniors would have to successfully complete the project in order to graduate.

A David and Goliath Story

For Parker, who had witnessed the abuses of test-driven schools in his state for so long, who had harangued state educational officials every chance he got to put an end to the nonsense, the commission's proposals radiated with hope for genuine reform. That such reforms were being contemplated at the highest levels of policymaking, Parker figured, was momentous.

If the commission's recommendations were enacted, then maybe what happened one memorable year for many people in nearby Northampton County Schools, where Parker had worked prior to taking a new job in Roanoke Rapids, could be repeated frequently and systematically across the state. Perhaps the commission's reforms could make it okay for teachers to take risks, the way it happened in Northampton.

In the early 1990s at Northampton High School, Parker's reform-mindedness found its beginning, in the poor, rural, and mostly black county in which Parker had been born and raised. Then director of instruction at Northampton High, Parker was approached one day by Randy Shillenburg, an executive at the local North Carolina subsidiary of Virginia Power. Shillenburg wondered, would Parker be interested in Shillenburg's company sponsoring Northampton High's entry into a regional electric vehicle competition?

The Richmond Eastern Regional Competition would include schools from throughout the eastern seaboard, including the elite schools from Virginia, Pennsylvania, Washington, D.C., and North Carolina. Surely, Northampton would be out of place in such a competition, being one of the lowest-achieving schools in North Carolina on the state's standardized tests. Nevertheless, Parker took up Shillenburg's offer, figuring there would be little to lose for his students and possibly a lot to learn from just trying. Parker recruited an unlikely pair of teachers to oversee the project, who for unusual but fortuitous reasons turned out to be fairly immune to the state's test-score mandates: A longtime auto shop teacher, Harold Miller, whose subject rarely required him to fret about the state's accountability tests; and a young science teacher fresh out of UC-Berkeley named Eric Ryan. For Ryan, having come to Northampton through the recently created Teach for America program, the need to jack up his students' test scores was also not a pressing need.

"We thought we'd just build this car, take our kids up there to Richmond just for the experience. None of us had any hopes of winning," Parker told me. "We knew what we were up against."

Over the next several months leading up to the big event, Parker watched the auto shop and science students take their physics and auto design lessons from Ryan and Miller and figure out how to build their electric-powered car, which they called *Shocker 1*. The requirements of the competition kept the Northampton students focused on what they needed to accomplish. There would be a ten-minute presentation about their car, evaluated by a panel of judges; a track test of *Shocker 1*'s electrical efficiency; and two team members, randomly selected by the judges, who would explain how *Shocker 1* was designed and built.

In spring 1994, the Northampton Electric Automobile Team traveled to Richmond as planned. The story that followed would become part of local legend. The team won easily, with *Shocker 1* and its creators crushing the elite eastern seaboard schools in most of the events. The unimaginable result qualified the *Shocker 1* team to compete in Arizona Public Service's national electric vehicle competition the following year, the oldest such event in the nation. With the $5,000 the team had won in Richmond, they raised a total of $25,000 to build another car and travel to the Phoenix event.

Again, Parker watched the team do what most observers believed impossible. He watched their young driver, Katrina Deloatch, patiently circle the track eighty-nine times, including ten laps alone as the other teams' vehicles one by one ran out of steam. She never wavered from the designated forty-five miles an hour the team had calculated for maximum fuel efficiency. The Northampton team placed first among dozens of teams from throughout the country. "Everybody was bawling," says Parker. "It was David and Goliath right in front of your eyes."

Clearly, a new kind of teaching and learning was going on here, and when the competitions were over, Parker was determined to try to incorporate its features into the school's curriculum. Here were these students from a school considered an educational wreck who had not just learned physics and auto mechanics but had used that knowledge to outperform students from the best math and science programs in the country. "I had been in this business twenty-six years, and I feel like I've had some wonderful educational experiences, but to me this whole electric car thing was the ultimate," Parker says. "We wanted to develop a whole junior and senior curriculum based on projects like this. Eric and I were dreaming about expanding the ideas to other areas where students could produce something, write about it, and talk about it."

Parker scoured the teaching staff looking for recruits to experiment with project-oriented teaching. But he ran into resistance from teachers who were unwilling to take risks with their test scores. Again, the same state accountability mandates loomed over their heads. "The bottom line was you're not going to get people to take the chances," Parker told me. "Everybody was so narrowly focused on the tests; there's just incredible pressure on them to make sure kids do well on the tests. You think, 'If teachers were just broad-minded enough to try something else,' but it's a hard sell."

Growing it Locally

When Parker's great ambitions that arose from the Northampton experience seemed to die on the vine for lack of interest, the Standards and Accountability Commission seemed a last, best hope for reformers.

However, as the drumbeat for school reform gained pace in the mid-1990s, the commission's time began to run out. Under marching orders from the public to "make schools accountable," the General Assembly wanted a new, sharp-toothed accountability system, and it wanted it now. In purely pragmatic terms, the ABCs model proved to be far less complicated than the sweeping NCANC plan to develop and implement. You don't do a bottom-to-top overhaul of the state's entire educational philosophy and practice without years of development, professional training, trial and error, and a bit of public education to boot. Into that mix came proponents of school vouchers nipping at legislators' heels. If the General Assembly didn't pass something immediately workable, even if antithetical to political moderates, vouchers would take center stage.

In the end, the Standards and Accountability Commission didn't have the requisite political clout. After the Senate beat back House proposals to go full-bore into vouchers, lawmakers saw the ABCs as the quick fix to which most of the political players could agree. Multiple-choice measurement by the numbers, severe sanctions for poor numbers, and more attractive rewards for ever higher numbers—these were the modern tools of education reform in the United States. As far as the General Assembly was concerned, authentic assessment was dead on arrival.

Meanwhile, Parker took his new job as assistant superintendent at Roanoke Rapids. There, he embarked on a new path to find local money and simply build a local network of teachers committed to doing authentic assessment from the ground up, with or without state support. As part of the strategy, Roanoke Rapids joined forces with a small faction of other districts across the state that wanted to launch local performance-assessment initiatives, despite the disincentives to do so in the state's ABCs accountability plan. "We decided to try to grow it locally," Parker told me.

Indeed, besides formidable disincentives presented by the ABCs for teachers and schools to innovate with authentic assessments, Parker and his allies faced the intractable power of tradition in the teaching profession. For his part, Parker had been a science and math teacher for two decades, mostly in Northampton County. Parker realized that even recently hired teachers had graduated from education schools without practical knowledge in performance assessment beyond a mention or two in a teaching methods course. Moreover, teachers left teaching programs to embark on thirty years of teaching with precious little professional development along the way.

Parker also understood that *how* you assessed pupils and what information you were looking for from testing could imply radically different kinds of teaching and learning. Traditional, standardized test-driven systems seemed to go hand-in-glove with habits of classroom organization and method that had existed for a century or more in American education. There was a teacher and there were her pupils, and the teacher commanded from a spot at the front of the classroom, imparting facts, formulas, and information to all those blank slates in her pupils' heads. A multiple-choice test that could be taken by hundreds if not thousands of pupils in one sitting was the logical extension of teachers' old habits in the classroom. One implied the other, and vice versa.

If one transformed the method of assessment to emphasize all that standardized tests were not, such as performance, application, creativity, problem solving, inventiveness, open-endedness, muddiness, and so forth, then one would be calling for a very different sort of teaching and learning, possibly even a different idea of what a classroom should be. Were North Carolina's schoolchildren to become at least proficient in the seven competencies that the Standards and Accountability Commission had called for, not just the tests would need to change. If students were to become proficient communicators, problem solvers, and team players, then teachers would have to give them ample opportunities to learn how to become good communicators, problem solvers, and team players. Just as standardized tests wouldn't cut it in this new universe, neither would teachers' 100-year-old teaching methods.

Thus, central to Parker's "grow it locally" plan in Roanoke Rapids would be some sorely needed professional development money for teachers. Parker was able to cobble together about $300,000 from various grant sources for training teachers in using performance assessment. Mainly, the money would go to teachers willing to test performance assessment projects with their pupils. Parker started asking for volunteers, but few teachers were willing to take the plunge in light of the whole array of institutional incentives not to. What would a few extra dollars mean if their jobs were put in jeopardy because of poor performance on the ABCs exams?

Specifically, Parker asked teachers if they would be willing to try out one of a few performance projects with their students, depending on the grade level. One, for instance, was titled Green Groceries, and it posed the following challenge to students: As an environmentally conscious grocery story chain with 112 stores in the Southeast, the Green Groceries Company wanted to design a twelve-ounce cylindrical container for an herbal soft drink that would minimize the amount of waste in production. The students, that is, market researchers for the company, were to report their findings to their supervisors in the marketing department. Besides designing the package, the students were to provide a written report, create a mock-up of the container, and produce a video commercial that would position Green Groceries and the new design in the marketplace. In the end, the students' efforts would be evaluated in terms of the quality of their written reports, model containers, and the commercials, as well as how well they worked together in teams.

Clearly, Parker figured, this performance task would be suitable for highschoolers, so he pitched the project idea to his high school math teachers to try on their regularly progressing algebra students. No dice, the teachers replied. Their higher-level math students, such as those in the geometry or trigonometry classes, might be able to do the task, the teachers told Parker. Maybe even the advanced algebra students. But their regular algebra students? No way.

Desperate for teachers to train with his newfound grant monies, as a last resort Parker turned to a less than ideal group of mostly poor and academically at-risk eighth-graders.

Plunging into Performance Assessment

An eighth-grade teacher at the Chaloner Middle School in Roanoke Rapids, Ann Hayes had spent fifteen years teaching in some of the most challenging educational circumstances any teacher can face. A special education expert, Hayes worked both ends of the academic spectrum, from teaching gifted and talented children to working with the pupils most at risk of failing in the school system.

In 1997, Hayes was in charge of an experimental class of fifteen pupils. Virtually all of them were considered to be poor, that is, eligible for free lunches under federal definitions. The experimental class was designed to keep the at-risk kids together, immersing them as a whole group in their math and language arts remediation. The district wanted to see whether any academic and personal gains in such a cloistered setting might offset any stigmatization the kids might experience being separated from the rest of the school.

One day, Parker approached Hayes with the Green Groceries challenge. "He asked me if I was willing to experiment with something," Hayes told me, "Something different that might work with my kids. I had no idea what he had in mind."

Parker showed Hayes his Green Groceries task and told her, with all the optimism of the salesman he was becoming, that the project could be completed as a three-week unit. By doing the project, Parker told Hayes, she could beef up her students' skills in math, language arts, communications, and teamwork. Moreover, they'd have real purpose for doing the project, with a genuine audience for their efforts. Hayes and Parker knew full well that these fifteen students would be a particularly hard group to crack—and not because they lacked the intellectual ability to do the work. In recent years, both educators had noticed many, many students were bored and disengaged from academics, believing schoolwork was completely irrelevant to their particular circumstances and aspirations. To be sure, the general problem of student disengagement from school was an old one, but it seemed to have become particularly acute in recent years. "The kids I teach don't think school is important, and they don't think it has anything to do with what they will end up doing in life," Hayes told me. "They've never seen algebra as something they will use. For them, school has always been a punishment they have to live through."

Realizing she had little to lose with her perennially low achievers, Hayes signed on to Parker's proposal, and the class launched into the Green Groceries project in November 1997. A task that was initially thought to require less than a month to complete evolved into a six-month effort, taking on a life of its own. Once her students bought into the idea that they *owned* the project at hand, the miraculous happened. They *wanted* to solve the problem of creating a can for the herbal drink that would conserve raw materials; and they understood the importance of presenting their findings as professionally as they could and persuading their audience of their solution's feasibility. Hayes's pupils immersed themselves in requisite lessons and exercises in geometry, algebra, writing, and other subjects because those lessons took on new meaning. Suddenly, all that boring stuff became necessary tools to complete the project. "They were in charge of what they needed to know," Hayes says. "John and I had plans, but it never ended up where we thought it was going to go. The students had their own agendas."

Indeed, by doing the Green Groceries project, Hayes's class covered all six "strands" of the North Carolina mathematics curriculum for eighth-graders, including geometry, problem solving, algebra, and so forth. But the kids always kept in mind their final objective to successfully complete the project. One student asked Hayes one day, " 'Tell me again, what does this have to do with solving the problem?' " she recalls. "Just like buying a new house, if you've never measured a wall in your life, the task suddenly is interesting to you when you need to put in furniture. It has to do with real life. My kids are motivated by solving an interesting problem. It makes them feel like they are real adults, and these problems are the kinds of problems adults solve, and they like that idea. These are the kinds of things that might mean something to someone."

That point crystallized one day when the class was working on a fairly standard lesson on determining the numerical value of *pi* by measuring circles. Off to the side, Hayes noticed one student, Caleb, furiously punching digits into his calculator, solving the *pi* problem on his own with mathematical reasoning (Caleb is not his real name).

By the usual measures of academic achievement, especially on standardized tests, Caleb proved himself to be just another unremarkable low achiever, the usual role the school system had designated for him and others like him. Indeed, Caleb could hardly read until he reached the sixth grade. His teachers had suspected he might have a learning disability in reading, but his schools never followed up on that hunch because of an arcane and probably absurd rule common in American education. According to policy, a child couldn't be accommodated for his or her learning disability unless there was a wide enough gap between "ability to learn," measured by IQ tests, and actual achievement, measured by standardized test scores—the theory being that a learning disability was the cause of the IQ-achievement gap. Because Caleb's IQ was measured at below average—in all likelihood *because* of his reading disability—he did not qualify for help for his reading disability.

In any case, Caleb's work on the Green Groceries project demonstrated an aptitude for mathematical reasoning that the schools had never before been able to tap. "He was over there with his calculator while the rest were plodding through the circles. He kept going and going until he got *pi*," says Hayes. "I would never have known he could have done that. I think it even surprised him. He was just hooked, and he began to really shine." Hayes continued, "On regular standardized tests, he didn't shine at all. But I noticed when we would sit down to talk and I'd ask him to show me how he did something, he knew exactly how to do it. What I've realized from doing authentic assessment is that on most traditional tests, we ask students just a small fragment of what they know and in a way that they may not be able to tell us what they know."

Throughout the project, Hayes's eighth-graders relied on their sense of logical relationships and ability to think things out rather than on strict mathematical formulas. They started with a big picture of the whole problem, and broke it down into smaller tasks and details. Hayes knew that letting them work this way was far different than how most American teachers approach their subjects. Most teachers begin with the details, the formulas and proofs, then work up, maybe, to a concrete application of those details. In this new universe of learning, the details and the application become inseparable. "My children are pretty naive with formulas and things like that," Hayes told me. "You couldn't get formulas across to them if you wrote it on their arms. These kids are really bad with details. So often, 'normal' teaching starts with the details and builds up to a big idea. With my kids, it somehow works to take a big idea and work down."

And so, this Dickensian bunch of middle-schoolers, considered the "lowest of the low" in the Roanoke Rapids academic hierarchy, accomplished what few thought possible, completing a project widely believed to be only within the reach of the top math students in the district.

The following year, Hayes continued to use the Green Groceries and other performance assessment projects with a new crop of low-achieving eighth-graders. The Green Groceries task had involved a fictionalized chain of food stores, while the next year's class took on projects with connections to the real world and genuine public controversies. When I spoke with Hayes, the class was just then working on a study of the Cape Hatteras Lighthouse, a state historical treasure located on the coast some four hours' drive from Roanoke Rapids. Owing to years of erosion of the long strand of land dividing Pamlico Sound and the Atlantic Ocean, the lighthouse was in danger of being washed away to sea. State residents and public officials were unsure whether to move the lighthouse to a new spot, or to try to preserve its existing location by shoring up the seawalls protecting the structure from the Atlantic.

Hayes's performance assessment task required her students to study the problem and become grounded in the scientific and economic issues, build scale models of the 208-foot lighthouse, and finally synthesize their findings with a research report in which they would make their recommendation about the lighthouse's fate to the North Carolina Historical Society. When finished, Hayes told me, she would score each element of the students' projects—the scale model, the research paper, and so on—according to clear and agreed-upon standards of quality, such as the degree of mathematical accuracy of the scale models or how well a student supported his or her position on the lighthouse's fate.

Having plunged headlong into authentic assessment, Hayes says the transformation of her classrooms to something entirely new to her experience seemed complete when she realized she had discarded most textbooks from her teaching. Everything about her new approach violated traditional expectations but for one remarkable thing. When the 1997 school year came to a close, her students took the statewide, end-of-course standardized tests required by the ABCs, and the kids produced the best test scores Hayes had ever seen in years of remediation work with at-risk students.

Profoundly, Hayes had discovered an enigmatic phenomenon about authentic assessment that flew in the face of conventional wisdom. According to the cookbook, the more you focused on the bottom-line test results, directly imparting test-savvy facts, information, and formulas, the better students would perform on standardized tests. Indeed, they might, but the real question remained: Did students trained to achieve in this way really *understand* what they were doing?

By using projects and performances for evaluating what her students could do, Hayes discovered just the opposite: The less heed she paid to test scores, the more attention she paid to the *process* of learning, the more her students understood. Hayes could tell whether the kids understood, because she *watched them* in the process of gaining understanding. That the same students demonstrated remarkable improvements on later standardized test scores proved to be a surprising bonus, frosting on the authentic assessment cake.

"I can tell you the difference," Hayes confidently said to me. "I taught math to these kids for eight years, and I never got the scores that I had last year. . . . I believe the Green Groceries project was largely responsible for that. I think we can do (authentic assessment) and still get the test scores."

The Movement Spreads

When successes like Hayes's began to accumulate from the bottom up, the authentic assessment idea refused to die in North Carolina, as a handful of go-it-alone districts kept taking risks and finding success. Mack C. E. McCary III, the assistant superintendent for instruction in Elizabeth City–Pasquotank Schools, was among Parker's allies in the drive to make authentic assessment happen at the local level, despite the ABCs law and the demise of the Standards Commission.

McCary had the sort of background that, those in the business world might say, allowed him to think outside the proverbial box. He'd been an educator for more than twenty-five years, but with stints in between as an inner-city social worker, computer entrepreneur, and director of a foster care training program in Tennessee. His first job out of Yale in 1970 was teaching first-graders; thirteen years later, McCary earned his education doctorate at Harvard. As a research and testing director at Durham County schools in North Carolina in the late 1980s, McCary got his first exposure to performance assessment ideas through the work of Grant Wiggins, who provided the philosophy, and Richard Stiggins, whom many considered a leading authority on the nuts and bolts of implementing performance tasks in schools. "I had gotten really fed up with the 'game' of standardized test scores, which seemed to have little to do with the quality of instruction and learning in classrooms," McCary explained.

Like Parker, McCary encountered the same political difficulties that innovative districts faced trying to implement performance assessment in test-heavy North Carolina. "I've described it as swimming upstream," McCary told me. "It's a high-stakes environment for many teachers, and they feel not just pressure, but downright fear. When that occurs, then teachers tend to go toward solutions they believe will work. If they get good results on the state's measure, then they're not willing to examine whether there's a better way."

Whereas a key part of Parker's strategy was to obtain outside funding for persuading teachers to try performance assessment and slowly build a network of experienced staff, McCary realized another possible strategy was to *require* students to do performance-based projects as a matter of district policy. Thus in the late 1990s, the Elizabeth City–Pasquotank school board, with McCary's urging, launched a major performance-based graduation requirement for the district's high-schoolers.

As a requirement for graduation, high school seniors had to conduct a senior project, in which they were to conceive, plan, research, write, and formally present their findings before a panel of faculty judges. The entire project consisted of four components to be evaluated, and the seniors would have to pass all four in order to meet the graduation requirement. Students had to complete the research paper; present the paper to a panel of judges; document at least fifteen hours of project work outside the classroom; and compile a portfolio containing materials documenting the journey.

McCary described as "unbelievable" some of the student projects, in terms of their impact on the high-schoolers' lives. For instance, one young man, struggling for an idea, sat down one day with McCary and said he wanted to do a project on cooking. "I'll just fix a meal," he told McCary, who urged him to take that kernel of an idea and broaden it into something more significant. "Have you thought about cooking on a cruise ship?" McCary wondered. One thing led to another, and the young man found an opportunity to help a master chef prepare a banquet on a cruise ship. That experience became the basis of the student's senior project, which in turn led to his obtaining a mentorship with a professional chef at the Johnson and Wales Cooking School. That led to a cooking school scholarship. Originally intending to be a fast-food cook, the young man now expected to become an executive chef earning upward of $80,000 a year.

In another case, a young woman researched fashion design for her senior project, putting on a small show with original designs for her presentation. The judges asked her if she intended to become a fashion designer. "Not right away," she told the panel. "The best preparation is to become a buyer first," she said, which would permit her to learn the business side of design before launching her own business. Says McCary, "She had her career all laid out."

Not all senior projects have been vocationally oriented. McCary told me about another young woman who talked her parents into letting her spend two weeks in a hut in the middle of the Ecuadoran rain forest to study a species of spider. She went on to the University of North Carolina in Chapel Hill to work on a degree in environmental studies. There was also the young man who had a passion for Civil War history. His project was to research and re-create the full-battle gear and attire of a Civil War soldier, and present himself as such to the judges. Later, he was invited to participate in a full-blown re-creation of a Civil War battle with other accomplished aficionados.

By the late 1990s, several North Carolina school districts had adopted the senior project requirement as an important milestone for high-schoolers, in order to, say, pass senior English, or even earn a diploma. One of the earliest adopters of the idea was the Charlotte-Mecklenburg School District. In its case, the investigative project—as the district described it for students and parents—counted 20 percent of the final English grade. This wasn't easy stuff. With the formality and safeguards the district required of the process, the senior projects were not unlike mini-doctoral dissertations. Indeed, the district sought parents and community members to be part of review boards, the panels of faculty, parents, educators, and others who evaluated the students' projects and oral presentations according to scoring guidelines provided by the district.

What is more, McCary told me his district has implemented another authentic assessment technique, known as portfolio review, as a check against using the state's ABCs tests for deciding whether children in third, sixth, and eighth grades should be held back and sent to summer school. In an effort to minimize the often educationally devastating effect on children of flunking a grade, the district decided to begin keeping portfolios of student achievement that would include a range of students' work besides test scores. At those key grades, the district chose to do complete portfolio reviews of children with very low test scores to ensure that no important decisions were made about children on the basis of test scores alone. (The policy stood in sharp contrast to the policy implemented by Johnson County schools.) McCary told me that fully 25 percent of the district's students would have been denied promotion and sent off for remedial summer work if local officials had abided strictly by the state requirements.

The portfolio check, McCary says, "told us what we knew" about the ABCs tests as unreliable indicators of individual achievement, because of inherent problems with most standardized tests. Although the ABCs were perhaps adequate indicators of broad-based achievement at the district or state level, using the tests to make decisions about individuals was rife with danger. "The tests have tremendous error for individual children," McCary says. "You can't take a measure like the state test and apply it to individual children as an absolute measure of what they are capable of doing."

"It's Real"

Nobody in Pike County Public Schools, in Millard, Kentucky, taught school the way Adkins and Adkins taught school.

Karen Adkins and her husband, Roy Dale Adkins, taught kindergarten through third grade at Millard Elementary in this economically struggling part of the once-thriving rural Kentucky coal belt. Ann Hayes's remarkable finding that paying attention to genuine achievement rather than test scores somehow produced good test scores was nothing new to this pair of teachers. They'd built a districtwide, even statewide reputation as performance assessment experts whose pupils annually exceeded all expectations for their performance on the statewide tests. Nay, their kids were some of the top scorers in the district at their grade level.

Adkins and Adkins even had a waiting list.

On a given day, you'll see the Adkins's class engaged in some performance assessment task—like five-year-olds working on a project called Autumn. They collect fall things, such as leaves, nuts, and corn; they group together and count up their supplies of each. Then the children draw bar graphs illustrating the results of their fall survey.

A recent performance assessment project had the class study each of the five classes of animals for five weeks. Each week, they learned about mammals, reptiles, birds, amphibians, and fish. The Adkinses set up different learning stations for the children to read about each animal. They had to learn about habitat, shelter, and food sources. At one station, the teachers discussed the report each child was to write about one animal from one of the five kinds—their choice. Finally, the children created models of their animal's habitat, including all important elements for the animal's survival. Where's the food, the water, the shelter? No project was complete without the self-evaluation. The Adkinses always asked the children: *Did you like the task? What did you learn? If you could do it again, what would you do differently? What have you learned that you can use again?*

As primary school teachers, the couple didn't have standardized tests to worry about exclusively; Kentucky prohibited as inappropriate such testing at the K–3 level. Still, their children would be subject to statewide tests when they entered fourth grade. Meanwhile, the Adkins's primary concern was abiding by the strictures of the Kentucky Elementary Learning Profile. KELP provided strong incentives for doing performance-based assessment for pupils in kindergarten through third grade. The law required teachers to document the children's learning according to nine types of performances. These wide-ranging kinds of performances included children having to pose a question on a topic and do research to get an answer; to communicate through an "aesthetic project, performance, or reflection"; to read for "literary experience" or to gain factual information; to solve "real-life" problems; and to complete and present a long-term project that integrated several subject areas at once.

Though KELP didn't specify how a teacher should implement its nine performance criteria, the path ahead was clear to Karen Adkins. In Adkins's mind, the nine criteria all added up to authentic assessment and a new classroom learning environment that was more compatible than traditional approaches with doing performance tasks. "It was show me what you can do, demonstrate, create, explain," Adkins told me. "That's what we're looking for in the primary program."

Adkins got her first exposure to authentic assessment methods a year after graduating with a teaching degree from Berea College in the late 1980s, when she attended a Mellon Foundation seminar on the topic. I asked Adkins what appealed to her about performance assessment, and why she kept at it. She told me:

> It's real. Paper-and-pencil tests don't show you very much. . . . They promote a type of learning that's just factual, with lots of regurgitation. I knew from my own schooling that that's not what learning is. . . . The goal of school should be to create lifetime learners. That's the way we believe. By the success of our children, they're telling us, 'If you just let me do it, just show me how, let me be involved in the process.' When you do that, they can become lifelong learners.

But despite their successes with the new assessments, the Adkins and Adkins team has remained something of an outlier in their school system. The irony isn't lost on the couple: other K–3 teachers in the district have known of the Adkins's methods, which produce students who obtain fine scores through a focus on learning and understanding, not tests. Nevertheless, other teachers have held steadfastly to their usual teaching methods, with lots of drilling students for factual regurgitation and, of course, pencil-and-paper tests that are supposed to prepare children for school life beyond the third grade.

Other K–3 teachers' unwillingness to try what the Adkinses are doing boils down to fundamentally opposed philosophies about the ability of children to learn, Karen Adkins said. Rooted in the very act of their doing authentic assessment, she says, was a simple belief about children's great capacities to learn. That belief allowed their unique little learning academy to create an environment in which both children and their teachers were allowed to take risks that were unheard-of in traditional settings.

"We are very well known," Adkins says matter-of-factly. Most teachers, she says, "do not believe in authentic assessment. Not because it doesn't work. It's a lack of want to. We have good teachers, some really good teachers, but I'm afraid most do not believe—at least, they have not been taught to believe—that all children can learn. I was convinced from the very beginning, that all children *can* learn."

Great Ideas, But Do They Work?

By the late 1990s the anecdotes and case studies started piling up from teachers in schools across the country who had found success with various kinds of authentic assessment. From the beginning of the performance assessment movement, many educators and scholars advocated it as an antidote to standardized, multiple-choice tests. Many believed—with ample justification, the evidence suggested—that if policymakers were to *try* to engineer an assessment system that would most effectively dumb-down and superficialize teaching and learning, then large-scale, multiple-choice tests with big stakes for schools and schoolchildren would be that system.

Many educators and researchers speculated that shifting to authentic tasks for assessing schools and schoolchildren might stop the educational calamity. However, little systematic evidence beyond anecdotal testimonials supported the claims for the new assessments. There was little hard data to suggest authentic assessment really worked or that it was not just another educational fad advocated by well-meaning educators who had more hope going for them than actual evidence. Recently, however, some empirical studies by research scholars suggests that there may be more than want-to and hope-for going for the new assessments.

Does authentic assessment have positive effects on learning and teaching? The short answer to this question appears to be that it does, significantly so, and we find evidence supporting that conclusion from studies of teachers, parents, and students themselves. Consider:

Vermont's Portfolio Review System. In 1992 the RAND Corporation examined Vermont's unique, even cutting-edge, system of portfolio review intended to assess students in writing and mathematics. As opposed to a one-time performance snapshot provided by achievement tests, the portfolios included a range of students' writing and mathematical performances over time. As the RAND report described the Vermont system, the portfolio assessments were the centerpiece of the state's entire assessment program, which relied minimally on multiple-choice tests. According to the RAND study, the portfolio assessment system was proving to be particularly beneficial in the mathematics arena. Surveying Vermont teachers, RAND discovered the portfolio process was doing for math teaching and learning just what it was intended to do: lessen the amount of drilling on mathematical routines and formulas and push children to think, solve problems, and apply mathematical reasoning. Some particulars:

- Fully eight in ten fourth-grade and eighth-grade teachers reported spending more time than before on problem-solving activities.
- About 50 percent of teachers in both grades said they were spending more time on the study of patterns and relationships of mathematics than previously.
- Nearly six in ten Vermont fourth-grade teachers were often or always more enthusiastic about teaching math and said their goals for math instruction had become considerably more focused. Forty-three percent said their pupils' attitudes toward math were often or always better than during the preportfolio era; most of the remaining teachers believed students were occasionally more sanguine about doing math.
- Perhaps more important, more than eight in ten of Vermont teachers said they had changed their minds about students' mathematical skills through the use of portfolios to evaluate student performance. Teachers "felt the portfolios demonstrated students' logical thinking and problem-solving abilities better than standardized tests," the RAND researchers noted.

School principals, too, viewed the portfolio assessments as doing well by the schools and schoolchildren. Burdensome, yes; a departure from the usual, yes; but nevertheless, educationally worthwhile, principals said.

"Principals offered a long and diverse list of attributes of the program that sparked positive responses by their teachers," the RAND authors said. "Many cited its effects on curriculum and instruction, while others noted its value for within-class and within-school assessment purposes. Perhaps the most telling sign of support for the portfolio program is the finding that it had already been extended beyond the grades targeted by the state in about half the schools." (2)

Kentucky's "Standards-Based" Assessment. In 1991, as part of the Kentucky Education Reform Act, the state created a new assessment system that placed heavy reliance on "on-demand" performance tasks, portfolios, and open-ended test items to assess schoolchildren against several new high-level standards. Enacted to rectify historical inequalities in the state's public schools, the new system's credo was that "all children can learn at high levels" and was intended to promote "a complete transformation of the entire learning environment," according to state officials.

A 1998 study, again by the RAND Corporation, evaluated the extent to which the new program enabled Kentucky schools to meet those goals. RAND's findings rang similar to the Vermont experience. Consider the effects on mathematics. According to RAND's opinion survey of Kentucky's fifth- and eighth-grade teachers, the new performance assessments meant math teaching and learning were no longer such abstract experiences for schoolchildren. Under the standards-based, performance-assessment system, teachers reported improvements in terms of:

- *Real-world applications.* More than nine in ten fifth-grade teachers reported using "examples of real-world applications of mathematical skills" on a weekly basis. Almost seven of every ten showed pupils "connections between mathematics and other subjects" at least weekly. And, eight in ten fifth-grade teachers said that, over a three-year period, they were asking students to do more open-ended performance tasks.
- *Teaching for understanding.* Whereas 33 percent of fifth-grade teachers said they were asking students to "memorize mathematical facts, rules, or formulas," on a weekly basis, more than seven in ten said the new assessment methods were requiring students to "explain why they solved a problem a certain way," at least once a week. Some 60 percent of teachers said students were at least weekly now required to write about mathematics in order to gain insight and understanding of math concepts. Just 3 percent of teachers reported a three-year increase in the pupils having to work the formulaic problems typically presented in textbooks, while 57 percent reported a three-year gain in children having to explain how they solved problems.

To be sure, Kentucky's teachers' views of math portfolio assessments were not uniformly positive. The heavy emphasis placed on writing and process turned off many teachers, with 90 percent saying all the writing demands "caused students to become tired of writing." Too, the portfolios demanded a great deal of teachers' time. Though two-thirds of teachers said they had become "more innovative" in their math teaching, they were evenly split on the perceived burden of finding good portfolio tasks. Further, though teachers said they were confident in the portfolio tasks to keep tabs on individual children's learning progress, the teachers remained skeptical of their use as a high-stakes accountability tool.

Although students might have tired of all the writing required by the new assessments, they became better writers, mainly because Kentucky's testing reforms evoked less superficial approaches to the teaching and learning of writing skills than in the past, RAND found. Whereas multiple-choice and even short-answer testing systems of many states had created incentives for teachers to pay most attention to mechanical aspects of writing such as grammar, punctuation, and spelling, as well as formulaic models of writing like the proverbial "five-paragraph essay," the new assessments were compelling Kentucky's teachers to broaden and deepen their teaching of writing.

For example, RAND found that under the new program, roughly 80 percent of teachers placed more emphasis on helping students "communicate clearly through writing" than teaching them writing mechanics. Matters of "purpose and audience" in writing had become more vital to these teachers than a focus on spelling and grammar. Indeed, more than 75 percent of Kentucky's fourth- and seventh-grade teachers believed that their overall goal in the teaching of writing was to encourage development of students' critical thinking and reasoning skills.

Most important, teachers believed the new assessments, particularly the writing portfolios, were improving the quality and quantity of student writing. Some 80 percent of Kentucky's fourth- and seventh-grade teachers told RAND their students "are writing more and better as a result of portfolios." Again, RAND concluded that the teachers viewed the writing portfolios as being "burdensome" for the teaching staff and moreover, caused students to get "tired of writing." (3)

What Parents Think. Conventional wisdom has it that parents of schoolchildren and the taxpaying public believe standardized testing is sacrosanct as a good measure of the quality of American schools and go hand in hand with maintaining high academic standards. Any efforts of schools to do more authentic assessment at the expense of garden-variety achievement tests would be met with wide disapproval, common wisdom might suggest.

Indeed, national polling data have lent support to this view. However, polling numbers beg the question: Just how much, if anything, do members of the public really know about standardized testing and its alternatives? In particular, how would moms and dads judge the new assessments relative to standardized tests once they became better informed about both methods?

In 1995, Lorrie Shepard and Caribeth Bleim of the University of Colorado sought answers to these questions. Generally, the researchers discovered that, once parents learned how the assessments actually worked, they preferred them over traditional multiple-choice testing for their children. The study worked this way: First, the researchers drew from a sample of schools from working-class and lower-middle-class suburbs of Denver, schools that were both ethnically diverse and had much experience with high-stakes testing. Next, the researchers showed parents and schoolchildren typical questions from widely used achievement tests and authentic performance tasks.

When the parents made informed, side-by-side comparisons between the new assessments and the standardized tests, the outcome belied the conventional wisdom that many observers have drawn from national polling data. The Colorado researchers discovered that about six in ten parents approved of standardized testing for measuring math achievement; however, seven in ten parents favored using the performance tasks as well. For assessing reading achievement, parents' preferences for the performance tasks over traditional tests were even stronger.

In one revealing question to the parents, Shepard and Bleim pointed out research evidence showing that teaching to tests had become all too common in American schools. If that is true, the researchers asked, what then did parents think would be the best indicator of their children's achievement? For math classes, 44 percent of parents preferred the performance assessments, some strongly so, compared to 31 percent who favored traditional testing. For measuring reading achievement, nearly six in ten parents would choose performance tasks compared to just two in ten who would stick with the familiar standardized tests.

Reasons that parents gave for preferring the performance assessments were even more revealing. In follow-up interviews with the study's subjects, one parent told the researchers: "There's more of an understanding why it's right and wrong, you know, with (performance assessments). And the kids, I think, should be taught in math and reading and stuff like that, they should be taught to understand the rights and wrongs of it." (4)

The meaning of all this seems clear. Opinion polls about public views of standardized tests and its alternatives need to be interpreted cautiously, because those opinions may well be founded on misinformation and folk wisdom rather than on reliable evidence. When parents in the Shepard and Bliem study actually were able to inspect the two types of assessments for making direct comparisons, they saw performance assessment in a new light.

"When parents in this study had a chance to look closely at performance assessment problems, most endorsed their use for district purposes and especially preferred their use in classroom contexts," the researchers say. "Therefore, survey data like the Gallup Poll showing approval" of standardized tests "should not be taken to mean that parents are opposed to the use of alternative measures."

What Students Think. Furthermore, there is the important question of how students themselves judge the relative merits of the new assessments relative to standardized tests. Pertinent evidence on this question came from a 1997 study of some 800 students in thirteen representative California schools, before the state dismantled its performance-based California Learning Assessment System (CLAS). Generally, the study suggested, students understood performance assessments were fundamentally different than standardized tests, and called on pupils to approach learning in fundamentally different—and often more challenging—ways than traditional tests. Mostly, the researchers found, the students appreciated the benefits of performance assessment, but at the same time, when students preferred multiple-choice testing they did so out of self-interest: They were easier.

For example, when students were asked which type of test they found more interesting, more than half picked performance tasks, compared to 29 percent who chose multiple-choice exams, with the rest having no preference. Asked which type made them try harder, 55 percent picked the performance items, compared to just 11 percent who said they tried harder on multiple-choice tests. Conversely, when asked which type of test students liked better, fully six in ten preferred the multiple-choice variety.

The researchers uncovered further support for performance assessments in follow-up interviews with individual students. Indeed, eight in ten students in the sample told the researchers that performance assessment "makes you think harder or is more challenging." By contrast, just 8 percent thought the multiple-choice tests forced them to think harder. The follow-ups indicated that the students' preference for standardized testing was less marked than they'd indicated on survey forms.

Moreover, there's the question of which kind of testing might encourage mathematical reasoning and thinking skills of the type that, according to a growing chorus of mathematics educators, schools must vigorously promote if American math and science achievement is to rise above mediocrity. Chapter 6 discussed how the often-superficial style of mathematics teaching in many American schools probably explains why U.S. twelfth-graders fared so poorly on international comparisons of mathematics performance in the late 1990s. Moreover, mathematics educators have warned, the widespread turn toward big-stakes testing and accountability programs has only worsened the "mile wide and inch deep" tendency of American mathematics education.

On this matter, too, the California study found, performance tasks did promote the sorts of thinking and reasoning skills mathematics education reformers have been advocating. The researchers discovered this by investigating whether students used mathematical reasoning to solve problems or instead guessed at solutions by trial and error. An example of guessing would be this student's description: *"I looked at the answers, and I thought four or nine would be all right, but I wasn't sure, so I picked four feet."*

As it turned out, trial and error and guessing were relatively common on traditional standardized tests in the study. About 35 percent of the interviewed students admitted to guessing on multiple-choice items. That's compared to just 4 percent who said they guessed or used trial and error to solve open-ended items calling for students to show and explain their solutions. In remarkable contrast, virtually all students in the study deployed mathematics-based reasoning skills to solve open-ended tasks, according to the researchers.

All considered, the California students might not have liked alternatives to multiple-choice tests all that much, but that is probably to be expected when the same students also indicated they found the performance assessments a tougher standard to meet. The alternative assessments, the researchers concluded, were more interesting and challenging than multiple-choice tests, requiring them to try harder, think harder, explain better, and reason more mathematically than they were accustomed to. (5)

Performance-Assessment and Accountability Politics

Whether such empirical evidence demonstrates beyond a doubt that performance assessment does significantly improve teaching and learning may be a matter of interpretation. Many educators and scholars believe there is ample evidence to back up the earlier promises and claims for authentic assessment. When combined with the many case studies and anecdotal testimonials from teachers and school officials in various states, the case for authentic assessment surely cannot be easily dismissed.

That many states have, to some degree, lessened their reliance on traditional multiple-choice exams in recent years demonstrates their belief that their schools need alternatives to old measures of merit and achievement. According to the Council of Chief State School Officers, for instance, standardized tests remained the most popular assessment tool for schools in the late 1990s; some forty-one states continue to rely on the old tests. But many states were also complementing the traditional tests with alternatives such as test items requiring extended written responses and short answers. Still, the transformation has been slow. Just nine states required full-blown performance tasks in their statewide systems, and even fewer called on students to complete major performance projects. (6)

Indeed, just as grassroots reformers in North Carolina discovered, accountability politics has been their most formidable roadblock. A handful of states in recent years did manage to transform their testing and accountability systems in response to the almost open-and-shut case against heavy reliance on standardized tests. These states shelved their old testing programs, replacing them with elaborate performance-assessment systems, only to see the authentic assessments fall victim within just a few years to the explosive politics of school accountability.

Two of the most glaring performance-assessment flameouts occurred in Arizona and California. In those states and in Kentucky to a lesser degree, newly enacted assessment systems that placed unprecedented emphasis on performance tasks were tossed out, rolled back, or shelved indefinitely in the late 1990s. The particular reasons for the backlash in each state differed, but the commonalties were eye-opening and instructive:

- *Accountability mandates.* Performance assessment systems that held great promise to raise the level of children's classroom performance were shoved into existing high-stakes accountability paradigms. Lawmakers simply wound up replacing one punishing testing system (standardized tests) with another (performance assessments) to which equally high stakes for students and schools were attached.

Responding to legislative mandates to reform schools, states often rushed the new assessments into use before ironing out technical details related to their validity and reliability. State politicians proved to have little patience for the careful gestation needed for the new authentic assessments.

What's more, lawmakers' demands on authentic tasks—that they be used to make important promotion, certification, graduation, and other vital decisions about schools, teachers, and schoolchildren—made their validity and reliability of paramount importance. In the admixture of accountability politics, conservatives wanting a return to traditional testing thus exploited any unsettled issues about the statistical accuracy of the new assessments, charging that the assessments were flawed beyond repair and should be replaced.

- *The "objectivity" myth.* When students' performance-assessment results finally got around to parents, the new methods ran headlong into the age-old shibboleth of objectivity. Certainly, the new assessments lacked the apparent unambiguity of the former standardized test scores. However, parents and lawmakers misunderstood both types of tests. For one, scoring of performance assessments was far less subjective and considerably more accurate than folk wisdom would have it. Nor were multiple-choice test scores the reputedly pure measures of an individual's true achievement that they were commonly believed to be.

Moreover, in cases where states scrapped their commercial standardized tests in favor of performance assessments, they also gave up the ability to compare an individual child's test score to national norms for the same grade level. Although such norm-referenced standardized tests were practically useless to most teachers for making informed professional judgments on their own students' educational progress, parents wanted those percentile rankings—showing *not* how well Johnny read but how well he read in comparison with other third-graders across the country.

- *Culture clash.* Dismantling the new performance assessments in states like California and Arizona also revealed angry clashes of cultural values. Power struggles ensued between cultural conservatives and the professionals in state departments of education. Although the latter placed their trust in research and evidence to guide educational policy, the former often harbored deep mistrust of the educational bureaucracies. One revealing public statement by Arizona governor Fife Symington, reaching far to the right for his political survival, underscored the nature of the culture clash that the new assessments had fallen victim to. Coming out against the performance-based "fads and foolishness" being pushed by the "pointy-headed" people with Ph.D.s at the Department of Education, Symington stated, in part:

> We have casually cast aside the settled and true in favor of the trendy and allegedly exciting. (Other than technology) there is almost nothing new about a high quality primary education, and very little new in secondary education. Most of the social and academic "innovations" the so-called professional educators have brought to our classrooms are wasteful at best and insidious at worst.(7)

There's more. Through the lens of cultural values, some religious conservatives in both California and Arizona injected themselves into the testing wars by claiming the new performance assessments intruded on family values. Condemning the assessments as "outcomes-based education," religious conservatives believed educators wanted to reshape children's basic values rather than teach pupils how to count and spell. "Under the umbrella of 'Citizens for Education Excellence,'" writes *Arizona Republic* reporter Michael Murphy, "the groups warn of secret conspiracies at the Department of Education, including one to establish computer files like those used in China to collect data on each pupil's thoughts and feelings." (8)

The Missing Link

To be sure, it may be tempting for education reformers to see authentic assessment in messianic terms, as the answer to all that might be wrong with American schools. But authentic assessment has been shoved into the same trap as all school testing has from its inception: that it be all things to all people. Lawmakers want a test they can use to sort good performers from bad ones, whether they be schools, teachers, students, or administrators. Reformers want tests that elevate the level of teaching and learning rather than dumb them down. Schools and teachers want tests that give them feedback on individual children's progress in school; but they also want tests that provide them with any signs of weaknesses in their curriculum and teaching methods. Many parents may want all those things, and they also want tests that give them individual scores by which to see how their children measure up with other children.

Whether it is a standardized test or a performance assessment, no one test could possibly be all those things to all the various constituencies. Indeed, it is probable that any one of those objectives is wholly incompatible with any of the others. Ultimately, Americans must make some difficult but crucial choices about what they want their public schools to be. As the 1990s came to a close, the apparent political consensus was that Americans wanted schools to be held accountable for children's learning.

However, few people dared question the implicit assumption that accountability measured on the basis of tests, whether standardized multiple-choice tests or performance assessments, is a good thing. School accountability has been viewed in the exceedingly narrow perspective that the public must get the most achievement-score bang for the taxpayer buck. That schools should also be held accountable for creating opportunities to ensure children's deeper *understanding* of what they have learned and chances to *apply* what they have learned in meaningful ways has not been what lawmakers have meant by the catch-all term, accountability. Under the assumption that accountability is generally a good thing in a democratic society, it may be useful to view accountability in different ways for different purposes:

- *Systemwide accountability.* It's true that authentic assessment in some cases has not been provided an adequate chance to succeed on a statewide basis. However, it remains unclear whether the new assessments, in light of the highly politicized environment of public schools, can be fitted into the same role occupied by traditional tests, as a statewide measure of individual and school performance to be used for anything ranging from retention to high school graduation. Standardized tests do have considerable weaknesses. However, traditional testing does have a comparative advantage that policymakers might do well to exploit. As broad indicators of system performance, with just enough test items to cover the whole array of knowledge and skills covered in a given grade, the easily scored, highly reliable, multiple-choice test could continue to have a useful role rather than the damaging one it now too often plays.

For traditional tests to properly fill this function as system barometer, it would be imperative that the tests be disarmed, disassociating the exams with the dangerous game of rewards and punishments. As soon as standardized test scores are attached to educational crimes and punishments, bad things happen. Using the National Assessment of Educational Progress as a model, states could test fewer schoolchildren less often and less expensively than prevailing systems of universal testing in which many children are tested *at least* once a year for every year they're in school. Moreover, this barrage of testing has led to many unsavory effects on teaching and learning.

- *Accountability for student understanding, learning, and engagement.* In terms of comparative advantage, it would seem that performance assessments are especially useful as indicators of real, individual classroom achievement. They provide teachers and parents with a window that shows in great depth what students are learning and how well they are learning it. But, performance assessment probably will never be able to provide individual percentile scores on an annual basis. Instead, parents and taxpayers might well focus on the real problems of the schools and decide what they really want America's schools to be for their children. Do Americans want schools primarily to be educational regulators and evaluators of pupil performance, or rather to be crucibles for the alchemy of learning, understanding, and engagement?

Were the public to choose the latter model for the schools, authentic assessment will not likely go away anytime soon. That is owing to perhaps its most compelling feature, which might well be part of the answer to the one intractable problem in American schools about which many lawmakers tend to be unaware and professional educators would just as soon not think about: the student "engagement question."

Most educators have rarely publicly acknowledged the engagement problem and the strong tendency of test-heavy environments to reinforce a certain disinterest among growing numbers of students in almost all things academic. Indeed, when you get to the subtextual strata where the real problems of American schools become exposed, one finds educators relatively unconcerned about the abilities of pupils of all races, classes, and ethnicities to excel in school. What they fear most is that too many kids hate school for all the reasons anybody would hate institutions that tend to be boring, unengaging, regimented, and run by adults saturated with the fear engendered by accountability politics. The adults' test-driven classrooms exacerbate boredom, fear, and lethargy, promoting all manner of mechanical behaviors on the part of teachers, students, and schools, and bleed schoolchildren of their natural love of learning.

By putting context above abstractness, understanding over recollection, process over the bottom line, and performing over filling in Number 2 pencil bubbles, teachers who have used the new assessments have demonstrated an uncanny ability to engage students in learning, indeed, to instill a love of learning and a continuing desire to learn. For all its other merits, performance assessment may be the missing link to solving the engagement problem, perhaps drawing kids' attention from *Buffy the Vampire Slayer* and redirecting it back toward algebra and reading.

That lesson was vividly and somewhat tragically underscored for Chris Gustafson, a sixth-grade teacher at North City Elementary School in Seattle. A teacher in the economically and ethnically diverse urban school, Gustafson had become an enthusiastic advocate of authentic assessment in her classes. In recent years, her classes completed major performance projects that integrated several subjects. In one effort, for example, classes over a period of three years worked on various stages of producing a museum display for one of the city's best-known black civil rights leaders, Edwin Pratt, who had been shot and killed some years ago at his Shoreline home, under suspicious circumstances believed to be racially motivated.

Then there was the newspaper project. At one class's insistence, Gustafson put together a performance task that required the sixth-graders to create and publish a class newspaper. The kids wrote articles about school sports, activities on the school playground, reviewed movies, and wrote opinion pieces on subjects of local or personal concern. Others volunteered to be editors, "keepers of the vision for their sections," says Gustafson. To assess the students' work, Gustafson used performance rubrics for standards of journalistic quality for different types of articles—standards the students themselves created and approved with Gustafson's guidance. "They were tough on themselves," Gustafson told me. "I was very pleased with the rigor of the standards they chose."

Through it all, one student, Laurie, shined as a member of the newspaper staff, and her self-confidence in her abilities blossomed. With the newspaper to motivate her, Laurie worked hard with Gustafson to improve. In fact, she began to see herself as a *writer*, and started experimenting with the use of dialogue in her stories.

Then, Laurie took the standardized achievement test that was required by the state of Washington in the late 1990s. Laurie received her test scores at home, and approached Gustafson the next day.

"I didn't score very well in language," Laurie told her teacher. "So I guess I'm not really a writer."

When I spoke to Gustafson, her dismay and anger over what happened to Laurie were palpable.

"I was just furious," Gustafson told me. "She was doing just fine. That test wasn't a test of her writing ability. It was whether she could answer multiple-choice questions about writing. She didn't believe me any more. She believed that test score that came to her parents' house."

In what should Americans place *their* trust in their children's abilities? A child's actual performance on efforts for which she is highly motivated to succeed or an abstract indicator of pseudo-achievement on a pencil-and-paper exam, the results of which become matters of bureaucratic convenience and necessity to politicians, the press, and school accountability managers?

"The one thing that performance tasks address that traditional tests don't tap is motivation," North Carolina's Mack McCary told me. "That's the heart of it. That's one of the biggest problems educators face, the 'won't do' kids, who have the ability but choose not to. The number of kids who just refuse school, who just won't, who may or may not end up at community college, that's a significant part of the problem. Also, I've been amazed at the alienation of the best and brightest kids. They won't outright fail, but they'll get through with minimal effort. We're hearing a giant message from kids: They don't think most schoolwork is worth doing. That's where I see hope in performance assessment."

12

Harmful Admissions: Why the Meritocracy Needs Fixing

As the dean of admissions at Bates College, William Hiss had worked the trenches of the American meritocracy for some twenty years. Like expert handicappers of race horses in Del Mar or Saratoga Springs, Hiss and his admissions staff at this prestigious liberal arts college in Lewiston, Maine, believed they knew how to pick the winners and losers of the college admissions game.

Chiefly, they employed high school grades and standardized test scores—lots of test scores. These, of course, were the usual and widely prescribed indicators of an American eighteen-year-old's academic promise. Bates College was big on test scores, having required a full-blown testing package that included both the SAT verbal and math sections in addition to three SAT achievement tests, now called the "SAT II" subject tests. High school grades and SATs would be complemented by other, second-order indicators of a high-schooler's potential for success at Bates. Such nonacademic indicators as playing on the soccer team or participating with the debate squad were surely pluses for a would-be Batesian's chances, but rarely determinative. Rather, they nicely rounded out the college's student body.

In short, Hiss and his crew knew the drill, and they did it well. SAT scores of high-schoolers admitted to Bates were indeed impressive, averaging more than 1,200. The college and its admissions staff were full-fledged participants in the prevailing ideology about the meaning of merit, prescribed by the Educational Testing Service, the College Board, and thousands of American colleges and universities.

That deeply entrenched ideology held that a young person was worthy of passing through the ivy-covered walls of wonderful places like Bates because he or she had the right statistical profile. Because this view of merit could be boiled down to the universal language of numbers, Hiss's job as chief gatekeeper was rendered a relatively straightforward exercise of sorting the beans with the highest numerical values.

Efficient as this process was, Hiss and others at Bates began to notice several disturbing aspects to the picture. The usual drill was yielding results inconsistent with the ideals of an institution founded by civil rights activists and abolitionists 143 years ago. Nor was the exercise sitting right with Hiss, himself a Bates graduate who went on to study ethics at Harvard Divinity School and religion in his doctoral work at Tufts.

First, Hiss said, he and his staff began to notice that the college's SAT requirement and its dauntingly high published test scores for students admitted were screening out or scaring off many capable kids who would do well at the college. According to rough figuring, the admissions tests were not predictive for about a quarter to a third of the applicants to Bates each year.

What's more, high-schoolers and their parents were becoming obsessed with scoring high on standardized tests as the ticket into Bates. The high demand for test-coaching companies underscored the problem. Firms such as Kaplan, the Princeton Review, and scores of other local consultants promised big gains in test scores in exchange for hefty fees.

"Test scores were simply occupying too much intellectual and emotional capacity in young people," Hiss told me. "We believed kids were misusing their time because of testing. When kids pay as much as five hundred dollars to spend the afternoon being coached on taking the SAT, they are not being the captain of the soccer team or not working in an AIDS clinic. What we came to feel was that to the extent that we required the SAT, we were throwing young people into the arms of Kaplan or the Princeton Review, and that was the wrong thing to do ethically. We began to think that what we should require was in fact what we valued. Therefore, for us to be tacitly supporting the whole coaching industry seemed like the wrong thing to do."

In 1984, Bates made SAT verbal and math scores optional for its applicants, but continued to require a few of the SAT II subject tests. After more careful study (Bates continued to ask for all sets of test scores among admitted applicants for research purposes), Hiss and his staff confirmed beyond doubt what they had suspected all along: The lower-scoring students who opted out of the SATs performed just as well at Bates as the higher-scoring ones who did submit scores. That prompted the college to make the next step, going completely test-optional in 1990.

"We decided we were going to try another way," Hiss says. Hence, those once secondary considerations that went into the equation of somebody's potential for success at Bates would no longer be relegated to a complementary role. Along with actual academic performance rather than a formulaic prediction of later performance on the basis of standardized tests, once-secondary considerations would now be the whole story of one's likelihood of accomplishment at Bates.

As it turned out, the Bates experiment would become immensely successful—for reasons that will be taken up in detail in Chapter 13. Through the years, however, Hiss, now a vice president at the college, continued to put a carefully worded spin on the college's successes with its test-optional program.

Bates, after all, was a small liberal arts college in Maine, and its discoveries about the questionable utility of standardized tests versus the costs of more complex and information-rich systems of determining merit could hardly be applied to much larger public institutions where most Americans go to college. Indeed, having garnered considerable public attention to the Bates program, Hiss would frequently be asked whether he believed the Bates experiment could be replicated elsewhere.

"I would simply defer the question and say that every institution has to do its own research, decide what they want their predictors to be, and make up their own minds," Hiss told me. "I ducked the issue."

Revelation

Hiss no longer ducks. The answer, he now says, is an unqualified yes. The Bates model not only can be replicated, but he contends, it *must* be. In fact, Hiss can pinpoint almost the exact moment in which he came to that realization. It happened at a meeting of the Congressional Advisory Committee on Student Financial Assistance, on which Hiss served as one of eleven members. Under Title IV of the Higher Education Act of 1965, the committee's purpose is to recommend policies and strategies to Congress for enhancing the prospects of higher education to children of families with low and moderate incomes.

One day, the committee was shown an innocuous sheet of paper with a graph on it. The graph was titled "Educational Attainment by Family Income 1970 to 1994." The piece of paper showed how the college graduation rate of people in the four quartiles of the income distribution had changed over the past quarter century. The picture depicted by the numbers was chilling. (1)

The poorest Americans, families earning less than $22,000 a year, had seen no long-term change whatsoever in the chance of completing a four-year degree by the age of twenty-four. In the mid–1990s, well under 10 percent of the children from the poorest families had completed college, unchanged in a generation. Even individuals of modest means saw no improvement. For instance, those from families earning from $22,000 to $41,000 saw their college graduation prospects hardly budge from 1970 through 1994: 10 percent of people in this moderate-income group completed a bachelor's throughout that period.

On the other hand, wealthier Americans made great progress in getting their children through college during that period. The third-highest income group, consisting of families earning $41,000 to $68,000, saw their children's chances of completing a bachelor's degree double in just a generation, climbing from about 15 percent to nearly 30 percent.

Most staggering of all, however, were the gains recorded by the richest Americans. Families earning more than $68,000 watched their children's college-graduation rates surge from about 40 percent to more than 80 percent in the span of twenty-five years.

Two more graphs handed out to members at the advisory committee meeting put the finishing touches on William Hiss's personal transformation about the proper roles of the gatekeepers to higher education. One showed that a high school dropout could expect to earn about $500,000 in her lifetime. Obtaining a bachelor's degree would more than double her lifetime earnings, while going to graduate school would triple lifetime income to more than $1.6 million.

Hiss also saw how educational attainment affected one's economic fortunes over the past twenty years. Americans without academic credentials got clobbered, particularly those who dropped out of high school; they saw their inflation-adjusted family income drop almost 40 percent from 1970 to 1993. College graduates saw incomes neither increase nor decrease. Only Americans with five or more years of college improved their economic prospects, as their real incomes rose 15 percent over two decades. (2)

For Hiss, the narrative contained in those few pieces of paper was profoundly disturbing. Poor—and even middle-class Americans—had seen their chances of going to college hardly budge over the span of almost three decades. At the same time, well-off Americans were obtaining college degrees for their children at ever-increasing rates. Moreover, diminishing economic fortunes of many Americans suggested that the chances of breaking the cycle and narrowing the education gap between the rich and nonrich were becoming increasingly slim.

At the same time, it was becoming all too apparent to Hiss that traditional admissions practices of higher education would not be sufficient to help narrow the opportunity gap. Indeed, colleges and universities, beyond their laudable efforts at affirmative action, were actually worsening the problem with their predominately narrow perspective on the question of merit. Institutions were not blameless in perpetuating the long-standing schism between the life chances for the richest Americans and everyone else.

"In the last three years especially, it was becoming quite clear that we (educators) have not had much success with regard to access to higher education among low income kids," Hiss told me. "Low-income kids are largely being hammered by testing. It's that old song that the SAT correlates with the number of cylinders in the family car and the number of books on the family bookshelf.

"These kids who go to Highland Park High School," Hiss continued, referring to the exclusive Chicago suburb on the shore of Lake Michigan, "have all the opportunities. They are sort of the nonhereditary dukes of this system. My college is full of those kids. We have hundreds of those kids. Looking out my window now, I can see the Cherokees in the college parking lot, and that's the family's *third* car. They'll make it fine. We get lots of applications from full-paying, educationally ambitious families."

Rather, Hiss says he began to realize the connection between educational inequality and the long-held practices and habits in the admissions world of placing too much weight on easily crunched, bureaucratically convenient, and predictively dubious test scores. "I have no problem with giving points for high scores," he says. "I just don't want to make the opposite assumption that kids with a couple of 520s (about average) couldn't do the work.

"What I've seen happening," Hiss continued, "is that a lot of institutions haven't done the research. They honestly don't know" how useful standardized admissions tests really are at their own institutions. "Very few have actually done the analysis to determine whether tests are good predictors or not. They talk a good game."

The Broken Meritocracy

Since Congress passed the Higher Education Act of 1965, U.S. policymakers have placed more equitable access to college for children of low and moderate incomes on the pedestal of their educational policy and rhetoric. Even thirty years later, their efforts have yielded limited overall success. In fact, the opportunity gaps between the wealthy and the not-wealthy have only gotten worse. The bar graphs that Hiss and the advisory committee saw that day tell only part of the story. Here are the persistently brutal facts of class and race in the American pseudo-meritocracy:

- *Academic tracks.* Of American eighth-graders from the wealthiest 25 percent of families, almost eight in ten are rigged up to the "academic" tracks of schooling that most likely lead to college. Well under half of eighth-graders from the poorest quarter of families are routed toward college preparatory courses. (3)
- *Achievement test scores.* Nearly 7 in 10 eighth-graders scoring in the bottom quartile on academic achievement tests come from poor and middle classes. Just over 6 in 100 of the poorest eighth-graders rang up achievement scores in the top quartile. That is compared to 50 in 100 who had top scores among the wealthiest 25 percent. (4)
- *SATs and selective admissions.* Fully one-third of wealthy high school seniors make SAT scores of at least 1,100, a likely cutoff point for some selective colleges and universities. That is twice the rate at which kids from moderate backgrounds make the cut and four times the rate of the poorest high school students. (5)
- *The class effect.* Wealthy high school seniors meet the five criteria considered necessary for admission to selective colleges more often than less privileged seniors in all five categories (including a GPA of at least 3.5; 1,100 SAT; necessary math and language courses, and so on.) But socioeconomic class confers the largest effect on SAT scores. For instance, while there's just an eight percentage point difference between middle- and high-income seniors in the frequency at which they meet the GPA requirements for highly selective colleges, a fifteen percentage

point gap separates the two classes on the rate they meet the test-score cut. (6)

- *SATs and the black-white score gap.* In 1976, 119 points separated black high school seniors and their white peers on the verbal part of the SAT. By the mid-1990s, the difference had narrowed but a gap of 91 points remained. (7)
- *College attainment and race.* In 1971, roughly 13 percent of young black people had completed four or more years of college by their twenty-ninth birthday. Twenty years later, in 1991, not much had changed. Although blacks made no progress in twenty years in the rate at which they earned college degrees, about 25 percent of young whites had completed four or more years of college by their twenty-ninth birthday in 1971. By 1991, a third of them had. (8)
- *Getting into college.* Nearly nine of ten high school seniors from high-income families with earnings of at least $75,000 a year meet the qualifications for acceptance to four-year colleges or universities, based on standardized test scores, grades, class rank, and so on. For low-income seniors in families earning less than $25,000, just about half do. (9)

In other words, the great American meritocracy machine has run amok. There is little doubt that the prevailing paradigm about merit has consistently reproduced social and economic advantages for the "dukes of the system," the relatively few who conform to widely held views of merit. This has been true from the very origins of the meritocracy in its current guise, from the birth of large-scale IQ testing at the turn of the century, to the rise of standardized achievement tests in American schools, to the sanction-filled school accountability mechanisms recently invented by the states, to employers' use of tests in the workplace.

To be sure, the American turn to such "objective" measures as test scores as the means to sort the fit from the unfit for higher education and career success was juiced up with democratic appeal. Standardized testing, rendered with complete objectivity and couched in terms of an empirical "science," would be the death knell to the insidious influences of class privilege perpetuated by the blueness of one's blood. And yet, yawning test-score gaps existed among social classes at the birth of the meritocracy, and they persist today, no matter what the test, no matter that it's given in grade school, high school, or graduate school.

Adherents to the present paradigm have told Americans that inequalities to educational opportunity will erode when the underlying social and economic conditions that influence a child's life prospects are improved. That's been the constant refrain from the Educational Testing Service and other defenders of the present system of merit. The tests don't lie, they tell us. They may not be perfect, but they're the best we have. Don't kill the tests because you don't like their unfortunate message. The implication, then, is that once less privileged Americans catch up to the dukes in economic and educational opportunity, that will be reflected in standardized test scores.

Perhaps so, and perhaps the use of test results as an educational and socioeconomic barometer makes sense. Whether it also makes sense to make life-altering decisions about individuals based on those scores is another question altogether and forces a moral question: Is it legitimate to keep punishing the already punished? Nevertheless, that has been our educational opportunity strategy. Keep making decisions based on test results, punishing as the outcomes might be to some, and someday, maybe, things will be better. As John Maynard Keynes told free market conservatives when capitalism was on the brink of slipping into oblivion during the Great Depression, "In the long run we're all dead."

Adherents to the widely held views about merit include people on both the left and right. Many liberals and institutions of higher education pin their hopes for equal educational opportunity on maintaining affirmative action policies. Adherents also include conservatives who are opposed to conferring any preferences based on race. These virtually codified perspectives of the left and right—and the public attention paid to that conflict—are obscuring a more necessary and unresolved debate over the very meaning of "merit" in American society.

There is little evidence to suggest any significant large-scale change in the educational attainment between white and black and rich and poor, should the standard liberal position hold sway and affirmative action admissions be maintained. Moreover, there is little doubt that equating test scores with academic merit will only serve to erect bigger and an unnecessarily tougher gates to higher education. Without preferences of any sort, even small and insignificant differences in test scores will prove decisive and deadly for the educational prospects of many people.

So the debate as currently framed will either overtly serve to worsen the opportunity gaps we have observed for the past thirty years or indirectly maintain the status quo, itself a choice that will wind up repeating the past and compound the persistent and staggering inequalities William Hiss saw on the bar graphs.

In the meritocracy's present form, one has merit, in large part, if he or she exhibits superior cognitive and academic abilities and traits, variously measured by IQ tests, employment aptitude tests, college admissions tests, and achievement tests. Whatever the kind of standardized test, the exams have at least one key feature in common. All are cognitive abstractions, ghostlike doppelgangers for real things and situations, compelling problems and genuine accomplishment.

At bottom, they are mind games. Employers and educational institutions are in the bizarre situation of trying to predict someone's future success by relying on cognitive abstractions rather than looking at demonstrations of real accomplishment. Standardized exams pitifully grope for a sense of reality.

A new paradigm for merit is poised to erupt in American society. This new sort of merit will not be based on distant abstractions of reality but on reality itself. In such a world, one's actual accomplishments and real performance on endeavors that matter, not test-taking skills, will be of central importance in demonstrating one's merit, rather than the secondary role that accomplishment and performance now occupy in the meritocracy.

The immediate task, however, is to show why the prevailing view of merit in American colleges and universities needs a complete overhaul. I will do so, first, on the basis of empirical evidence on the validity of gatekeeping tests. Second, I examine the staggering changes recently wrought by politics and the courts that may be rendering the present merit system virtually incompatible with a democratic society.

Gatekeeping Tests Do Not Work

Under the helping hands of school counselors, parents, and teachers, more than 1.2 million high school seniors took the Educational Testing Service's SAT in 1998. ETS makes and administers the aptitude test for the College Board, a nationwide consortium of colleges and universities. But for all practical purposes, this is a monolithic SAT organization. Call it the ETS/College Board alliance. Besides the SAT, an additional one million seniors took its Iowa City cousin, the ACT college admissions test, produced by ACT Inc.

In either case, students, parents, and counselors have been subjected to the relentless message that the tests—although not infallible, of course—are good predictors of one's prospects for college success.

That has been the take-home message of the admissions testing industry's sales force for decades, and little has changed in recent years. For example, a sampling of ETS and College Board statements in 1998 about the relative merits of its SAT I (the verbal and math reasoning test) includes the following:

- *The ETS:* "High school grades have great value, but they are subject to variability from place to place. Standardized admissions tests offer colleges and universities a fair and impartial way to compare students from different school situations. Literally thousands of studies have found that the combination of grades plus test scores is a more effective predictor of the students readiness than either one alone." (10)
- *The College Board:* "No one can accurately predict with 100 percent certainty what your grades will be in college. . . . However, colleges use SAT I scores to help estimate how well students are likely to do at its school." (11)
- *The College Board:* "Many colleges require the SAT I because it is a *standard* way of measuring a student's ability to do college-level work." (12)
- *Donald M. Stewart, former president, The College Board:* "SAT scores provide a vital piece of information about a student's ability to perform college-level work." (13)

Taken together, those statements—the official ones carefully worded, Stewart's decidedly not so careful—leave counselors, parents, and high-schoolers with the highly misleading impression that the SAT is an adequate predictor, or even a good predictor, of college success. There is also the clear implication that the test has great utility to colleges in screening applicants.

Moreover, the ETS/College Board alliance has exacerbated those misleading statements about the SAT's predictive validity in their public reporting on the question of test bias. For instance, the ETS/College Board alliance, in an attempt to counter public rhetoric that the SAT is biased against women and minorities, has gone to great lengths to show that the SAT actually overpredicts freshman grades for blacks and that it actually somewhat underpredicts the academic performance of whites. Their studies have also shown that freshman grades for women are slightly underpredicted by the SAT. (14)

However, to a public unfamiliar with the technical argot of the testers, the ETS/College Board test-bias studies have led people to naively assume that the test is a good predictor of academic success. After all, if it is not biased against minorities, it must be valid.

However, the test-bias issue, which is subject to a great deal of public controversy and misunderstanding, is a red herring. The attention paid to test bias permits test makers and users to avoid the far more compelling issue of the predictive validity admissions tests. The fact that the tests are not biased against particular ethnic groups—in the sense that they do not significantly underpredict their academic performance—says absolutely nothing about how well the tests predict success for *all* individuals.

As it turns out, from scores of independent studies over the years by well-respected researchers in highly-regarded journals, the prevailing view of merit has been erected on a rather shaky foundation of scientific evidence about the real usefulness of admissions tests for predicting accomplishment in college or even graduate school. It is worthwhile looking at some of this evidence in detail, because the public's generally favorable views about the validity and utility of the tests surely has sustained the privileged position that college and university entrance testing continues to occupy in the American meritocracy.

Validity Evidence

By far, the bulk of the evidence about the power of college admissions tests to predict academic success comes from examinations of the SAT, particularly what is known as the SAT I exam of verbal and math "reasoning." A fewer number have investigated the ACT, and a smattering of occasional studies have looked at various other sorts of admissions tests as well as tests intended to help institutions place college students at the proper academic level. Mostly, researchers have studied the relationship of SAT scores and the one outcome for which the SAT is actually designed to predict: freshman year grades. In other words, counselors, parents, students, and colleges cannot make any inferences about one's chances of success beyond the freshman year based on SAT scores.

Even by that restricted criteria, the SAT falls well short of the ETS/College Board's implicit claims. To get a flavor for what the researchers have concluded about the validity of admissions tests, consider a handful of studies from a variety of academic settings.

Public colleges and universities. Consider the California State University System, consisting of several campuses in cities throughout the state. At CSU, freshman are admitted according to an eligibility index of high school grades and test scores. Students earning a high school grade point average of at least a B, or 3.0, are not required to submit standardized test scores. Estimates show, however, that as many as 90 percent of seniors submit test scores nevertheless.

Sheila Cowen and Sandra Fiori set out to evaluate the relative utility of test scores and high school grades at CSU's Hayward campus in a study of the academic performance of 762 regularly progressing students and another 210 "slower progressors," considered to be at greater risk for academic failure.

Overall, for both males and females and all ethnic groups, high school grades were the most powerful predictor of the academic performance of Cal State university freshman. In statistical terms, high school grades accounted for about 18 percent of the variance in freshman grades. SAT scores did help improve upon that prediction, but the gain was barely measurable—just five one-hundredths (from 18 percent to 23 percent). For the slower progressing students, the SAT's added value was virtually zero.

Nevertheless, the researchers found no evidence of test bias in the SAT. That is, the test didn't significantly over- or underpredict freshman grades for any ethnic group. Absence of bias, the researchers concluded, is no reason not to scrutinize the SAT's usefulness to Cal State. Indeed, the authors say, their study "leads to the conclusion that educators need to intensify the search for better predictors of college performance."(15)

Another recent study looked at the predictive power of the other popular college entrance exam, the ACT, at Chicago State University. This time, however, researcher Sandra Paszczyk was interested in determining whether the ACT could help the university assess a student's chance of success in broader terms than just freshman GPA, instead looking at one's grade point average at graduation from the university.

At both extremes of very high and low test scores, the ACT had modest powers of prediction. However, for the majority of the university's graduates who scored in the middle range of the test as high school seniors, the test could explain merely 3.6 percent of the differences in final grade point averages. That means, of course, that factors besides the ACT—from grades to motivation to work habits, and so on—accounted for virtually all the variance in grades.

Indeed, in one case the ACT proved to be *counterpredictive.* In the Chicago State study, the fall 1992 graduating class had the highest average ACT score (17.9) among the 428 students studied between 1990 and 1993. Among the graduates, that class also produced the poorest academic performance during their years at the university." (16)

Highly selective institutions. Even among the elite American colleges and universities, which admit a relatively small fraction of the number of high school seniors who apply each year, standardized admissions tests have not lived up to the implied validity claims of their proponents.

Consider a study at the University of Pennsylvania. Jonathan Baron and M. Frank Norman looked at the outcomes for some 3,800 students admitted to the university, who majored in fields ranging from engineering, business, and nursing to the arts and sciences.

Specifically, the researchers wanted to determine which explanations of academic performance actually gave Penn most additional predictive value, the most bang for the buck. The factors included class rank in high school, SAT II achievement scores on various academic subjects, and SAT I scores on general verbal and quantitative reasoning—the SAT most high school seniors take.

Among the predictors, the SAT I reasoning test was by far the weakest, able to explain just 4 percent of the changes in academic performance of students at Penn. The SAT II subject tests were somewhat better, accounting for 6.8 percent in the variation in grade point averages. Rank in high school was the clear winner, however, able to explain 9.3 percent of changes in cumulative GPAs, a predictive punch more than twice that of the SAT.

Now, the usual drill at many institutions, particularly highly selective ones, is to combine SATs and grades into a predictive index in accordance with the ETS/College Board advice that test scores add significantly to predictive power of grades alone. In Penn's case, that turned into a highly debatable proposition. When Baron and Norman added SATs to class rank, the prediction rose by just 0.02. When combined, class rank and SATs could still account for only 11.3 percent of the Penn students' grade differences. The subject tests, however, were a bit stronger than the SAT reasoning tests. Combined with class rank, the achievement tests boosted the explanatory power to 13.6 percent. Even then, almost 90 percent of the differences in academic performance remained unexplained.

Among the ETS/College Board defenses against such poor results for the SAT is the so-called "restriction of range" objection, which says that the test-score profile of the applicant pool will be much wider than the pool for admitted candidates. Because the range of test scores for the admitted pool is limited, the observed relationship between test scores and academic performance will be depressed below the "true" correlation, according to the argument. At highly selective institutions such as Penn, which admit students with relatively high test scores, the restriction of range problem would even more severely truncate the true power of the tests, according to the argument.

Therefore, Norman and Baron investigated precisely that possible technical objection to their findings. Contrary to SAT defenders' supposition, however, the researchers tell us, "it was concluded that restriction of range does not seem to explain the nonsignificant weight of the SAT." (17)

In another broad investigation of more than 10,000 students at eleven choosey private and public institutions, a high-schooler's predicted freshman performance estimated by the SAT proved to be of only modest predictive value. Fredrick E. Vars and William C. Bowen, reporting their results in 1998, found that a full 100-point gain in combined math and verbal SATs, holding race, gender, and field of study constant, was associated with about one-tenth of a grade point gain in an elite college student's grade point average.

Vars and Bowen's analysis of socioeconomic factors was particularly striking for these top students. For instance, a 100-point increase in the SAT I mathematics score was associated with GPA gain of 0.08 grade points. One could predict the same effect on college grades by simply observing whether the student's dad had a graduate degree, which also conferred a GPA gain of 0.08 grade points. If mom completed college, the addition to her offspring's GPA at an elite institution proved to be more powerful than either one's math or verbal SAT score.

Overall, the researchers' evidence suggested, the usual model of grades and test scores that institutions have used to prognosticate one's academic performance have proven to be less than satisfactory. In their own relatively comprehensive model that included test scores, grades, and several personal and socioeconomic variables, Vars and Bowen were able to predict just a quarter of the differences in the academic performances of these students.

"Clearly, much remains to be explained," the researchers tell us. "The relatively weak relationship between SAT scores and academic performance, especially for black students, underscores why admission officers must be free to consider factors other than grades and SATs when choosing among candidates." (18)

Even the ETS's own studies tell a similar story, but a school counselor or parent might not know it from the College Board/ETS public statements on the SAT's predictive power. To help illustrate this, it is worth noting that all the statistical relationships between test scores and academic performance cited above are in terms of what's known as the coefficient of determination, the *r-squared* statistic, which is an estimation of the amount of change in one variable (academic performance) that can be attributed to a predictor variable (SAT scores). Obtaining the *r-squared* is a considerably more useful and intuitively sensical indicator of the predictive value of standardized tests than looking at the simple correlation between the variables, or the *r* value. (One calculates the *r-square* by simply squaring the simple correlation between the two, then multiplying by 100 to translate to percentage terms.)

Yet, that seemingly arcane technical distinction between the *r* and *r-squared* can convey significantly different impressions about the predictive punch of test scores. The College Board and ETS know this. But parents or school counselors would be hard-pressed to find any *r-squareds* for the SAT reported in College Board/ETS public literature on the test. Rather, the alliance chooses to report its SAT's predictive validity in terms of the simple *r*, which has great potential to mislead the public into believing the test is considerably more powerful than it really is.

For example, the College Board's 1997–1998 *Counselor's Handbook for the SAT Program* reports an ETS study that calculated the simple correlation, or *r*, between test scores and freshman grades at 0.42, for the bulk of SAT I scores around the median. That figure appears to be strong evidence for the predictive value of the SAT. On that basis, some students, parents, or counselors might well conclude that the SAT correlates 42 percent with college grades. (19)

In fact, squaring the correlations reported in the College Board handbook shows that SAT scores accounted for just 17.6 percent of the variation in freshman grades in the ETS study of more than 600 colleges and universities—leaving more than 80 percent of the variance unexplained. What is more, any number of factors falling in that unaccounted-for variance could by itself have greater predictive punch than the test score.

Indeed, it is almost always the case in studies of the SAT's effectiveness that high school grades are more powerful than any test score. As indicated in the College Board counselor's handbook, high school grades are a significantly better indicator of college performance. One's high school performance, in fact, could explain almost a quarter of the differences in grades among freshman.

Adding SATs to high school grades in those 600-plus studies improved prediction of college performance, but barely. In terms of simple *r*, the supposedly tried-and-true formula of SATs combined with high school grades nudged up the correlation over high school record alone by just 0.07 (from 0.48 to 0.55). That means the variance in academic performance accounted for by the combination of test scores and high school grades, at 30 percent, was seven percentage points greater than for high school grades by themselves. (Squaring 0.55 equals 0.30; that times 100 equals 30 percent. Squaring 0.48 equals 0.23; that times 100 equals 23 percent. The difference equals 7.)

Proponents of standardized entrance tests have argued that even such marginal improvements on the predictive value of the high school record is better than nothing, and hence, the SAT and its ilk remain beneficial to colleges and universities. However, that claim has been shattered by the work of James Crouse and Dale Trusheim, who have shown in a number of ways that the SAT adds virtually no value for colleges in forecasting student performance in college.

Consider, for instance, two prime objectives for undergraduate admissions offices: They want students who maintain good or passing grades and obtain a bachelor's degree. Admissions officers want to maximize their "correct" admissions; that is, the numbers of students who perform at or above some academic level.

Crouse and Trusheim have shown, for example, that the use of high school rank by itself for admissions results in 62.2 percent "correct admissions," when the academic standard is set at a college GPA of at least 2.5. When the SAT is combined with high school performance, colleges make 64.6 percent "correct" admits—just an additional 2 in 100 correct decisions. When the admission's office goal is having lots of students who successfully complete a bachelor's degree, the SAT's added benefit is even worse. Consideration of the high school record results in 73.4 percent correct admissions, compared to 72.2 percent with the addition of SAT scores.

"From a practical viewpoint," Crouse and Trusheim conclude, "most colleges could ignore their applicants' SAT score reports when they make selection decisions without appreciably altering the academic performance and graduation rates of the students they admit." (20)

But wait, one might object. From a societal perspective, such findings might overlook a key benefit of standardized admissions tests. Although certainly not precise—no single measure can possibly be—the tests could serve as a broad indicator to help society distinguish the brightest people likely to accomplish far more in college than their intellectually mediocre peers. Surely, a good standardized test can help institutions sort out the cream of the crop, right?

That question actually has been examined in several investigations. Leonard Baird, for instance, compared "very bright" National Merit Scholarship finalists—who are eligible for college scholarships on the basis of standardized test scores—with a representative sample of ordinary college students. On some thirty-five various measures of accomplishment in college, Baird found "very little difference between the two groups."

Baird performed a similar analysis on the Michigan Scholarship Program, which awarded funds on the basis of ACT scores. He compared the academic performance and accomplishments of more than 14,000 scholarship-eligible students—with ACTs averaging 25.5 out of a possible 30—with some 10,000 others not eligible for the scholarships because their ACTs averaged a mediocre 18.

That is a significant difference, and a good test of the theory that bright students, as indicated by test scores, ought to shine in all aspects of college relative to not-bright ones. After all, students scoring in the eighty-sixth percentile of all ACT test takers nationwide were being compared to those scoring in just the thirty-fifth percentile. But in terms of actual accomplishments, there were few discernible differences between the two groups. Says Baird: "In no case did academic ability (ACT scores) account for as much as 1 percent of the variance in accomplishment." (21)

Results like this have compelled other researchers to consider the effects of different models of selection for students besides the prevailing method of grades and test scores, followed only secondarily, if at all, by accomplishments in and out of school.

For instance, when two researchers looked at the effects of several different admissions scenarios, they concluded that selection based on aptitude tests did not lead to superior academic performance. Also, picking students on the basis of high school rank did produce superior students in academics, but not other sorts of accomplishment. On the other hand, the study also found that admissions based on "a broad range of high school achievements results in a broad range of achievement in college without lowering the level of academic performance." (22) Commenting on these remarkable findings, Baird provocatively suggests:

> Admission on creative accomplishment would result in college classes that would include many students who would write stories and essays, develop their own science experiments, create their own music, take part in college and non-college plays, submit works of art to art contests, and run for campus offices. The students selected by this strategy would be also somewhat less likely to drop out but were not more (or less) likely to have good grades. (23)

In short, a new paradigm for choosing who has and has not merit for going to college is likely to enhance the overall educational quality of academic institutions and do so with no sacrifice in academic performance of students. Chapter 13 explores how some institutions are actually putting that remarkable realization into practice.

FOCUS: BATES COLLEGE RUNS THE NUMBERS

As might be expected of a highly regarded college, a member of the College Board and full-fledged user of admissions tests, Bates College did not bow out of mandatory admissions testing without serious study. Under the workmanship of Bates professor Drake R. Bradley, the college's Committee on Admissions and Financial Aid carried out carefully controlled studies on the effects of dropping the SAT.

The crucial question for the committee was whether Bates's storied academic excellence would be endangered by not requiring gatekeeping tests. Did the SAT do a good job of predicting academic performance at Bates? Moreover, did students who chose not to submit their SATs fare worse academically than those who did file their SATs for scrutiny? Here is what the committee discovered, as reported in its final report to the college on February 13, 1990:

SATs and grades. As the numerous studies for many other institutions have shown, the SAT turned out to be a poor indicator of later academic performance at Bates as well. Bradley's group found that SAT math and verbal scores combined to explain just 9.6 percent of differences in grades among Bates's students. The SAT subject tests were slightly better. Still, all three SAT scores combined could account for just 13.6 percent of the variation in grade point averages at the college.

In the analysis, the Bradley group noted some of the absurd results obtained from trying to predict grades from test scores. For even the best predictor among the tests, the SAT achievements, the committee discovered that a score of 610, for instance, predicted "GPAs which ranged from a low of 0.6 to a high of 4.0!"

Test score submitters versus nonsubmitters. Another indicator of the SAT's real benefit to Bates could be ascertained by comparing academic performance of high-schoolers who submitted their scores relative to those who chose not to. The situation was all the more interesting in that the test filers had significantly higher SATs than the nonfilers. (Nonfilers actually did submit scores for research purposes only.)

After Bates dropped its admissions testing requirement, SAT submitters got average test scores that consistently ran about 160 points more than those who did not submit scores (about 80 points on both the math and verbal subtests). And, while submitters scored considerably above national averages on the SAT, Bates's nonsubmitters *underperformed* national averages.

With that magnitude of difference in the supposed academic aptitude—the "developed abilities," in ETS parlance—between Bates's SAT submitters and nonsubmitters, one would expect the high scorers among the former to far outshine their supposedly duller peers among the latter.

Again, actual data disproved the mythology. Over a study period of six years that included a total of about 1,880 students, about a quarter of Bates's applicants chose not to submit test scores each admissions cycle. In terms of indicators of academic standing, such as rates of dismissal and probation, the two groups were virtually identical. Indeed, the committee's report indicated, out of fifteen students whom Bates booted for poor academic performance, fully fourteen of them were SAT *submitters.*

As for college grades, no statistically noticeable differences between the two groups surfaced over six years of study, as both submitters and nonsubmitters earned GPAs of about 2.8. In fact, the academic achievements of the nonsubmitters belied

(continues)

(continued)

the formulaic expectations colleges typically use to translate SAT scores into predicted grades. Consistently, the SAT turned out to overpredict actual grades for the test filers and woefully underpredict GPAs on nonfilers, in some years by as much as two-tenths of a grade point.

All told, none of this evidence favored the continued use of the SAT at Bates. Evident from the rigor with which the group assessed the effects of its test-score mandates, the Drake committee clearly had bent over backward to be open to any possible counterevidence. But the data simply didn't exist to support the widely held view that test scores were a valid proxy of academic merit at the college. With open eyes, the Bates group took a good, long look at the SAT emperor and found that it, indeed, had no clothes. Their report concluded:

> There is nothing in the data to suggest that we would benefit by returning to the pre-1985 policy, which required applicants to submit both their SAT and achievement test scores. In fact, there is much in the data that would call into question the policy of requiring *any* standardized test scores, given how poorly they predict academic performance at Bates.

With that, Bates faculty voted to quit the SAT requirement for good in 1990, a move that would give all applicants the opportunity to have their credentials fully considered, with or without test scores. As Bates vice president William Hiss put it to me, "this little college in Maine was going to try another way."

The Graduate Record Exam

If the SAT's (or ACT's) usefulness as an indicator of later performance in college remains dubious, then the commonly used entrance exam for American graduate studies borders on the ridiculous.

There's little doubt that what is known as the Graduate Record Examination, or GRE, yet another ETS test, has achieved central importance in the lives of the increasing numbers of Americans who would like to go on for a master's or doctorate degree. Indeed, graduate or professional training has proved to be one key credential enabling highly educated Americans to remain relatively untouched by, and even thrive in, the vast economic and technological changes rippling through the U.S. economy in recent years.

Yet, the class and racial differences among those who obtain graduate education are striking. In 1996, for example, almost three out of four of all graduate students were white. The same year, far less than 1 percent were Hispanic, and about 7 percent of the some 1.7 million students enrolled in graduate school were black.

At the same time that graduate education may be viewed as the necessary credential for success in the American economy, the Graduate Record Examination has evolved into a formidable gatekeeper into the world of graduate studies.

Graduate programs are typically far more selective than undergraduate ones, and the GRE almost always plays a decisive role.

The GRE has deeply penetrated American graduate education. One study of 7,000 graduate programs figured that more than six in ten programs required the GRE, and almost seven of ten graduate programs in the health sciences mandated the test. (24) Further, the GRE typically carries enormous, even pivotal weight in admission and financial aid decisions. It is common for admissions committees to sort prospective graduate students on the basis of rankings according to an index of undergraduate grades and GRE scores. A cutoff point for the index is established, either explicitly or tacitly, below which applications are rarely considered. Only applicants making the numerical cutoff receive the luxury of having their application even read, for either admission or for graduate fellowships.

This common usage of numerical cutoffs means, too, that someone applying to a graduate program or for a graduate assistantship, who has very good undergraduate grades but low or moderate test scores, "will either be completely eliminated from further consideration, or will have a low probability of being selected for admission," say Edith Goldberg and George Alliger, professors at the State University of New York at Albany. (25) Similarly, Robert J. Sternberg and Wendy M. Williams reveal that, in the screening process for the graduate psychology program at one major research university:

> Applications for admission are sorted upon arrival into four boxes labeled *GRE Below 1200, 1200 to 1300, 1310 to 1400, and Above 1400.* . . . The first applications to be read and considered come from the box labeled Above 1400. Applicants scoring below 1310 are rarely admitted, and applicants scoring below 1200 are almost never considered—their applications are often merely skimmed! (26)

For its part, the Graduate Record Examinations Board, which like the College Board contracts with ETS to produce the test, advises universities not to place excessive weight on the GRE. In fact, the GRE Board and ETS dutifully inform test users that the exam should be just one of multiple criteria, as no test score can be an exact indicator of one's chances of success in graduate study. "A cutoff score based only on GRE scores should never be used as a sole criterion for denial of admission," the GRE Board's test guidelines say.

At the same time, the GRE Board sounds a lot like the College Board in its claims about the validity of the test to predict success in graduate school. As a "common measure" for comparing applicants, the GRE "when used properly, can improve graduate admission and fellowship selection processes," the board informs the GRE's users. "Research indicates that GRE scores are valid predictors of success in the first year of graduate school for all students." (27)

Thus, users and customers of the test are told that the GRE should be used judiciously—but not to fret because the exam is still a quite decent indicator of later achievement. That so many graduate programs appear to have flouted guidelines on proper use of the GRE renders the board's counsel as so much boilerplate, not unlike the surgeon general's warning labels on a pack of cigarettes. The Graduate Record Exam might cause the equivalent of educational cancer if not used properly, but it is still highly usable, valid for predicting grades in the first year of graduate school. It is worth taking time to examine the claim.

According to the Educational Testing Service's own data, the various GRE subtests (verbal, quantitative, and analytical reasoning) do predict first-year grades, but the power of the relationship is feeble. According to the ETS, in studies of 1,000 graduate departments nationwide and 12,000 test takers, the GRE could account for just *9 percent* of the variation in their first-year grades. In the natural sciences, the GRE analytical test predicted 7 percent of the differences in first-year graduate performance. In engineering departments, the GRE quantitative test explained a mere 4 percent of the variability in graduate grades. The proportion of variation in graduate business grades was just 6 percent for the GRE analytical test.

And so on. Overall, undergraduate grades in the ETS studies proved to be well superior to the test scores, able to predict 14 percent of the variability in academic performance. Adding all three GRE scores to undergraduate grades bumped up the predictive power only marginally (0.07) to 21 percent. (28)

Scores of studies of the GRE by independent scholars underscore the patterns found in the ETS's own data. At the State University of New York at Buffalo, for instance, researchers evaluated the admissions policy of the Nursing School, which required a minimum GRE of 900 and an undergraduate GPA of 3.0. Only candidates having at least those numerical credentials would be considered.

The SUNY researchers revealed amazingly low associations between the entrance test and academic performance in graduate nursing. They found, for instance, that the three GRE subtests predicted from 1.6 to 2.2 percent of the differences in first-year graduate nursing grades. The correlations were so weak that they did not rise to a level of acceptable statistical significance.

In fact, the researchers noted, the *only* statistically meaningful relationship proved to be between first-year graduate grades and graduation from the nursing program. *Actual performance* in the first year of graduate nursing accounted for fully 64 percent in the differences in graduation. By contrast, GRE scores could explain about 4 percent of the variation in graduation rates.

An admissions scenario that paid closer attention to actual performance rather than test performance, the researchers suggest, would likely improve the nursing school's ability to select the most capable candidates. At the same time, doing so would diminish barriers the GRE presents to members of ethnic groups hurt most by the tacit or explicit use of minimum GRE scores.

"Because the results show that GRE scores are weak predictors for success in graduate nursing education, success may be better predicted by undergraduate GPA, which showed a strong correlation with success," the researchers concluded in their report in the *Journal of Professional Nursing*. "The verbal and quantitative GRE scores have some relationship to later performance, but they are marginal at best in their predictions." Furthermore, they say, because the GREs "can have a negative impact on decisions to admit minority students, older students, and women, the use of these tests by nursing programs is questionable." (29)

At Glassboro State College, researcher Thomas C. Monahan seemed taken aback at the GRE's weakness to predict academic performance throughout the New Jersey college's graduate departments. The GRE verbal test could account for well less than even 1 percent of grades in graduate school (0.5 percent, actually); quantitative GREs explained 3 percent.

"These correlation coefficients indicate that the relationships among these variables are not particularly strong," Monahan reports. "In fact, a surprising statistic is the correlation between GRE verbal scores and the graduate grade point average. . . . One would think that the correlation between these two variables at the graduate level would be greater." (30)

In a broad assessment of the GRE's ability to predict grades in graduate psychology and counseling programs, Edith Goldberg and George Alliger conducted a meta-analysis of several dozen studies covering more than 1,800 test takers. For all studies combined, Goldberg and Alliger found that GRE scores explained "virtually zero" of the differences in specific course grades. What's more, the test's verbal and quantitative sections predicted no better than 2 percent of the variance in total graduate grade point averages.

"Overall, the results from this meta-analysis do not paint a particularly favorable picture for the validity of the Graduate Record Examination," they report in the journal *Educational and Psychological Measurement.* (31)

In 1995, Todd Morrison and Melanie Morrison took just seven pithy pages in the same highly regarded journal to decimate the GRE's credibility as a predictor of graduate school grades in many fields. In their meta-analysis of twenty-two studies covering more than 5,000 test takers from 1955 through 1992, the researchers reported that the combined GRE verbal and quantitative score could explain just 6 percent of variation in the academic achievement of graduate students. In no uncertain terms, they tell us:

> The average amount of variance (in graduate grade point average) accounted for by performance on these dimensions of the GRE was of such little magnitude that it appears they are virtually useless from a prediction standpoint. When this finding is coupled with studies suggesting that performance on the GRE is age-, gender-, and race-specific . . . the use of this test as a determinant of graduate admission becomes even more questionable. (32)

Groping for Significance

In response to the exceedingly poor showing of the GRE in predicting first-year grades in graduate programs, researchers have groped for other sorts of outcomes on which to assess the exam's adequacy as an indicator of achievement. Grades, some researchers have suggested, are undesirable indicators of success on at least two counts.

The first objection to grades is related to the same restriction of range problem encountered earlier, the statistical quirk alleged to explain the low correlations of freshman grades with SAT scores. In the graduate setting, because the lowest grade a student can typically get in most graduate programs is a 2.0—with the bulk of grades ranging between 3.0 and 4.0—then grades, according to this objection, may lack sufficient variability to yield meaningful relationships to test scores.

Furthermore, other researchers have suggested, grades in academic subjects may be an overly narrow criterion for measuring success in graduate school. Why not look at faculty ratings of students' performance, quality of doctoral dissertations, and master's theses, or how quickly students complete a master's or doctorate?

Even when researchers use alternative measures of success besides grades, the GRE comes up short. For example, in 1994, educational researcher Christine Onasch hypothesized that higher GRE scores would lead to faster completion of a master's degree in geology at Bowling Green State University. To Onasch's surprise, she found just the opposite—that high scorers on the exam actually took longer to complete the degree.

Like many other studies have revealed time and again, Onasch discovered that a geology graduate student's undergraduate grades were the far better predictor of his or her obtaining the master's in a timely fashion. The GRE, Onasch concluded, "is but a one-time measure of the student, which does not realistically indicate (his or her) future success in graduate school." (33) It should be noted that Bowling Green's graduate geology program has continued to require the GRE, despite Onasch's remarkable finding.

For fairly obvious reasons, the GRE Board and the Educational Testing Service have long sought to find academic outcomes for which their GRE might obtain better success as a predictor than its dismal record on first-year grades. For instance, in a recent board technical report, ETS researchers Mary Knight and Donald Powers examined the GRE's ability to predict faculty members' ratings of a student's graduate performance. The researchers assembled findings from earlier studies covering a total of a couple of hundred graduate departments. The results showed that GRE scores were hardly better indicators of faculty opinions of students than they were of first-year grades. Although GRE quantitative scores, for instance, could explain anywhere from 2 to 8 percent of the variation in first-year grades in graduate school, the test predicted 5 to 7 percent of the differences in faculty ratings. (34)

Robert Steinberg and Wendy Williams's investigation of the GRE's performance as a predictor of success in graduate psychology at Yale University sought to broaden perspective of the problem still further. What kinds of individual traits, knowledge, skills, and abilities should graduate admissions committees really be looking for if their goal is to produce good psychologists, not just stars in academic courses? Are the logical and analytical reasoning abilities assessed by such standardized tests as the GRE sufficient for this broader purpose of screening prospective practitioners?

The researchers hypothesized that the GRE would perform better as an indicator of success in first-year graduate courses than it would as a predictor of accomplishment in more real-world kinds of performances where creative abilities, practical sense, and independent thinking come into play.

Why so? "Because introductory graduate-level psychology courses, as they are typically taught, require most of the same kinds of fairly abstract and often context-lean memorization and analysis that are required by conventional tests of ability and achievement," Sternberg and Williams say. "Success in psychology as a career, or even in the later years of graduate training in psychology, may require creative and practical abilities more than do conventional psychology courses. . . . Thus, one might expect the GRE to be weaker as a predictor of success as a psychologist, or even as an advanced graduate student, than one would expect it to be as a predictor of initial graduate grades." (35)

And so, Sternberg and Williams compared the GRE's performance at predicting three outcomes for Yale graduate psychology students: overall faculty ratings of the quality of a student's performance in graduate school; faculty evaluations of dissertation quality; and grade point averages for the first two years of graduate work. Their findings:

- GRE quantitative, verbal, and analytical tests, per usual, showed slight relationships with grades, accounting for, at best, about 3 percent of the variances (*r* values ranging from 0.03 to 0.18).
- The exam's performance as a predictor of success on the broader measures of success was even worse. The GRE's average proportion of variance explained for all the alternative measures combined was 1 percent, meaning the test left *unexplained* 99 percent of the differences in student performance on real-world assessments. The authors tell us that "there just was not enough relation in many of the correlations to be significantly different from zero."
- Indeed, in some instances, the correlations of GRE scores and graduate performance were actually negative. This was particularly true of women's performance at Yale's graduate psychology program.

Anticipating the usual objections that the GRE's proponents trot out in its defense, the researchers showed that possible protests of their findings on technical grounds amounted to red herrings. The vaunted restriction of range problem was not a significant problem in their data and "cannot be fully blamed for the pattern of correlations we obtained." Alleged unreliability of faculty ratings could also be dismissed; after all, the ratings systematically correlated with several variables in the study. And so forth, leaving the investigators to conclude:

> We believe that our results underscore the need for serious validation studies of the GRE, not to mention other admissions indexes, against measures of consequential performances, whether of students or of professionals. Psychologists need to apply the same standards of falsifiability in their admissions process as in their scientific

> work. Too often, we believe, the use of a test becomes self-perpetuating, without serious attempts to verify its effectiveness. Our study suggests the need to reflect on the use of tests before they become firmly—and, as it sometimes seems, irrevocably entrenched. (36)

What makes the highly questionable validity of the GRE all the more disconcerting is the stark relationship between one's class background and test performance. Even the GRE's maker, the Educational Testing Service, has vividly demonstrated the effects of economic class on test performance. In a January 1994 report for the Exxon Foundation, ETS found that parental income and education have especially strong correlations with test scores.

For example, of the nearly 7,000 test takers who scored between 750 and 800 on the analytical part of the GRE, fewer than 4 percent had fathers who had not completed high school. However, fully half of these high scorers had fathers with a bachelor's degree or more. Of these, some 90 percent had fathers with graduate or professional degrees. Moreover, when the ETS study held income constant, the often stark differences in test scores between races diminished dramatically in some cases. For instance, with family income of $15,000 to $25,000, 25 percent of whites scored 550–599 on the GRE verbal section—identical to the percentage of blacks with those scores in that income bracket. (37)

In a March 1993 report to the Graduate Record Examinations Board, the ETS's Lawrence Stricker and Donald Rock concluded that "it is striking that parental education generally had the most consistent and strongest associations" among several variables, including sex, ethnicity, geographic location, and age. (38)

A "Conspiracy of Lethargy"?

In truth, there is no shortage of serious, independent validity studies on the usefulness of college and university entrance tests like the SAT and GRE. Furthermore, despite finding after finding showing indisputable weakness in the exams to perform even the minimal function of predicting grades, the tests remain firmly ensconced as a principal measure of merit for university admissions.

What, then, possibly explains institutions' continued reliance on these standardized tests of exceedingly doubtful benefit? This question has been raised at various points in this book in many of the various contexts in which Americans are required to take standardized tests in education and the workplace. In all contexts of standardized testing, part of the answer surely can be found in the American predilection for quantification and the reductionist urge to put human complexity in the argot of "psychometrics." Related to this is the American love of the black and white, the cut-and-dried bottom line as the one and only indicator of the quality of some one or some thing. A business is a good business when its profits are maximized. A nation is a good nation when its gross domestic product is rising. A movie is a good one when its box-office receipts soar.

Americans have been witness to a culturewide embrace of abstractions of reality in so many aspects of the technological age. In the era of postmodernity, images and abstractions of reality, like a pencil-and-paper test, are somehow seen as more powerful and compelling than reality itself.

Furthermore, gatekeeping tests have remained entrenched as a matter of bureaucratic efficiency and perceived convenience for the gatekeepers. Besides the talismanic hold that scores and percentiles have on American culture, institutional bureaucrats view gatekeeping tests as a brutally efficient means to sort, classify, and rank. Because the gatekeepers themselves don't pay a price for the testing they require, the economic and social costs of all this sorting, classifying, and ranking are shifted to the consumers of tests and the public at large.

Equally important, in a country obsessed by numerical rankings as the measure of quality, GRE and SAT scores can confer institutional prestige upon colleges and universities vying for the attention of prestige-seeking constituencies, including students, parents, and even state legislatures.

There may be other reasons as well for this unmerited entrenchment of standardized tests. Wendy Williams, a human development specialist at Cornell, says colleges and universities will not quit the GRE habit because they are afflicted by a "conspiracy of lethargy." Too many graduate school aspirants for the number of slots available provides graduate programs little incentive to innovate and to seek alternative strategies to sticking people into boxes labeled by their GRE performance. (39)

Certainly, institutional laziness and the mere habit of conforming blindly to the agenda-setting counsel of such formidable institutions as the College Board and the Educational Testing Service can't be dismissed. However, there may be more to it than bureaucratic inertia and the power of tradition.

John A. Muffo, now the director of academic assessment at Virginia Tech, has been working the trenches of institutional research on assessment for some twenty-five years at various major universities. Over the years, Muffo told me, many academic departments have asked his counsel on setting up systems to help departments ensure students entering their programs are capable of doing the work.

Once, for instance, an English Department came to him wanting to use SAT scores to place students at their proper level of study, contrary to the existing open-admission policy. "Let's use verbal SAT scores as a predictor," the English faculty told Muffo. "I said, 'We could do that, but you're wasting your time,'" Muffo now recalls. "'If you were to put SAT scores in one column and student English grades in another, you could eye-ball it and immediately see there is no relationship.' They didn't believe me."

Nevertheless, faculty in the English Department insisted, and Muffo ran the numbers. They discovered for themselves what Muffo already knew. "You're right, there is no relationship," the faculty members conceded. "What do we do?" Muffo advised them to develop their own assessment that fit their own standards and expectations for their students in their courses, as opposed to an off-the-shelf standardized test like the SAT.

In another case, an accounting department chairman got a notion that accounting students seemed more highly skilled in the 1980s compared to those in the 1970s, believing the "greed revolution" had driven many bright students who would have gone into the sciences instead toward business. So, he asked Muffo to prove the theory using SAT scores. Although Muffo ended up proving the hypothesis wrong, he thought the department chairman might also want to know an interesting fact he had uncovered, which would render the underlying assumptions of the whole exercise suspect. The assumption was that student quality was measurable by SATs. "'By the way,' Muffo told the department head, 'there's no relationship between the SAT and accounting grades.' But when I told him that, he wasn't interested."

Time and again, when Muffo would show people on various campuses the numbers they asked for on SATs or GREs, and their relationship to actual academic performance, people would often simply refuse to believe him. Muffo's description of these incidents makes evident the not very subtle irony that a certain parochial, anti-intellectualism can thrive even in the most enlightened quarters. Amazingly, these academics were able to so compartmentalize their abilities as scientists and skeptics that they would seem to leave those traits behind whenever the subject of GREs or SATs arose. The academics' refusal to hear Muffo's news seemed an act of blind faith in a tradition they had been raised to believe in.

"Most of their notions about this stuff were formed when they were teenagers," Muffo says of his colleagues. "They're all going on historical misinformation, and they just do not want to hear that their information might be wrong. They don't because it contradicts everything they've been taught. They don't want their lives disrupted this way. . . . I think it's just plain ignorance."

"We Are Failing"

Altogether, then, several immensely powerful cultural influences have combined to sustain the privileged status of standardized testing in the American meritocracy. Cultural values and habits in the society at large have overwhelmed the scientific case against the use of gatekeeping tests. As a result, they have continued to play a central role in what amounts to a pseudo-meritocracy. The pseudo-meritocracy reproduces itself because it chiefly serves the interests of American elites, who can justify their superior economic and social positions on the basis of objective evidence of merit provided by indisputable numbers.

In recent decades, educational policymakers have sought to diminish unequal access to higher education among Americans via one principal remedy: affirmative action policies that permit consideration of race and ethnicity in admissions decisions. That's the good news. However, important as affirmative action has been for many individuals, these policies never could and never will substantially alleviate vast disparities in access between ethnic majorities and minorities and between the rich and not-rich. Commenting on some thirty years of ever-expanding inequality between elites and those of low and moderate means in terms of access to higher education, higher education policy analyst Thomas Mortenson tells us:

> In fact, we are doing very poorly, we are failing. As measured by the national commitments of 1965 to eliminate poverty, we are failing badly. As measured by the commitments through 1992 to equalize higher educational opportunity we have failed. . . . By any of these measures, the growing needs for postsecondary education and training are not being adequately met, and they are certainly not being adequately met for those on whom federal policy is targeted.(40)

The Problem with Affirmative Action

Although affirmative action has been necessary to redress higher education's past sins against racial minorities, race-based preferences have *judiciously sidestepped the larger question of the legitimacy of the nation's prevailing definition of merit.* Indeed, a persuasive circumstantial case can be made that affirmative action, which permits gatekeepers to use one's race as a criterion for some admissions, may be a tool of American elites that enables them to preserve the social definition of merit that primarily serves their own interests. Why? Affirmative action permits alternative views of merit only at the margins, for a relatively few number admissions for some ethnic minorities, while leaving the far greater bulk of admissions unaffected, subject to the same hegemony of test scores and grades. Hence, even under affirmative action, the vast majority of the openings remain subject to the prevailing views about merit that primarily benefit children of the well educated and well-to-do.

The law school at the University of California at Los Angeles is a remarkable case in point. In 1991, despite its efforts on affirmative action, UCLA law school's student body had a socioeconomic profile that placed them in the upper crust of American society. The students' fathers had graduate degrees considerably more often than the average American dad; their moms were far more likely to have obtained bachelor's degrees. Their parents' income were more than double the national median.

"If one considers the national population of people in their twenties, those from families with incomes over $200,000 were about fifty times more likely to end up as students at our school than were those from families below the poverty line," says Richard H. Sander, a law professor at UCLA. Further, he says, UCLA's socioeconomic profile wasn't at all unusual among top law schools, public or private. A 1995 survey of 6,000 students at the top thirty law schools, for instance, showed that 41 percent of their dads and 25 percent of their moms had earned graduate degrees. Sander notes that, for all Americans aged forty-five through sixty-four, however, just 8 percent of men and 4 percent of women had graduate educations. (41)

Of course, many unavoidable social and economic barriers to equal opportunity may well contribute to such schisms. I'm not suggesting some utopian society and the elimination of all barriers to success for the sake of some overly idealized democratization of educational opportunity. However, it's another matter altogether when those socially constructed barriers are illegitimate. Gatekeeping tests frequently are not objective, fair, or accurate, and often amount to artificial and arbitrary barriers for some Americans and keys to the kingdom for others. This state of affairs cannot be sustained in any society that purports to be a democracy.

Why the Current Paradigm Cannot Be Sustained

Unlikely as it might seem in the face of such so much cultural horsepower propping up the present system of merit, there is good reason to suspect the present-day equilibrium is about to be permanently altered. The guardians of the meritocracy may be about to be shaken from their conspiracy of lethargy, their bureaucratic laziness, and their long-held beliefs about merit.

In one of the great ironies of recent American history, the very existence of affirmative action itself—and the recent legal and popular attacks on it—will force the hands of educational decision makers regarding the real utililty of gatekeeping tests. Only then will the prevailing merit system be officially rendered obsolete.

Institutions understood early on in the affirmative action era that strict adherence to the prevailing merit formula for all applicants—owing principally to significant and persistent test-score gaps between whites and most minorities—would cause a whiteout, in violation of their legal and ethical obligations to bring diversity to their campuses and to eliminate the vestiges of generations of racial exclusion. As a result, institutions devised what amount to two sets of gatekeeping rules, one for ethnic groups supposedly not penalized by test-score-based decision rules and another one for ethnic minorities who are damaged by them.

The effect of the separate sets of rules has been to admit some minorities with lower test scores than some whites. In recent years, however, a number of popular and legal challenges to such two-tiered gatekeeping systems have prevailed, directing institutions in no uncertain terms to stop basing admissions decisions on racial classifications. As a result, colleges and universities have been provided an alarming glimpse of the future where merit is defined strictly by grades and test scores, a future without even the slightly ameliorating effects of affirmative action. Colleges and universities most affected by the backlash have watched minority admissions plummet, threatening to re-create a pre-1965 era of public higher education whose sole beneficiaries were upper-middle-class whites.

As the millennium was coming to a close, affirmative action as the one official remedy for vastly unequal access to higher education among Americans appeared to be in its death throes. Should affirmative action ultimately be dismantled, its demise may well lead to the widespread acknowledgement in the American democracy that the prevailing paradigm of merit, which is so highly dependent on standardized test scores of highly dubious value, can't be sustained or tolerated. Here's why:

The California backlash. In July 1995, the Board of Regents at the University of California voted 14–10 to phase out over three years all consideration of ethnicity and gender in admissions to the nation's most prestigious public university system. A year later, California voters passed Proposition 209, which effectively ended affirmative action in public agencies and public higher education throughout the state.

Governor Pete Wilson, whose short-lived presidential campaign was based largely on abolishing all affirmative action in hiring and college admissions, made certain utterances that appeared to resonate with the public. Through a spokesman, he told the *New York Times* in 1996 that, in essence, affirmative action was cheating the children of white families because they had higher SAT scores, that is, more "merit," than blacks or Hispanics. "It was wrong thirty years ago when African Americans were denied access to public universities," the spokesman said. "It is equally wrong when non-preferred racial groups, who might have higher SAT scores and better qualifications, are denied admission to public universities based on the color of their skin." (42)

By 1998, effects of the changed political environment on affirmative action in the UC system had become glaringly evident. At UC–Berkeley, the number of blacks admitted to the freshman class—already quite low compared to whites and Asians—was down to 255, a drop of nearly 60 percent from the prior year. Hispanic admissions to Berkeley's freshman class were off 40 percent. At UCLA, UC–San Diego, Davis, Irvine, and Santa Barbara, black admissions had dropped anywhere between 14 percent and 46 percent. Hispanic admissions to those campuses had declined anywhere from 9 to 33 percent.

The Hopwood decision. In March 1996, the Fifth Circuit of the U.S. Court of Appeals ruled that the University of Texas School of Law's use of race as a factor in its admissions equation was prohibited by the U.S. Constitution. Employing a common admissions formula, the law school compiled a so-called Texas Index consisting of grades and scores on the Law School Admission Test (LSAT), and rank-ordered the applicants on that basis. But the law school used a separate schedule of cutoff points on the index for white and minority applicants. The white plaintiffs, including one Cheryl J. Hopwood, sued because the law school passed them over in favor of ethnic minorities with lower numbers.

Although the judges agreed that promoting diversity may be necessary for public institutions, they also said using racial classifications to achieve diversity cannot pass constitutional muster. A university, the judges said:

> may properly favor one applicant over another because of his ability to play the cello, make a downfield tackle, or understand chaos theory. An admissions process may also consider an applicant's home state or relationship to school alumni. Law schools may specifically look at things such as unusual or substantial extracurricular activities in college, which may be atypical factors affecting undergraduate

> grades. Schools may even consider factors such as whether an applicant's parents attended college or the applicant's economic and social background. . . . We only observe that "diversity" can take many forms. To foster such diversity, state universities and law schools and other government entities must scrutinize applicants individually, rather than resort to the dangerous proxy of race. (43)

After the U.S. Supreme Court refused to consider the decision, it soon became apparent to colleges and universities that the Fifth Circuit's sweeping decision would apply, at a minimum, to all institutions of higher education in Texas, Louisiana, and Mississippi.

The immediate impact of the Hopwood ruling was devastating. In Mississippi, historically black colleges, which had established their own rules for grades and test scores, were instructed to make their admissions standards conform to the more restrictive ones to be applied to all Mississippi colleges. At the predominately black Jackson State University, applications plummeted 60 percent. (44)

At the University of Texas School of Law, where all this began, just eleven blacks were admitted in fall 1997, the first new class after Hopwood, compared to sixty-five the prior year. That translated to an admissions rate of about 4 percent for blacks, down from 18 percent in 1996. Admissions of Mexican Americans declined from seventy to forty, and the proportion of admissions to applicants also took a dive. Law School Dean M. Michael Sharlot reacted to the news by saying the school "is greatly distressed by the sharp reduction in the number of Mexican-American and, most dramatically, of African American students enrolled in the 1997 entering class." (45)

At the same time that the Fifth Circuit judges told institutions what they could not do, the judges, in essence, also provided the region's colleges with a road map for what they *could* do. Chapter 13 will revisit the state of Texas to examine what the University of Texas has done in the aftermath of this landmark case.

The backlash spreads. Institutions across the country became awash in legal challenges to their affirmative action policies. In all instances, the issues turned on the existence of different sets of gatekeeping rules for different ethnic groups. The University of Michigan's law school faced a lawsuit brought by four Michigan legislators that essentially duplicated the issues in Texas. In Washington State, voters replicated California's Proposition 209, approving a ballot measure in November 1998 that prohibited all government entities in the state from considering race in any hiring or college admissions decisions.

In addition to all these attacks, yet another compelling legal event suggested affirmative action in higher education was in legal trouble at the end of the 1990s. This one came in another federal appeals court decision in the Northeast. On November 19, 1998, the U.S. First Circuit Court of Appeals outlawed as unconstitutional an elite Boston public school's use of racial categories in its admissions. Although the case pertained not to higher education per se, the issues it presented to the appellate judges were nearly identical to what the Hopwood court contended with in law school admissions.

The Boston case turned on the admissions procedure of the Boston Latin School. The most selective of three public "examination schools" in the city, Boston Latin picked the best and brightest on the basis of standardized test scores. However, the school also used a system of proportional representation for ethnic groups, which raised the hackles of the court on constitutional grounds.

Boston Latin denied its policy amounted to a quota system, of the sort banned by the U.S. Supreme Court under the 1977 *Bakke* decision. The First Circuit's opinion stated that quota or not, the policy rested on racial preferences to pick students. "Attractive labeling cannot alter the fact that any program which induces schools to grant preferences based on race and ethnicity is constitutionally suspect," the court's majority opinion stated.

Like the University of Texas law school, the court's opinion said, Boston Latin's argument for diversity among its students would not be served viewing diversity through racial lenses alone. "We do not question the School Committee's good intentions," the majority stated. "The record depicts a body that is struggling valiantly to come to terms with intractable social and educational issues. Here, however, the potential for harmful consequences prevents us from succumbing to good intentions. The policy is, at bottom, a mechanism for racial balancing—and placing our imprimatur on racial balancing risks setting a precedent that is both dangerous to our democratic ideals and almost always constitutionally forbidden." (46)

Lowering "Standards"?

All totaled, these legal and popular broadsides against institutions' use of different gatekeeping rules for different races and ethnic groups threatened to kill off affirmative action, and, further, set back the movement for more equitable access to America's colleges and universities by decades.

The backlash against racial classifications, in turn, was greeted with dismay by affirmative action's adherents and practitioners in the universities, many of whom vowed to keep the principles of affirmative action alive at their institutions. Still, most institutions were not willing to confront or open up a discussion of the most basic question of all: *What is merit?*

Shortly after the Hopwood court rendered its landscape-altering decision, sixty-two major research universities, under the mantle of the Association of American Universities (AAU), took out a full-page ad in the *New York Times*. "As members of the (AAU), we therefore want to express our strong conviction concerning the continuing need to take into account a wide range of considerations—including ethnicity, race, and gender—as we evaluate the students whom we select for admission," the universities pledged. (47)

Even some former hard-liners who had always been against racial preferences were coming to affirmative action's aid, arguing that such preferences were better than the alternative: a whiteout of America's universities. For other so-called pragmatists, their reaffirmation of racial preferences went even further, claiming that affirmative action's demise would, in effect, spell doom for academic standards at America's colleges and universities. Race-blind admissions, this specious reasoning suggested, would mean lower academic standards applied to everyone, thus lowering average SATs, GREs, and LSATs, and diminishing the intellectual stature of the nation's coveted system of higher education.

"If affirmative action is ended, inevitable political, economic, and legal forces will pressure the great public universities to lower admissions standards as far as necessary to avoid resegregation." So warned three law professors at the University of Texas in a legal brief they filed in one federal case, an assessment imbued "with cool-eyed accuracy," in the words of the *New Yorker*'s legal writer, Jeffrey Rosen. (48)

In short, these pragmatists clearly understood that one of most profound, unintended effects of affirmative action has been to shore up a merit system led by test scores and grades. Having enjoyed the escape valve of affirmative action to vent societal and legal pressure on institutions to open access to underrepresented groups, selective colleges and universities still were able to compete in the marketplace for prestige by keeping average test scores up for the people they allowed in.

How so? Consider the highly selective admission system that's been used at the UCLA School of Law. One block of admittees, the far largest one, would consist of students who ranked highest on a so-called "predictive index" (PI) of test scores and grades. A second, relatively small bunch would include the affirmative action candidates who most likely would be admitted with significantly lower test scores. As long as the affirmative action block was small relative to those admitted on the PI, the law school could maintain its prestigious statistical profile of high LSAT averages. At the same time, however, one could be sure that such a system would ensure that the publicly-funded UCLA would remain an island of privilege for children of American elites.

A cynical but perhaps well-deserved interpretation of the pragmatic view is that maintenance of the status quo will keep the beasts at bay, as it were, those unworthy hordes who would depress test scores and lead to the academic ruin of America's great universities. Arguably, the pragmatic view is the "test scores equals academic quality" argument all over again, issued under the protective ideals of affirmative action.

Were the present gatekeeping system to really help decision makers differentiate those who will succeed at the university from those who will not make it, then the doomsday scenario above might actually be something to fear.

However, there is ample reason to suspect that a post–affirmative action world, which also shunned the prevailing merit rules, would not be apocalyptic. Based on what is known about the poor quality of the present merit system to judge human potential—in which the lion's share of the variation in people's achievement is *not* accounted for by scores and grades—one can take comfort knowing that changing the gatekeeping rules for all college-bound Americans will surely not measurably erode academic quality.

Indeed, there may be silver in the lining of affirmative action's demise, as we shall now take up in the following chapter. As colleges and universities struggle to reinvent themselves and their gatekeeping rules, and to institutionalize far broader and more complete perspectives of merit, then educational quality may be poised for a new renaissance in America. And now the beauty part: This renewal of the meritocracy may come not at the cost of racial and ethnic diversity, but may actually enhance the goals of affirmative action and equal opportunity.

13

Beyond the SAT: Merit that Matters

LIKE ALICE IN WONDERLAND, THE INNER WORKINGS of the American merit system have been getting curiouser and curiouser. And, Bob Zenhausern might say, even Catch–22ish.

A professor of psychology at St. John's University in New York, he has seen the merit system's eye-opening, nonsensical contradictions repeated annually with the entry of two tracks of students in the school's graduate psychology programs, one for doctoral psychology students and another for those planning to stop at a master's degree.

As it turns out, the master's students are not required to take the Graduate Record Exam, the ubiquitous standardized test most graduate programs in dozens of fields require to judge an applicant's worthiness. On the apparent theory that the Ph.D. students should have greater intellectual power than the master's candidates, people applying to the doctoral program must submit GRE scores. The master's and Ph.D. students take the same courses from the same professors and compete in their courses on exactly equal terms.

The scenario has made for an interesting test of the Psychology Department's assumptions about merit, particularly when master's students change their plans and decide they want to continue on for a Ph.D., as some inevitably do. No matter what one's *actual* performance in the graduate-level classes has been, those master's students wanting to go on for a Ph.D. must take the GRE. Why? *In order for the department to predict their first-year grades for graduate courses they've already taken.* The absurdity has not been lost on Zenhausern.

"You get these people in the same courses as the Ph.D. students and even when they're getting A's, the Ph.D. admissions committee wants them to take the GRE," Zenhausern told me. "Now, the GRE does a poor job, and the poor job it does is to predict graduate school grades." But even *if* the GRE were to do a good job of prediction, he says, "why do we have to predict them when we already have them?"

Without hesitation, Zenhausern promptly answers his rhetorical question. "In this case, they're worthless. We don't need to predict what we already have in actuality. What then happens is that you find people who are great, who perform very well, but they're not accepted because their standardized tests are not good."

This is the sort of curiosity one encounters when merit resides in the gamey, abstract universe of standardized tests that are only vaguely and remotely connected to the real one of actual deeds and genuine accomplishments. In the case of St. John's Psychology Department, graduate admissions committees have been so enchanted by this way of thinking that its glaringly absurd outcomes seemed coated by Teflon.

When Zenhausern or others would object to the GRE's use in the department, the test's defenders usually resorted to the testocracy's equivalent of the Pentagon's claims of "national security." At St. John's, as well, it was an invocation of a policy on the basis of tradition and authority alone, irrespective of whether the claim was justifiable by reason or evidence. "It's (the GRE) got to be included," was the usual answer, says Zenhausern. "It's done everyplace else. . . . We need something objective."

Zenhausern remains unwavering in his view that American higher education ought to come up with a better justification than that pseudo-argument in the face of the overwhelming evidence that the present merit system makes little sense. There are better ways to assess human talent, he insists, ways that get to what is really the whole point of any selection system.

It is a simple idea, really. To know how someone might do in medicine, undergraduate English, or law school, then look for evidence of achievements on real-world tasks and personal characteristics that may actually pertain to medicine, English, or law school. Give her the opportunity to demonstrate what she can do.

"Get rid of standardized tests, period," Zenhausern said. "What you put in its place is an evaluation that makes sense. . . . These standardized tests evaluate what somebody *can't* do. That's because it's easier to find out what somebody doesn't know. They give you a bunch of questions and count how many mistakes you make. We need instead to measure what somebody *can* do."

American colleges and universities are beginning to do just that. Some institutions, particularly those in Texas and California, are doing so because they have had little choice, under the cloud of legal attacks against their affirmative action programs. Many others, such as Bates College in Maine, have mounted a direct challenge to the assumptions underlying the current merit system out of enlightened self-interest.

Although many of the innovations are fledgling, still trying to swim against the powerful currents of our test-obsessed culture, they are proving that the merit system's current gatekeeping rules can be modified or even radically changed without risking a collapse in academic civilization as we know it.

Changing the Rules in Texas, California, and Beersheba, Israel

After the Hopwood court had its way with the University of Texas School of Law's affirmative action program, directing Texas to stop using race as an admissions factor, state policymakers found themselves between the proverbial rock and a hard place. Texas was trapped by its own history of segregation.

Like other southern states, Texas's higher educational system in the 1970s had been subjected to intense federal scrutiny. The U.S. Office of Civil Rights, in fact, determined that Texas operated a dual system of higher education that kept blacks, in particular, out of the mainstream of Texas institutions. Thus was born the so-called Texas Plan in 1983, whereby the state agreed with federal authorities to remove the stains of segregation from its colleges and universities.

Partly because of the Texas Plan's federal pressure, the 1997 Texas legislature took a bold step to ward off a potentially disastrous whiteout arising from the Hopwood decision. Senate Bill 588 was a landmark piece of legislation, establishing a uniform admissions policy for all colleges and universities in the state.

Most notably, the legislation, sponsored by House Democrats, required all of Texas's public institutions to automatically accept any Texas high-schooler who ranked in the top 10 percent of his or her graduating class. Further, the bill left to each campus's discretion whether to extend its automatic admissions to the top 25 percent of high school classes. Governor George Bush, Jr., a Republican, signed SB 588 into law the same year.

And that's how the professional life of Bruce Walker was turned upside down. As the director of admissions at the sprawling campus of nearly 50,000 students at the University of Texas at Austin, Walker oversaw the transformation of the university's gatekeeping system from a process driven by the crunching of numbers to one managed by people making professional judgments and decisions, one applicant at a time.

Certainly, the "10 percent solution" to the pending crisis in Texas was huge in the annals of major research universities. That change in itself marked a quantum break in the evaluation of merit at the university, sending the message to all Texas high-schoolers, no matter how poor, black, or Hispanic their schools and their neighborhoods, if they worked hard and made good grades, they would have a shot at Texas's flagship university.

The new law meant that a black or Hispanic high school senior from a struggling urban school in San Antonio, who achieved in the top 10 percent of her class, would be on an equal footing with her top 10 percent counterpart at elite Highland Park High in Dallas. The new system also meant that a poor showing on the SAT would not preclude a top 10 percent high-schooler from attending any Texas university, including UT–Austin, as a matter of law.

In effect, lawmakers were listening to the research about the relative value of standardized tests, compared to the more useful indicator of grades, to predict college success. In sum, that research suggests, if you want to know how someone will do in school, then look to their past record of actual performance in school. Policymakers were also sending Texas teenagers a profoundly different message about merit than most American students typically were exposed to: Show us what you can do and what you can accomplish, not necessarily how well you take college admissions tests.

It all meant that a student in the "top ten" could not be denied admission because of a test score. The effect was immediate and dramatic at UT. In previous years, even many "top ten" students were not actually admitted owing to deficiencies in their admissions test scores or high school curriculum. Under the new rules, virtually all "top ten" students got into UT. For the few who were denied admission, it was because of glaring problems in their high school courses or other aspects of their application.

But the 10 percent rule was only part of the transformation at UT–Austin. For the fall 1998 class of new freshman, UT received about 12,000 applications. Some 4,600 of those were students ranking in the top 10 percent of their high school classes. So, about 40 percent of UT's applicants ranked in the top 10 percent. That left a block of about 7,400 applications that Walker's admissions staff evaluated according to an elaborate list of eighteen pieces of evidence incorporated into state law, of which standardized test scores were just one. The eighteen items reflected the Hopwood road map for the wide range of nonracial factors the university could legitimately consider in its admissions decisions.

Further, many of the items were themselves objectively verifiable measures, providing UT's admissions staff with a far broader picture of a high-schooler's background than academic measures alone. Topping the list of the eighteen items was the applicant's academic record in high school. That was followed by a broad array of socioeconomic indicators, such as the degree to which a family's income was above or below the poverty level; household income; mom's and dad's level of education; and whether the high-schooler would be the first in his family to attend college.

The new admissioins equation even factored in such information as whether a student worked part time in school or helped the family to raise children. The law permitted UT to rate the financial status of an applicant's school district; the performance of his or her school on various state measures; and whether the school was operating under a court-ordered desegregation plan. Rounding out the list was consideration of an applicant's community involvement and activities outside school.

"They all help us put student achievement into some kind of context," Walker told me. "If a student is not involved in any activities, you see if they worked or not. Then you see the low (socioeconomic status) rating and you begin to understand why they weren't as involved in extracurricular activities."

After nineteen months of debate among the faculty, UT added one more element into the mix: the applicant's personal essay, which Walker says became a central element in the admissions decision. The university wanted to send a message that writing mattered for its prospective freshmen. With help from the

English Department, the admissions staff received special training in how to score essays to achieve a high degree of reliability among the readers. Called "holistic" scoring, the method has become common in the evaluation of writing in schools and colleges. First, readers agreed to guidelines, called "rubrics," for what features various quality essays should minimally include. In an admissions scenario, essays could be scored for such features as the writer's sense of purpose about going to college; the focus and organization of the piece; concrete detail and specific examples that reveal something appropriate about the applicant; and so on. Typically, highest quality essays are scored a six, and lowest quality a one.

UT's essay scoring was highly consistent among the readers. Prior to the scoring, Walker's group met in consensus-building sessions to evaluate a random sample of 300 essays. This enabled them to develop crystal-clear examples of each level of essay quality, and more important, to agree with each other about those judgments. A UT study showed that readers agreed within one point among themselves nearly 90 percent of the time.

In November 1998, Walker had ten staffers gearing up to read 8,000 to 10,000 applications and essays from the block of applicants not in the top 10 percent, and the reading staff was expected to double by mid-January. Each application would receive two scores, one for the essay and another one through six rating on the academic and socioeconomic factors. To accommodate the extra workload, the university boosted Walker's $5 million budget by $350,000 in 1997, the first year of the new admissions scheme.

Of course, policymakers and observers nationwide will be watching UT in coming years to determine whether such new-fangled perspectives on merit are worth the cost and trouble. Prior to talking to Walker, I'd been warned by various people that the frontliners in the admissions trenches at large public institutions, people like Walker, would not look favorably on any changes to the status quo that messed with the bureaucratic convenience and efficiency provided by numerical indexes and cutoffs. However, that was far from the case with Walker. Indeed, early indications suggested the 10 percent solution was working as hoped.

First, it appeared the new system—which explicitly could not take race or ethnicity into consideration—not only prevented the feared Hopwood whiteout but actually helped bolster the quest for diversity at UT.

For instance, according to data Walker provided, the admission rate for African American students who graduated in the top 10 percent of their high school classes rose from 87 percent in 1995—prior to the effects of Hopwood—to 97 percent by 1998. That meant more blacks in the top 10 percent were actually getting in, because low SATs were no longer a roadblock.

In 1995, 63 percent of black applicants were admitted to UT. In 1997, the first year of the new admissions system, about two-thirds of black applicants were admitted—still, however, well below the admission rates for whites and Asian Americans. The fall 1997 enrollment of Mexican Americans at UT was up 4.5 percent over the 1996 level. Moreover, fully 96 percent of Mexican Americans in the top ten were admitted, compared to 90 percent or so in previous years.

"We're holding our own in terms of minorities," Walker told me. "In the face of Hopwood and the affirmative action debates around the country, I think we can hold our own, and are probably doing very well. The top ten percent law has allowed us to hang in there."

Walker acknowledges that the new system is not as bureaucratically convenient as the old, numbers-driven process. Whereas the old system was technology intensive, so that decisions could be rendered by the clinical efficiency of computers, the new method is considerably messier and more labor-intensive. However, it is also a labor of considerably more love, Walker says, especially when he has got so many essays to read that he does them during evenings and on weekends. Walker says:

> It is a lot of work. But in my opinion, it's more satisfying work. You come to know a great deal more about the class than using a computer to make decisions for you. What they're thinking about, and so on. You just get a better feel for the class. . . . It would be easier and faster to do all this by computer. There was a time that we could process an application and render a decision within 48 hours. Now, we can only promise to let a student know by March 25. It's because they're in that great mass in the middle, the great mass that we're reading. . . . When you move from a numbers-driven process, you do have to ask yourself the question, 'Is it worth it?' Our faculty seem to think so. And, using this method, we can control our numbers. Nobody is guaranteed admission, except those in the top ten percent. We're able to determine for ourselves where we draw the line. It is a costly process, and there's more room for error than computer-driven formulas. But we believe it will be our best chance to control our enrollment and have a diverse class.

Using its "10 percent solution," the University of Texas thus modified its gatekeeping rules for undergraduate admissions—and its definitions of merit—to put a premium value on solid evidence of accomplishment—one's high school performance. At the same time, UT downgraded the importance of potential accomplishment as indicated by test scores. The new system complemented that core value with a "class-based" admissions model that placed a high-schooler's academic performance into a meaningful social and cultural context.

Other institutions both in the United States and outside the country have also turned to alternatives to the traditional view of merit, where test scores and grades are considered central, while all other considerations and individual accomplishments are deemed merely complementary, if considered at all.

Institutions are beginning to exploit a remarkably consistent finding that has been encountered throughout this book: The pool of available talent, who would accomplish much in school and beyond, is almost always far larger than permitted under the excessively narrow and faulty view of merit commonly employed in selective admissions. Here are various solutions to the equity dilemma that have modified the traditional rules of gatekeeping:

- *Boalt Hall.* The University of California–Berkeley law school appears to be perhaps in the early stages of a renaissance. In 1997, Boalt Hall was a bleak place. In the wake of the affirmative action wars in California, minority admissions plummeted owing to the school's continued heavy reliance on LSATs and undergraduate GPAs for admission.

In prior years, the admissions system's damage to minority applicants had been somewhat mitigated by racial preferences. Still, Boalt was an all-too-typical example of a highly selective institution that pretty much disregarded all the cautions about the appropriate use of standardized tests: that test scores should never be decisive by themselves, but should be considered along with many other factors that bear on an applicant's chances of success; and that small differences in test scores are not meaningful, statistically or otherwise.

Up against the wall, Boalt did the academic equivalent of attending an Alcoholics Anonymous meeting, beginning with the selection of the fall 1998 entering class. Its name was Boalt and it was an admitted test abuser. The school completely overhauled its gatekeeping engine, removing parts that were not working and adding elements that would increase the chances both of maintaining the diversity of its students and holding up academic quality.

First, the school abandoned the odious practice of sorting applicants by cutoffs and indexes composed of LSATs and undergraduate GPAs. That move alone meant low LSAT scores would not automatically eliminate one from consideration. Related to that change, the admissions committee quit making life-altering inferences about applicants based on meaningless, small differences in test scores. Henceforth, all LSATs would be reported to the admissions staff only in terms of a score band, to reflect the statistical truth that, because of measurement error, one's "true" score falls within a range of scores. That meant, for instance, a candidate with an average LSAT of about 150 would be considered to be no less worthy than another with a slightly above-average score of 155.

In another remarkable move, Boalt made a concerted effort to permit applicants with relatively low LSATs to present evidence about their past history with standardized tests in relation to their actual academic performance. Thus, applicants with good college grades and relatively poor SAT results would be provided an official forum to show how the test may have mispredicted their accomplishments.

Such alterations might at first glance appear subtle, but if Boalt Hall actually continues to do what it claims it is doing, these seemingly modest changes could prove to be profound. One's record of poor showings on standardized tests compared to their actual performance and accomplishments at jobs or at school would no longer be relegated to the incidental, anecdotal stuff that Boalt Hall in the past may or may not have even listened to.

At the same time, reworking the rules of merit did not mean Boalt Hall was becoming any less choosy. In fact, 857 people were admitted out of an applicant pool of more than 4,500, resulting in an admissions rate of just 18 percent, making Boalt still a very highly selective law school.

In terms of regaining lost ground on diversity goals, Boalt Hall's new regard for broader views of merit appeared to be going in the right direction. Whereas just one African American was admitted to the 1997 class, nine blacks were admitted to Boalt under the new race-blind paradigm in 1998. Mexican American enrollment shot up from six to sixteen. In all, minority enrollment for the 1998 class exceeded the prior year's by nearly 40 percent. (1)

- *Texas A&M School of Medicine.* Drop the Medical College Admissions Test? In a post-Hopwood world, that is exactly what the Texas medical school has done—in part. Concerned that the Hopwood ruling would worsen the already difficult problem of getting doctors to practice in underserved rural areas, in 1998 A&M's medical school launched its Partnership for Primary Care program. For college students of any ethnicity who pledged to work in rural areas, Texas A&M would waive the MCAT requirement. Also, participating students, who agreed to attend workshops and take internships in rural settings during college, and who maintained a 3.5 grade point average, would be automatically admitted to the medical school. On the other hand, applicants to A&M who did not participate in the partnership would still have to submit their MCATs. (2)

Texas A&M's dramatic move represents yet another highly selective institution that has chosen to at last act on what researchers have been telling medical educators for some time. The essence of that message is that the wholesale reliance of medical schools on MCATs and undergraduate grades to pick and choose the succeeding generation of doctors has been deeply flawed.

Indeed, the magnitude of the MCAT-achievement relationship is weak, at best, accounting for no more than about 9 to 16 percent of the variation in medical students' first-year grades. Beyond that, as medical students enter the real-world, clinical phases of their training, the MCAT prediction vanishes. "Data from numerous studies show that the presumed link between aptitude for medical education (measured by MCAT scores and college GPA) and medical school achievement (measured by grades and National Board of Medical Examiners examinations) is tenuous," writes William C. McGaghie in the journal *Academic Medicine*.

Several reasons can account for the MCAT's inability to predict overall success in medical school and beyond. First, classroom aptitude is a far cry from competence in real professional settings. "No physician answers pages of multiple-choice questions when he or she practices clinical medicine," says McGaghie. Further, any positive correlations that do exist between predictors and later performance is more a function of the measure than individual ability. "Grades predict grades, test scores predict test scores, ratings predict ratings, but attempts to demonstrate scientific convergence among such indicators of professional competence have not been successful," McGaghie tells us. (3)

That Texas A&M will waive the MCAT requirement for only some candidates, however, presents school officials with a problem. Clearly, they know and believe MCAT scores tell them virtually nothing about the quality of doctors they will produce. Surely the school would not risk dropping the MCAT for the partnership participants if officials thought otherwise. Retaining the MCAT for all other applicants exposes the standardized test for what it is and always has been: a sorting machine powered by myth.

- *The UCLA School of Law.* Without race to consider, many American colleges and universities in states like Texas and California have been searching for other answers to their equity dilemmas, presented by the fact that standardized test scores continue to be formidable roadblocks for many minorities. In California, the UCLA School of Law is one highly selective institution that has recently experimented with "class-based" admissions, and with some success.

In the aftermath of Proposition 209 and the University of California Regents' move ending racial, ethnic, and gender preferences in admissions, the UCLA School of Law embarked on its new path during the 1997 admissions cycle. The school had in the past maintained a system driven by undergraduate grades and test scores using what it called the "predictive index" or PI. At the same time, the school had set aside a portion of each entering class for what it called "diversity admissions."

As law professor Richard H. Sander describes in the *Journal of Legal Education,* the law faculty studied the problem for several months before settling on the new admissions scheme. In addition to the PI, the school created a new, separate index called the "combined index" or CI, which effectively replaced its former raced-based affirmative action program.

The class-based affirmative action system, as the law school calls it, worked like this: Combining LSAT scores and grades, the school first calculated a PI of between 0 and 1,000 points for all 4,000 or so applicants. Going by past experience on those admitted under the old system, the school determined that PIs of about 800 or above would stand, unadjusted, in the admissions process. Applicants with PIs of less than 625 would automatically be denied admission. However, applicants with PIs between 625 and 815 would receive a modest number of extra points depending on how they fared on a range of objectively measured and verifiable socioeconomic factors. These applicants would be the so-called CI group. The lower their level of socioeconomic status, the more extra points individuals would receive.

The family background measures that were systematically thrown into the mix included mom's and dad's educational attainment and income; measures to assess the economic status of the applicant's neighborhood, such as the rate at which neighbors received welfare payments; and the percentage of adults in the neighborhood who had not graduated from high school. Again, these measures were intended to be verifiable to the greatest extent possible, and independent databases categorized by census tracts aided the analysis.

In any case, the school's class-based experiment proved to be remarkably promising in terms of eroding barriers to law school for people from poor and moderate economic circumstances. In terms of family income, the admitted CI candidates looked vastly different from their PI counterparts—the ones admitted solely by rank on LSAT scores and undergraduate grades. Just 3 percent of the PI group had family incomes under $15,000, for instance, compared to 22 percent of the CI group. Although 7 percent of the PI group fell into the lower-middle-class category of $25,000 to $35,000, 17 percent of the CIs did so. Overall, the PIs came from families with annual incomes almost twice the national average, at $78,000, compared with $31,000 for the CI group—which was about $10,000 less than the national average.

On all the other measures of socioeconomic status, the CIs ended up approximating national norms. On the other hand, says Sander, "the parents of the PIs are a true educational aristocracy, with over half the fathers and 41 percent of the mothers holding graduate degrees." By contrast, just 5 percent of the CI moms had graduate degrees, roughly equal to the U.S. average.

Sanders says he was "surprised and delighted" by those outcomes. "I was surprised that a relatively modest regard for socioeconomic status could produce a class that looked pretty similar to the general American population," he told me.

In terms of racial diversity, the class-based approach also appeared to hold some promise. To the extent that underrepresented groups like blacks and Mexican Americans came from poorer families and neighborhoods than other ethnic groups, they were more likely than others to get socioeconomic boosts in the point system.

In the case of Mexican Americans, the boosts were sufficient to maintain their admissions rates even without affirmative action. In the former race-based setup, Mexican Americans were admitted at an average rate of 9.8 percent between 1990 and 1996. In the class-based system, 7.3 percent of Mexican American applicants got in. Sander says the admissions rates for Anglos and Asians increased substantially, owing to the socioeconomic boosts added to their already relatively higher test scores and grades. Native Americans held steady.

Blacks fared worst among the ethnic groups, going from a 10 percent rate of admissions during the recent years of affirmative action to a 2.1 percent rate under the class-based program. Blacks got hit, Sander explains, partly because of the moderately high cutoff point for minimum test scores and grades, at 625, which eliminated many more blacks from consideration than under the old race-based rules, when the cutoff was set at about 550. The socioeconomic status boost actually benefited only about a quarter of the blacks eligible for extra points. What's more, the school received many fewer applications from black students, a decline of 27 percent from the prior year, under the chill of affirmative action's demise in the state.

Still, compared to what black admissions *would have been* without the points for socioeconomic status—that is, under a strict selection system of LSATs and grades—the class-based program proved its worth. Black admissions, in fact, were more than twice the rate they would have been under a test-score cum grades setup.

Finally, there is the important question of the academic performance of the students admitted with lower test scores. Sander told me the UCLA students who were provided a leg up because of their relative socioeconomic disadvantages performed better in the first year of law school than their counterparts entering through the former race-based system.

Overall, Sander says, UCLA law's experiment with class-based admissions "produced a class that, in socioeconomic terms, resembled the general American population on many dimensions. It produced a significant amount of racial diversity, and its main failing in this area—the small number of blacks—would not have been significantly remedied even by much larger SES preferences, since larger preferences would have admitted other groups at high rates, swamping most of the gain in black admissions." (4)

Despite hopeful signs that class-based admissions can tear down old barriers to law school for Americans of poor and moderate economic means, it is worth noting that UCLA's experiment still largely embraced standardized test scores as a decisive measure of one's merit to study law. UCLA's new gatekeeping system basically replaced race with socioeconomic considerations, meaning that implicit assumptions about test scores and merit remained unaffected.

Just as for UCLA's former "diversity admissions" candidates, test scores carried relatively less weight for the CI candidates whose LSATs tended to be significantly below the school's PI group. Under the UCLA plan, test scores could still either automatically eliminate a candidate or virtually guarantee one's entry, regardless of other considerations.

Black students, as always, were damaged most severely by the school's continued reliance on minimum cutoffs for test scores and grades. Indeed, the school's class-based plan erected significantly higher cut points than the old race-based rules.

However, there is some wiggle room. The school could lower the cut points to at least the level they had been under the old affirmative action rules, without affecting the quality of the lawyers they graduate. Time will tell whether the present form of the UCLA plan can be sustained without such modifications, which would permit more African Americans to be included in the selection pool.

- *Ben-Gurion University of the Negev.* Perhaps no other higher education institution in the world has taken to heart the lessons about academic aptitude tests to a greater extent than this "medical school that could" in Beersheba, a city of 160,000 in the heart of Israel's Negev Desert.

Opened in 1974 soon after the Yom Kippur War, the medical school aims to train caring and highly competent physicians committed to community medicine, under the overarching idea that patients are people, not diseases. Indeed, that philosophy is reflected in every aspect of the school, from the yearly admissions process for the first-year class to how they learn and practice medicine.

The school's method of selecting students presents a particularly compelling example that challenges the myth, evident in physician training especially, that only the "cognitive elite," as measured by IQ scores and their ilk, are fit to succeed at the rigors of medical school and in later professional practice.

"The hidden assumption of most medical schools would seem to be that the goal of selection is to admit potential Nobel prize winners," wrote the late Aaron Antonovsky, who had been a driving force behind the Israeli medical school's pathbreaking admissions process.

"Alternatively, it is assumed that none but the very top scorers on ability and achievement have the cognitive potential to perform well as medical students and physicians. Despite the massive evidence that the predictive value of scores, with the narrow range of those that allow admission, is at best marginal for even the first years of school, this assumption has continued to guide most selection procedures." (5)

The Ben-Gurion University of the Negev (BGU) embarked on another path, making a far different set of assumptions about merit than suggested by what might be called the "Nobel Prize model." Based on the research evidence, the school hypothesized instead that the pool of physician talent was in fact far larger than yielded by traditional selection methods. The program would remain just as selective as more traditional schools, but the narrowest part of the passageway would not come from test scores.

"The goal of the medical school selection process," says medical school professor Shimon Glick, "is not to choose outstanding medical students but rather to select ideal doctors." (6)

Ben-Gurion's model of selection is based on the "threshold" principle, which says that fairly modest cognitive abilities, as measured by tests, may be important for success in medical school, but measured "aptitude" beyond that modest threshold shouldn't be accorded undue weight.

This implied that if BGU wished to pick people who would be the best doctors, consistent with its institutional values centered on community, humanity, and professional competence, then its selection system should focus on methods to ascertain those traits in people. The school settled on a model that placed crucial weight on structured personal interviews with candidates. Here's how the selection method works:

At the first stage of selection, the school broadly screens applicants for modest levels of intellectual and academic ability. The first threshold is high school grades, which must be the equivalent of an American grade of B. The second cognitive screen is an IQ-type test. Compared, say, to Hunter College Elementary's cutoff of about the ninety-eighth percentile on the Stanford-Binet IQ test to get into the New York school's elite public *kindergarten,* applicants to this Israeli *medical school* have only to score in the sixtieth percentile to pass this initial screen.

This means anyone with average "intelligence" is considered to have sufficient cognitive ability to perform well in medical studies. For every 10,000 or so candidates, about 80 percent survive this phase. At this juncture, the test is never looked at again. So it is a loose screen, indeed.

Next comes the first interview of candidates, conducted by teams of four faculty members on the admissions committee. Over the years, says Professor Glick, local judges, clergy, teachers, community leaders, and others besides physicians have volunteered to serve on the interview teams. Antonovsky says the interviews have been crafted as a "serious, reliable and valid interaction appropriate to its intended purpose."

In other words, BGU interviews are decidedly not casual conversations between applicants and high-powered medical researchers who are perhaps unskilled or untrained at establishing rapport and obtaining useful information about the candidates. The school's interview is a structured process that efficiently elicits information from applicants as to their suitability to study medicine at Ben-Gurion. Admissions committee members receive special training on the interview process, and new members are always teamed up with experienced ones.

The interviewers also become well practiced in avoiding the potential pitfalls such a process often presents. One is the potential for bias, particularly against women and minorities, the latter of whom would typically be Israelis of Arab descent. Institutional values and norms, however, have been sufficient to drown out any particular ethnic or gender biases that interview team members may harbor, says Antonovsky.

"If anything, we have leaned over backwards," he says. "Thus, the proportion of women and ethnic minorities selected has invariably been a bit higher than these groups constituted of the applicant population." Not only that, but their representation has been "considerably higher than the proportion who pass the 'objective' tests," he tells us.

A second potential pitfall of information-gathering interviews is the "smooth talker." Here, too, the interview teams have been well trained not to fall prey to simply charming personalities. Foremost, interviewers are trying to solicit from a candidate information about his or her actual accomplishments. "We focus on deeds, on life experience, and not on the right words," says Antonovsky. "Woe to the candidate who is dying to be a primary care practitioner in a development town, but who has never gone out of his or her way to do something for anyone or to know anything about people in other social classes or ethnic groups than his own."

Not unlike the "holistic" evaluation of admissions essays we found earlier at the University of Texas, BGU interview teams rate an applicant's performance in interviews on a one-through-five scale. Whether it is in writing or interviews, the method must yield highly consistent results not dependent on who's doing the scoring. Over the years, says Antonovsky, BGU interview teams have achieved an impressive degree of agreement on the candidates through the interviews. In a study of 3,000 interview sessions, team scores were in agreement about 99 times in 100.

The interviews last about fifty minutes. If all four team members approve the candidate, she's passed to the next stage. About 44 percent of the candidates who make the cognitive threshold stay in the running after the initial interview session. (Out of some 10,000 applicants over a ten-year period, about 3,400 passed this milestone.)

The remaining candidates are invited for a second interview. Again, four thumbs up means the candidate enters the final selection phase. About 36 percent of the remaining candidates survive this test. (Over a period of ten years, of the 3,400 who made the first interview cut, about 1,100 remained standing after the second interview.)

In order to pick the final group for each first-year class, Ben-Gurion then rank-orders the interview scores for the remaining group. At this point, Antonovsky says, the admissions committee focuses most of its discussions on the marginal candidates who may not have won unqualified enthusiasm from all team members.

The school's main goal in the endgame is to avoid making false rejections. This is contrary to the usual mission or highly selective admissions to avoid false acceptances. About 36 percent of the candidates who passed the second interview are chosen for the new class of medical students. Out of 10,000 applicants to Ben-Gurion over a period of ten years, slightly more than 400 actually made the final cut, resulting in an average yearly admission rate of about 4 percent, exceedingly selective by any measure.

In essence, then, Ben Gurion has turned on its head the usual method by which medical students are chosen, not just in the rest of Israel but in the United States and most other nations as well. Typically, the lion's share of medical students are eliminated from competition by means of exceedingly high thresholds of academic aptitude—as are most applicants for graduate and professional studies in the United States. The so-called "noncognitive" traits come into play as mere tributaries to this cognitive river.

Ben-Gurion, however, eliminates relatively few candidates on the basis of test scores and academic records. Its elites are those people who demonstrate the sorts of personal characteristics, traits, and real-world accomplishments that, in the school's experience, lead to fine physicians.

An important test of Ben-Gurion's model is whether the people whom the school picks really do perform well in their medical studies. "After all," Antonovsky notes, "some 50 percent to 60 percent of our students could not be accepted, by virtue of their grades and test scores, in any of the other Israeli medical schools." Still, the intellectual demands placed on Ben-Gurion students through six years of training are equal to any medical school in the country, Antonovsky says.

Thus, the dropout rate at Ben-Gurion compared with other medical schools would be a good indicator of the efficacy of BGU's unusual admissions system. Over a period of six years, just thirteen students dropped out because of academic failure. Some 17.8 percent of BGU students did not finish in six years, whether for academic or personal reasons, which was roughly equal to the dropout rate at the Jerusalem medical school with its more traditional model of merit.

"Perhaps most important of all," Antonovsky tells us, "a self image of BGU medical students as being different has emerged," but in this case, "being different" has been widely viewed as a good thing. "The most consistent 'complaint,' voiced with pride, of graduates coming home to receive their MDs after internships throughout the country, is that department heads invariably expect more of them than their peers from other schools."

Even without the usual definitions of merit to carry on its traditions, BGU has established an enviable international reputation in the years since its founding. Recently, the school joined forces with Columbia University to set up an M.D. program in international health and medicine. Countries worldwide have sought BGU's counsel and expertise on community medicine practice. In a resource guide put out by the Association of American Medical Colleges in 1993, the AAMC said: "While Ben-Gurion's admission process is more time consuming than most schools . . . the results are worth the effort."

Quitting the SAT

Bates College was right about Karen Fletcher. This academically rigorous college in Maine never saw the California woman's SAT scores, and she still earned straight As at Bates. The college was right about Amanda Colby, too. The star volleyball player and biochemistry major from Connecticut attributed her A average to her dogged determination, curiosity, and critical thinking skills. Her SATs? Bates never saw them, but admitted her anyway.

As it turns out, Bates College's admissions committees over the years, since quitting the SAT mandate, have been right most of the time about young people they decide to admit, even without the standardized test scores that the Educational Testing Service and the College Board suggest colleges simply cannot live without. How is this possible?

Having fully eliminated standardized testing requirements in 1990, Bates has been a pioneer in a recent but growing cohort of colleges and universities loosely known as the "test-optional movement." The National Organization on Fair and Open Testing in Cambridge, Massachusetts has kept tabs on the number of test-optional four-year institutions for several years. In 1990, the organization says, some 236 four-year schools had to some degree either rolled back or dropped their SAT or ACT requirements. By 1998, 281 schools had done so. In the United States, there were a total of about 2,200 four-year schools in 1997, so although the test-optional movement is expanding, still only 12 percent of the nation's four-year institutions have quit or significantly reduced the test burden.

Without strictly numeric credentials to punch into computers, how has Bates managed to evaluate a high-schooler's Batesworthiness?

William Hiss, Bates's former dean of admissions who helped to engineer the college's test-optional transformation, now a vice president at the college, described the college's overarching philosophy about finding talent in the pool of some 3,600 high-schoolers who apply to Bates each year. Although it is the college's job to provide the young people with a fair and effective forum, Hiss told me, the high-schooler's task is to demonstrate his or her talents and achievements.

Hiss likens the process to the theatrical lighting for a dramatic play. Bates provides the open stage, but students, he says, "show us in detail what they have done. Their job is to get all the lights on that apply to them. If you've overcome unbelievable troubles but have still shown up on the top of every list, that is what we're trying to find out with our admissions process."

In practice, that means Bates elicits information from high-schoolers that amounts to a portfolio review process, but without actually using the word "portfolio," because students invariably think of portfolios as sticking art projects and the like into leather or plastic folders.

"We run a portfolio system without calling it that," Hiss says. "We simply tell students, 'We strongly recommend you provide us with evidence of your talents.'" That evidence, of course, can take a great number of forms, and the admissions office does not presume it has the requisite knowledge to judge whether a work of art or a science project is done well.

That is where the entire Bates faculty gets involved. As the frontline owners and defenders of Bates's standards for academic quality, the faculty help the admissions staff answer those questions. After the admissions "portfolios" arrive at Bates, the admissions staff channels its various elements to the experts on campus who *are* in a position to make informed judgments about the quality of the materials in the portfolios.

"It's sort of a complicated, multiple tip system going on," Hiss says. As the faculty input is returned, the admissions staff reassembles the information and gives the portfolios an overall rating, based on a five-point scale. As in any holistic scoring process, the staff must agree to standards for their scale and ways to ensure the reliability and integrity of the process.

Hence, the basic message to people vying for a spot at the college is carried by the simple dictum to applicants, which boils down to this: "Show us." The Bates model, sans mandatory SATs, remains a highly selective merit system, but one based on accomplishment, performance, and personal characteristics of individuals. The effects of this sea change throughout the college have been extraordinary.

After going test-optional, public interest in Bates took off. Until 1984, the college was getting about 2,300 applications a year. After Bates decided to require just the SAT achievement test that year, an additional 700 applications annually started coming over the transom. Then, in 1990, after eliminating all testing requirements, applications started running about 3,600 each year.

An additional 1,300 applicants every admissions season, a 60 percent jump from the pre-1984 levels, supercharged Bates's already high academic profile. "The grumpy question is always, 'If you make testing optional, aren't you undercutting the academic quality of the entering class?'" Hiss says. "When you have 60 percent more applicants to work with, quality goes up, class rank in high school goes up, diversity goes up, special talents, test scores, you pick, they all go up.

You'd have to be a fool of an admissions officer not to get a better class when you have an applicant pool that is 60 percent larger."

Consider the diversity question. After Bates went test-optional, the college promptly established itself as a sort of magnet for many minorities and Maine working-class kids for whom attending a college of Bates's academic stature would have been improbable under the old gatekeeping rules.

At first, Bates officials were unsure what sorts of young people would take advantage of the policy, but common folk wisdom that it might attract more women, people of color, and students of moderate economic means—all the sorts of people most damaged by test-heavy admissions—proved to be accurate. Women nonsubmitters have outnumbered men two to one; half of all Hispanics who have applied to Bates haven't submitted test scores; 60 percent of blacks have not; and 35 percent of Asian Americans have not.

As a result, the college has become more diverse in terms of race, ethnicity, and social class. In 1999, enrollment of Americans of color and international students reached a high of about 18 percent of the total. Mostly blue-collar kids from Maine have been running about 13 percent. (Hiss says that many factors beyond the college's control, such as geographic and demographic constraints of its Maine location, has somewhat limited how much racial diversity Bates can achieve.)

Further, locals and students of color take great advantage of the test-optional policy. Although 13 percent of each freshman class comes from Maine, about a fifth of all applicants who do not submit test scores are Maine locals, often of moderate economic circumstances. Hiss describes them as those "rock-ribbed, disciplined, and sensible students (who) will outperform all the predictors to graduate disproportionately on the Phi Beta Kappa and Latin Honors Lists."

In 1992, by then well convinced that the great Bates experiment was exceeding anyone's highest expectations, both in terms of academic and social considerations, Hiss presented the college's evidence to his fellow admissions professionals in the *Journal of College Admissions*. "Bates's policy," Hiss wrote, "while making no claim for political correctness, is an attempt to open windows, to take some chances, to see young people in more multifaceted individual lights."

The news was out. This small college in Maine had "gone naked" on standardized admissions tests, as it were, no longer relying on the SAT crutch as a major reference point of academic merit. Contrary to all fears, the college's academic foundations did not come tumbling down. Indeed, Hiss told his fellows, Bates's students and Bates as an institution were stronger than ever.

The Test-Optional Movement Spreads

Among those watching and listening carefully to the Bates experiment from the beginning was Gail Berson, the admissions director at Wheaton College in Massachusetts. The former women's college in the town of Norton made the test-op-

FOCUS: GETTING A CHANCE

Karen Fletcher's calculus teacher just knew his star pupil had done superbly on her SATs. After all, as a student at Campolindo High, in a small East Bay town near San Francisco, Fletcher was first in her graduating class, maintaining a perfect 4.0 grade average. Not only that, she had aced his calculus class, so mere algebra on the SATs must have been a breeze for her, the teacher believed. "You got about a 1,600 (a perfect SAT score), right?" the teacher asked Fletcher one day, in all seriousness.

Not exactly, she had to tell him. In fact, not even close.

When I spoke to her, Fletcher told me her SAT score, but I'd prefer not say what it was. Doing so might tempt irrational judgments about her, the very sorts of inferences many people and institutions like to make about people whose test scores do not measure up. Whatever the test's proven flaws; parents, counselors, colleges—and yes, even calculus teachers—continue to believe that the magical, all-meaningful numbers describe the intellectual firepower of people like Fletcher. Let's just say her scores were quite modest, in ETS terms, nowhere near what her calculus teacher fully expected of his star pupil.

Meanwhile, Fletcher began her college search. Having been born in Massachusetts, Fletcher thought she might like to go to college back east. She applied to a handful of schools on both coasts, including Haverford College, Willamette College in Oregon, the University of Puget Sound, and UC–Santa Cruz.

True, her SATs might harm her chances, but Fletcher figured her superb classroom performance plus her nonacademic activities would surely help her cause. She was a varsity cross-country runner and swimmer and treasurer of the Earth Club as a high school freshman. For that effort, Fletcher set up a recycling program to raise money for preserving Costa Rican rain forests. She and the club's other officers held fundraisers enabling them to travel to Costa Rica for a ten-day field study of the country's rain forest ecology.

Eventually in her hunt for the right college, a family friend told her about a small liberal arts institution in Maine called Bates College. Academically, Bates sounded good, making all the guidebooks' lists of highly regarded liberal arts colleges and having a student-to-faculty ratio of just eleven to one. The college also was in a beautiful place in a smaller community near the ocean. The college even owned a 600-acre seaside conservation area.

But mom didn't like the idea. "My mom discouraged me from applying," figuring Fletcher might feel too isolated from big-city life. "You won't like it there," she told Karen.

Then came the kicker in Bates's favor. According to all the college guides, Bates was considered to be a very choosy place because only a relatively small percentage of applicants won acceptance. *Barron's*, in fact, rated Bates as among the most competitive in the country. Typically, that meant a college's requisite SAT scores would be quite high in ETS terms, as in the 1,300 and above category, a level at about the ninetieth percentile and considerably higher than Fletcher's modest scores. But then, as she was looking over the materials Bates had sent her, Fletcher came across item number four of Bates's admission requirements, as stated in the Bates annual catalog:

> 4. Standardized Test Scores. The submission of standardized testing (the SAT I, SAT II, and the ACT) is optional for admission. Independent of the admission process and solely

for the purpose of the College's research, students who have taken the standardized tests must submit the official results of these tests upon matriculation.

Bates's test-optional admissions policy, therefore, meant its selectivity derived entirely from assessing its applicants' academic record and other accomplishments. For Fletcher, that meant her rank of first in her high school class of 200 would be enormously important, as would all her nonacademic accomplishments. These would not be supplemental afterthoughts for the admissions committee to consider only after she'd passed certain test-score thresholds. They would be crucial from the get-go.

Even Fletcher's lifelong history of doing poorly on standardized tests would matter. She would have the opportunity to tell Bates that standardized tests have rarely reflected what she's been capable of doing and learning, that the multiple-choice format didn't seem to capture how she approached problems and solutions—the ways she *thought*. Fletcher could tell Bates how, as a third-grader, she was tested for her school's gifted and talented program, because her teachers figured she would qualify since she was such a good pupil. Even now, she remembers failing the test's cutoff point and being denied acceptance into the program.

"The tests always seemed too mechanical to me, not very broad-based at all," Fletcher told me. "For me, learning is reading books, analyzing them, having a good discussion, learning how the body works, and integrating things into how they fit in the big picture."

Thus, that one small passage in the Bates College catalog thrilled Fletcher. "I just felt the SAT didn't reflect me at all," she says. "If colleges were going to depend on that instead of anything else, I'd have trouble. It definitely made me happy to see that Bates didn't see that tests were necessarily a good reflection."

Fletcher was in her final semester as a senior at Bates College when I spoke with her in November 1998. Mom, of course, had relented, and Karen ended up applying to Bates, choosing not to submit an SAT score she felt had demeaned her.

Four years later, Fletcher had provided Bates's faculty and administration plenty of opportunity to prove the admissions committee had erred by letting her in. Through nearly four years at Bates, Fletcher maintained a 4.0 grade average, studying anthropology with a concentration in Chinese studies. Following the nominations of faculty members and other students, she had been chosen as one of ten women to be named a Dana Scholar for her first-year accomplishments at the college.

This dynamo even turned a personal illness into an academic project at Bates. During her first year, Fletcher was forced to take a medical leave from Bates, and she went back to California for her recuperation. She saw several doctors, including a Chinese medicine specialist, and the experience led her to take a course in medical anthropology at UC–Berkeley as well as to her interest in non-Western medicine.

As a junior, Fletcher traveled to Taiwan to study Chinese and Chinese medicine at Tung Hai University on the west coast, about a two-hour drive south of Taipei. Fletcher traveled again to Taiwan in summer 1998. This time, with a grant from the college, Fletcher zeroed in on the traditional Chinese postpartum technique, a month-long ritual bringing to bear a host of Chinese cultural traits and practices. Based on her research, she would write a report she would later develop into her senior thesis.

Thus, the young woman had gone from sickness to seeing a Chinese doctor to taking a medical anthropology course to forging a senior thesis project. Clearly, these were not the habits of an idle mind.

tional leap in 1991, soon after Bates and another Maine innovator, Bowdoin College, had gone public with their remarkable results.

Although Wheaton initially took a wait-and-see approach to the test-optional solution, the college has since forged ahead into the new era, and in the process has virtually revolutionized its entire educational mission.

For Wheaton, going test-optional became just a piece—a crucial one—of a sweeping change of its core values. Wheaton transformed itself into a tangible illustration of the profound reformulation of merit now occurring in some corners of higher education. Eschewing an ideology of merit based on such culturally powerful totems as "aptitude" and "academic potential," Wheaton instead chose to embrace the world.

In practice, that meant Wheaton's abandonment of standardized testing rules would be relatively meaningless without an overhaul of something as basic as the college application form. Central to the new application process was a new essay that college officials designed to elicit more useful information about prospective students than they often got from bland essays about what "Martin Luther King, or Jesus or FDR means to me," Berson told me.

Instead, the new essay prompt asked applicants to project their present lives out ten years, and write a letter to a high school friend that reflects on the opportunities, challenges, and obstacles they faced after graduation. The exercise would permit a teasing out of the personal characteristics, family backgrounds, and life experiences of applicants that placed their achievements—or lack of them—into some meaningful context.

Wheaton's new views about merit meant institutionalizing another, perhaps even more crucial element, to its application process. If Wheaton was to actually create an accomplishment-based merit system, then the school would have to send that message loudly and clearly to the some 2,500 high school students who applied for admission each year.

Thus, although Wheaton would no longer require SATs, the college would strongly encourage students to submit what it called a Personal Academic Portfolio, consisting of an assemblage of materials, documentation, evidence, products, and projects demonstrating what students have done and can do. In short, Wheaton wanted young people whom Berson calls "active learners," individuals who love to create, perform, accomplish, and do something with their learning.

Indeed, like a chicken and egg problem, it is hard to ascertain in Wheaton's transformation what came first, dropping the SAT rules or adopting the Personal Academic Portfolio. In a sense, the crucial institutional values embodied in the Personal Academic Portfolio concept quite naturally implied that Wheaton would have to significantly reduce its reliance on standardized test scores.

"We wanted to encourage students to send us material that was not routinely required as part of a college application, to provide them the opportunity to demonstrate who they are that three lines on an application form can't get at," Berson told me.

"We wanted a way of saying, 'This matters. . . . That this is so important to us that just to underscore it we are going to be SAT optional.' We didn't want young people applying to us feeling like Hester Prynne and telling us, 'I'm sorry, I had a 530 verbal.' That isn't how we wanted students to think of themselves as learners."

Wheaton's move toward an achievement-based merit system also permitted the admissions staff to discover amazing gems among applicants, who might have gone undetected in the past. Like the young woman who started an orphanage in Peru while still in high school. Or another who worked as a sheepherder in Maine. Says Berson, "This wasn't some 4-H stuff; it was her job."

What is more, the transformation in Wheaton's gatekeeping rules also allowed staff and faculty to simply know their students better, to understand what the new generations of students were thinking about college in relation to the world at large. This was hardly an idle benefit. In fact, not understanding what made students tick was turning into a costly epidemic throughout academia.

As the 1990s were coming to a close, college professors and administrators across the country were becoming increasingly concerned that recent cohorts of new college students had become alienated from the academic experience as their professors had known it, to unprecedented degrees. Record numbers of freshman were reported to be bored in class and generally disengaged from academic concerns. Wheaton's new model, however, proved useful for gaining insight about possible reasons behind students' growing disenchantment with academic life.

As it turned out from the new essays and the material students submitted for the Personal Academic Portfolio, Wheaton College discovered that recent high-schoolers were unusually fascinated with the world of work and harbored a keen interest in making connections between their classroom lives and work lives.

"We've discovered many wonderful things," Berson says. "You can start with the obvious, that teenagers nowadays have complicated and complex lives. . . . Kids are so interested in stuff outside of school. Most are oriented toward their work, and they are engaged by the work they do. They show enthusiasm when they talk about it. Even for the best students, high school can be a very boring place, either too rigid or a lot of unevenness among the faculties. But as an underlying theme, kids get really excited at the world outside of the classroom, and work is one of the big ones. There's a much higher level of consciousness among kids I meet about doing interesting work."

Thus came the final piece of the Wheaton merit revolution. In addition to quitting the SAT and revamping the whole application process, the college forged far more explicit connections than ever before between its classrooms and the outside world of work, jobs, and community service. Thus, through the college's Filene Center for Work and Learning, students were required to find outside jobs or volunteer experiences that complemented their classroom work, experiences in which students actually applied what they learned in Wheaton's classrooms.

"It's more than just a career center, and they are not just internships," Berson explained to me. "It's a whole process, and such a crucial academic requirement that each student must have at least one evaluated work experience. You establish goals, you find a place and a supervisor, and you close that chapter by reflecting on what the experience meant to you."

The tangible result of these experiences is what the college calls a Second Transcript, a "work and service transcript," says Berson, considered to be coequal to the academic transcript. In narrative form, the second transcript evaluates the students' out-of-class experiences. "The reality is, most kids have multiple Second Transcripts," Berson says. "They get hooked on them." In one recent case, for instance, twelve Wheaton students participated in a project at Robert College in Istanbul, where they taught English to Turkish children. Through the project, Wheaton students were provided a $2,000 stipend and air fare to enable them to participate.

When added together, the four tangible, interrelated pieces of Wheaton's transformation—the new essay, the Personal Application Portfolio, the integration of the academic and the nonacademic—all have sent the college's constituency a profoundly different message about the nature of teaching, learning, and the whole notion of going to college.

The new message being sent to anyone interested in applying to Wheaton was clear. Of course, academic subjects are important, but they may deserve no more privilege in the Wheaton hierarchy than the world outside college. Learning by doing is not just desirable, it is crucial. Someone can be a near genius at taking pencil-and-paper tests, but if he or she has not done anything with that apparent ability, so what? At the same time, poor test scores would no longer indelibly brand a young person as a failure waiting to happen.

Thus far, Wheaton College has not been disappointed with the results of its reformation. Having made the institution a far more interesting place, a more intellectually and culturally diverse bunch of students have also proven themselves worthy by any genuine definitions of academic merit.

Numbers of Wheaton students receiving Latin Honors or getting on the Dean's List have held steady. Freshman retention has improved. The proportion of Wheaton grads going on to graduate school has increased. Academic credentials of its applicants, in terms of grades and high school class rank, have surged. Moreover, the number of people applying to Wheaton has shot up some 300 percent from pre-1991 levels.

"We have become a more desirable place for many students," Berson told me. "Yet, we have become more selective; with more applications, we are getting stronger kids."

No More "Wincing"

True, one could heavily discount all this were the successes at Bates and Wheaton merely quirky, isolated examples. But their stories have also become the stories of many other institutions that have quit equating standardized test scores with academic excellence.

Indeed, that the Bates and Wheaton ideas about merit have been replicated elsewhere has led to the discovery of the rather eye-opening phenomenon that almost rises to the level of a new educational principle: Institutions can actually bolster their academic stature *and* their ethnic, class, and racial diversity by looking at merit from a different angle than in the past, by viewing young people not as "students" so much as people who may, or may not, love to learn and love to do.

For instance, there's Franklin and Marshall College of Lancaster, Pennsylvania, one of a handful of test-optional four-year schools in that state loosely known as the Keystone Group. The college dropped its SAT requirement in 1991, instead permitting applicants to submit two graded writing assignments.

Since then, the college has watched its applicant pool not just expand but glisten. For the freshman class that will graduate in 2001, nearly two-thirds were among the top 10 percent of their high school classes. High-schoolers who did not submit test scores were admitted 10 percent more often than test-score filers, "outperforming the norm of the class," says former Admissions Director Peter Van Buskirk. (7) Van Buskirk explained to the *New York Times* in 1991, after Franklin and Marshall quit the SAT:

> We weren't convinced that the SAT is a necessary predictor for high achievers. In a highly selective school, you end up looking at a group of students in which many are in the top 10 percent and you can't take them all. If you're wincing because you see a modest SAT score, then you're not being fair to a candidate who should be evaluated on other factors. What this decision does is take the wincing out of the process. (8)

Clearly, test-optional policies like these have provided gatekeepers with the institutional legitimacy to admit highly accomplished young people who nevertheless might have found the schools tough places to crack under the old gatekeeping rules, and do so without second-guessing their decisions.

However, the newfound freedom to really judge young people on their merits has led to certain costs. The downsides have not risen from any substantive shortcomings in the new systems themselves but rather *only* because these innovations fly in the face of academia's entrenched ideologies about merit and notions of academic quality most Americans have been weaned on.

Colleges like Bates and Wheaton still must contend with public misunderstanding about the meaning of standardized tests. Pressures remain to maintain high published test scores for all the guidebooks. Finally, what happens after college to young Batesians or Wheatonites, who have gone through college in their test-optional worlds? What will happen to them when it is time to graduate and, perhaps, go on to graduate or professional schools that will inevitably classify and sort them by scores on the GRE or the LSAT or the MCAT?

What happens to people like Karen Fletcher? Close to earning her diploma from Bates, Fletcher was mulling her immediate career options when I spoke with her. She told me she was seriously considering going to graduate nursing school to become a nurse practitioner, focusing on women's health. Then I asked her about what I suspected might be a sensitive subject for her, the prospect of having to take the Graduate Record Exam, and the need to score well enough to get into a graduate nursing program.

Her response was enough to break my heart. She believed that graduate nursing programs would treat her the way Bates had treated her, and would take into account a full picture of her achievements and personal characteristics, which enabled her to end up "near the top of every list," as Bates vice president William Hiss put it, despite relatively poor performance on standardized tests.

"I'm a little concerned about taking the GREs," Fletcher said to me. "I think it's similar to the SAT. I'm not too concerned about it though. I think having an interview and having a chance to highlight other parts of my application will work in my favor."

I suppose places like Bates make one hopeful about the future of merit in America. Karen Fletcher believed that, of course, she would have the opportunity to interview at the nursing schools she would apply to. She naturally assumed graduate nursing programs, like Bates, would not simply stick her into a file labeled "presumed denial," based on a GRE score. I wasn't about to tell her otherwise.

Retiring the Pseudo-Meritocracy

Brutal as these cultural imperatives can be, one hopes they will not prevent colleges like Bates, Wheaton, and other innovators from continuing to tell the public the truth about such matters and test scores and merit.

Understanding the realities of the world outside its walls, Wheaton has chosen to deal with the downsides of its merit system by fighting fire with fire. Since going test-optional, Berson told me, the college has recently embarked on an intensive test-coaching program to prepare its graduates for the test-obsessed world they will encounter after Wheaton. "The rest of the world hasn't caught up with us yet," Berson sighs.

For his part, William Hiss of Bates has turned defiant on these matters. He was not always so. After Bates dropped its SAT requirement, Hiss would inevitably be asked how an experiment at a small private college in Maine could possibly apply to, or be replicated at, larger and equally competitive institutions. In the late 1980s and early 1990s, Hiss preferred to dodge the question, and simply answer that each institution must determine the proper role of standardized testing for itself. When I spoke to Hiss in late 1998, he had just returned from the annual meeting of the Educational Records Bureau, an organization that administers standardized testing programs for private elementary and secondary schools in New York. In attendance were the admissions deans from such prestigious places as Columbia, Yale, Connecticut College, and the University of Chicago. On the table was a discussion of the continued role of admissions testing for these highly selective schools. Yet again, Hiss says, he listened to the usual refrain that Americans have heard time and again from the large swath of American higher education led by the College Board and the Educational Testing Service: No, the tests aren't perfect; yes, they are the only objective measure in the entire admissions process.

In light of discoveries to the contrary at colleges and universities ranging from the University of Texas to Franklin and Marshall College, in light of a mountain of empirical evidence showing these "objective" tests often bear minimally upon a young person's real achievements, the old refrain begins to sound disingenuous and hollow.

Indeed, the purported bureaucratic convenience to those who would sort and classify their applicants based on test scores no longer seems tolerable in a nation of vast and growing inequalities in access to higher education: inequalities between the rich and not rich, between highly-educated elites and those of the working class, between privileged whites and unprivileged people who are not white.

The example of California, the nation's most populous state, is staring the rest of the country in the face on these questions. California provides Americans with a startling illustration of what the United States *must* come to terms with if higher education is to survive as a democratic institution into the next millennium.

California's problem, nay, our problem, boils down to this: By the year 2000, young Latinos are projected to make up fully 50 percent of the enrollment in California's K–12 system. And yet, over the past decade or so, just 4 percent of the state's Latino high school graduates were deemed to have met the academic eligibility and test score rules of the *public* University of California system.

The nation's pseudo-meritocracy will continue to reproduce such horrific outcomes unless Americans finally lose patience with hollow-sounding arguments about the impossibility of change. That will not happen until the public begins to understand the fundamentally political nature of the meritocracy—that real people and real institutions with high stakes in the outcome set the rules of its game. That the rules until now have benefited handsomely a relatively few while punishing many others is all the more reason to shift the vantage point. All the better to see what merit in America might truly be.

Like I said, Hiss is among those who have turned defiant at the old excuses. "We've got to change the lenses," he told me. Once states like California and their educational institutions change the lenses through which they judge people's worth, miraculous things begin to happen. Speaking from experience, weary of all the excuses he has heard over the years, Hiss says to California and the rest of the country that, were they to change the lenses:

"You'll see the Latino applicant pool expand like a giant hot air balloon. Then, if admissions people can't figure out who is really good, the state ought to fire them and get some people with imagination, to read essays, to look at artwork, to examine whole transcripts rather than the usual quick glance at the GPAs. There are twenty different ways you can dramatically open up the system, and if you really want to, you'll figure out a way. And don't complain to me about the cost, that we can't afford it. How much are you paying for all those prison guards? What are the total costs of *not* changing the system?"

Notes

Chapter 1

1. The Nader report focused its attack. . . . Allan Nairn and Associates, *The Reign of ETS: The Company that Makes Up Minds*, The Ralph Nader Report on the Educational Testing Service, 1980.

2. Although the testing arena and the stakes. . . . Teresa A. Dais, "An Analysis of Transition Assessment Practices: Do They Recognize Cultural Differences?" in Teresa Dais and others, *Selected Readings in Transition: Cultural Differences, Chronic Illness and Job Matching* 2, 1993; ERIC Document No. ED 372 519.

3. Consistently similar results on test scores. . . . Mark E. Fetler, "Pitfalls of Using SAT Results to Compare Schools," *American Educational Research Journal* 28, no. 2, Summer 1991, pp. 481–491.

4. At the K–12 level, teachers often don't believe. . . . Timothy C. Urdan and Scott G. Paris, "Teachers' Perceptions of Standardized Achievement Tests," *Educational Policy* 8, No. 2, June 1994, pp. 137–156.

5. However, the main purpose of standardized testing. . . . Bruce C. Bowers, "Alternatives to Standardized Educational Assessment," ERIC Clearinghouse on Educational Management, Eugene, Oregon, 1989, ERIC Document no. ED 312 773.

6. By fall 1996, as many as thirty-six states. . . . Council of Chief State School Officers, *Trends in State Student Assessment Programs*, Fall 1996, Washington, D.C.

7. According to one recent estimate. . . . Walter Haney, George Madaus, and Robert Lyons, *The Fractured Marketplace for Standardized Testing* (Boston: Kluwer Academic Publishers) pp. 61, 87.

8. It seems reasonable to question whether. . . . Office of Technology Assessment, *Testing in American Schools: Asking the Right Questions*, Washington, D.C.: U.S. Government Printing Office, February 1992.

9. When such opportunity costs are factored in, Americans' annual. . . . Walter Haney, George Madaus, and Robert Lyons, *The Fractured Marketplace for Standardized Testing* (Boston: Kluwer Academic Publishers 1993) p. 95.

10. But the economic payoff for minorities. . . . David Lavin and David Hyllegard, *Changing the Odds: Open Admissions and the Life Chances of the Disadvantaged* (New Haven: Yale University Press, 1996) pp. 114–115.

11. Similarly, our culture places. . . . Frank Miele, "Interview with Robert Sternberg," *Skeptic Magazine* 3, no. 3, 1995, pp. 72–80.

12. At the peak of America's antitesting. . . . College Board News, June 1978, p. 5, quoted in Allan Nairn and Associates, *The Reign of ETS: The Company that Makes Up Minds,* 1980, p. 75.

Chapter 2

1. "An accurate measurement of everyone's. . . . Charles Spearman, *The Abilities of Man* (New York: Macmillan, 1927), p. 8.

2. Galton once said. . . . quoted in Brian Evans and Bernard Waites, *IQ and Mental Testing: An Unnatural Science and its Social History* (London: Macmillan, 1981), p. 41.

3. A fellow member of the British upper class, Spearman was a great admirer of Galton . . . *Encyclopedia of Human Intelligence,* s.v. "Francis Galton, Robert J. Sternberg, editor (New York: Macmillan Publishing, 1994) p. 1009.

4. In his landmark 1904 paper . . . Charles Spearman, "'General Intelligence,' Objectively Defined and Measured," *American Journal of Psychology* 15 (1904) p. 206.

5. Whenever branches of intellectual activity are at all dissimilar, ibid., p. 273.

6. ". . . here would seem to lie the long wanted rational basis for public examinations . . ." ibid., p. 277.

7. In what's considered his greatest work . . . Charles Spearman, *The Abilities of Man* (New York: Macmillan, 1927) p. 411.

8. Harvard astronomer David Layzer. . . . David Layzer, "Science or Superstition? A Physical Scientist Looks at the IQ Controversy," *The IQ Controversy: Critical Readings,* edited by N. J Block and Gerald Dworkin (New York, N.Y.: Pantheon Books, 1976) pp. 194–241.

9. That problem alone would suggest. . . . ibid., p. 58.

10. In addition to the Binet-Simon Scale being heavily slanted toward verbal and language . . . Alfred Binet and Th. Simon, *The Development of Intelligence in Children* (Baltimore: Williams and Wilkins Co., 1916), p. 124.

11. "Consequently," they write, "we have felt justified in supposing. . . . ibid., p. 320.

12. "It is to be supposed," Binet and Simon tell us. . . . ibid., p. 317.

13. Reminiscent of Spearman's "g," the unseen and. . . . ibid., p. 42.

14. Binet intended the Scales .. . . quoted in Leon J. Kamin, *The Science and Politics of IQ* (Potomac, Md.: Lawrence Erlbaum Associates, 1974), p. 5.

15. "Binet would have resisted vigorously. . . ." *Encyclopedia of Human Intelligence,* s.v. "Alfred Binet," Robert J. Sternberg, editor (New York: Macmillan Publishing, 1994), p. 188.

16. Of the "feeble-minded," Terman wrote. . . . Lewis M. Terman, *The Measurement of Intelligence* (Boston: Houghton Mifflin 1916), pp. 6–7.

17. Among his practical innovations. . . . ibid., p. 4.

18. Indeed, this mode of thinking has become institutionalized. . . . National Research Council, Board of Testing and Assessment, *The Use of IQ Tests in Special Education Decision Making and Planning* (Washington, D.C.: National Academy Press 1996), pp. 20–21.

19. Terman's data showed. . . . Lewis M. Terman, *The Measurement of Intelligence* (Boston: Houghton Mifflin, 1916) ibid., p. 115.

20. The higher Terman climbed. . . . ibid., p. 94.

21. Among the intellectually superior. . . . ibid., p. 97.

22. Findings from his study on the new intelligence scale. . . . ibid., p. 115.

23. "It would, of course, be going too far. . . . ibid., p. 116.

24. Those results "show clearly that the foreign born are intellectually inferior. . . . Carl C. Brigham, *A Study of American Intelligence* (Princeton: Princeton University Press, 1923), p. 87.

25. In terms of the percentage who scored higher than the average American. . . . ibid., p. 119.

26. "It is sometimes stated," he snapped, "that the examining methods. . . . ibid., p. 96.

27. Further, there was the matter .. . . ibid., p. 190.

28. Brigham hammers home his conclusions. . . . ibid.

29. Like Terman's Stanford-Binet Scale. . . . ibid., p. 180.

Chapter 3

1. School board president Marie Warnke. . . . *The (Bergen) Record*, April 6, 1994.

2. For Herrnstein and Murray, this meant—absurdly, it might seem. . . . Eleanor A. Hubbard, "The IQ Caste and Gifted Children," *Roeper Review* 18, no. 4, pp. 258–260.

3. That is especially evident in the policy implications. . . . R. J. Herrnstein and C. Murray, *The Bell Curve: Intelligence and Class Structure in American Life* (New York: The Free Press, 1994).

4. Further, says Michael J. Feurer, a testing expert. . . . Michael J. Fuerer, "Social Policy, Intelligence, and Testing," *Encyclopedia of Human Intelligence*, Robert J. Sternberg, ed., (New York: Macmillan Publishing Co., 1994), p. 985.

5. Ability grouping and special programs for children . . . Mary Ruth Coleman and James J. Gallagher, "State Identification Policies: Gifted Students from Special Populations," *Roeper Review*, May/June 1995, p. 269.

6. Ibid., p. 269.

7. Stephen J. Ceci, a human development expert. . . . Stephen J. Ceci, "How Much Does Schooling Influence General Intelligence and Its Cognitive Components? A Reassessment of the Evidence," *Developmental Psychology* 27, no. 5 (1991), p. 708.

8. Despite the warnings of child development experts that standardized testing. . . . Lorrie A. Shepard, Grace A. Taylor, and Sharon L. Kagan, *Trends in Early Childhood Assessment Policies and Practices,* published on the web page of the National Educational Goals Panel, negp.gov, October 1996.

9. "The examination requires students. . . ." New York ACORN Schools Office, *Secret Apartheid II: Race, Regents, and Resources,* May 5, 1997, appendix.

10. The top five feeder districts, for instance . . . ibid., pp. 17–18.

11. For instance, in District 3, Independent School 54. . . . New York ACORN Schools Office, *Secret Apartheid III: Follow Up to Failure,* June 15, 1998, p. 18.

12. "At PS 72, a tester was told that his address . . . ibid., pp. 10–16.

13. Somewhat recent and large-scale studies of families. . . . Robert Plomin and John C. DeFries, "The Genetics of Cognitive Abilities and Disabilities," *Scientific American*, May 1998, pp. 62–69.

14. "There is little doubt. . . ." Greg J. Duncan and others, "Economic Deprivation and Early-Childhood Development," ERIC Document No. ED356076, January 25, 1993, pp. 20, 29.

15. Consider the effects of long bouts of being poor. . . . Judith Smith and others, "Consequences of Living in Poverty for Young Children's Cognitive and Verbal Ability and Early School Achievement," in *Consequences of Growing Up Poor,* edited by Greg J. Duncan and Jeanne Brooks-Gunn (New York: Russell Sage Foundation, 1997), pp. 132–167.

16. "What our analyses do show," .. . . Jeanne Brooks-Gunn, Pamela K. Kebanov, and Greg J. Duncan, "Ethnic Differences in Children's Intelligence Test Scores: Role of Economic Deprivation, Home Environment, and Maternal Characteristics," *Child Development* 67, 1996, pp. 397–408.

17. Indeed, while the young children. . . . Stephen J. Ceci, "How Much Does Schooling Influence General Intelligence and Its Cognitive Components? A Reassessment of the Evidence," *Developmental Psychology* 27, no. 5, 1991, pp. 703–722.

18. "When one considers the entire corpus of correlations. . . ." ibid., p. 711.

19. Another item on the Stanford-Binet. . . . Lee J. Cronbach, "Review of the Stanford-Binet Intelligence Scale, Fourth Edition, in *Psychological Assessment in the Schools*, edited by James C. Impara and Linda L. Murphy (Lincoln, Nebr.: The Buros Institute of Mental Measurement, 1994) p. 245.

20. For instance, the test rewards. . . . Stephen J. Ceci, "How Much Does Schooling Influence General Intelligence and Its Cognitive Components? A Reassessment of the Evidence," *Developmental Psychology* 27, no. 5, 1991, pp. 717–718.

21. In France, for instance, I.Q. gains from 1949 to 1974 . . . James R. Flynn, "Massive Gains in 14 Nations: What I.Q. Tests Really Measure," *Psychological Bulletin* 101, no. 2, 1987, pp. 171–191.

22. "The Dutch do feel. . . ." ibid., p. 187.

23. I.Q. tests don't measure intelligence. . . ." ibid., p. 188.

24. What test makers view as general intelligence, says Yale psychologist Robert Sternberg. . . . .Sternberg and others, "Identification, Instruction, and Assessment of Gifted Children: A Construct Validation of a Triarchic Model," *Gifted Child Quarterly* 40, no. 3, Summer 1996, p. 136.

25. " . . . A general factor is bound to be present. . . ." Brian Evans and Bernard Waites, I.Q. and Mental Testing (London: The Macmillan Press Ltd.1981) p. 130.

26. "The most widely accepted explanation. . . ." A. Harry Passow and Mary M. Frasier, "Toward Improving Identification and Talent Potential Among Minority and Disadvantaged Students," *Roeper Review* 18, no. 3, February/March 1996, p. 198.

27. "In spite of efforts to address this issue. . . ." Ruth Coleman and James J. Gallagher, "State Identification Policies: Gifted Students from Special Populations," *Roeper Review* 17, no. 4, May/June 1995, p. 271.

28. Rather than choosing test items. . . . Robert Sternberg and others, "Identification, Instruction, and Assessment of Gifted Children: A Construct Validation of a Triarchic Model," *Gifted Child Quarterly* 40, no. 3, Summer 1996, p. 129–137.

29. "Although most researchers understand. . . ." National Research Council, Board on Testing and Assessment, *The Use of I.Q. Tests in Special Education Decision Making and Planning* (Washington, D.C.: National Academy Press 1996) p. 27.

Chapter 4

1. Those early test takers got barely 30 percent. . . . David Tyak and Elisabeth Hansot, *Managers of Virtue: Public School Leadership in America, 1820–1980* (New York, N.Y.: Basic Books, 1982) p. 35, quoted in U.S. Office of Technology Assessment, *Testing in America's*

Schools: Asking the Right Questions (Washington, D.C.: U.S. Government Printing Office, March 1992), p. 109.

2. The idea underlying the implementation. . . . ibid., p. 108.

3. In 1991, for example, the former Chrysler Chairman. . . . James Moffett, "On to the Past: Wrong-Headed School Reform," *Phi Delta Kappan* 75, no. 8, April 1994, p. 587.

4. "Just as mass immigration was a symbol for .. . . " Paula S. Fass, "The IQ: A Cultural and Historical Framework," *American Journal of Education* 88, no. 4, August 1980, p. 433.

5. For example, in 1908, Harvard President. . . . David Tyak and Elisabeth Hansot, *Managers of Virtue: Public School Leadership in America, 1820–1980* (New York, N.Y.: Basic Books, 1982) p. 35, quoted in Office of Technology Assessment, *Testing in American Schools*, p. 115.

6. By 1920, some 500,000 published tests existed . . . OTA report, p. 122.

7. Watching in horror. . . . David Tyak and Elisabeth Hansot (note 6), quoted in the OTA report, p. 116.

8. Congress has tweaked Title 1. . . . OTA, p. 84.

9. "(Title 1) has helped create. . . . OTA, p. 85.

10. Our nation is at risk. . . . National Commission on Excellence in Education. . . . *A Nation at Risk: The Imperative for Education Reform* (Washington, D.C.: U.S. Government Printing Office 1983) p. 5.

11. Left unquestioned, of course. . . . *A Nation at Risk*, Appendix A.

12. "Standardized tests of achievement. . . . ibid., p. 29.

13. It was an inauspicious beginning. . . . Jerome T. Murphy and David K. Cohen, "Accountability in Education—The Michigan Experience," *The Public Interest* 36, Summer 1974, pp. 53–81.

14. In famous last words. . . . ibid., p. 60.

15. Such rankings invariably reveal. . . . Ernest House and others, *An Assessment of the Michigan Accountability System*, a report to the Michigan Education Association, March 1974, pp. 17–18.

16. The authors concluded that. . . . ibid., p. 23.

17. "So it is no small wonder . . . .David C. Berliner and Bruce J. Biddle, *The Manufactured Crisis* (Reading, Mass.: Addison-Wesley Publishing Co., 1995), p. 4.

18. What David C. Berliner and Bruce J. Biddle would later condemn . . . ibid., p. 3.

19. In 1982, just 14 percent of high schoolers. . . . U.S. Department of Education, *The Condition of Education* (Washington, D.C.: U.S. Government Printing Office, 1996), p. 98.

20. In March of 1979, fully 85.6 percent . . . ibid., p. 92.

21. Moreover, consider international . . . National Center for Education Statistics, *International Education Indicators: A Time Series Perspective* (Washington, D.C.: U.S. Government Printing Office, December 1996), p. 66.

22. If there were deep problems . . . ibid.

23. "NAEP is forbidden by law . . . Catherine A. Shaughnessy, Jennifer E. Nelson, and Norma A. Norris, *NAEP 1996 Mathematics Cross-State Data Compendium for Grade 4 and Grade 8 Assessment* (Washington, D.C.: National Center for Education Statistics, December 1997), p. 1.

24. In complete contradiction. . . U.S. Department of Education, *1997 Condition of Education* (Washington, D.C.: U.S. Government Printing Office, 1997), p. 72.

25. In what amounted to a stern . . . International Monetary Fund (IMF), *World Economic Outlook 1998* (Washington, D.C.: IMF, April 1998), pp. 3–5.

26. "We keep expecting a slowdown . . ." Sylvia Nassar, *New York Times*, May 1, 1998, p. A-1

27. These developments placed the United States . . . International Institute for Management Development (IMD), *World Competitiveness Yearbook* (Lausanne: IMD, April 1998), Executive Summary.

28. In 1993, the RAND Corp. . . . R. Sturm, *How Do Education and Training Affect a Country's Economic Performance?: A Literature Survey* (Los Angeles: RAND Corp. Policy Brief, 1993).

29. The answer, Cuban says, is that the politically charged . . . Larry Cuban, *Education Week*, June 15, 1994, editorial page.

30. If lax American schools were the culprit. . . Stanley Fischer, "Symposium on the Slowdown in Productivity Growth," in Zvi Griliches and others, "Symposium: The Slowdown in Productivity Growth," *Journal of Economic Perspectives* 2, no. 4, (Fall 1988), p. 4.

31. Some historical figures give us a flavor . . . Frank B. Womer, "State-Level Testing: Where We Have Been May Not Tell Us Where We Are Going," *New Directions for Testing and Measurement* 10, 1981, pp. 2–3.

32. More recently, according to the latest figures . . . Council of Chief State School Officers (CCSSO), *Trends in State Student Assessment Programs* (Washington, D.C.: CCSSO, Fall 1996), p. 1.

33. Indeed, a similar analysis. . . National Center for Fair and Open Testing, *FairTest Examiner*, "High-Stakes Tests Do Not Improve Learning," vol. 12, no. 1, Winter 1997–1998.

Chapter 5

1. At the Wilson Mills School, Eric had been coming home. . . . *Eric V. et al v. Dr. James Causby and the Johnson County Board of Education*, Complaint no. 5-97-CV-587, filed July 28, 1997, in U.S. District Court for the Eastern District of North Carolina, parents' affidavits.

2. On that first test of Johnson County's new accountability policy. . . . Memorandum in Support of Motion for Temporary Restraining Order, ibid., p. 8.

3. In a thirty-year career of research and teaching about testing, Jaeger. . . . Jaeger Affidavit, *Eric V. et al. v. Johnson County Board of Education.*

4. "Measurement error alone," says Hattie. . . . *Eric V.et al v. Johnson County Board of Education*, affidavit of John A. Hattie, August 24, 1997, p. 20.

5. But that's not the conclusion reached .. . . Hattie affidavit, p. 13.

6. Validity is the most important consideration in test evaluation. . . . American Educational Research Association, American Psychological Association, National Council on Measurement in Education, *Standards for Educational and Psychological Testing*, July 1996, p. 9.

7. Said Jaeger, "Johnson County Public Schools have provided no evidence. . . . *Eric V. et al. v. Johnson County Board of Education*, Jaeger affidavit, p. 8.

8. That body of work, says Jaeger . . . ibid., p. 26.

9. Hattie, who performed one such analysis, says . . . Hattie affidavit, *Eric V.et al. v. Johnson County Board of Education*, p. 2.

10. Indeed, Steven Holmes, a professor and expert on the effects of grade retention . . . Steven Holmes affidavit, *Eric V.et al. v. Johnson County Board of Education*, p. 2.

11. According to the Texas Education Agency, "the implementation of TAAS shifted the focus . . . Texas Education Agency, *TAAS Technical Digest*, Chapter 1.

12. In fiscal 1998, the state allocated $19 million just for testing . . . Joey Lozano, Texas Education Agency, personal communication, March 12, 1998.

13. According to the Council of Chief State School Officers' most recent comparisons, Texas's assessment budget for 1995–1996 . . . Council of Chief State School Officers, *Annual Survey of State Assessment Programs* (Washington, D.C.: CCSSO, Fall 1996), p. 87.

14. School bonuses in Texas have ranged. . . . Texas Education Agency, *Development of Accountability Systems Nationwide and in Texas*, Statewide Educational Progress Report no. 1, April 1996, p. 20.

15. According to recent figures, about one in three people in the district, who are predominately Hispanic, lived in poverty. . . . Government Information Sharing Project, Oregon State University, School District Data Book Profiles: 1989–1990.

16. "As a predictor of future performance in the classroom and the workplace. . . . GI Forum, Image De Tejas, *Plaintiffs 1–7 v. Texas Education Agency,* Civil Action no. SA97CA1278, United States District Court for the Western District of Texas, San Antonio Division.

17. Differences in failure rates among racial and class groups startle. . . . GI Forum, Image De Tejas, *Plaintiffs 1–7 v. Texas Education Agency.*

18. As a result of the poor predictive. . . . Texas Education Agency, Division of Student Assessment, *Texas Assessment of Academic Skills and End-of-Course Examinations, Student Performance Results,* Fall 1994, p. 165; *Student Performance Results 1994–1995*, p. 179; *Student Performance Results 1995–1996*, p. 201; *Student Performance Results 1996–1997*, p. 227.

19. It turns out that TAAS's measurement error. . . . James Parsons, personal communication, May 15, 1998.

20. Schools, Bush asserted in the who-could-disagree. . . . *San Antonio Express-News*, "Bush, Mauro focus on education," March 22, 1998, p. 1A.

Chapter 6

1. The turnaround in test scores in Northampton County. . . . Office of Testing, Northampton County Schools, North Carolina, Internal document, May 30, 1998.

2. By 1990, the following tests were in place. . . . Public Schools of North Carolina, correspondence dated March 16, 1998, from Mildred Bazemore to Kathy Newbern.

3. North Carolina budgeted some $72 million. . . . *The* (Charlotte, N.C.) *News and Observer,* "Schools find value, vexation in ABCs program," October 26, 1997.

4. In 1985, North Carolina spent some $3.1 million. . . . Public Schools of North Carolina, correspondence dated April 22, 1998, from Becky McConkey to Kathy Newbern.

5. "The primary basis for my concern is the correlation that is being implied. . . . John Parker, correspondence to the North Carolina Testing Commission, November 16, 1992.

6. Again, in 1997, Parker told the State Board of Education. . . . John Parker, correspondence to the North Carolina State Board of Education, January 20, 1997.

7. Coaching of students on specific test content . . . North Carolina Division of Accountability Services/Testing, Department of Public Instruction, "Testing Code of Ethics," 1988 and the 1996 revision.

8. Consider a 1991 study by Lorrie Shepard and Katherine Cutts Dougherty. . . . "Effects of High-Stakes Testing on Instruction," Annual Meeting of the American Educational Research Association, April 1991, Chicago, ERIC Document no. ED 337 468.

9. Instances of cheating, of course, do occasionally. . . . *New York Times*, May 1, 1996, p. A9.

10. "Teaching to the test. . . . Daniel Koretz, "Arriving in Lake Wobegon: Are Standardized Testing Exaggerating Achievement and Distorting Instruction?" *American Educator*, Summer 1988, p. 15.

11. Herman and Golan found that teachers frequently gave students. . . . Joan Herman and Shari Golan, *Effects of Standardized Testing on Teachers and Learning—Another Look* (Los Angeles: UCLA Center for Research on Evaluation, Standards and Student Testing, 1990).

12. At a grade school in the state's Roanoke Rapids school district. . . . Bob Williams, personal correspondence, May 7, 1998.

13. As observers, it appeared to us that the most vibrant .. . . " Thomas O'Shea and Marvin F. Wideen, "The Impact of External Examinations on Science Teaching," paper presented at the National Association for Research in Science Teaching, Atlanta, April 1993, ERIC Document no. ED 363 497.

14. In the Lorrie Shepard study I quoted above. . . . See note 8 above.

15. "According to the old theories" of learning. . . . Lorrie Shepard, *Will National Tests Improve Student Learning?* (Los Angeles: UCLA Center for Research on Evaluation, Standards and Student Testing, 1991), Technical Report 342.

16. "What is remarkable," Forgione said . . . National Center for Education Statistics, "Responses to the Recently Raised Issues Regarding 12th-Grade TIMSS," at www.ed.gov/NCES/timss/.

17. Japanese lessons "came closer to implementing the spirit. . . . Third International Math and Science Study, "Videotape Classroom Study" (Washington, D.C.: National Center for Education Statistics) www.ed.gov/NCES/timss/.

18. James Ridgeway of Michigan State University. . . . James Ridgeway, *NISE Brief*, National Institute for Science Education, vol. 2, no. 1, January 1998.

19. After obtaining test-score data from the thirty-two other states. . . . Cannell, J. J., *Nationally normed elementary achievement testing in America's public schools: How all fifty states are above the national average* (Daniels, W.Va.: Friends for Education, 1987), quoted in D. Koretz, see note 10, p. 10.

20. "In my opinion, there can be no doubt . . . D. Koretz, see note 10, p. 11.

21. Versions of the California Achievement Tests. . . . Buros Desk Reference, *Psychological Assessment in the Schools*, edited by James C. Impara and Linda L. Murphy (Lincoln, Nebraska: The Buros Institute of Mental Measurements, University of Nebraska Press, 1994), p. 6.

22. "Standardized mathematics test scores are not, however, a sound basis. . . . Robert Stake, "The Invalidity of Standardized Testing for Measuring Mathematics Achievement," in *Reform in School Mathematics and Assessment,* edited by Thomas A. Romberg (State University of New York Press, 1995) pp. 173, 211.

23. For instance, if a school happened to use versions "E" or "F" of the California Achievement Tests. . . . Buros Desk Reference, see note 21, pp. 7, 29.

24. In one analysis of *Scoring High*.. . . Lorrie Shepard, "Inflated Test Score Gains: Is the Problem Old Norms or Teaching the Test?" *Educational Measurement: Issues and Practice* 9, no. 3, Fall 1990, pp. 15–22.

25. Researchers have quantified the effects. . . . ibid., p. 20.

26. The results of their study, Koretz told his peers. . . . Daniel Koretz and others, "The Effects of High-Stakes Testing on Achievement: Preliminary Findings about Generalization Across Tests," a paper presented at the Annual Meeting of the American Educational Research Association and the National Council on Measurement in Education, Chicago, April 5, 1991.

27. One observer said in a pithy summary of the problem . . . G. Sutherlund, *Elementary Education in the Nineteenth Century* (London: Historical Association, 1971) p. 52. Quoted in T. Kellaghan and G. Madaus, "National Testing: Lessons for American from Europe," *Educational Leadership* 49, no. 3, November 1991, p. 91.

28. "Lackluster. Mediocre. Disappointing. Frustrating," remarked the paper's editorial . . . *Morning News-Tribune*, "Tacoma Test Scores Disappoint—Again," December 23, 1992, p. A6.

29. In December 1993, Crew told. . . . *Morning News-Tribune*, "Three School Districts Seek Answers to Drop in Test Scores," December 9, 1993, p. A1.

30. But, "there was one bright spot. . . ." *Morning News-Tribune*, "Crew's Right on Test Scores: They Won't Do," December 12, 1993, editorial page.

31. Then came the fall 1994 scores. . . . *Morning News-Tribune*, "Tacoma Test Scores Drop," November 20, 1994, p. A1.

32. According to the 1997 Abt Associates. . . . Abt Associates Inc., *Evaluation of the Efficacy Initiative: A Retrospective Look at the Tacoma School District*, vol. 1 (Bethesda: Apt Associates, October 1997).

33. Horn described the approach teachers took under Crew's . . . Leon Horn, personal interview, March 4, 1998.

34. Besides that, Wilhoft maintained. . . . Joe Wilhoft, "Sound Reasons for Dramatic Turnaround in Test Scores," district memorandum published as an op-ed piece in the *Morning News-Tribune*, June 11, 1995, p. G1.

35. A senior vice president at the testing company. . . . *Morning News-Tribune*, "Soaring Test Scores on the Up and Up, School Official Says," June 14, 1995, p. B1.

36. New York came calling. . . . *Morning News-Tribune*, "Chief Says He'll Stay in Tacoma Job," September. 21, 1995, p. A1.

37. The *News-Tribune*'s editorial board begins to turn sour. . . . *Morning News-Tribune*, "Tacoma Test Scores Don't Make the Grade," December 12, 1996, p. A12.

38. Except for listening, fewer than one-half. . . . Office of the Superintendent of Public Instruction, Washington Assessment of Student Learning, District Summary of Student Performance, Spring 1997.

39. "It's a numbers game. . . . *Seattle Times*, "Lesson from Tacoma: Stress the tests and scores improve," December 3, 1995, p. A12.

Chapter 7

1. "We have been, frankly, inundated. . . . *Education Week on the Web*, "The Push for Accountability Gathers Steam," February 11, 1998.

2. All the state's parishes but New Orleans had complied. . . . *Education Week on the Web*, "Challenge to La. Accountability Law Heads to Trial," March 13, 1998.

3. In an example of school achievement levels determined . . . *Idaho Statesman*, "Testers rethink kids' reading scores," May 13, 1998, p. A1.

4. Illustrative of a disturbing lack of concern. . . . *The Journal Sentinel*, "MPS may hire firm to help 'teach to test,'" April 22, 1998.

5. In Chicago, 1 in 10 of Chicago school's 424,000 students . . . *Education Week on the Web*, "The Push for Accountability Gathers Steam," February 11, 1998; and *Catalyst*, "It's test time! IGAP down, CASE, TAP on tap," April 1998, vol. 9, no. 7.

6. In California, the performance-based assessment system . . . National Center for Fair and Open Testing, FairTest, in *Examiner*, "California Adopts Regressive Testing Program," Winter 1997–1998, p. 8.

7. Compared to rich schools, poor schools. . . . ibid., p. 26.

8. "We can be almost certain," writes Jencks. . . . Christopher Jencks and others, *Inequality: A Reassessment of the Effect of Family and Schooling in America* (New York: Basic Books, 1972), p. 148.

9. "Overall, the data lead us to three general conclusions. . . ." ibid., p. 141.

10. Consider the Cleveland City School District. . . . James F. Lanese, "Statewide Proficiency Testing: Establishing Standards or Barriers," paper presented to the annual meeting of the AERA, San Francisco, April 1992.

11. Even then, Gallagher found both income and poverty were significantly. . . . Michael Gallagher, "Proficiency Testing and Poverty: Looking Within a Large Urban District," paper presented at the annual meeting of the AERA, Atlanta, April 1993.

12. Summing up his team's remarkable findings in *Phi Delta Kappan*. . . . Bruce J. Biddle, "Foolishness, Dangerous Nonsense, and Real Correlates of State Differences in Achievement," *Phi Delta Kappan*, Internet site, September 1997.

13. To what benefit? .. . . Joan Herman and Shari Golan, *Effects of Standardized Testing on Teachers and Learning—Another Look* (Los Angeles: UCLA Center for Research on Evaluation, Standards and Student Testing, 1990), p. 62.

14. Indeed, a 1997 public opinion poll. . . . *Phi Delta Kappan*, "The 29th Annual Phi Delta Kappa/Gallup Poll of the Public's Attitudes Toward the Public Schools," August 25, 1997.

15. Still, the take-home message of *Risk II* was the same as its progenitor . . . Center for Education Reform, *A Nation Still at Risk: An Education Manifesto,* April 30, 1998, at the Internet site of the Center for Education Reform.

16. "The designers of the NAEP project took extreme care. . . . Office of Technology Assessment, *Testing in America's Schools: Asking the Right Questions* (Washington, D.C.: U.S. Government Printing Office, March 1992), p. 91.

17. Commenting on the safeguards built into the NAEP. . . . Lyle V. Jones, "National Tests and Education Reform: Are They Compatible?" William H. Angoff Memorial Lecture Series, Educational Testing Service, 1997.

Chapter 8

1. Other studies have shown that about half of American employers. . . . Michael Selmi, "Testing for Equality: Merit, Efficiency, and the Affirmative Action Debate," *UCLA Law Review* 42, no. 5, June 1995, p. 1256.

2. The Bureau of National Affairs .. . . *Encyclopedia of Human Intelligence*, "Testing in Government and Industry," Robert J. Sternberg, editor (New York: Macmillan and Co. 1994), p. 1068.

3. Of course, there are the garden variety. . . . ERIC Clearinghouse on Assessment and Evaluation, *Test Review Locator*, on the Internet at www.ericae.net.

4. The session lasted about 30 minutes. . . . *Carmelo Melendez v. Illinois Bell Telephone Co.,* U.S. Court of Appeals for the Seventh Circuit, Decided March 27, 1996; and attorney Elaine Siegel, personal interview, September 29, 1998.

5. But, as it turned out, the most daunting gatekeeper . . . *Melendez v. Illinois Bell,* appeals court decision.

6. Indeed, according to the company's own records. . . . *Melendez v. Illinois Bell*, appeals court decision, footnote 2.

7. What is more, when Illinois Bell hired an outside consulting. . . . ibid.

8. Test takers have just twelve minutes . . . Kevin R. Murphy, "The Wonderlic Personnel Test," *Test Critiques*, vol. I (Kansas City: Test Corporation of America,1984), p. 769.

9. There's little question many employers. . . . Leslie Braunstein, "The Right Stuff," *Electric Perspectives*, November/December 1995, pp. 46–53.

10. Michael Selmi, writing in the *UCLA Law Review*.. . . Michael Selmi, "Testing for Equality: Merit, Efficiency, and the Affirmative Action Debate," *UCLA Law Review* 42, no. 5, June 1995, p. 1252.

11. "It can turn a first-round pick into a third-round. . . ." Richard Hoffer, "Get Smart!" *Sports Illustrated*, September 4, 1994, p. 74.

12. "I've seen guys who have scored very. . . ." ibid., p. 75.

13. "A player needs a baseline mental capacity to play this game. . . ." *Milwaukee Journal Sentinel*, "Iowa State's Davis Alarms NFL with Test Score," quoted in the *San Diego Union-Tribune*, February 27, 1997, p. D3.

14. Hunter concluded that the GATB. . . . National Academy of Sciences, *Fairness in Employment Testing: Validity Generalization, Minority Issues, and the General Aptitude Test Battery*, edited by John A. Hartigan and Alexandra K. Widgor (Washington, D.C.: National Academy Press,1989), p. 5.

15. What's more, Hunter came up. . . . ibid., p. 235.

16. The NRC reanalyzed. . . . ibid., pp. 5, 153.

17. On the question of the economic benefits. . . . ibid., p. 241.

18. "The claim of omnipotence for the GATB. . . . ibid., p. 3.

19. Relatively poor showings for the predictive validity. . . . Leonard L. Baird, "Do Grades and Tests Predict Adult Accomplishment?" *Research in Higher Education* 23, no. 1, 1985, p. 10.

20. In brief, the results of several studies of highly creative scientists. . . . ibid., pp. 16–17.

21. Consider the biologists. . . . ibid., p. 20.

22. A huge study of some 6,300 doctorates. . . . ibid., p. 22.

23. A study of 239 chemists, 142 historians. . . . ibid., p. 25.

24. On the other hand, a manager's. . . . ibid., p. 36.

25. Like Baird's review, their findings from some fifty years. . . . Terry W. Morris and Edward M. Levinson, "Relationship Between Intelligence and Occupational Adjustment and Functioning: A Literature Review," *Journal of Counseling and Development* 73, May/June 1995, p. 506.

26. Thus, when the results of these many I.Q.-occupation studies. . . . ibid., 512.

27. But even then, with the clear weight of the explanatory. . . . ibid., 510.

28. But when the shoe-size and salary data for men. . . . Fred B. Bryant and Elaine K. B. Siegel, "Junk Science, Test Validity, and the EEOC Guidelines for Personal Selection Procedures: The Case of Melendez v. Illinois Bell, unpublished manuscript, 1998.

29. "We all want the best people. . . . *Boston Globe*, "Several States Saw High Failure Rates with New Tests," June 27, 1998, p. B4.

30. "I think our school system's policy will be. . . ." personal correspondence, August 1998.

31. "National Evaluation Systems has offered no proof. . . ." R. Clarke Fowler, testimony before the Joint Committee on Education, Arts and Humanities, July 15, 1998.

32. "The failure of the standardized test scores (CBEST and NTE).. . . Iris M. Riggs and Matt L. Riggs, "A Test of the Validity of Selected Predictors of Student Success in a Teacher

Education Program," paper presented at the 1990 Annual Meeting of the American Association of Colleges for Teacher Education, February 22, 1990, ERIC Document 324 324, pp. 13–14.

33. The implication then is that admissions decisions. . . . American Association of Colleges for Teacher Education, "Academic Achievement of White, Black, and Hispanic Students in Teacher Education Programs," Washington, D.C., 1992, ERIC Document 353 259, p. 37.

34. To put the results of the teacher testing validity studies. . . . Boehm, V. R., "Are We Validating More but Publishing Less?" *Personnel Psychology* 33, 1982, p. 495–502, quoted in Riggs, Iris M., and others, "An Assessment of the Selection Criteria for a Teacher Education Program," paper presented at the annual meeting of the American Educational Research Association, San Francisco, 1992, ED 353 291, p. 11.

35. "Contrary to what many test takers and test users. . . ." Terry S. Salinger, "The Gatekeepers: Tests at Entry to and Exit from Teacher Education Programs," in *Assessment, Testing, and Evaluation in Teacher Education*, edited by Suzanne Wegener Soled, (Norwood, N.J.: Ablex Publishing Corp.,1995) p. 138.

36. "We reject any important role for innate ability. . . ." K. Anders Ericsson, Ralf Th. Krampe, and Clemens Tesch-Romer, "The Role of Deliberate Practice in the Acquisition of Expert Performance," *Psychological Review* 100, no. 3, 1993, p. 399.

37. For instance, one frequently cited 1945 investigation. . . . quoted in Leonard L. Baird, "Do Grades and Tests Predict Adult Accomplishment?" *Research in Higher Education* 23, no. 1, 1985, p. 63.

38. When one complicates the analysis. . . . ibid., p. 22.

39. "Since the social structure enforces. . . ." Brian Evans and Bernard Waites, *I.Q. and Mental Testing* (London: The Macmillan Press, LTD, 1981) p. 139.

Chapter 9

1. Here's a small sample from one reading passage. . . . *Boston Globe*, "Another Look at the Mass. Teacher Test," June 28, 1998, p. B5.

2. But while women typically have fared consistently worse. . . . Marcia C. Linn and Cathy Kessel, "Success in Mathematics: Increasing Talent and Gender Diversity Among College Majors," *CBMS Issues in Mathematical Education*, vol. 6, 1996, pp. 104–105, drawing on various studies, including: M. Clark and J. Grandy, *Sex Differences in the Academic Performance of Scholastic Aptitude Test Takers*, ETS/College Board Report no. 84-43, 1984; UC Office of Student Research, *Berkeley Campus Statistics* 1992; S. Frazier-Kouassi and others, *Women in Mathematics and Physics: Inhibitors and Enhancers* (Ann Arbor: University of Michigan, 1992); and R. Hughes, "Calculus Reform and Women Undergraduates," *Calculus for a New Century: A Pump, Not a Filter*, edited by L. Steen, *MAA Notes*, no. 8 (Washington: Mathematical Association of America, 1988).

3. "Whatever the explanation of our findings. . . ." Niall Bolger and Thomas Kellaghan, "Method of Measurement and Gender Differences in Scholastic Achievement," *Journal of Educational Measurement* 27, no. 2, Summer 1990, pp. 165–174.

4. Another investigation of the effects of test format. . . . Brent Bridgeman and Rick Moran, "Success in College for Students with Discrepancies Between Performance on Multiple-Choice and Essay Tests," *Journal of Educational Psychology* 88, no. 2, 1996, pp. 333–340.

5. Results gleaned from more than 560 studies. . . . Dieter J. Schowetter, "Academic Success in College: An Empirical Investigation of Gender Differences by Test Anxiety Interaction," paper presented at the Annual Meeting of the American Educational Research Association, San Francisco, April 18–22, 1995, ERIC Document ED 391 840.

6. As Cathy Kessel and Marcia Linn of UC-Berkeley. . . . Cathy Kessel and Marcia Linn, "Success in Mathematics: Increasing Talent and Gender Diversity Among College Majors," *CBMS Issues in Mathematical Education*, vol. 6, 1996, p. 129.

7. "When I do work for my classes. . . ." Karina Moltz, personal communication, November 16, 1998.

8. The researchers speculated that the high scoring. . . . Melissa Hargett and others, "Difference in Learning Strategies for High, Middle, and Low Ability Students Measured by the Study Process Questionnaire," paper presented at the Annual Meeting of the National Association of School Psychologists, Seattle, March 1994, ERIC Document 376 402.

9. The apparent contradiction between. . . . Eric Anderman, "Motivation and Cognitive Strategy Use in Reading and Writing," paper presented at the Annual Meeting of the National Reading Conference, San Antonio, December 1992, ERIC Document 374 402.

10. Indeed, applicants' scores on the multiple-choice. . . . Sari Lindblom-Ylanne and others, "Selecting Students for Medical School: What Predicts Success During Basic Science Studies? A Cognitive Approach," *Higher Education* 31, 1996, pp. 507–527.

11. Take the verbal section of the SAT I. . . . The College Board, *Counselor's Handbook for the SAT Program, 1997–1998* (New York: The College Board), p. 38.

12. Alan S. Kaufman, an IQ testing expert. . . . Alan S. Kaufman, "The WIPPSI-R: You Can't Judge a Test by Its Colors," *Journal of School Psychology* 28, 1990, pp. 387–394.

13. According to Kaufman, fully 40 percent .. . . Alan S. Kaufman, "Evaluation of the WISC-III and WPPSI-R for Gifted Children," *Roeper Review* 14, no. 3, pp. 154–158.

14. To answer this question, the researchers. . . . Ann Fishkin and John Kampsnider, "WISC-III Subtest Scatter Patterns for Rural Superior and High-Ability Children," March 1996, ERIC Document ED 394 783.

15. And so, gender mattered on the speeded. . . . Shelagh Gallagher and Edward Johnson, "The Effect of Time Limits on Performance of Mental Rotations by Gifted Adolescents," *Gifted Child Quarterly* 36, no. 1, Winter 1992, pp. 19–22.

16. But Sadler contends that children. . . . Philip M. Sadler, "Psychometric Models of Student Conceptions in Science: Reconciling Qualitative Studies and Distractor-Driven Assessment Instruments," *Journal of Research in Science Teaching* 35, no. 3, 1998, pp. 265–296.

17. On the other hand, so-called left-brain. . . . Jerome Schiele, "An Epistemological Perspective on Intelligence Assessment Among African American Children," *Journal of Black Psychology* 17, no. 2, Spring 1991, pp. 23–36.

18. What's more, studies of brain assymetry. . . . Karen Davidson, "A Comparison of Native American and White Students' Cognitive Strengths as Measured by the Kaufman Assessment Battery for Children," *Roeper Review* 14, no. 3, March 1992, pp. 111–115.

19. Norman Anderson, as admissions dean at Johns Hopkins. . . . Norman Anderson, "The Mismeasure of Medical Education," *Academic Medicine* 65, no. 3, March 1990, pp. 159–160.

20. When thinking becomes standardized. . . . Wolff-Michael Roth, "Tests, Representations and Power," *Journal of Research in Science Teaching* 33, no. 8, 1996, pp. 817–819.

21. "An education system that puts inordinate emphasis. . . . Arthur R. Jensen, "How Much Can We Boost I.Q. and Scholastic Achievement," *Harvard Education Review* 39, no. 1, 1969, pp. 116–117.

Chapter 10

1. All told, Americans take anywhere. . . . Walter Haney, George Madaus, and Robert Lyons, The Fractured Marketplace for Standardized Testing (Boston: Kluwer Academic Publishers, 1993), pp. 61, 87.

2. By 1997, standardized achievement test sales in the K–12 market. . . . *The Bowker Annual*(New Providence, N.J.: R. R. Bowker), various years; and U.S. Department of Labor, Bureau of Labor Statistics, Consumer Price Index, 1913–1997.

3. Indeed, Nader F. Darehshori, chief executive. . . . Houghton Mifflin Co., Second Quarter Conference Call Comments, July 23, 1998.

4. Testing and related businesses have been very good .. . . Harcourt General, "Harcourt General Announces Higher Earnings for Fourth Quarter and Full Year," Company press release, December 9, 1998.

5. Again, as the late 1990s brought. . . . Houghton Mifflin Co., SEC Form 10-K, December 31, 1997; Nader F. Darehshori conference call comments, January 27, 1998; and third-quarter earnings report, October 22, 1998.

6. Often, NCS works as a subcontractor. . . . NCS, "NCS Awarded Two Contracts with Michigan Department of Education," press release, November 11, 1998.

7. While McGraw Hill doesn't report. . . . McGraw-Hill Companies, "The McGraw-Hill Companies Reports 16.2 Percent Increase in Net Income for 1997," press release, January 27, 1998.

8. Rich non-profits that sell. . . . *New York Times*, "Testing Service, Expanding and Competing, Draws Fire From All Sides," September 30, 1997.

9. Fully recognizing the implications. . . . Educational Testing Service, *1997 Annual Report*, Consolidated Financial Statements (Princeton: Educational Testing Service).

Chapter 11

1. Replicates or simulates the ways. . . . North Carolina Education Standards and Accountability Commission, Third Annual Report, July 1996, pp. 23–24.

2. "Principals offered a long and diverse. . . . Daniel Koretz, Brian Stecher, and Edward Deibert, RAND Corporation, *The Vermont Portfolio Assessment Program: Interim Report on Implementation and Impact, 1991–1992 School Year* (Los Angeles: National Center for Research on Evaluation, Standards, and Student Testing, Technical Report 350), August 1992.

3. Most important, teachers believed. . . . Brian M. Stecher and others, RAND Corporation, *The Effects of Standards-Based Assessment on Classroom Practices: Results of the 1996–1997 RAND Survey of Kentucky Teachers of Mathematics and Writing* (Los Angeles: National Center for Research on Evaluation, Standards, and Student Testing, Technical Report 482), May 1998.

4. "When parents in this study had a chance. . . . Lorrie Shepard and Caribeth Bleim, *"An Analysis of Parent Opinions and Changes in Opinions Regarding Standardized Tests, Teacher's Information, and Performance Assessments* (Los Angeles: National Center for Research on Evaluation, Standards, and Student Testing, Technical Report 397), February 1995.

5. All considered, the California students. . . . Joan Herman and others, *American Students' Perspectives on Alternative Assessment: Do They Know It's Different?* (Los Angeles: Na-

tional Center for Research on Evaluation, Standards, and Student Testing, Technical Report 439), July 1997.

6. That many states have, to some degree. . . . .Council of Chief State School Officers, *Trends in State Student Assessment Programs* (Washington, D.C.: Council of Chief State School Officers, Fall 1996).

7. We have casually cast aside the settled. . . . Press Release, Office of the Governor, March 25, 1996, quoted in Mary Lee Smith and others, *The Politics of Assessment: A Case Study of Policy and Political Spectacle* (Los Angeles: National Center for Research on Evaluation, Standards, and Student Testing, Technical Report 468), May 1997.

8. "Under the umbrella of. . . ." Michael Murphy, "Symington Moves to Right Seeking Votes," *Arizona Republic*, May 5, 1996. Quoted in Mary Lee Smith and others, *The Politics of Assessment: A Case Study of Policy and Political Spectacle* (Los Angeles: National Center for Research on Evaluation, Standards, and Student Testing, Technical Report 468), May 1997.

Chapter 12

1. One day, the committee was shown an innocuous sheet of paper. . . . .*The Mortenson Research Letter on Public Policy Analysis of Opportunity of Postsecondary Education*, vol. 41 (Iowa City, Iowa: November 1995).

2. Ibid.

3. Of American eighth-graders from the wealthiest 25 percent. . . . National Center for Education Statistics, *National Educational Longitudinal Study (NELS): 1988–1992* (Washington, D.C.: U.S. Department of Education).

4. Nearly 7 in 10 eighth-graders scoring. . . . ibid.

5. *SATs and selective admissions..* . . National Center for Education Statistics, *Making the Cut: Who Meets Highly Selective College Entrance Criteria* (Washington, D.C.: U.S. Department of Education), Pub. no. 95–732, August 1995.

6. The "class effect," test scores and selective admissions.. . . . ibid.

7. SATs and the black-white score gap. . . . National Center for Education Statistics, *The Educational Progress of Black Students* (Washington, D.C.: U.S. Department of Education), Pub. no. 95–765, May 1995. p. 5.

8. *College attainment and race*. . . . ibid., p. 16.

9. *Getting into college..* . . . National Center for Education Statistics, *National Education Longitudinal Study: 1988–1994* (Washington, D.C.: U.S. Department of Education).

10. "High school grades have great value. . . ." Educational Testing Service, "Frequently Asked Questions about ETS," *ETS-net*, on the Internet at www.ets.org (1998).

11. "No one can accurately predict with 100 percent . . . " *College Board Online* (1998).

12. "Many colleges require the SAT I . . . ," ibid.

13. Donald M. Stewart, president. . . . Donald M. Stewart. . . . "Why Hispanic Students Need to Take the SAT," *The Chronicle of Higher Education*, January 30, 1998, p. A48.

14. Moreover, the ETS/College Board alliance. . . . The College Board, *Common Sense About SAT Score Differences and Test Validity* (New York, N.Y.: The College Board), Research Notes: RN-01, June 1997.

15. Nevertheless, the researchers found no evidence. . . . Shiela Cowen and Sandra J. Fiori, "Appropriateness of the SAT in Selecting Students for Admission for Admission to California State University, Hayward," paper presented at the Annual Meeting of the Cali-

fornia Educational Research Association, San Diego, November 14–15, 1991. ERIC Document no. 343 934.

16. Indeed, in one case the ACT proved .. . . Sandra Paszczyk, "A Comparative Analysis of ACT Scores and Final GPA's of Chicago State University Undergraduate Students," April 1994, ERIC Document no. 370 519.

17. And so, Norman and Baron investigated. . . . Jonathan Baron and M. Frank Norman, "SATs, Achievement Tests, and High School Class Rank as Predictors of College Performance," *Educational and Psychological Measurement* 52, 1992, pp. 1047–1055.

18. "Clearly, much remains to be explained. . . ." Fredrick E. Vars and William C. Bowen, "Scholastic Aptitude Test Scores, Race, and Academic Performance in Selective Colleges and Universities," in *The Black-White Test Score Gap*, edited by Christopher Jencks and Meredith Phillips (Washington, D.C.: Brookings, 1998) pp. 457–479.

19. For example, the College Board's 1997–1998 . . . The College Board, *Counselor's Handbook for the SAT Program 1997–1998* (New York, N.Y.: The College Board), p. 42.

20. On the basis of actual data, Crouse and Trusheim. . . . James Crouse and Dale Trusheim, *The Case Against the SAT* (Chicago: University of Chicago Press, 1988), pp. 40–69.

21. But, in fact, there were few discernible. . . . Leonard L. Baird, "Do Grades and Tests Predict Adult Accomplishment?" *Research in Higher Education* 23, no. 1, 1985, pp. 3–85.

22. Results like this compel one to consider. . . . ibid., p. 54.

23. Admission on creative accomplishment. . . . ibid., p. 55.

24. First, the GRE has deeply penetrated. . . . Mattie L. Rhodes and others, "The Graduate Record Examination as an Admission Requirement for the Graduate Nursing Program," *Journal of Professional Nursing* 10, no. 5, September-October 1994, pp. 289–296.

25. At many master's and doctoral programs. . . . Edith L. Goldberg and George M. Alliger, "Assessing the Validity of the GRE for Students in Psychology: A Validity Generalization Approach," *Educational and Psychological Measurement* 52, 1992, pp. 1019–1027.

26. Applications for admission are sorted upon arrival. . . . Robert J. Sternberg and Wendy M. Williams, "Does the Graduate Record Exam Predict Meaningful Success in the Graduate Training of Psychologists?" *American Psychologist,* June 1997, pp. 630–641.

27. On one hand, the GRE Board. . . . Educational Testing Service, *GRE Guide to the Use of Scores, 1998–1999* (Princeton: Educational Testing Service).

28. And so on. Overall, undergraduate grades .. . . ibid., p. 22.

29. An admissions scenario that paid. . . . Mattie L. Rhodes and others, "The Graduate Record Examination as an Admission Requirement for the Graduate Nursing Program," *Journal of Professional Nursing* 10, no. 5, September-October 1994, pp. 289–296.

30. "These correlation coefficients indicate. . . ." Thomas C. Monahan, "Using Graduate Record Examination Scores in the Graduate Admission Process at Glassboro State College, February 1991, ERIC Document no. 329 183.

31. "Overall, the results from this meta-analysis. . . . Edith L. Goldberg and George M. Alliger, "Assessing the Validity of the GRE for Students in Psychology: A Validity Generalization Approach," *Educational and Psychological Measurement* 52, 1992, pp. 1019–1027.

32. The average amount of variance. . . . Todd Morrison and Melanie Morrison, "A Meta-Analytic Assessment of the Predictive Validity of the Quantitative and Verbal Components of the Graduate Record Examination with Graduate Grade Point Averages Representing the Criterion of Graduate Success," *Educational and Psychological Measurement* 55, no. 2, April 1995, pp. 309–316.

33. As many other studies have revealed. . . . Christine Onasch, "Undergraduate Grade Point Average and Graduate Record Exam Scores as Predictors of Length of Enrollment in

Completing a Master of Science Degree," Bowling Green State University, June 1994, ERIC Document no. 375 739.

34. Enright and Power's own study. . . . Mary K. Enright and Donald E. Powers, *Validating the GRE Analytical Ability Measure Against Faculty Ratings of Analytical Reasoning Skills* (Princeton, N.J.: Educational Testing Service, GRE Board Report no. 86-06P), January 1991.

35. Thus, the researchers hypothesized. . . . Robert J. Sternberg and Wendy M. Williams, "Does the Graduate Record Exam Predict Meaningful Success in the Graduate Training of Psychologists?" *American Psychologist,* June 1997, pp. 630–641.

36. We believe that our results underscore. . . . ibid., pp. 638–639.

37. Consider, again, the Graduate Record Exam . . . Maria Pennock-Roman, *Background Characteristics and Future Plans of High-Scoring GRE General Test Examinees*, research report ETS-RR9412 submitted to EXXON Education Foundation (Princeton, N.J.: Educational Testing Service), March 1994.

38. In another, March 1993, report. . . . Lawrence J. Stricker and Donald A. Rock, *Examinee Background Characteristics and GRE General Test Performance*, GRE Board Report no. 89-07R (Princeton: Educational Testing Service), March 1993.

39. The unmerited entrenchment of standardized tests. . . . Wendy M. Williams, "Reliance on Test Scores is a Conspiracy of Silence," *The Chronicle of Higher Education,*" October 10, 1997, p. A60.

40. In fact, we are doing very poorly. . . . Mortenson Research Seminar on Public Policy Analysis of Opportunity for Postsecondary Education, no. 75, Oskaloosa, Iowa, September 1998.

41. "If one considers the national population. . . . Richard H. Sander, "Experimenting with Class-Based Affirmative Action," *Journal of Legal Education* 47, no. 4, December 1997, pp. 472–503.

42. A spokesman for Governor Pete Wilson. . . . *New York Times*, "California Regents Criticized as Hasty on Affirmative Action," June 3, 1996, p. A11.

43. While the judges agreed that promoting diversity. . . . *Cheryl J. Hopwood et al. v. State of Texas et al.,* U.S. Court of Appeals for the Fifth Circuit, March 18, 1996.

44. The impact of the Hopwood ruling .. . . *New York Times*, "Mississippi Alters College Rules," April 24, 1996, p. A8.

45. At the University of Texas School of Law. . . . University of Texas at Austin, Office of Public Affairs, News Media Advisory, August 27, 1997.

46. And, like Hopwood, the court's opinion suggested. . . . U.S. First Circuit Court of Appeals, Sarah P. Wessman, p.p.a., *Henry Robert Wessman v. Robert P. Gittens, Chairperson of the Boston Latin School Committee, et al.*, no. 98-1657, November 19, 1998.

47. All totalled, these legal and popular broadsides. . . . *New York Times*, "On the Importance of Diversity in University Admissions," advertisement by the American Association of Universities, April 24, 1997, p. A17.

48. "If affirmative action is ended. . . . Jeffrey Rosen, "Damage Control," *The New Yorker*, February 23, March 2, 1998, p. 58.

Chapter 13

1. In terms of regaining lost ground. . . . Boalt Hall, UC—Berkeley, News Release, August 17, 1998.

2. *Texas A&M School of Medicine.. . . The Chronicle of Higher Education,* "Texas A&M's Medical School Will Allow Some Applicants to Avoid Admission Test," February 5, 1998.

3. "Data from numerous studies show".. . . William C. McGaghie, "Perspectives on Medical School Admission," *Academic Medicine* 65, no. 3, March 1990, pp. 136–139.

4. Overall, Sander concludes. . . . Richard H. Sander, "Experimenting with Class-Based Affirmative Action," *Journal of Legal Education* 47, no. 4, December 1997, pp. 472–503.

5. "The hidden assumption of most medical. . . ." Aaron Antonovsky, "Medical Student Selection at the Ben-Gurion University of the Negev," *Israel Journal of Medical Sciences* 23, 1987, pp. 969–975.

6. "The goal of the medical school. . . ." S. M. Glick, "Selection of Medical Students: The Beer-Sheva Perspective," *Medical Education* 28, no. 4, 1994, pp. 265–270.

7. For instance, there's Franklin and Marshall. . . . Charles Rooney, National Center for Fair and Open Testing, *Test Scores Do Not Equal Merit: Enhancing Equity & Excellence in College Admissions by Deemphasizing SAT and ACT Results* (Cambridge, Mass.: FairTest, September 1998), pp. 20–23.

8. We weren't convinced that the SAT is a necessary. . . . *New York Times,* "Some Applicants Will be Permitted to Skip the S.A.T.," June 2, 1991. Quoted in ibid., p. 21.

Index